Anti-Judaism
and the
Gospels

Anti-Judaism
and the
Gospels

EDITED BY
William R. Farmer

TRINITY PRESS INTERNATIONAL
Harrisburg, Pennsylvania

Trinity Press International, P.O. Box 1321, Harrisburg, PA 17105
Trinity Press International is a division of the Morehouse Group

Library of Congress Cataloging-in-Publication Data
Anti-Judaism and the Gospels / edited by William R. Farmer.
    p.   cm.
  Includes bibliographical references and index.
  ISBN 1-56338-270-9 (pbk. : alk. paper)
  1. Judaism (Christian theology) – History of doctrines – Early church, ca. 30–600. 2. Bible. N.T. Gospels – Criticism, interpretation, etc. 3. Christianity and antisemitism – History. I. Farmer, William Reuben.
  BS2555.6.J44A58 1999
  261.2′6′09015 – dc21   99-20631

Printed in the United States of America

99 00   01   02   03   04   10 9 8 7 6 5 4 3 2 1

CONTENTS

ABBREVIATIONS

AB   Anchor Bible

ASTI   *Annual of the Swedish Theological Institute*

BBB   Bonner biblische Beiträge

BHT   Beiträge zur Historischen Theologie

BibInt   *Biblical Interpretation*

BJRL   *Bulletin of the John Rylands University Library of Manchester*

BTS   Biblisch-Theologische Studien

CBQ   *Catholic Biblical Quarterly*

CCARJ   *Central Conference of American Rabbis Journal*

CTSR   *Chicago Theological Seminary Review*

CurTM   *Currents in Theology and Mission*

EvT   *Evangelische Theologie*

HSCP   *Harvard Studies in Classical Philology*

HTR   *Harvard Theological Review*

HUCA   *Hebrew Union College Annual*

JAAR   *Journal of the American Academy of Religion*

JBL   *Journal of Biblical Literature*

JES   *Journal of Ecumenical Studies*

JJS   *Journal of Jewish Studies*

JSJ   *Journal for the Study of Judaism*

JSNT   *Journal for the Study of the New Testament*

JSNTSup	*Journal for the Study of the New Testament* Supplement Series
JSOTSup	*Journal for the Study of the Old Testament* Supplement Series
JTS	*Journal of Theological Studies*
NovT	*Novum Testamentum*
NovTSup	*Novum Testamentum,* Supplements
NTR	*New Theology Review*
NTS	*New Testament Studies*
RevExp	*Review and Expositor*
SBLDS	Society of Biblical Literature Dissertation Series
SBLMS	Society of Biblical Literature Monograph Series
SBLSymS	Society of Biblical Literature Symposium Series
SC	Sources chrëtiennes
SCJ	Studies in Christianity and Judaism
SJLA	Studies in Judaism in Late Antiquity
SOR	Studies in Oriental Religions
SP	*Studia Patristica*
SPB	Studia postbiblica
TDNT	*Theological Dictionary of the New Testament,* ed. G. Kittel and G. Friedrich
ThRes	Theological Resources
TR	Theology and Religion
TS	*Theological Studies*
USQR	*Union Seminary Quarterly Review*
ZNW	*Zeitschrift für die neutestamentliche Wissenschaft*

INTRODUCTION
William R. Farmer

This volume is the fruit of a three-year research project that began with a series of conversations early in 1994 between Professor
Joseph Tyson and myself. The question at issue was whether it would
be worthwhile to bring together in the Southwest persons competent in Gospel studies to discuss, reflect upon, and research the topic
"anti-Judaism and the Gospels."

An educational agency that wishes to remain anonymous responded
positively to the offer to organize the project, and the University of Dallas accepted the responsibility of sponsorship. From the beginning there
was an educational component to the project, under the direction of
Dr. Sarah Baumgartner Thurow of the Center for Critical Issues, which
made it possible for students and the public to benefit from the presence
of scholars who came to the University of Dallas to participate in the research program. The provost of the university, Dr. Glenn Thurow, served
as chairman of the executive committee for the project and dispersed all
funds. I served with Dr. Sarah Baumgartner Thurow on the executive
committee and was responsible for the research component of the project.

The research program was carried out in three stages. Stage one
served to organize a research planning committee that accepted responsibility for carrying the research program to completion. Stage two
served to explore the topic, identify the nature of disputed matters, and
make research assignments that would advance the discussion. Stage
three culminated in a scholarly conference where the research papers
were presented, responded to, and discussed. Once stage three was
completed, the research planning committee proceeded to publish the
resulting papers, the result of which the reader now has in hand.

ANTI-JUDAISM AND THE GOSPELS

Anti-Judaism and Jesus

Although Jesus has frequently been perceived as being in conflict with
various Jewish groups and individuals, it is clear that he was a Jew,

1

lived as a Jew, and died as a Jew. His teaching and actions were opposed by some Jews (among them Pharisees, Sadducees, and priests) but were admired and accepted by many Jews, some of whom made lifetime commitments to him.

In the case of Jesus, the term "anti-Judaism" is not only anachronistic but historically incorrect, for it would mean identifying certain Jewish individuals or subgroups, contemporary with Jesus, with the whole of Judaism at his time, and excluding, against his intentions, him and his disciples from the Jewish people.

The Death of Jesus

The causes leading to the death of Jesus are not totally clear, but the following can be said with some measure of confidence. The judicial conviction and execution was carried out with the sanction and under the authority of Roman governmental officials. It appears that some Jewish leaders were probably involved in the proceedings leading up to Jesus' crucifixion. The immediate opportunity for the arrest of Jesus may have been caused by one of his disciples who had defected.

The Gospels and Anti-Judaism

The Gospels were formed in the span of roughly sixty years after Jesus' crucifixion. They contain missionary preaching about Jesus' teaching, deeds, death, and resurrection. They codify and solidify oral tradition preached to a growing number of disciples that included at first mostly Jews but with the progress of time an increasing number of Gentiles.

Destined to specific readers, the individual Gospels reflect to different extents the growing separation between Christians and Jews. While in its infancy, Christianity thought itself to be an extension of Judaism; as the proportion of Gentile converts grew and the Jewish-Christian communities eventually dwindled, the notion of distinction and separateness between Christians and Jews began to take shape in both groups.

The four Gospels were written to converts of *both* Gentile and Jewish origins. It is likely, however, that the Gospels of Mark, Luke, and John envisage congregations of preponderantly Gentile backgrounds.

Along with this development, Jesus' relations with his compatriots were pictured in the Gospels in a progressively simplified way, with stereotypical language, so that his conflicts with various Jewish groups were presented as "us against them." "Jesus and his followers" came to stand for "Christians," and the opponents eventually began to be seen as "the Jews." This development reaches its peak in interpretation of the Fourth Gospel, where, as a rule, polemics are said to take place between Jesus and "the Jews," although it is clear throughout the texts that even friendly interlocutors are Jewish.

The Gospels As Used and Perceived after the Jewish Wars

The decades between and after the two Jewish wars (in 70 and 135 C.E.) constitute the period in which the distinction between Christianity and Judaism comes to completion on both the factual and the conscious levels. This is the time when a new interpretive framework is *superimposed* upon the Gospel narratives: Christian readers see themselves as heirs and followers of the disciples and see in contemporary Judaism the successors of those who rejected Jesus. A famous illustration appears in the second-century *Martyrdom of Polycarp*, in which the Jewish community of Smyrna, under their leader Herod, cooperates in the killing of the bishop Polycarp. From this time on, a new and superimposed paradigm becomes operational in understanding the opposing factions in the Gospel narratives.

New Forms of Jewish-Christian Confrontation Beginning in the Second Century

The events of the second century are not entirely negative with regard to Judaism. In the Gnostic crisis, the church not only rejects Marcion's option to discard the Jewish Scriptures, but even takes an opposite step. It continues to claim the Jewish Scriptures as its own and, in such terms, expands and streamlines the practice of apologetic confrontations with Judaism about their interpretation. A framework for intellectual debates is created. Christians in the second century not only produce new literary works but also begin to discuss their distinction and separation on a theological level and maintain their awareness of a heritage common to the two distinct religions. The fruits of this activity must not be underestimated; the activity documents common concerns that go beyond hostilities and provide a framework for some cooperation. Numerous Christian ecclesiastics through the patristic and medieval eras, from Origen (third century) through Jerome (fourth century) to Stephen Harding (twelfth century), frequent Jewish experts in order to learn Hebrew and correct their Greek or Latin texts to conform to the *Hebraica veritas* (a term coined by Jerome).

Conclusion: So What?

1. Jesus was a Jew who lived and died as a Jew.

2. Neither Jesus nor his supporters nor his opponents can be said to "represent" the Jews and Judaism of his day or any other.

3. The switch in perspective as a result of religious separation needs to be addressed in scholarly studies and popular publications.

4. With the separation of Christianity from Judaism and Judaism from Christianity, stories of Jesus' conflicts were interpreted as conflicts between Christianity and Judaism. Jesus' Jewishness was forgotten; he became a "Christian" and was understood to be criticizing Judaism from without. This tendency became normative in Christianity.

5. Thus the conflict stories in particular, and the Gospels in general, became anti-Jewish in the history of Christianity. It must be emphasized, however, that this makes neither Jesus nor the original tellers of the Jesus tradition anti-Jewish. Nonetheless, Christians should not take false comfort from this fact. On the contrary, they should take particular pains to avoid denial of the injury to Jews that has come as a consequence of anti-Jewish use of certain Gospel texts, and to seek appropriate ways to stop such use.

6. The questions of the why and how of the separation of Christianity from Judaism and of Judaism from Christianity must be addressed and responded to from both Jewish and Christian points of view. The theological debate as it began after the separation needs to be studied from both sides; the opposing theological views need to be explained, critiqued, and reexamined in the spirit of an ecumenical exchange.

7. Most importantly, anti-Judaism and the Gospels must not be regarded as essentially connected, but rather entwined in the course of a history that can be understood differently. Meanwhile, one must learn to affirm the legitimacy of theological debate that both connects and separates Judaism and Christianity while denying, in the name of both religions, the anti-Jewish or anti-Christian sentiment or attitude, which is incompatible with respect for human dignity.

8. Anti-Judaism refers not to negative attitudes toward Jewish people generally speaking, but to a specific "Christian" form of anti-

Judaism, which in time came to quintessential expression in the cruel charge leveled by some Christians against Jewish people that they are "Christ-killers."

THE RESEARCH FOSTERED IN THIS BOOK

It is undisputed that certain texts in the Gospels have been interpreted in a manner that feeds "Christian" anti-Judaism. Matt. 27:25 is a classic case in point. The research fostered in this project focuses on the historical question: When and under what circumstances did these Gospel texts begin to serve anti-Jewish ends? Specifically, for example, can it be said that the evangelists were anti-Jewish? Are there texts or tendencies in the Gospels that were originally intended by the evangelists to injure the Jewish people or their religion, or to work against the interests of the Jewish people and/or their religion?

If so, it is important to document such facts carefully and completely. Scholars who offer answers to such questions bear a heavy responsibility at this point. Conversely, if a passage traditionally interpreted in an anti-Jewish way does not on a careful reading appear to call for an anti-Jewish attitude or action on the part of the intended readers of the Gospels, the reasons for coming to this conclusion also need to be laid out carefully and completely. The burden scholars bear in both cases is equally heavy.

ACKNOWLEDGMENTS

Obviously, a research project such as the one that produced this volume requires the cooperation and dedication of many people.

The members of the research planning committee and the institutions they represented were as follows:

> Ted Cabal, Southwestern Baptist Theological Seminary
> Mark Goodwin, University of Dallas
> Edward John McMahon II, Texas Christian University
> David Naugle, Dallas Baptist University
> Jordan Ofseyer, Congregation Shearith Israel, Dallas
> Daryl D. Schmidt, Texas Christian University
> Joseph Tyson, Southern Methodist University
> William R. Farmer, University of Dallas (Chair)

The organizing meeting of the first stage took place at the University of Dallas on 3 October 1994. One of the first actions of the research

planning committee was to decide to bring into its consultative process
two experts from outside the Southwest having extensive knowledge of
Judaism in the Second Temple period. These two scholars were Shaye
Cohen of Brown University and E. P. Sanders of Duke University.

Each member of the research planning committee was asked to recommend colleagues in the Southwest they thought competent to make
meaningful contributions to the research project. These scholars were
then invited to participate with the request that they in turn send names
of colleagues they could recommend. In this way the committee was
put in touch with a total of over thirty New Testament scholars in the
Southwest who were recommended by one or more of their colleagues.
Each scholar so recommended was invited to participate in stage two
of the project, which centered around a series of research conversations
with Professors Cohen and Sanders. In the end, the following scholars
were willing and able to join members of the committee and Professors
Cohen and Sanders as participants in the research conversations that
took place on the campus of the University of Dallas from 31 March to
2 April 1995:

> Norman A. Beck, Texas Lutheran College
> Paul Coke, Episcopal Theological Seminary of the Southwest
> Denis Farkasfalvy, Cistercian Abbey, Irving, Texas
> William Frank, University of Dallas
> Sidney Hall, Methodist Minister, Austin, Texas
> Roch Kereszty, University of Dallas
> Philip L. Shuler, McMurry University
> Todd Still, Dallas Baptist University

By special invitation, also participating in one or more of the research
conversations were the following:

> Sarah Baumgartner Thurow, University of Dallas
> Margaret Obrecht, Office of Church Relations of the U.S.
>   Holocaust Museum
> Susannah Heschel, Case Western Reserve University

In addition to those already named, I would especially like to acknowledge Cynthia Stewart for her work in organizing and coordinating
the physical facilities necessary for stage two and stage three and for her
role in bringing this volume to press. Her input throughout the project
has always been appreciated. Thanks also go to Susan Earles and Duane

Edinger for their help in coordinating the activities of the stage three conference.

The contributions of Professors Shaye Cohen and E. P. Sanders at an early and formative stage in the development of this research project are especially to be acknowledged. At the end of the project both were invited to examine the five major research papers in this book as well as the responses thereto, with a request that they would thereafter consider offering contributions of their own to the published volume. Each agreed to receive a set of the papers, but with the stipulation that, because of the time constraints, no promise could be made to submit a contribution. As it turned out, only Professor Sanders was able to make room in his schedule to prepare an essay. This introduction closes by citing a few words from the introductory paragraph of his essay:

> In the spring of 1995, I attended the planning conference on anti-Judaism and the Gospels. . . . Unfortunately, I was unable to attend the full conference that resulted in the publication of this volume, but I am pleased to have been associated, if only in a preliminary way, with the project. This book succeeds in giving a comprehensive view of the problem it addresses, and the essays are clear, forthright presentations that will help the reader see what the issues were when the Gospels were written and what they still are.

❧ O • N • E ❧

ANTI-JUDAISM AND
THE GOSPEL OF MATTHEW
Amy-Jill Levine

BY ASSIGNING THE TOPIC of anti-Judaism and the Gospel of Matthew, the conference conveners have left me, like the disciples, "greatly distressed." Each of the terms is problematic, overdetermined, and methodologically conflicted. Definitions of "anti-Judaism" appear throughout biblical, sociological, and literary studies; "Gospel" can refer to the narrative text, its sociological origins, or the history of reception and application; even "and" signals a dialectic between Matthew and anti-Judaism rather than presupposes the presence of anti-Judaism in the Gospel. Moreover, how one term is defined has substantial implications for the understanding of the others. Finally, any discussion of anti-Judaism and the New Testament faces the intractable problems of who makes the decision, and on what criteria.

Were the matter of anti-Judaism as it relates to the New Testament not vital to ecumenical relations, Christian theology, and even the *Shoah*, I would forsake this task and flee. But, like those Matthean women at the tomb, I shall proceed with fear and great joy. My fear is based in my conclusion that there is, on my reading, an anti-Jewish component to the First Gospel. My great joy results from my conclusion that there is less anti-Judaism in Matthew's text than has sometimes been suggested.

A CONJUNCTION OF INTERESTS

Appropriate to a study of Matthew's origins, the title of this essay is not "Anti-Judaism *in* the Gospel of Matthew." The "in" formulation already insists that anti-Judaism is inherent to the Gospel's sayings and tone,[1] and it matches one of the definitions of anti-Judaism provided by the conference conveners: Anti-Judaism "is a thought form or attitude hostile toward Jews as such, thus virtually toward all Jews of all times — or, in this context, all Jews since the time of Jesus of Nazareth."[2] There is no doubt that Christians, and Jews, have interpreted the Gospel as anti-Jewish, but the question of whether it should be so labeled when analyzed in terms of its historical context and narrative presentation remains debated.

Some students of Matthew insist that the Gospel, rhetorically and socially, replaces ethnic Judaism with the "new" or "true" Israel of the church, that it removes the Jews as a nation from soteriological privilege and possibility, that "all the [Jewish] people" (Matt. 27:25) are responsible for Jesus' death, that only the Gentiles will inherit the dominion of G-d, the *basileia*.

Other students distinguish between the intention of the text and its reception,[3] and they frequently find the former to be innocent of anti-Judaism. Asserting that Matthew has been misread by those who would label it anti-Judaic, they insist to the contrary that the Gospel as text and message proclaims love and grace. This benevolent disculpation (if one agrees with it) or apologetic (if one does not) derives from several exegetical perspectives: Matthew's Gospel has been historically contextualized such that its polemic becomes understandable and even expected when viewed in the setting of synagogue persecution.[4] It has been psychologically contextualized as the excess of the church's attempts at self-definition in light of perceived or actual oppression. It has been generically contextualized as containing conventional prophetic excoriation and/or Hellenistic polemic. It has been religiously contex-

---

1. See Lillian C. Freudmann's introductory comments in her book with the telling title *Antisemitism in the New Testament* (Lanham, Md.: University Press of America, 1994), 3.

2. See note 10 below for another conference-generated definition.

3. Daniel Patte, "Anti-Semitism in the New Testament: Confronting the Dark Side of Paul and Matthew's Teaching," *CTSR* 78 (1988): 31–52; Adele Reinhartz, "The New Testament and Anti-Judaism: A Literary-Critical Approach," *JES* 25 (1988): 524–37. See also the discussion by Scot McKnight, "A Loyal Critic: Matthew's Polemic with Judaism in Theological Perspective," in *Anti-Semitism and Early Christianity: Issues of Polemic and Faith*, ed. Craig A. Evans and Donald A. Hagner (Minneapolis: Fortress Press, 1993), 57 n. 5. On such attempts to "do away with the anti-Judaism of Christian origin," see Gerd Lüdemann, *The Unholy in Holy Scripture: The Dark Side of the Bible* (London: SCM, 1997), 80–81.

4. Craig A. Evans and Donald A. Hagner, preface to *Anti-Semitism and Early Christianity: Issues of Polemic and Faith*, ed. idem (Minneapolis: Fortress Press, 1993), xix. They define "anti-Semitism" as "against the Jewish people" and "anti-Judaic" as "opposed to Judaism as a religion" (see in the same volume Evans's "Faith and Polemic: The New Testament and First-Century Judaism," 1).

tualized as a criticism of particular Jewish practices and beliefs, such as those associated with a reified Pharisaism, rather than a wholesale condemnation of Judaism. It has been hermeneutically contextualized as instructions to the church, or more broadly, as a parable about humanity writ large.[5] Such contextualizations frequently lead to domestication, and "to explain" becomes "to explain away." The burden of the anti-Jewish implications of the text is either erased, or it is placed not in the Gospel but on the readers.

For example, in its 1974 "Guidelines and Suggestions on Implementing the Conciliar Declaration Nostra Aetate (2)," the Vatican Commission for Religious Relations with the Jews observed, "With respect to liturgical readings, care will be taken to see that homilies based on them will not *distort* their meaning, especially when it is a question of passages which *seem* to show the Jewish people as such in an unfavorable light. Efforts will be made so to instruct the Christian people that they will understand the *true* interpretation of all the texts and their meaning for the contemporary believer."[6] The issue for me hinges on the italicized expressions. Unclear is how to determine whether a text says something or only seems to say something. If the problem is sufficiently severe that such guidelines are needed, then perhaps the qualification "seems" should be removed and the presence of anti-Judaism in the church's canon acknowledged.

On the question of the New Testament and anti-Judaism, the Vatican's commission and I have the same *telos* — the elimination of anti-Judaism from the church — but our subject positions and our conclusions differ. Such competing truth claims are inevitable; there can be no fully objective interpretations, because meaning is obtained in the conjunction of the text, its readers, and the communities of interpreta-

---

5. James A. Sanders suggests that "the Bible, as canon and as parable, is ultimately not about Jews and non-Jews in any of its parts, but reflects normal, human protagonists and antagonists in many kinds of situations on this rapidly shrinking globe" (foreword to Evans and Hagner, eds., *Anti-Semitism*, xvii). While politically appealing, this quotation leads ultimately to an erasure of Judaism and Jews. Better would be a both/and configuration: The Bible — the *Tanakh* — is about human relationships, but it is in particular about the relationships and the self-definition of a specific people. To universalize a group in the majority, such as Christians, plays into the hands of triumphalism — their story becomes everyone's story. To universalize the minority has the same function, since now what provides the minority its unique social identity is removed and, again, co-opted.

6. Italics added. Cited in Philip A. Cunningham, *Proclaiming Shalom: Lectionary Introductions to Foster the Catholic and Jewish Relationship* (Collegeville, Minn.: Liturgical Press, 1995), 2. Cunningham himself (p. 1) justifies his study by noting that "certain lectionary selections can promote anti-Jewish attitudes if they are heard outside of their historical contexts." Such a comment might, however, simply indicate that the text, heard by any competent listener, is itself anti-Jewish.

tion within which the readers live.[7] While anti-Judaic readings of the First Gospel may be declared in error from the perspective of contemporary ecumenical theology, I do not find them wrong from either a literary-critical or historical-critical standpoint. Whether my argument is, like the Vatican's, influenced by or even compromised by my own subject position — not only as a student of Christian origins, but also as a Jew who, at age seven, was told by a playmate, "You killed our Lord" — is a question I must leave to the readers of this essay.

DEFINING THE PROBLEM

Discussions of the relationship of Gospel narratives in general and the Gospel of Matthew in particular to anti-Judaism are not recent phenomena.[8] The sixties and seventies witnessed a spate of texts addressing the topic of anti-Judaism and the gospels.[9] Several of these volumes sought to demonstrate that any Gospel text even hinting at anti-Judaism, however defined, was (merely!) rhetorical and therefore not true or legitimate in a historical sense. Corollary to this was the

---

7. For helpful discussions of both postmodern implications for scriptural interpretation and the concern for the social location of the reader, see Daryl D. Schmidt, "Anti-Judaism in the Gospels and in Biblical Scholarship: Are the Gospel Narratives, Especially Matthew, Inherently 'Anti-Jewish?' (Or Is It Only Matthean Scholarship)?" I thank Professor Schmidt for providing me a copy of his text.

8. William R. Farmer suggests that nineteenth-century German biblical interpretation was affected by the society's need to accommodate cultural differences: "All scripture passages that had fed anti-Semitism had to be discounted. This meant that the words in Matthew 'let his blood be upon our heads' needed to be relativized, as did the condemnations of the Pharisees in Matthew 23" (*The Gospel of Jesus: The Pastoral Relevance of the Synoptic Problem* [Louisville: Westminster/John Knox, 1994], 152). The goal was accomplished by removing Matthew from its foundational place and by positing pre-Matthean sources with a less polemical stance. See also Farmer's "State *Interesse* and Markan Priority: 1870–1914," in *Biblical Studies and the Shifting of Paradigms 1850–1914*, ed. H. G. Reventlow and W. Farmer, JSOTSup 192 (Sheffield: Sheffield Academic Press, 1995), 15–49. Today, one finds instead supporters of the two-source hypothesis who claim — correctly, if their model of the synoptic problem is followed — that Matthew increases the anti-Jewish tone of Mark (see in particular Norman Beck, *Mature Christianity: The Recognition and Repudiation of the Anti-Jewish Polemic of the New Testament* [Selinsgrove, Pa.: Susquehanna University Press, 1985]). The comparison of "Matthean redaction" (e.g., Matt. 12:11–12; 16:2–3; 21:45) to the ostensibly more benign Mark confirmed the judgment. In a study of the First Gospel from a socio-historical perspective, the comparison with Mark is finally irrelevant; it is unlikely members of Matthew's community compared texts.

9. A helpful summary appears in William Klassen's "Anti-Judaism in Early Christianity: The State of the Question," in *Anti-Judaism in Early Christianity*, vol. 1, *Paul and the Gospels*, ed. P. Richardson and D. Granskou (Waterloo, Ont.: Wilfrid Laurier University Press, 1986), 1–19.

question of how Matthew's narrative could be anti-Jewish when it was in fact the "most Jewish" of the Gospels.

Scholarship's initial attempt to rescue Matthew from charges of bigotry was a historically appropriate as well as ecumenically profitable move. Anti-Judaism, a theological category, was initially distinguished from anti-Semitism, a racial one. For Matthew, Jesus is a Jew; the Holy Family, the women who follow Jesus from the Galilee, the eleven who receive the Great Commission, all remain (ethnic) Jews. One could confidently and happily proclaim that the Gospels were not anti-Semitic.[10]

But the exorcism of racial anti-Semitism was followed by the visitation of its fellow demons, a legion of definitions of anti-Judaism, and some of these were found to inhabit the Gospel. Whether Matthew is "anti-Jewish" depends on how one defines that term. One definition emphasizes the charge that Jews collectively are responsible for the crucifixion of Jesus.[11] Another stresses soteriology: Anti-Judaism is "a purely theological reality; it rejects Judaism as a way to salvation but not the Jews as a people."[12] Biblical scholars who focus on a particular text or writer tend to speak in their own discipline's language, with a particular emphasis on covenantal terms. McKnight, for example, uses the expression "anti-Judaism" for the "religious polemic exercised especially by early Christians who thought rejecting Jesus as Messiah was abandoning God's covenant with Israel."[13] The expression "anti-Judaism" evokes a range of meanings, from condemnation of Jewish leaders, to scorn for Jewish practices, to the elimination of the covenant between the Jews and their God, to the view that the Jews "killed both

---

10. See, among others, John Rousmaniere, *A Bridge to Dialogue: The Story of Jewish-Christian Relations* (New York and Mahwah, N.J.: Paulist Press, 1991), 6–7. A 15 February 1996 note from William Farmer to the conference participants makes this distinction explicit: "As distinct from the term Anti-Semitism, Anti-Judaism is a specifically Christian, theologically driven attitude toward Jews, including concepts of divine rejection and punishment of Jews, as well as Christian supersessionism and triumphalism."

11. Rousmaniere, *Bridge to Dialogue*, 7.

12. E. H. Flannery, "Anti-Judaism — Anti-Semitism: A Necessary Distinction," *JES* 10 (1973): 582, cited as "commonly employed" by George Smiga, *Pain and Polemic: Anti-Judaism in the Gospels* (New York and Mahwah, N.J.: Paulist Press, 1992), 11. Smiga offers a concise overview on the problem of definition.

13. McKnight, "Loyal Critic," 56–57. This notice of use by "Christians" requires emphasis, given the odd permutations of how Jewish "practice and belief" have been configured in the secondary texts. I want to avoid extending the inference, drawn by McKnight (p. 78) that "Matthew saw nonmessianic Judaism as itself 'anti-Judaism' because, in his view, true Judaism is messianic." With this definition, the problem of anti-Judaism ceases to be that of the church and becomes that of the synagogue, with those Jews who do not accept Jesus labeled the true "anti-Jewish faction." McKnight's point, narrowly construed, is valid but finally, not helpful for the concerns of this essay, since it allows the Christian gospel to define the term.

the Lord Jesus and their own prophets, and drove out [Jesus' followers]; they displease God and oppose everyone.... They have constantly been filling up the measure of their sins" and justly suffer punishment for their actions (1 Thess. 2:15–16).

To bring order to this spectrum and to facilitate biblical interpretation, Douglas R. A. Hare proposes three categories of varying intensity: prophetic anti-Judaism, an internal critique that resembles biblical prophecy in its hopes for the salvation of the Jewish people; Jewish-Christian anti-Judaism, also an internal critique, but one that replaces central Jewish symbols such as Torah and Temple with christology; and Gentilizing anti-Judaism, an external polemic that removes Jews from the hope of salvation and replaces Judaism with the "new," or "true" Israel of the church.[14] Because the first two categories presuppose a monolithic system called "Judaism" and the third suggests that only (ethnic) Gentiles would condemn those who keep Jewish practice, George Smiga refines the categories under the rubrics "prophetic polemic," "subordinating polemic," and "abrogating anti-Judaism."[15]

I locate particular passages in Matthew's Gospel as subordinating polemic, but I find the text as a whole conforms more closely to abrogating anti-Judaism. Consonant with subordinating polemic, the text proclaims that any practice or belief that lacks such a christological center is contrary to the will of heaven. Yet Matthew does not remove Jews from the missionary purview of the church and therefore from the hope of salvation; the Great Commission (28:18–20) extends the mission to "all the Gentiles" (πάντα τὰ ἔθνη), but it does not abrogate the original mission to the "lost sheep of the house of Israel" (Matt. 10:6).[16] The Jews do not lose any soteriological privilege; rather, in light of the change in Jesus' status (28:18), the Gentiles gain the privilege that they did not have prior to the cross and resurrection (Matt. 10:5b; 15:24). For the First Gospel, salvation is dependent not on ethnic identity or even confession, but on "doing the will of the Father" (Matt. 7:21,

---

14. Douglas R. A. Hare, "The Rejection of the Jews in the Synoptic Gospels and Acts," in *Anti-Semitism and the Foundations of Christianity*, ed. A. T. Davies (New York: Paulist Press, 1979), 28–32.

15. Smiga, *Pain and Polemic*, 12–23. See John Gager's similar concerns about the monolithic structure implied by "prophetic anti-Judaism" in his *Origins of Anti-Semitism* (New York: Oxford, 1985), 9. For yet another series of classifications, see Miriam S. Taylor, *Anti-Judaism and Early Christian Identity: A Critique of the Scholarly Consensus*, SPB 46 (Leiden: Brill, 1995); Taylor offers very helpful analyses of scholarly positions regarding patristic sources (Justin, Melito, Tertullian, and so on) and cultural contexts.

16. Amy-Jill Levine, *The Social and Ethnic Dimensions of Matthean Salvation History: "Nowhere among the Gentiles" (Matt. 10:5b)* (Lewiston, N.Y.: Edwin Mellen, 1985).

cf. 25:31 46), as defined by Jesus. Positively depicted are Jews (from Joseph of Bethlehem to Joseph of Arimathea, the women who follow Jesus from the Galilee and the eleven disciples who return to the Galilee to meet him) and Gentiles (the magi, the centurion of Matt. 8:5–13, the Canaanite woman of Matt. 15:21–28, Pilate's wife). Negative depictions encompass both as well (the [Jewish] population of Jerusalem that cries out for Jesus' crucifixion; the Gentile soldiers who mock him). Were the analysis to stop here, the evangelist would seem to be no more, and no less, anti-Jewish than anti-Gentile.[17]

However, the Gospel's presentation of Jewish and Gentile systems and figures reveals a qualitative difference. Gentile characters are, overall, positive; even Pilate is at worst cowardly rather than malevolent. Gentile culture provides a relatively innocuous foil (e.g., Matt. 5:27; 6:7, 32), and the injunction that the sinning member of the church be "as a Gentile and a tax collector" (Matt. 18:17) has a positive result: it is precisely the "Gentiles" (Matt. 8:10; 28:19) and the tax collectors (Matt. 9:9; 11:19) who prove receptive to the "good news" of Jesus. The Gospel's relationship to Judaism — defined according to the people, the culture, view of Scripture, ritual practice, and so forth — is more complex and, finally, more pernicious. As narrative, Matthew stands outside of the Jewish community's structure — apart from its leadership, its institutions of synagogue and Temple, its interpretation of Torah, its geographical centrality in Jerusalem, even its ethnic basis. Further, the evangelist co-opts and redefines these Judaic concerns. Going beyond the polemic of the Qumran scrolls in relation to the Sadducean Temple and Pharisaic practice, or the Pharisees in debate with Sadducees, the christocentric, *ekklesia*-oriented First Gospel moves toward abrogating anti-Judaism.

I am therefore satisfied with neither subordinating polemic nor abrogating anti-Judaism as an appropriate label for Matthew. The Gospel does more than subordinate, but it does not reject the Jews as a race or people. Indeed, at times I feel, as does Gerd Lüdemann, that the labels, and qualifications, and then more qualifications, are more distracting than helpful.[18]

---

17. This reading nuances Rosemary Ruether's claim that anti-Semitism is at the heart of Christianity (*Faith and Fratricide: The Theological Roots of Anti-Semitism* [New York: Seabury], 1974). For a more benevolent reading of Christian theology, see T. A. Idinopulos and R. B. Ward, "Is Christology Inherently Antisemitic," *JAAR* 45 (1977): 193–214.

18. See Lüdemann (*The Unholy*, 80–81) on instances where "a distinction is made between numerous forms of anti-Judaism, and the reader no longer experiences or knows

Nevertheless, exploration of how Hare's various categories can be and have been applied to the gospel remains helpful in determining where the salient issues are. The application, finally, brings me to shift the emphasis from the dialectic "Matthew *and* anti-Judaism" to the embedded "anti-Judaism *in* Matthew."

ABROGATION OF INTERNAL CRITIQUE MODELS

Prophetic polemic is an internal critique spoken from within the community and in some measure accepted by that community. The assignment of the First Gospel to this category — an assignment not infrequently made by well-meaning ecumenical interpreters — absolves the evangelist from the charge of anti-Judaism. The argument runs as follows: Amos caviled against the wealthy in Israel; Ezekiel condemned his fellow Judeans for placing their hopes in false gods. The prophets challenged the status quo; so does Matthew's Jesus.[19] Social and religious critique was part of the culture: The Pharisees did it, the Qumran scrolls do it,[20] birds do it and bees do it. Consequently, "If all negative statements about Jews and Judaism are to be designated anti-Semitic, then, absurdly, we will be forced to designate the prophets of Israel as anti-Semitic."[21]

Related to this approach is the identification of Matthean polemic as consistent with conventional first-century rhetorical modes. The vituperative language is harsh only to ears unfamiliar with the polemic arts of the agora. While the charges may sting, and while honor may be lost, there need be no underlying hatred.

Application of the models of prophetic polemic and conventional rhetoric to Matthew's Gospel is for at least three reasons compromised. First, the quantity or popularity of a particular manner of discourse does not keep that discourse from being abusive. It may be conventional to

---

whether historically there was any religiously motivated repudiation of the Jews in early Christianity at all."

19. See the observations by Sanders, foreword to *Anti-Semitism*, xiv–xvi; and in the same volume, Evans, "Faith and Polemic," 3–7.

20. Evans, "Faith and Polemic," 6–8; McKnight, "Loyal Critic," 55–79.

21. D. A. Hagner, *The Jewish Reclamation of Jesus: An Analysis and Critique of Modern Jewish Study of Jesus* (Grand Rapids: Zondervan, 1984), 289; cited, approvingly, by McKnight, "Loyal Critic," 56 n. 3. Less felicitous is the phrasing of Richard E. Menninger: "Matthew was not anti-Semitic but rather against Judaism (as were the OT prophets)" (*Israel and the Church in the Gospel of Matthew*, TR 162 [New York: Peter Lang, 1994], 22 n. 115); the description presumes a Judaism that is necessarily reified, sterile, and otherwise unpleasant.

imprecate one's opponents, but if there is no indication of reconciliation to be found, if the presentation is entirely one-sided, and if the targets of the rhetoric are eventually described as killing the speaker, the matter of its typicality is irrelevant. The rhetoric needs to be seen in its wider narrative context. Matthew has produced a narrative Gospel, not a speech in the agora.

Appeals to conventional polemic in order to absolve Matthew of anti-Judaism on occasion also misdirect the analysis toward comparison. In a discussion of the New Testament and anti-Judaism, it is not helpful to observe that "in contrast to Qumran's esoteric and exclusive posture, the early church proclaimed its message and invited all to join its fellowship. Never does the New Testament enjoin Christians to curse unbelievers or opponents."[22] The comparison of Matthew's polemic with that of the Qumran scrolls falters: The Gospel, not the Dead Sea cache, was (and is) disseminated to the making of new converts; the Gospel, not the scrolls, presupposes an audience outside of Judaism broadly defined. There is no First Church of Qumran hurling invective against Presbyterians. The point also should not be that the Gospels are "better" than the scrolls: Torquemada was probably "better" than Eichmann, and *The Dearborn Independent* "better" than *Der Stürmer.*

Second, the prophetic analogy fails to hold within the narrative. The prophets and the objects of their attacks (Hebrews, Israelites, Judeans, Jews) all recognized membership in a community centered around a common set of symbols, confessions, history, and traditions. This is not the case with the Gospel of Matthew and its opponents. The center of the Gospel is not Israel or even G-d; it is Jesus. Nor does Matthew attempt, as do the prophets, to bring the people back to a proper relationship with the Deity. The focus of Matthew is not entirely on *tshuvah,* repentance, with turning back toward good and away from evil. Matthew advocates a turn to something new.

The Gospel as genre is also distinct from the prophetic corpus. Amos, Isaiah, Jeremiah, Malachi offer separate oracles spoken by an individual. The Gospel, on the other hand, intensifies the polemic by distributing it through various speech mechanisms: the omniscient narrator presents a guise of objectivity, and so eliminates the possibility of reading the text

22. Evans, "Faith and Polemic," 8. The text does not need to enjoin Christians to do this; the curses are already present in the text, from the labeling of the scribes and Pharisees as "snakes" and "brood of vipers" and killers of prophets (Matt. 23:33–35), to John's insisting that the "Jews" are the devil's children (John 8:44) to the various condemnations of groups opposed to the seer of the Apocalypse (Rev. 2:6, 9, 20–21, and so on).

as hyperbolic or metaphorical. The narrator then couples third-person description with the direct discourse of Jesus: The opponents — the Jews who reject Jesus' message — are tackled from two sides. Even without taking into consideration the preservation by and placement of the Gospel in the church's canon as opposed to *Nevi'im* preserved by the Jewish community, the prophetic analogy fails.

Third, Matthew's Jesus does not simply follow current rhetorical practice, and it is unlikely that "the denunciations contained in this literature were a tolerable religious rhetoric designed to shock and revive."[23] To the contrary, the Gospel portrays Jesus as being condemned by his opponents in great part because of what he says. "When the chief priests and the Pharisees [a very unlikely combination epitomizing Jewish leadership] heard his parables, they realized he was speaking against them. They wanted to arrest him" (Matt. 21:45–46a). If the characters in the Gospel do not find the rhetoric tolerable, then why should those outside the Gospel?

Nor is it clear that Matthew sought to "shock and revive" Jews outside the church; the Gospel is more an in-house manual than a missionary tract addressed to the synagogue.[24] Those being revived are those already in the church, just as today one group can gain strength by listening to the vilification of another. Last, as Elaine Pagels observes, "Philosophers did not engage, as Matthew does here [chapter 23], in demonic vilification of their opponents....It is only the Essenes and the Christians who actually escalate conflict with their opponents to the level of cosmic war."[25]

Unlike those responsible for the scrolls, the followers of Jesus fought their battle for self-definition in the same neighborhood as the synagogue. This observation moves the discussion from one of rhetoric

---

23. McKnight, "Loyal Critic," 56.

24. On the in-house function of polemical rhetoric in antiquity, and for a general assessment of the forms and functions of ancient polemic, see Luke T. Johnson, "The New Testament's Anti-Jewish Slander and the Conventions of Ancient Polemic," *JBL* 108, no. 3 (1989): 419–41, esp. 433.

25. Elaine Pagels, *The Origin of Satan* (New York: Random House, 1995), 84; cf. Douglas R. A. Hare on Matthew 23: "The kind of anti-Pharisaism here evidenced is far too intense to be a matter of literary convention, as it is in Luke" (*The Theme of Jewish Persecution of Christians in the Gospel According to St. Matthew* [Cambridge: University Press, 1967], 96). See also Michael J. Cook, "Anti-Judaism in the New Testament," *USQR* 38 (1983): 127. Even Evans and Hagner (preface to *Anti-Semitism*, xix) acknowledge that the texts can be "abusive [but] not anti-Semitic." This difference in terminology may lack distinction. To be abusive against Jews is, it seems to me, to be anti-Jewish. Nevertheless, Johnson ("Anti-Jewish Slander," 441) finds, in conclusion, that "by the measure of Hellenistic conventions, and certainly by the measure of contemporary Jewish polemic, the NT's slander against fellow Jews is remarkably mild."

to one of sociology. In this neighborhood as well, the designation of Matthew's polemic as internal prophetic polemic finds no home.

Benno Przybylski neatly summarizes another common, and to a great extent correct, view among biblical scholars: "The true nature of the anti-Jewish polemic in the Gospel of Matthew can only be ascertained once the question of its historical setting has been settled."[26] With knowledge of such diverse topics as the theological and ethical contributions of the Pharisees, the pluriform nature of formative Judaism, and the relation of the Gospel to the local synagogue, readers can, it is claimed, see Matthew as the "most Jewish" of the evangelists and as engaged in a debate with fellow Jews.[27] Thus sociologically as well as rhetorically the First Gospel has been read as consistent with prophetic polemic.

The analogy to the ethnic joke is somewhat apt.[28] Jackie Mason tells stories about bumbling rabbis, and his audience laughs; Richard Pryor jokes about inept African-American men, and his audience laughs. But were the two to use each other's material, neither the NAACP nor the Anti-Defamation League would be amused. This observation is the flip side of Evans's citing Matt. 3:7–10; 23:27–33, 34–36, 37–38 with the observation, "Consider the bigoted tone that the passages have if we assume that the New Testament is a gentile book expressing criticism of the Jewish people."[29]

Such historical-critical reading emphasizes less the text (the narrative available to any reader) and its canonical placement (the equally available Christian Bible) than its — hypothetical — social context. At this point the analogy to the ethnic joke breaks down. We have more familiarity with the social contexts of a Jackie Mason and a Richard Pryor

---

26. Benno Przybylski, "The Setting of Matthean Anti-Judaism," in Richardson and Granskou, eds., *Anti-Judaism in Early Christianity*, 183. Too mild is Johnson ("Anti-Jewish Slander," 441) in concluding, "Readers today hear the NT's polemic as inappropriate only because the other voices are silent." The polemic may be "inappropriate" — regardless of its conventionality — even if the other voices were heard, if that polemic leads to violence or hatred.

27. Cunningham, *Proclaiming Shalom*, 3; and idem, "The Synoptic Gospels and Their Presentation of Judaism," in *Within Context: Essays on Jews and Judaism in the New Testament*, ed. D. Efroymson et al. (Collegeville, Minn.: Liturgical Press, 1993), 51–57; Rousmaniere, *Bridge to Dialogue*, 7–18.

28. See, among others, Joel Marcus, epilogue to Evans and Hagner, eds., *Anti-Semitism*, 292.

29. Evans, "Faith and Polemic," 1. On the "primarily Jewish internal struggle," see B. Vawter, "Are the Gospels Anti-Semitic?" *JES* 5 (1968): 473, 483; Evans and Hagner, eds., *Anti-Semitism*, xix. Evans's "assumption" is understated: The New Testament, by definition a canonical collection deemed sacred by the church, *is* a Gentile book.

than we do with the author of the First Gospel. We can see their audiences, we recognize the groups to which their shows and tapes are
marketed, and we know from their various public statements and private works that they are committed to, rather than dismissive of or
disparaging toward, their own ethnic communities (hatred of one's own
group is not an unfamiliar phenomenon). Unknown is Matthew's relationship to the Jewish community, however defined: debate still exists
as to whether Matthew is inside, outside, in between. There are no
definitive criteria for, and no end of the debates concerning, locating
Matthew's assembly geographically (the Galilee, Syria), demographically
(mostly Jewish, Jewish and Gentile both, increasingly or primarily Gentile), or in relation to the synagogue (did confessors of Jesus remove
themselves from the synagogue; was the evangelist encouraging them to
leave; were they thrown out; how is the synagogue to be connected to
the category of Judaism in the first place?).[30] Each configuration, and
set of configurations, leads to a different perspective on the topic of
Matthew and anti-Judaism.

If it is difficult to define anti-Judaism, how much more so is it difficult
to define Matthew's, or anyone's, Judaism? The First Gospel is seen as
being Jewish because it uses the circumlocution "kingdom of heaven,"
has five teaching discourses that may suggest a new Pentateuch, emphasizes a comparison of Jesus with Moses, retains rather than dismisses
Torah, restricts the initial mission to the "lost sheep of the house of
Israel" (Matt. 10:6; cf. 15:24), and even endorses the following of Pharisaic teaching (Matt. 23:3a).[31] Neither individually nor collectively do
these points or others make a definitive case for the First Gospel being
a part of Judaism; in some instances, they may support an anti-Judaic
impression.

If Judaism is to be equated with the term "Jew," then Matthew
rhetorically may be separate (cf. Matt. 28:15).[32] Then again, the single reference to the Ἰουδαῖοι may be to "Judeans" rather than "Jews,"
and Matthew offers no definitive alternative self-designation.[33] If Juda-

---

30. Best evidenced in the extremely diverse conclusions drawn by the contributors to
David L. Balch's edited collection, *Social History of the Matthean Community: Cross-
Disciplinary Approaches* (Minneapolis: Fortress, 1991).

31. A convenient summary of the "Jewish features of Matthew's Gospel" appears in
Smiga, *Pain and Polemic*, 52–57.

32. The title of Graham Stanton's major work, *A Gospel for a New People: Studies in
Matthew* (Edinburgh: T. & T. Clark, 1992), makes clear his view of separation, including
"a period of prolonged hostility" (p. 156). See also the summary of Stanton's scholarship
on this question in Schmidt, "Anti-Judaism in the Gospels," 14–15.

33. See Samuel Sandmel, *Is the New Testament Anti-Semitic?* (Philadelphia: For-

ism means association with synagogues, then again Matthew is removed ("their [αὐτῶν] synagogues" [Matt. 10:17]).[34] Yet the covenanters at Qumran did not favor the self-designation "Jews," and they too were separated from synagogues. If organizational autonomy (e.g., Matt. 16:19; 19:28) separates Matthew from Judaism, it also removes Qumran and probably a good many other groups and individuals in Judea, the Galilee, and the Diaspora. If separation is to be equated with synagogal persecution, there is again counterevidence: The synagogue used such discipline to keep people in, and if the synagogue were able to impose its will on an individual, then both parties had to agree that in some sense the individual was Jewish. Even more problematic for determining the relation of the First Gospel to Judaism: Hare argues that the synagogal persecution to which Matthew refers was an event of the past.[35]

Arguments for the evangelist's Jewishness, based on the text's concern for Torah, Jesus-Moses analogies, intensive concern with Pharisees, and so forth are equally fuzzy. The Gospel is replete with explicit fulfillment citations, references to biblical instruction, appeals to biblical characters. These references are almost unanimously positive: Moses and Elijah are ideal figures; not one jot or tittle of the Law is to pass away; the ancient prophets are inspired and their voices valid for the time of the Gospel; the covenant with Israel is preserved. The Gospel can seem so redolent with such "Jewish" concerns that one wonders if the five thousand were fed with pickled herring and a nice piece of challah.

Yet redolence need not be benevolent, and what is aromatic to one perspective may be rancid to another. True, Matthew makes frequent, almost incessant appeals to the Hebrew Bible. But there is no reason to assume such appeals serve as counter to a charge of anti-Judaism. The matter is one of exclusive and definitive interpretation of Torah: No scribes, Pharisees, Sadducees, no "Jews" can interpret Torah properly unless they read through christological lenses;[36] the only proper

---

tress Press, 1978), 69; and the developed argument by Anthony J. Saldarini, *Matthew's Christian-Jewish Community* (Chicago: University of Chicago Press, 1994).

34. Hare, *Theme of Jewish Persecution,* 104–5; cf. Menninger (*Israel and the Church,* 27): "Matthew's church was no longer part of Judaism because it was no longer part of the synagogue." The claim equates the institution with Judaism and naively presupposes (p. 25) that after 70 C.E., "If a group remained a part of Judaism (unlike Qumran) then this group would be directly influenced by Yavneh."

35. Hare, *Theme of Jewish Persecution,* 105, 114.

36. On the role of scriptural interpretation in the self-definition of the Matthean community, see Sean Freyne, "Vilifying the Other and Defining the Self: Matthew's and John's Anti-Jewish Polemic in Focus," in *"To See Ourselves As Others See Us": Christians, Jews,*

interpretation is through Jesus or one of his representatives. Rather than a sharing of sacred Scripture between church and synagogue, Matthew presents a co-optation. The parallels the evangelist draws between Moses and Jesus support this interpretation: While the status of each is enhanced through the comparison,[37] the juxtaposition reveals that Moses can be best understood through the main character of the Gospel, Jesus.

If to be a Jew means to cherish or even adhere to Torah, then Matthew fits. Then again, according to this definition, so do those foolish Galatians. The same point holds for the exhortation to heed the teachings of the scribes and Pharisees who "sit on Moses' seat" (Matt. 23:2–3). Those Galatians would have done the same. The problem is the scholarly tendency to equate Judaism (not only various movements in the Second Temple period but also modern varieties) with the *Tanakh*.[38] The majority of Gentile churches also held these books as sacred. Moreover, Matthew's exhortation may be less an acknowledgment of the Pharisees' theological legitimacy than a matter of self-preservation (cf. Matt. 17:26–27).

The Gospel's discussion of the Temple tax (Matt. 17:24–27) is also not definitive. Peter responds that Jesus does pay the tax, yet Jesus himself argues that "the children are free from it." Complicating the discussion, the tax is paid first by a miraculously found stater and then by Jesus' accompanying comment, "So that we do not give offense to them" (ἵνα δὲ μὴ σκανδαλίσωμεν αὐτούς [Matt. 17:27]). The pericope may indicate separation from, or recognition of belonging to Judaism, an excuse for what the community continues to do, or even advice that all in the community — Jew and Gentile — should follow.

To proclaim that Matthew is "Jewish" thus produces an overly expansive definition of Judaism, since the descriptions would also fit

"Others" in Late Antiquity, ed. J. Neusner and E. Frerichs (Chico, Calif.: Scholars Press, 1985), 117–43, esp. 134–37.

37. Dale C. Allison Jr., *A New Moses* (Minneapolis: Fortress, 1993).

38. Some scholars and churches reject the expression "Old Testament" in favor of "Hebrew Scriptures," or use "First" and "Second Testament" (cf. the policy of *Biblical Theology Bulletin*). This approach equates the importance of the two volumes, or even emphasizes that of the first, which may well sell short the explicitly "Christian" message. More, the emphasis on redefining the "New Testament" in terms seen as "compatible with Judaism" need not lead to improved ecumenism. Cf. Clark M. Williamson and Ronald J. Allen on referring to the *Tanakh* as "the holy writings of the Jews" (*Interpreting Difficult Texts: Anti-Judaism and Christian Preaching* [Philadelphia: Trinity Press International; London: SCM, 1989], 116). First, the book is also the holy writing of the church. Second, Judaism is not Leviticus, although this is the impression such language invariably leaves members of church congregations.

Judaizers or the gentile heirs of an originally (ethnically) Jewish congregation. But to proclaim Matthew as "non-Jewish" may produce an overly narrow one. Countering various claims of the First Gospel's Jewishness are some works claiming that Matthew is at best a heretical Jew, and others insisting that the text had a Gentile final redactor. Representing the former view, Freudmann suggests that kneeling "before a person as if he were a deity" (Matt. 8:2, 17:14) is for a Jew "inappropriate and forbidden"; that Jesus' rejection of his biological family "runs contrary to the Jewish principle of filial duty (cf. Matt. 4:21–22; 10:34)"; that Matt. 5:7–13 indicates Jesus' practice of sorcery, another forbidden activity; that cures would be unlikely in synagogues or the Temple, since these locations "did not serve as the local infirmary," and so forth.[39] The problem here is less Matthew's relation to Judaism than it is ahistorical apologetic. Formative Judaism was marked by diversity: The covenanters at Qumran separated from their natal families; Jewish exorcists are known to Josephus as well as to the evangelists; worshipful poses and the presence of ill individuals in synagogues would not be unexpected. The claim that the Gospel's redactor was a Gentile, a view still popular in certain circles of Matthean studies, derives in good measure not only from the Gospel's emphasis on the Gentile mission, positive portraits of Gentile characters, explanation of Pharisaic practices (e.g., Matt. 15:2a), and so forth, but also from the very negative picture of Jews and Judaism that these scholars find in the Gospel.

The discussion has come full circle, from the view that Matthew offers in-house prophetic polemic to the claim that the evangelist is a Gentile fully removed from and rejecting of Jews and Judaism. The question "Who is a Jew?" has been vexing and will continue to be so. To some, "Jews for Jesus" are Jews; to others, they are simply and only Christians. Some Gentiles within the church may see themselves as the "true Jews," yet others, both Jews and Gentiles, would deny this claim (cf. Rev. 2:9). As with the question of Matthew and anti-Judaism, the answer to the question "Who is a Jew?" depends in great measure on the person giving the answer. Would Jews in Matthew's community have seen the "church" as "Jewish"? There is not enough information available to answer that question. Would those bound by the church have seen themselves as "Jews"? Again, there is no definitive evidence, although even those scholars who emphasize Matthew's Jewishness agree

---

39. Freudmann, *Antisemitism*, 239–41.

that the community was a body comprised of both Jews and Gentiles or, at the very least, one encouraged to welcome Gentiles (Matt. 28:19).

Both from lack of evidence and inappropriate use of the data available, the common assertion that Matthew is the "most Jewish" Gospel is, finally, not helpful in a discussion of anti-Judaism. The suggestion that to be Jewish precludes an attitude of anti-Judaism is naive if not racist. Even if Matthew's polemic is the product of a "family feud,"[40] the family may not be functional. We have here not James and John, or even Jacob and Esau, but Amnon and Absalom. The label "most Jewish Gospel" is, finally, for the purposes of this paper, ineffectual; the expression is a Christian category that implies a comparison of Matthew's text with those attributed to Mark, Luke, and John; it would not be meaningful if the comparative categories were Mishnah and Tosefta.

Sadly, arguments of in-house criticism, often offered by church members with the goal of eliminating anti-Jewish readings of the First Gospel, may contribute to rather than dispel the problem. Those who would reconstruct Matthew's social setting as within Judaism usually take a second step and attempt to describe the relationship of church to synagogue. Were these arguments to suggest that Matthew's polemic is occasioned by the success of synagogue-based Judaism, perhaps the anti-Judaistic impressions of the reconstruction would lessen. However, this is not the picture presented by perhaps the majority of studies. Once the "reasons" appear, anti-Judaism hangs by their fringes.

According to one prominent theory, Matthew had good reason to be so vicious: "On the Jewish side the rabbis were expelling Jesus-followers from synagogues, denouncing Christians to Roman authorities," and so forth.[41] "Matthew's community, although suffering tribulation at the hands of gentiles (24:9; 10:22), was experiencing even greater persecution at the hands of Jews" (cf. Matt. 5:10–12; 10:17, 23, 28; 23:34).[42] Less violent in its picture is the view that the polemic results from the

---

40. The term is Cunningham's, "Synoptic Gospels," 56. Daniel J. Harrington uses the same term to describe the setting of Matthew 23 and analogizes the chapter to the controversies between Protestants and Catholics in the sixteenth century ("Retrieving the Jewishness of Jesus: Recent Developments," *NTR* [forthcoming]; my thanks to Professor Harrington for providing me a copy of his manuscript).

41. Rousmaniere, *Bridge to Dialogue*, 18; cf. Menninger (*Israel and the Church*, 27): "Jewish-Christians were probably excluded from Jewish synagogues long before A.D. 85."

42. Kingsbury, *Matthew*, Proclamation Commentaries, 2d ed. (Philadelphia: Fortress Press, 1986), 22, 111 n. 64; cf. p. 103. Less extreme is Erwin Buck on the "pronounced anti-Judaism" of the Gospel as arising from a church in the position of "a minority in danger of either being swallowed up by Judaism, or of being deprived of the right to consider itself a part of the true Israel" ("Anti-Judaic Sentiments in the Passion Narrative According to Matthew," in Richardson and Granskou, eds., *Anti-Judaism in Early Christianity*,

"anger and frustration at the continuing rejection of Christian claims and at the continued hostility of Jews towards the new community."[43] Is the language anti-Jewish? Yes. Whose fault is that? The "Jews" are at fault, whether that fault be imposing synagogue discipline or simply refusing baptism. How synagogue "flogging" (a means of keeping individuals in the system [cf. Matt. 10:17]) relates to synagogue expulsion is not explained. How one distinguishes Matthean hyperbole from historical fact is not addressed.

In the effort to locate the "hermeneutic of prophetic criticism," Evans provides several examples that require reconstructions of Matthew's (Jewish) context. Here are two examples: "Jesus taught, contrary to widely held opinion, that the poor and various social and religious outcasts would have an easier time getting into heaven than the wealthy and the ostensibly pious"; "Further developing Jesus' remarkable practice of extending messianic invitations to the apparently disenfranchised (i.e., the uneducated, the rabble, tax collectors, and 'sinners'), the early church all but did away with the halakic prerequisites for proselytization."[44]

For all of Evans's protestations about the diversity and plurality of Judaisms in the formative period, these two quotations require a single Judaism, or at least a widely held Judaism, that taught something contrary to Jesus. The plurality therefore becomes, to a greater or lesser extent, a unity in opposition to Jesus (and, therefore, the Gospels), and a negatively stereotypical unity at that. Evans offers no sources to demonstrate that Jews "widely believed" that only the educated would be welcome in the world to come. Since most people in antiquity were not "educated," since most, including Jews, were among the crowds, since the Jewish canon included "uneducated" people such as Amos, this view would at best have been self-defeating. On the other hand, we lack sources to tell us what the attitudes of most Jews at the time — including those in Matthew's community, wherever it was — were. Worse, we do have sources that insist on concern for the poor, condemn the abuses of the rich, and speak of the righteous Gentile.

Similarly common is the assertion that Matthew is universalistic

179). How one is deprived of thought is not clear, and deprivation on the practical side is not detailed.

43. Stanton, *Gospel for a New People*," 157, and cited by Schmidt ("Anti-Judaism and the Gospels," 15) with discussion.

44. Evans, "Faith and Polemic," 10, 12. The citation also risks the collapse of historical Jesus and baptized evangelist, and it slides too easily between class distinctions and halachic demands (which by definition extend to all classes).

while Judaism is particularistic, and therefore Matthew goes beyond Judaism in the call to disciple the Gentiles.[45] The universalism of the Gospel is a curious concept. There is no necessary contradiction between Judaism and universalism; there is no indication that the Jews in Matthew's community had consigned all Gentiles to hell; there was no single Jewish view of Gentiles in antiquity. Jews for the most part did welcome proselytes, but they saw no reason to engage in missionary activities to Gentiles, since, as can best be determined from the various sources available for the Second Temple period, they did not believe that Gentiles needed to be Jews in order to be in a right relationship with heaven. Conversely, to evangelize the world is not a sign of universalism if the process is motivated by soteriological exclusivity.

Given the textual, comparative, generic, sociological, and historical problems with viewing Matthew's presentation of Jews, Judaism, and Jewish culture as in-house and tolerable, I cannot support the view that the First Gospel represents prophetic polemic or reveals the hermeneutics of prophetic criticism. Even if these terms are appropriate for a study of the historical Jesus — and I believe they are — they are not appropriate for the interpretation of the Gospel of Matthew.

Also dissatisfying, however, is the third category of polemic: the view that First Gospel completely rejects the Jews.

GENTILIZING ANTI-JUDAISM (ABROGATING ANTI-JUDAISM)

According to the third classification offered by Hare and refined by Smiga, Jews are rejected as a people, and Judaism is rejected as a practice. McKnight, with direct appeal to Hare, suggests that "Matthew's Jesus warns of a coming judgment by God that will be visibly demonstrated in the sacking of Jerusalem. This judgment illustrates the withdrawal of the national privilege of the Jewish people."[46] The church forms a "true" Israel,[47] a "new" Israel, a third race or a new people.[48] The matter of anti-Judaism, which is not inevitably stressed and which

---

45. See Menninger (*Israel and the Church*, 35) on "the Gentile (or universalist) character of the Gospel."

46. McKnight, "Loyal Critic," 61, with reference to Hare in n. 20.

47. W. Trilling, *Das wahre Israel*, 3d ed. (Munich: Kösel-Verlag, 1964), and, emphasizing the idea of the remnant, Menninger, *Israel and the Church*. Perhaps similar is Sandmel's classification of Matthew as offering "authentic Judaism" (*Is the New Testament Anti-Semitic?* 70). McKnight ("Loyal Critic," 69) offers "new" and "true Israel" as well as "new people of God."

48. So Hare, *Theme of Jewish Persecution*, 157. See also Robert H. Gundry, *Matthew: A Commentary on His Handbook for a Mixed Church Under Persecution*, 2d ed. (Grand

is not infrequently denied by those who offer these descriptions, enters with the attendant classification of "the Jews" on the other side of the borders as "false" Israel, the old (i.e., outdated, antiquated, ossified, surpassed) Israel. They are no longer "the people of God."

In abrogating anti-Judaism, Jews apart from the church forfeit their role as bearer of the covenant and are in turn rejected by God: "The whole of Israel proves itself to be 'an evil and adulterous generation' (Matt. 12:36–45; 16:4; cf. 11:16; 17:17; 23:36) that refuses to repent and receive the kingdom of heaven."[49] These people are no longer "Israel" but "Jews," who remain in the persecuting synagogue, proclaim that the body of Jesus was stolen by the disciples, and fail to follow Torah. Their recalcitrance is easily explained: "Israel has fallen under the rule of Satan."[50]

Debate continues on whether Jews remain within the church's mission. If they do not, then Matthew proclaims abrogating anti-Judaism. If they do, then Matthew may be nudged into the second category of subordinating polemic. Both models rest on the interpretation of specific pericopes: the accounts of the magi and Herod the Great (Matthew 2); the expulsion of the "children of the *basileia*" (Matt. 8:10–12); the restriction of the mission of Jesus to Jews (i.e., non-Gentiles and non-Samaritans) in Matt. 10:5–6 and Matt. 15:24 and the Great Commission's exhortation to make disciples of πάντα τὰ ἔθνη (Matt. 28:19); the parable of the vineyard (Matt. 21:33–44); the portrayal of the Jewish leaders (Matthew 23); and the Passion narrative. The Gospel does suffer from the myopia of anti-Judaism, but the case is not as severe as one might think at first glance. The following examples suggest where anti-Judaism has been located, and why such readings are sometimes extreme.

Herod and the Magi (Matthew 2)

Matthew's second chapter has been read as a foreshadowing of the passion, in which evil Jews persecute the righteous while good Gentiles seek their well-being. For example, J. C. Fenton asserts, "In this chapter Matthew introduces the major theme of the Gospel: the Jews have rejected the offer of salvation, but the Gentiles will accept it." Equating Herod

---

Rapids: Eerdmans, 1994), and Stanton (*Gospel for a New People*) on "new people" but not "true" or "new Israel."

49. Kingsbury, *Matthew,* 78.

50. Ibid., 80; cf. Hare (*Theme of Jewish Persecution,* 145) on "the theological cause, the obduracy of Israel."

and "all Jerusalem" with "the Jews," and the magi with "the Gentiles,"
Fenton concludes, "The Gentiles will be brought into the place which
the Jews had forfeited by their unbelief."[51]

One major problem with this conclusion is that it omits the other
groups mentioned in the pericope: the *Jewish* Holy Family; the *Jewish*
children killed by the soldiers. The magi provide a contrast to Herod
and Jerusalem, and so highlight the faithlessness of the Jewish leadership and of Jerusalem. Yet they also parallel Joseph's association with
the child, with travel, and with dreams and so underscore his righteousness. Thus the lesson of Matthew 2 is not a division between Jews and
Gentiles, but rather the division between static, faithless, elite Jerusalem
and its leaders on the one hand, and the mobile, righteous, powerless
residents of little Bethlehem and removed Chaldea.

Who's Coming to Dinner? (Matt. 8:10–12)

Following the display of the centurion's faith, Jesus announces, "Truly
I tell you, in not even one in Israel have I found such faith. I tell you,
many will come from east and west and will eat with Abraham and Isaac
and Jacob in the *basileia* of heaven, while the children of the *basileia* will
be thrown into the outer darkness, where there is wailing and gnashing
of teeth." The pericope identifies neither the many (πολλοὶ ἀπὸ ἀνα-
τολῶν καὶ δυσμῶν) nor the children (οἱ...υἱοὶ τῆς βασιλείας), but this
gap is often filled by scholars: The many are Gentiles; the children, the
Jews.[52]

The vagueness should give pause. "Many" may include Diaspora
Jews (cf. the "ingathering of the exiles") as well as Gentiles. The υἱοί
may, in turn, be identified also as (Gentile) members of the church,
whose salvation is not guaranteed until the last judgment (cf. Matt.
13:38, where the same phrase is used for those apparently inside the
church). Again, the phrase recollects Matthew's polemic against the
elite, the "sons," and praise of the humble removed from the centers
of power. Finally, the narrative context of the logion indicates more
a praising of the Gentile centurion's faith than a condemnation of all
Jews. To the contrary, among others displaying faith in Jesus are the apparently Jewish leper (Matt. 8:2–4), the mother-in-law of Peter (Matt.
8:14–15), a paralytic and his friends (Matt. 9:2–8), Matthew the tax

---

51. J. C. Fenton, *Saint Matthew* (Philadelphia: Westminster, 1963), 44; similarly,
Smiga, *Pain and Polemic*, 58–59. See additional references in Levine, *Social and Ethnic
Dimensions*, 89.

52. See listings in Levine, *Social and Ethnic Dimensions*, 125–26.

collector (Matt. 9:9) along with other tax collectors and sinners (Matt. 9:10), a woman suffering a hemorrhage and a local leader (Matt. 9:18–31), two blind men (Matt. 9:27–31), a mute demoniac (Matt. 9:32–33), and other Jews not only in the cities and villages, but also in the synagogues (Matt. 9:35). Might the Gentiles be more righteous, considering that they had farther to come to sit with the patriarchs? Yes. Are the Jews as a corporate community displaced from the table? The text does not say so.

Exclusivity Logia and the Great Commission (Matt. 10:5–6; 15:24; 28:18–20)

In Matt. 10:6 (cf. Matt. 15:24), Jesus in direct discourse announces that he has been sent to the "lost sheep of the house of Israel." The term "Israel" necessarily means ethnic Jews (or proselytes) and, more narrowly, Jews within the borders of Judea and the Galilee: Jesus also tells his disciples, "Go nowhere among the Gentiles and enter no town of the Samaritans. . . . You will not have gone through all the towns of Israel before the Son of Man comes" (Matt. 10:5b, 23). These sayings have most often been read as either pieces of narrow, Jewish-Christian exclusivism with which Matthew did not agree but felt constrained to preserve,[53] or as the first evangelist's means of both demonstrating the guilt of the Jews and justifying the shift in the covenant from the Jews to the (Gentile) church.

These diverse readings, all anti-Jewish in one form or another, are countered by both historical events and Matthean narrative. The assignment of the exclusivity statements to a "Jewish-Christian" source is frequently a prejudicial move in two steps. First, it suggests that the restriction is a necessarily negative and unfortunate vestige of ethnocentrism on the part of a Jewish writer; second, it implies that neither Jesus nor Matthew (here untainted with the term "Jew") would have been so restrictive.

The exclusivity comments in Matthew 10 and 15 need not be read as negatives at all: They are not anti-Gentile; they are rather, pro-Jewish as well as historically warranted. There is no reason to believe that a well-organized writer such as Matthew would include (Matt. 10:6),

---

53. McKnight ("Loyal Critic," 67) proposes that "this kind of particularism serves a larger universalism: Jesus is sent to Israel so that the nations can be reached." How the Pauline evocation (cf. Romans 11) works in Matthew's Gospel is not, however, explained. For extensive discussion of the logia and their interpretations, see Levine, *Social and Ethnic Dimensions*, 13–52.

emphasize (Matt. 10:5b), and then reiterate (Matt. 15:24) antithetical material. Rather, Paul anticipates well the import of Matt 10:5b-6 and Matt. 15:24 in light of Matt. 28:19 by his phrase "to the Jew first and also to the Greek." The Scriptures were given first to the Jews, and Jesus himself came to them; he did not take missionary trips to Antioch or Rome. Nor does Matthew restrict the mission in order to set up the guilt of a people foreordained to fail (so Matt. 13:10–17).[54] To the contrary, the mission to the Jews remains open. Jesus' final exhortation is not, "Go now only to all the Gentiles, and stay away from those damned lost sheep." The Great Commission extends rather than replaces the original command. The mission of the church remains to the house of Israel,[55] but in light of Jesus' own change of status as occasioned by the resurrection and his gaining of "all authority" (Matt. 28:18), the mission goes to "all the Gentiles."

This extension means, on the positive side, that the Gentiles have been elevated rather than that the Jews have been demoted. On the negative side, it still means that anyone outside the church, Jew or Gentile, will not be bound in heaven.

One might compare present-day reactions to the Southern Baptist Convention's initiative to evangelize Jews. From the perspective of the Baptists involved in the process, the mission represents the special love the church has for the Jewish people. However, in this soteriological configuration, the Jew who does not follow Jesus is damned to hell. Jews, as the focus of the mission, may well see in this initiative not love but lack of respect for the fullness and integrity of their own tradition. It is not a compliment to be labeled an "incomplete" Jew. For many Jews as well as Christians, such a missionary process may well be, and has been, judged anti-Jewish.

Sour Grapes (Matt. 21:33–43)

Vineyard parables are fertile fields for those who claim Matthew to be engaged in abrogating anti-Judaism. Those who see an ethnic anti-Jewish import to Matt. 21:33–43 concentrate on the conclusion of the narrative rather than on the parable itself or its narrative context. In Matt. 21:43, Jesus announces that "the *basileia* of God will be taken away from you and given to a nation (ἔθνει) producing the fruits of

---

54. On exclusion, see especially Hare, *Theme of Jewish Persecution*, 146–66; Lüdemann, *The Unholy*, 106.

55. On inclusion, see Kingsbury, *Matthew*, 101; Menninger, *Israel and the Church*, passim.

it." Commentators then tell their readers that this nation is the "Gentile church." Hare, for example, states that the unfaithful tenants "represent Israel as a whole, not its religious leaders.... What is taken away, therefore, is not the privilege of leadership but the status of being God's special people."[56]

However, the summary statements in Matt. 21:43–45 combined with the details in the parable suggest that Matthew distinguishes between leaders and sheep. The reidentification of the audience, the "chief priests and the Pharisees" (Matt. 21:45; cf. 21:23), indicates that the various leadership groups within Judaism have banded together against Jesus and his people. The impression conveyed by the joint leadership can be anti-Jewish, but since the crowds remain distinguished from the leaders — the leaders are afraid to arrest Jesus because he has the support of the crowds — the text need not be read as such.[57]

The characters in the parable confirm the distinction between faithless Jewish leaders and faithful Jews in the crowds. A division exists between faithless (Matt. 21:33–41a) and faithful (Matt. 21:41b) tenants, but the allegorical subject (cf. Isa. 5:1–7, the Jewish community) remains the same. So too within Matthew's narrative the Jewish community may be divided into two groups: On the one hand are the crowds, prostitutes, tax collectors, sinners, and those who follow Jesus and John the Baptist; on the other are those complacent leaders and residents of the capital. But at no time in Matt. 21:33–43 do Gentiles enter the vineyard, or the discussion. Again, the impression can be anti-Jewish, since the faithful are only those who follow Jesus. Nevertheless, these faithful, in the story line, are also Jews. The people who produce the fruits of the *basileia* (Matt. 21:43) are not (only) Gentiles.

Jewish Leaders (Matthew 23)

The First Gospel labels the Jewish leaders "hypocrites, children of hell, blind guides, blind fools, blind, children of those who murdered the prophets, serpents, brood of vipers." They are charged with failing to practice what they preach; refusing to lift the heavy burdens they place

---

56. Hare, "Rejection of the Jews," 38–39; cf. idem, *Theme of Jewish Persecution,* 151. Many other examples are given in Levine, *Social and Ethnic Dimensions,* 207–9; cf. Lüdemann (*The Unholy,* 88): "Matthew takes over all Mark's anti-Jewish sentiments; he gives them further point by emphasizing the explicit handing over of the vineyard to the Gentiles and denies Israel any promise." Also arguing for an abrogating anti-Judaism, as Warren Carter reminded me, is Ulrich Luz, "Matthew's Anti-Judaism: Its Origin and Contemporary Significance," *CurTM* 19 (1992): 405–14.

57. See the detailed argument in Levine, *Social and Ethnic Dimensions,* 207–9; and, in agreement, Smiga, *Pain and Polemic* , 86.

on others; doing all their deeds to be seen; seeking places and titles of honor; shutting others out of the *basileia;* leading their proselytes into evil; corrupting the practice of oaths; trivializing tithing; being full of extortion and greed; being inwardly dead and unclean; being full of hypocrisy and iniquity; killing, crucifying, scourging, and persecuting prophets, the wise, and scribes; being guilty for all the righteous blood shed on earth since the time of Abel; and murdering Zechariah the son of Barachiah. Finally, they are condemned to hell. These are not compliments.

To observe that this is a caricature of Judaism, that the Pharisees were great leaders, that Hillel the Pharisee had much in common with Jesus, and so on is correct, and it goes a long way toward decreasing anti-Judaism in the modern church. But such observations do not absolve Matthew of the charge of anti-Judaism. Caricature and stereotype are stock techniques of polemic.

The topic of anti-Judaism and Matthew must address whether the leaders are to be distinguished from, or whether they represent, all the people. The "scribes and Pharisees" may be read as a metonym for "all Jews." However, vilification of the leadership need not indicate vilification of the followers. The Gospel narrative separates the leaders from the people, Jerusalem from the outlying regions, the center from the periphery. The narrative then holds out hope for the entry of the Jewish people as a whole into the church and out of the fangs of the Pharisees. At this point, Matthew is engaged in subordinating polemic. Additionally, the anti-Jewish potential of the chapter is possibly mitigated by the evangelist's tendency to use anti-Pharisaic language for in-house instruction; as in the Matthew 8 reference to the "children of the *basileia,*" so in Matthew 23 the hypocritical Pharisee refers to the hypocritical Peter, or pastor, or professor of theology.

Nevertheless, any Jew who chooses not to follow Jesus but who instead opts to stand with the Pharisees and scribes — any Jew who is not, in effect, Christian (granting that the term is not Matthew's) — becomes "twice as much a child of hell" as they. The non-Christian Jew yet to hear the Gospel is a "lost sheep of the house of Israel"; the one who hears and rejects epitomizes the damned. Further, even if the polemic is seen as directed inwardly toward the church rather than externally toward the synagogue, the terms themselves that are employed are not neutral. The negative example remains the Jew.

The lament over Jerusalem (Matt. 23:37–39) provides the strongest case for those who interpret the First Gospel as rejecting Israel. In this scenario, the Jewish leaders are viewed not merely as having failed their people; rather, the "failure of Israel" is the result of the "failure of her self-appointed leaders."[58] Although many scholars do see the leaders as representative of all Jews, I disagree. First, the evangelist makes a consistent distinction between elites and marginals, the static and the mobile. Among the former are not only the Jewish leaders, but also Pilate and his soldiers, the complacent residents of Jesus' hometown, those unwilling to follow the Son of Man on the road, the residents of Jerusalem. Among the latter are the very mobile Holy Family, the Jews who follow Jesus from the Galilee, the centurion who is willing to submit to another's authority, Joseph from Arimathea. The former are condemned; the latter are welcomed into Jesus' new family.

It is possible, although given the severity of the rhetoric doubtful, that Matthew retains some hope that even the Jewish leaders might join the new group. The absence of the Pharisees from the Passion combined with the evangelist's recognition that the scribes and Pharisees sit on Moses' seat and the positive scribal language in Matthew 13,[59] may signal the possibility of rapprochement.[60]

The Death of Jesus (Matthew 27)

In the Roman Catholic tradition, Matt. 26:14–27:66 or 27:11–54 is the Cycle A reading for Passion Sunday. Both selections contain the infamous Matt. 27:25, and both therefore suggest that "all the people" — usually interpreted by church congregations as "the Jews" — are responsible for the crucifixion of Jesus.[61] As Williamson and Allen observe, "the Bible readings for the day are among the most vitriolic and anti-Jewish documents from the hand of the early church."[62] Three general approaches have been offered for understanding the verse: the historical, the idiomatic, and the literary critical. All should be noted during

---

58. David E. Garland, *The Intention of Matthew 23*, NovTSup 52 (Leiden: Brill, 1979), 116; cf. Hare (*Theme of Jewish Persecution*, 151–52), and p. 94, which describes Matt. 23:35 as indicating "apostate Israel" and a "corporate whole"; and Sandmel, *Is the New Testament Anti-Semitic?* 69. Additional references and discussion are in Levine, *Social and Ethnic Dimensions*, 215–22.

59. See David E. Orton, *The Understanding Scribe: Matthew and the Apocalyptic Ideal* (Sheffield: JSOT, 1989).

60. Suggested by Williamson and Allen, *Interpreting Difficult Texts*, 87.

61. Lüdemann (*The Unholy*, 98–99) first notes that Origen's *Commentary on Matthew* for Matt. 27:25 concludes, "Therefore the blood of Jesus came not only upon those who lived formerly but also upon all subsequent generations of Jews to the consummation," and then observes, "These words contain the average Christian view of the Jews."

62. Williamson and Allen, *Interpreting Difficult Texts*, 85.

liturgical reading, yet only the last bears on the matter of Matthew's anti-Judaism.

Scholars frequently observe that much of the Matthean Passion narrative is ahistorical: There was no custom of releasing a prisoner on Jewish holidays; Pilate likely did not wash his hands to absolve himself of Jesus' death; the heavens did not darken; the dead did not come forth from the tombs; and the (Jewish) crowds neither cried, "Let him be crucified" nor cursed themselves and their children. The theologian is wont to argue that Matthew's picture is not "appropriate to the Gospel" because "falsehood is never part of the Christian witness."[63] Would that Williams and Allen had written Matthew's account of the Passion.

While these observations are historically correct, they underscore rather than remove Matthew's anti-Judaism. At issue for this essay is not what happened, but what the evangelist states.

Historically, Matthew 27 may be the evangelist's reflection on the tragedies of the war against Rome in 66–70 and the resulting destruction of the temple in light of the cross. If so, Matthew does not blame all Jews in all locations at all times for the death of Jesus; the condemnation was a local matter internal to Jerusalem. To make this case for Matthew's Gospel, the approach must shift from the historical to the literary. In the purview of the narrative, a distinction can then be found between "all the people" who speak before Pilate, and "the Jews" as a community.

Consistently, Matthew establishes a pattern of condemning Jerusalem and those associated with it. In the infancy accounts, "Herod and all Jerusalem" oppose Jesus, but the mobile magi and Holy Family (i.e., Gentiles and Jews, both in contradistinction to Jewish as well as Gentile Jerusalem) support him. The faithful second Joseph is from Arimathea. He does not even "work" in Jerusalem; unlike Mark and Luke, Matthew identifies him not as a member of the Sanhedrin, the Jerusalem-based institution, but as a "rich man." The resurrection appearance to the male disciples is not in Jerusalem, but in the Galilee. These geographical markers complement Matthew's insistence that belonging to Jesus' new family is based on action rather than on ethnicity. Joseph of Arimathea, the women who follow Jesus and weep for him, and even the repentant Peter do not cease being Jewish. Thus "all the people" (Matt. 27:25) who stood to condemn Jesus cannot mean "all Jews." It rather means "all the people of Jerusalem."

---

63. Ibid., 88.

This survey indicates that for all of Matthew's anti-Judaic rhetoric, the Jews as a people are not removed from their position of soteriological privilege, and they remain part of the missionary focus of the church. The Gospel is therefore not on the extreme end of abrogating anti-Judaism. However, as the discussion of claims for prophetic polemic has indicated, the text is not a benign, in-house warning.

CONCLUSION

The First Gospel establishes the locus of truth to be that of Jesus: Abraham's lineage culminates in him; Moses' Law finds its fulfillment in him; the covenant community is that which is gathered in his name. Those who do not proclaim him remain a part of the church's missionary endeavor, but they are outsiders rather than insiders. And as outsiders their belief systems, interpretations of Torah, relationship to Abraham, and so forth are at best irrelevant and, in actuality, condemned as false and unfaithful.

The Gospel is not, in any traditional sense, ecumenical. It does not proclaim that those outside of a belief in Jesus and the attendant baptism into the Father, Son, and Holy Spirit are following the divinely appointed path; its theology is fully colored by its christology. It is unlike contemporary works in Jewish-Christian relations, which explicitly do not seek "to convert the other person or even to reach theological agreement; history has already seen too many demands made on Jews to conform to Christian standards."[64]

Matthew's narrative is rather a text that has been read by Jews and Christians, converts to the church and those baptized at birth, people from all nations. Wherever it has been read, anti-Judaism erupts — not from all readers, to be sure, but from a significant number in a significant variety of cultural contexts and geographical locations. This excrescence is not, I believe, simply the result of the text's being read through Gentile eyes unfamiliar with Jews or Judaism; I believe even in Matthew's own community, the Gospel would have stirred up hostility toward any Jew who favored the synagogue over the church, the teachings of the Pharisees over those of Jesus, the sacrifices of the Temple or deeds of loving-kindness over baptism and eucharist. Since modern Judaism views itself as the heir of the Pharisaic tradition through

---

64. Rousmaniere, *Bridge to Dialogue* , 3.

such rabbis as Hillel and Akiba, then by Matthew's own definitions its members are children of hell (Matt. 23:15).

For the Jew to be told that there is yet the hope of salvation, that damnation has not already been proclaimed, that the door to the church is open, is good news of only a very minimal sort. The better news, which both Christian and Jew can take from the Gospel, requires that the heart of the text be located not in the very real anti-Jewish rhetoric, but in the equally real ethical exhortations. Here, the evangelist provides some hope for humanity: For all those priests and pastors and "Christians" who preached on Matthew 23 or 27 during the Second World War, there were some — in convents, in camps, in Le Chambon — who opened their Bibles to Matt. 25:31–46.[65] Did these good souls believe that the Jews would go to hell? Some did. But I can be content with the knowledge that they did what they could to prevent the final judgment and journey from being premature.

This last example returns us, finally, to the problem with which we began. The Gospel of Matthew need not be, and has not inevitably been, read as anti-Jewish. Nevertheless, as I reconstruct both the sociological context of the Gospel and the implications of the language it uses, I find myself reluctantly concluding the opposite: Matthew's text reorients and redefines Jewish symbols in a christocentric manner; Matthew's text, addressed to both Jews and Gentiles, is more than prophetic polemic according to categories of audience, tone, and genre; Matthew's text offers baptism as the initiation rite into the community of those bound in heaven. While I do not see Matthew as condemning Jews as a people or a race — they are still part of the missionary purview — ultimately I am forced, with great reluctance, to conclude that this reading is insufficient to dismiss the question. Matthew's Gospel is, in my reading, anti-Jewish.[66]

---

65. On the diversity of interpretations, see A. K. M. Adam, "Matthew's Readers, Ideology, and Power," in *SBL 1994 Seminar Papers*, ed. E. Lovering (Atlanta: Scholars Press, 1994), 435–49.

66. My thanks to William Farmer, Daryl Schmidt, Warren Carter, Anthony J. Saldarini, Daniel Patte, and Jay Geller for insightful comments and needed encouragement.

RESPONSE TO
AMY-JILL LEVINE
Philip L. Shuler

NO ONE NEED BE REMINDED that we are rapidly approaching the end of the twentieth century and the entrance to the twenty-first. This transition period produces hopes and dreams for the future; at the same time, it provokes considerable introspection. Included in such reflections will be lists of the most significant events that serve to characterize our accomplishments and failures, both as a people and as individuals. One event that casts a dark shadow over our past and our future is the systematic eradication of six million Jews (including one and one-half million women and children) during the 1930s and 1940s. One may quibble over the precise number, but one cannot justly deny the monstrous moral evil callously implemented through Hitler's "final solution," or with the fact that it took place in the full view of a mostly silent world.

Along with one of the survivors, Elie Wiesel, I cannot begin to understand this event, nor can I begin to comprehend its severity and magnitude. All I can do is mourn the victims, weep with the survivors, and pledge all my efforts to seeing that such never happens again. The last twenty years have witnessed an explosion of information related to the details of the Holocaust, information made public with the expressed purpose of preventing future Holocausts. A plethora of novels and stories of and by survivors has been collected and published, numerous courses have been and are being offered on university campuses all over the nation, movies and television specials have been produced, and quality museums have been built — all with the expressed purpose of increasing the world's awareness of what one human being (and culture) is capable of doing to another.

My own school, McMurry University, has offered such a course for the past eighteen years. From the inception of the course, the most haunting and vexing question students ask is, "How could such an event

happen?" This was the question the fifteen-year-old Wiesel asked his father as they walked in line following the selection that separated him
and his father forever on this earth from his mother and little sister.
"How can this be? Humanity will not tolerate it, will it, father?"[1] As
troubling as the question is, some of the answers given, especially those
accompanied with little reflection, are even more disturbing. I well remember one of those early sessions during which I had spent almost
three hours "easing" into the subject of the Holocaust. As students were
leaving, one woman (a local minister's wife) commented, "I don't know
why we spent all of this time. I know why the Holocaust happened." I
responded by asking her to enlighten me. She simply replied, "Because
they killed Jesus, God's Son!" Equally horrifying is the personal account
of the author of the essay presently under consideration, when at the
impressionable age of seven years she was told by her then best friend,
"You killed our Lord!"

Professor Amy-Jill Levine of Vanderbilt University has presented an
excellent essay on the first book of the New Testament canon, the
Gospel according to Matthew. It attempts to examine and assess the
topic of anti-Judaism and Matthew's Gospel. Our author is a competent New Testament exegete who herself is Jewish. I personally owe
Professor Levine a word of thanks for the thoroughness and quality of
her work. That she can speak from experience about the cruel effect of
anti-Judaism serves to remind me of the seriousness of the topic we are
addressing, and of the high purpose of this particular collegial exchange.

The first portion of Levine's essay focuses on the secondary discussions and their interpretations of Matthew's Gospel. She distinguishes
between the terms "anti-Semitism" and "anti-Judaism," noting that the
racial connotation of the former is not relevant for a discussion of the
first canonical Gospel; rather, the theological category, "anti-Judaism,"
is the point of focus. In this regard, Levine respectfully notes the contributions of Douglas R. A. Hare's three categories of polemic, which
include "prophetic anti-Judaism," "Jewish-Christian anti-Judaism," and
"Gentilizing anti-Judaism"; but in her own analysis, she prefers George
Smiga's "prophetic polemic," "subordinating polemic," and "abrogating anti-Judaism" as the better terms. She is not totally comfortable
with these terms, but chooses to employ them in her presentation as
affording her the best way to bring clarity to the salient issues. The en-

---

1. Elie Wiesel, *The Night Trilogy: Night, Dawn, the Accident* (New York: Hill and
Wang, 1994), 42 (here paraphrased).

suing discussions of these categories by Levine highlight the plethora of ambiguities encountered in the consideration of anti-Judaism and Matthew's Gospel. For example, Levine writes, "Unknown is Matthew's relationship to the Jewish community, however defined; debate still exists as to whether Matthew is inside, outside, in between"; "If it is difficult to define anti-Judaism, how much more so is it difficult to define Matthew's, or anyone's, Judaism"; "The Gospel is replete with explicit fulfillment citations, references to biblical instruction, appeals to biblical characters. . . . Yet redolence need not be benevolent, and what is aromatic to one perspective may be rancid to another"; "The question 'Who is a Jew?' has been vexing and will continue to be so."[2] These quotations (and others within the discussion that could be cited) serve to reinforce the validity of an earlier comment made by Levine: "The Gospel's relationship to 'Judaism' — defined according to the people, the culture, view of Scripture, ritual practice, and so forth — is more complex and, finally, more pernicious."[3] Here, I read Levine's use of "pernicious" to refer to that anti-Judaism that may emanate from the ambiguity of Matthean meaning rather than from an intentional literary design imposed by Matthew upon his narrative.

To this point, Levine has rendered an important contribution. She has reviewed in an informative manner the discussions among scholars of the alleged anti-Judaic character of the Gospel of Matthew. The manner by which she has accomplished this task reminds the reader of the complexity of the subject. It is something like groping through a mine field in which one wrong step or turn evokes explosive results. Even in the attempt to clarify the issues by reference to the three types of anti-Judaisms found within the discussions (i.e., prophetic polemic, subordinating polemic, and abrogating anti-Judaism), one can appreciate Levine's reluctance to use the three (or, for that matter, any) such categories. In truth, reality no doubt lies not in any single category, but rather in the dynamic tension that exists between all three of these categories, a tension that tends to obscure the defining differences. Matthew contains materials that are parallel to prophetic invective, redefines basic religious symbols and soteriological focus, and reflects a separation from one community (Jews) while opening doors to another (Gentile). In any case, the issue of anti-Judaism and Matthew's Gospel cannot be settled

---

2. Amy-Jill Levine, "Anti-Judaism and the Gospel of Matthew," in this volume, 20, 20, 21, 23.

3. Ibid., 15.

by reference to the secondary discussions apart from examination of the Matthean text.

It is in the section "Gentilizing Anti-Judaism (Abrogating Anti-Judaism)" that Levine moves directly to the Matthean text from which to draw her own conclusions. What follows is a discussion of selected passages frequently identified in scholarly discussions as reflecting anti-Judaism.

In Matthew 2, Jewish characters are presented in both positive and negative imagery. Into this scene ride the magi, who "provide a contrast to Herod and Jerusalem, and so highlight the faithlessness of the Jewish leadership and of Jerusalem.... Thus the lesson of Matthew 2 is not a division between Jews and Gentiles, but rather the division between static, faithless, elite Jerusalem and its leaders on the one hand, and the mobile, righteous, powerless residents of little Bethlehem and removed Chaldea."[4] In "Who's Coming to Dinner? (Matt. 8:10–12)" Levine concludes, "Might the Gentiles be more righteous, considering that they had farther to come to sit with the patriarchs? Yes. Are the Jews as a corporate community displaced from the table? The text does not say so."[5] The Jews are not specifically excluded from the table. Likewise, Matthew maintains the openness of the mission to the Jews in Matt. 10:6, and extends it to the Gentiles in Matt. 15:24–28 (and Matt. 28:18–20). The vineyard parables (e.g., Matt. 21:33–43) point to various leadership groups within Judaism that have banded together against Jesus and his people. At the same time, those who are faithful also include Jews. Again, Matthew's story includes Jews as faithful: The people who produce the fruits of the *basileia* (Matt. 21:43) are not (only) Gentiles. In her focus on Matthew 23, Levine rightly observes that "vilification of the leadership need not indicate vilification of the followers. The Gospel narrative separates the leaders from the people, Jerusalem from the outlying regions, the center from the periphery," and "the 'failure of Israel' is the result of the 'failure of her self-appointed leaders.' "[6] Admittedly, however, the negative example is the Jew.

The account of Jesus' death in Matthew's Gospel serves as a capstone to the polemic linking Matthew to an anti-Judaism position. As Levine observes, the church tends to interpret "the Jews" as responsible for Jesus' crucifixion. The literary character of Matthew's Passion account notwithstanding, at issue for her essay is not what happened, but

---

4. Ibid., 28.
5. Ibid., 29.
6. Ibid., 32, 33.

what the evangelist states. Consistent with Levine's exegesis elsewhere, she observes that the phrase "all the people" (Matt. 27:25), in reference to those who stood to condemn Jesus, cannot mean "all Jews"; rather, it means "all the people of Jerusalem." In summarizing the section she states, "This survey indicates that for all of Matthew's anti-Judaic rhetoric, the Jews as a people are not removed from their position of soteriological privilege, and they remain part of the missionary focus of the church. The Gospel is therefore not on the extreme end of abrogating anti-Judaism."[7] In view of the results of Levine's work, and the manner in which her analyses of the Matthean texts does not yield a consistent and aggressive anti-Judaic character, one may be a bit surprised at her concluding statement: "While I do not see Matthew as condemning Jews as a people or a race — they are still part of the missionary purview — ultimately I am forced, with great reluctance, to conclude that this reading is insufficient to dismiss the question. Matthew's Gospel is, in my reading, anti-Jewish."[8] In view of her own analysis of the evidence generally cited to support the view that Matthew is anti-Jewish, how is such a conclusion possible?

Levine's conclusion derives from her analysis of the wider literary and the soteriological character of Matthew's Gospel. She perceives that the center of Matthew's Gospel is not Israel or even God, but Jesus, and that any Jew who stands with the Pharisees and scribes rather than with Jesus — any Jew who is not, in effect, Christian — becomes "twice as much a child of hell" as they. In her conclusion she writes, "The First Gospel establishes the locus of truth to be that of Jesus: Abraham's lineage culminates in him; Moses' Law finds its fulfillment in him; the covenant community is that which is gathered in his name. Those who do not proclaim him remain a part of the church's missionary endeavor, but they are outsiders rather than insiders. And as outsiders their belief systems, interpretations of Torah, relationship to Abraham, and so forth are at best irrelevant and, in actuality, condemned as false and unfaithful."[9] Levine's identification of the soteriological thrust of Matthew's Gospel and the literary manner by which this soteriological affirmation is narratologically conveyed can signal an anti-Judaism within the reader who is predisposed to receive it.

On the one hand, as Professor Levine will attest, my initial response to her presentation was overwhelmingly positive. I could see how a

---

7. Ibid., 35.
8. Ibid., 36.
9. Ibid., 35.

reader of Matthew's Gospel could, on a subconscious if not a conscious level, become at least a silent witness to, if not a perpetrator of, the Holocaust. On the other hand, I realized that I was reading both her text and that of Matthew through my experience of eighteen years of offering a course on the Holocaust, through my personal repulsion to the Holocaust, and over the fact that the present volume was organized in relation to that event. Over the past several months, I have had to literally tear myself away from my own personal emotional involvement and attempt to read both Levine's text and that of Matthew from a different perspective. The soteriological thrust of Matthew's Gospel is a fact: New Testament scholars have long affirmed that the kerygma has largely shaped the narrative. The question confronting us here, however, is this: Has such an authorial purpose on the part of Matthew led him to produce an anti-Judaic text? More specifically, the question is not whether or not Matthew's text may be read as an anti-Judaic narrative, but whether or not anti-Judaism is innate to that text and is in any meaningful sense a purpose of that text.

At this point I looked once more at the definitions produced by stage two of the research program (see the introduction). Here anti-Judaism was defined as "antipathy toward Jews based upon a perceived inferiority of Jewish ways and manners ('Judaism')." If one uses this criterion as a measure — and I understand there is still discussion precisely at this point — then I find myself in dialogue with Professor Levine.

Consider, for example, the Matthean text. Although she has referred indirectly to the genealogy in Matthew 1, Levine's first text for discussion is Matthew 2. As a genre critic who addresses the question of literary type and function, I find the starting point of Matthew 1 to be crucial. The first verse is concise and direct, and Matthew locates his story of Jesus within the traditions of Abraham and David. This tradition is not in any way denigrated nor minimized; on the contrary, it is this tradition that authenticates the person of Jesus, who is central to Matthew's narrative. Professor Levine would, I think, agree.

In Matthew 2, the portrayal of Jews in positive and negative roles is instructive, but the primary focus is upon the Moses typology that Matthew employs. At this point, at least, I am unable to agree with Levine's assertion that Moses is best understood through Jesus. At issue in Matthew 2 is kingship, and Matthew apparently believes that Jesus' "kingship" is to be best understood in relation to that of Moses, that is, as savior or deliverer (e.g., as Moses is portrayed in Philo's *On the Life of Moses*).

Matthew's account of Jesus' view of the Law as found in the Sermon on the Mount, reflects no animosity. There is no soteriological challenge to Law proposed. Indeed, Matt. 5:17–48 tends to offer a more radical form of Torah obedience for its readers. And the negative critique implicit in Matthew 6 with respect to almsgiving, prayer, and fasting is not aimed specifically at these practices but at the manner in which the practices are often observed.

Levine's discussion of "Who's Coming to Dinner? (Matt. 8:10–12)" stands with little comment. The Jews are not excluded from the table. In her discussion of "Exclusivity Logia and the Great Commission (Matt. 10:5–6; 15:24; 28:18–20)" what impresses me is the lack of precision with which the various types of anti-Judaism may be applied. The reference to the "lost sheep of Israel" as a title is similar to the words of Ezekiel and could be linked with prophetic anti-Judaism, which is a category already dismissed as an applicable description of the Gospel as a whole. Levine's conclusion with regard to the Christian mission, that the Great Commission extends rather than replaces the original command, seems correct to me. As Levine will agree, this corresponds with Paul's position of "first to the Jews, and then to the Gentiles." The discussion of Matt. 21:33–43 ("Sour Grapes") is well nuanced. Under discussion in this parable is the notion of who produces fruit and who doesn't, not the issue of Jews and Gentiles. I have little to add to Levine's discussion of Matthew 23. She rightly notes that vilification of the leadership need not indicate vilification of the followers. I might add that vilification of Judaic leadership need not mean vilification of Judaism (assuming that it includes not only those persons identified as Jews but also the belief system to be practiced). I find little difference between the situation of Jesus here and that of Jeremiah on the occasion of the Temple Sermon (Jeremiah 7). Neither do I find a great deal of difference between the reaction to that Temple Sermon as described in Jeremiah 26 and the reaction to Jesus that will lead to his death (with the exception that Micah's words saved Jeremiah from death, though they were of little assistance to Uriah, son of Shemaiah).

With Matthew's account of Jesus' death we come to the most potentially inflammatory statements of an anti-Jewish nature. Levine notes that her essay is concerned not with what happened, but with what the evangelist states. I agree, and I also agree that the real discussion is to take place on the literary level, not the historical one. Even here, though, I agree with Levine that the responsibility is more local, and centered in Jerusalem and its leadership than with all Jews.

With regard to Levine's conclusion, I agree that "the Jews as a people are not removed from their position of soteriological privilege, and they remain part of the missionary focus of the church."[10] I also agree that the text of Matthew is not a benign, in-house warning; but then again, neither is the text of Jeremiah (emphasis on *benign*).

Having reached this point, we must deal with "Anti-Judaism and the Gospel of Matthew." Whereas my first tendency was to accept without question an intrinsic anti-Judaic polemic in Matthew's Gospel, I am at this point not prepared to do so. Given the nature and characters of the story, I am not convinced that the case has been made. On a literary basis, Matthew (and his Jesus) reflects a deep respect for the authority of Judaism, its history, and its religious practices (when performed from the right motive). Jesus' Jewishness is fully affirmed without apology, and the reformer garb worn by Jesus is apparent to the reader. At this point, therefore, I am not prepared to agree fully with Levine that Matthew's readers would have had hostility stirred up against the Jews based simply upon a reading of his Gospel alone. That Matthew's Gospel *may be* read to justify hostility is another issue entirely; but such a reaction (based on my own work) need not be *the* initial, primary, or even secondary response resulting from a reading of Matthew's Gospel. What is central to the Matthean text, as Levine observes, is soteriology — it is about "Jesus Christ, the son of David, the son of Abraham" (Matt. 1:1). Perhaps at this point the real question to be posed for further discussion is this: What precisely are the criteria one is to use in order to determine whether or not a text, narrative, or document is anti-Jewish or intrinsically contains anti-Judaism?

I'm not sure it is within the scope of my response to go beyond what I have said to this point. But I believe that a few remarks are in order. First, I think Matthew serves as a transition Gospel, both internally with respect to Matthew's message and externally with respect to the canon. Matthew begins his narrative thoroughly grounded in Jewish belief and tradition, and moves to the proclamation of Jesus Christ among the Gentiles. It begins as Jewish, even if it does not end in that camp. The author is rightly referred to as an *evangelist*, and the narrative reflects this Christian perspective. Matthew's Gospel serves as a bridge from the Old Testament to a new era of salvation as reflected in Matthew's story of Jesus.

Second, both genre and canon play important roles in accounting for

---

10. Ibid., 35.

at least some of the confusion and ambiguities surrounding our topic. Levine acknowledges the importance of genre, but chooses not to develop it. She writes, "Matthew has produced a narrative Gospel, not a speech in the agora"; "The Gospel as genre is also distinct from the prophetic corpus"; "The gospel is more an in-house manual than a missionary tract addressed to the synagogue"; "The problem here is less Matthew's relationship to Judaism than it is ahistorical apologetic."[11] In each of these quotations, clearly the literary type is crucial to the discussion. At this point, two observations appear to be worthy of note. First, there was an alternative available to Matthew. He could have written his story without implicating the Jews directly. Consider, for example, the kergymatic hymn of Philippians 2. Here, God's plan of salvation is conveyed without reference to any but divine responsibility for Jesus' death. Or consider how in Exodus, pharaoh's heart is hardened, and how in the Gospel of Luke, the disciples' eyes were blind to the recognition of Jesus, who accompanied them on the road to Emmaus. But the drama of the story is greatly enhanced, and the requirement of decision and renewal more immediate as Matthew's narrative now stands. Second, without going into my own specific views, I observe that most of the works in and around the period of the Gospels, especially works structured around personages, employed numerous techniques of embellishment and amplification, frequently created through the use of comparison.[12] The good guys are good and the bad guys bad. Such literary procedures do not by themselves produce "anti-isms." For example, the depiction of Egypt's role in the Exodus and the celebration by the Hebrews on the occasion of the demise of pharaoh's horses, chariots, and drivers (Miriam's song in Exodus 15) need not be interpreted by Egyptians as "anti-Egyptian" polemic.

As if matters were not difficult enough, how is one to deal with a text that has become Scripture? When it has been included in the canon? The issues become more ominous. Sacred Writ is inspired by God; it comes from God. Scripture is self-vindicating. In Christian circles, Scripture *is* truth (Luke 1:4; John 21:24) to which nothing can be added or subtracted (Rev. 22:18–19). Although it teaches and brings life, Scripture in any religion may appear harsh and even abusive; it may be employed

---

11. Ibid., 17, 17, 18, 23.
12. Philip L. Shuler, *A Genre for the Gospels: The Biographical Character of Matthew* (Philadelphia: Fortress Press, 1982); Richard A. Burridge, *What Are Gospels? A Comparison with Graeco-Roman Biography* (Cambridge: Cambridge University Press, 1992).

harshly and abusively. In both Christian and Jewish communities, Scripture prescribes and justifies human action. It sets forth Law and provides keys to its interpretation. Under its auspices, rules of the community are specified and enforced, and the threats to its faith are identified. Outsiders are identified, and punishments are rendered. Within its sacred pages, Saul falls from Yahweh's favor for his failure to perform *cherem*, the destructive sacrificial ban; Ananias and Sapphira die because they lie to the Holy Spirit about the value of property they have sold.

Perhaps one solution to the dilemma of anti-Judaism lies in an observation by Levine. She writes, "There can be no fully objective interpretations, because meaning is obtained in the conjunction of the text, its readers, and the communities of interpretation within which the readers live."[13] (Here she offers an appreciative note to Professor Daryl Schmidt.) Whereas on the one hand her comment may affirm that "truth resides in the eye of the beholder," on the other hand it serves to alert us to the virtual impossibility of the task we face except through divine assistance to hear, understand, interpret, and reach out in affirming love to all to whom God has in one way or another spoken a word of life. We have heard the word of life in Professor Levine's work. May my response serve to perfect, not hinder, that word.

---

13. Levine, "Anti-Judaism," 11.

RESPONSE TO
AMY-JILL LEVINE
Warren Carter

I WANT TO BEGIN with a brief and genuine word of thanks to Professor Levine, first for her collaborative and collegial approach, and second for this helpful and wise essay. She has covered much material with clarity, perceptive insight, astute critique, and a deep sense of the importance of this topic. I have learned much. There is much here with which I agree, even though finally I will suggest a somewhat different approach.

A CATALOGUE OF HIGHLIGHTS

Her initial comment about the difficulty and importance of this issue, and her warnings about claims of "misreading" and the use of contextualization to "explain away" are well stated.

Her discussion of the crucial but difficult question of definition helpfully settles on Hare and Smiga's threefold understanding of anti-Judaisms,[1] at least as a way of determining where the salient issues are: (1) prophetic anti-Judaism, or prophetic polemic, "an internal critique spoken from within the community"; (2) Jewish-Christian anti-Judaism, or subordinating polemic, which proclaims a christological center in the place of Jewish symbols such as Torah or Temple; and (3) Gentilizing anti-Judaism, or abrogating polemic, which claims that all Jews are rejected by the divine and the church is the "new" or "true" Israel. Unlike Hare and Smiga (also Luz[2]), who vote for the third position, Levine locates Matthew between subordinating polemic and abrogating anti-Judaism.

---

1. D. R. A. Hare, "The Rejection of the Jews in the Synoptic Gospels and Acts," in *Antisemitism and the Foundations of Christianity*, ed. A. T. Davies (New York: Paulist Press, 1979), 27–47, esp. 29–32; G. M. Smiga, *Pain and Polemic: Anti-Judaism in the Gospels* (New York and Mahwah, N.J.: Paulist Press, 1992), 12–23, 52–96.

2. U. Luz, "Matthew's Anti-Judaism: Its Origin and Contemporary Significance," *CurTM* 19 (1992): 405–14.

She discusses models of internal critique, rejecting them on rhetorical and sociological grounds. The use of conventional polemic does not prevent its abusiveness. Typicality is irrelevant if it leads to hate. The prophetic analogy fails to account for the shift from a common set of symbols to christology. Matthew's Jesus does more than engage in rhetoric. Sociologically, reconstructions of the Gospel's historical setting and claimed Jewish nature are impossible to determine, thwarted by definitional and informational deficits. Worse, this line of argument may exacerbate the problem through arguments that blame Jews for the conflicts.

Levine refutes Hare and Smiga's third option, that the Gospel evidences Gentilizing or abrogating anti-Judaism, that it indicates the ethnic and religious rejection of Jews. Like Levine, I do not read the key texts (Matthew 2; 8:10–12; 10:6, 15:24 and 28:19; 21:33–43; 23; 26–27) as indicating rejection. I also read πάντα τὰ ἔθνη in Matt. 28:19 in an inclusive sense, indicating a mission to all people, including Jews.[3] I agree that the religious leaders do not represent all Jews. Attention to the various roles of diverse crowds belies such a claim.[4] Nor do all Jews call for Jesus' death.

The elimination of the first and third options leaves the second, that of subordinating polemics and christocentricity. Yet this focus does not exhaust the Gospel. Its center can be located in lifegiving ethical exhortations such as Matt. 25:31–45.[5]

Throughout her essay, Levine engages a spectrum of scholarly work to produce an extensive and well-informed discussion. The breadth of her essay has two immediate implications. One is that this response can engage but a small proportion of the rich fare she offers. The second is that we should not let this great range of scholarly opinion go unnoticed. The existence of such breadth of perspective offers an important insight that I will develop in this response.

---

3. See J. P. Meier, "Nations or Gentiles in Matthew 28:19?" *CBQ* 39 (1977): 94–102. Particularly convincing are the uses of ἔθνος/ἔθνη in Matt. 21:43, 24:7, 9, 14; 25:32. *Contra* D. Harrington and D. R. A. Hare, "Make Disciples of All the Gentiles" (Matthew 28:19)," *CBQ* 37 (1975): 359–69. Levine understands ἔθνη (Matt. 10:16) to refer to Gentiles, but without abrogating the mission to Israel (Amy-Jill Levine, "Anti-Judaism and the Gospel of Matthew," in this volume, 14).

4. See W. Carter, "The Crowds in Matthew's Gospel," *CBQ* 55 (1993): 54–67.

5. Because of space restrictions in the main text, I will note here my disagreement with this reading of Matt. 25:31–45. I understand this passage not to be a statement of judgment on the basis of good works, but judgment on the basis of response to Matthean missionaries (cf. Matt. 10:40–42). See G. Stanton, "Once More: Matthew 25.31–46," in idem, *A Gospel for a New People: Studies in Matthew* (Edinburgh: T. & T. Clark, 1992), 207–31.

Initial Questions and Issues for Discussion

Levine employs categories of definition that differ somewhat from the working definition circulated in a 15 February 1996 memo from William Farmer on behalf of the research committee. In that memo anti-Judaism is defined in this way:

> As distinct from the term Anti Semitism, Anti-Judaism is a specifically Christian, theologically driven attitude toward Jews, including concepts of the divine rejection and punishment of Jews, as well as Christian supersessionism and triumphalism.

With its emphasis on divine rejection and punishment, this definition seems to be closely akin to Hare and Smiga's third category of Gentilizing or abrogating anti-Judaism. Levine rejects this position, though recognizing that the Gospel moves toward it. That is, it seems that she would have to agree that on the basis of part of the distributed definition, Matthew is not anti-Judaic. Yet she finds Matthew anti-Jewish on other grounds, namely as a subordinating polemic that advocates christocentric soteriological exclusivity. That position might be construed as Christian supersessionism and triumphalism, though she does not use that language. In the light of this observation, we need to consider the adequacy of the distributed definition and of her argument.[6]

Levine discusses Hare and Smiga's first category of internal prophetic critique as an approach that "*absolves* the evangelist from the charge of anti-Judaism" (italics added).[7] Several questions can be raised: Is Levine right in arguing that the Gospel is not internal prophetic critique? Is it simply not possible to say anything about the Gospel's circumstances of origin and address, or has Levine overstated the difficulties and ignored something of a scholarly consensus that favors some sort of Jewish rather than Gentile context? Is this approach of internal prophetic critique better understood not as an attempt to absolve the Gospel of the charge of anti-Judaism, but as an attempt to identify the *type* or *types* of Judaism opposed in the Gospel? Is Matthew anti-some-type/s-of-Judaism and pro-other-type/s-of-Judaism? For example, some forms

---

6. It may also be helpful to note that Louis Feldman identifies three types of anti-Semitism in the ancient world: governmental, popular, and intellectual (Louis Feldman, "Anti-Semitism in the Ancient World," in *History and Hate: The Dimensions of Anti-Semitism*, ed. D. Berger [Philadelphia: The Jewish Publication Society, 1986], 15–42). What we are discussing here has perhaps some affinities with his last category. Might it perhaps constitute a fourth group, namely religious anti-Judaism?

7. Levine, "Anti-Judaism," 16.

of Judaism are strongly denounced (Pharisees and Sadducees, often not distinguished from each other), but that is not the sum total of first-century Judaism. Another form of Judaism, namely, disciples who follow the Jew Jesus, is highly commended. Numerous òther forms of Judaism are not engaged.

Is Levine correct in rejecting Gentilizing anti-Judaism? Does the Gospel disenfranchise and reject Jews and Jewish practices from God's purposes, from salvation, and from mission, and replace Jews with the (Gentile?) church as the new/true people of God? Levine answers no. Does her discussion of key texts and insistence on a distinction between the religious leaders and the crowds support this conclusion?

Is christocentric soteriological exclusivity anti-Judaic (Hare and Smiga's second position of subordinating polemic)? Levine answers yes. Does the Gospel present its soteriology as christocentric and exclusive? Or is it theocentric with several soteriologies? If its soteriology is christocentric and exclusive, and if that system is available to Jews (as Levine thinks it is), does that christocentric exclusivity necessarily render the Gospel anti-Judaic (any more than it would be anti-Gentilic if other Gentile salvific systems are not legitimated)?

Is there anti-Judaism *in* the Gospel, as Levine finally maintains, or is the question misdirected? Does anti-Judaism inhere in a text or do readers and audiences, constituted by different social locations, construct anti-Judaic readings from polyvalent textual markers? What do we make of the very existence of diverse scholarly and nonscholarly views on this topic? Is her formulation that "the Gospel does suffer from the myopia of anti-Judaism, but the case is not as severe as one might think at first glance"[8] sufficiently nuanced with respect to various reading strategies and interpretations (even within the first century)? Would it reflect more accurately the Gospel's possible historical circumstances of origin, its content, and the diverse strategies of its readers to claim instead that *parts of Matthew can be construed as anti-some-forms-of-Judaism by some readers at some times, but not all parts, not all Judaisms, and not by all readers?*

DISCUSSION OF HARE AND SMIGA'S FIRST OPTION

I want to comment on several aspects of Levine's fine critique of Hare and Smiga's first option as a step toward a restatement of the essay's the-

---

8. Ibid., 27.

sis. My claim is that anti Judaism does not reside *in* this text, as Levine argues, but can result from the interaction of socially constituted readers with the textual markers of this Gospel.

It seems to me that Levine's objection to this first position centers on its assumption that Judaism and Christianity were not yet irrevocably separated at the time of the Gospel's writing. Her critique seems to be guided by the understanding that Christians (Matthew's community) and Jews *were* irrevocably separated from each other.[9] Hence, in claiming that the prophetic analogy fails to hold, she writes, "The prophets . . . recognized membership in a community centered around a common set of symbols, confessions, history, and traditions. This is not the case with the Gospel of Matthew and its opponents. The center of the Gospel is not Israel or even G-d; it is Jesus."[10] But is the Gospel "Jesuscentric"? Many Christian interpreters have so read it. But polyvalent texts are capable of various readings, and this one can be read otherwise as another story of the relationship between God and Israel. That is, a theocentric reading is quite possible. The opening genealogy and conception story utilizes the primacy effect to locate God and God's history with Israel on center stage. Within this theocentric focus, and only within it, does Jesus have any significance, commissioned by God to carry out God's task of saving from sin and manifesting God's presence in accord with the scriptures (Ps. 129:8 LXX [Ps 130:8 NRSV]; Isa. 7:14). To be Christ and Son of God is to carry out this divine purpose. To follow Jesus is to experience the reign *of the heavens* (Matt. 4:17–22). To receive Jesus is to encounter God (Matt. 10:40). Disciples pray to God (Matt. 6:9), serve God (Matt. 6:24), trust God (Matt. 6:25–34), do God's will (Matt. 12:46–50). Of course, this will is taught by Jesus (Matt. 7:24–27) but "these words of mine" (Matt. 7:24, 26; cf. 24:35) are significant only in that Jesus is *God's* agent. Central to this teaching are familiar teachings for which Jesus can claim no originality (Matt. 9:13; 12:7; 22:37–39). That is, one can read from the "inside," recognizing that there are common symbols, confessions, history and traditions, while also recognizing that the significance of these commonalities is multivalent and disputed.

---

9. In addition to the parts of this section of her essay engaged in the main text, Levine's concluding comment reveals the same assumption: "Even if these terms ["prophetic polemic" or "hermeneutics of prophetic criticism"] are appropriate for a study of the historical Jesus — and I believe they are — they are not appropriate for the interpretation of the Gospel of Matthew" (Levine, "Anti-Judaism," 26).

10. Ibid., 17.

Levine reveals this guiding assumption, that Christians and Jews were irrevocably separated from each other, in her comment that the Christians "fought their battle for self-definition in the same neighborhood as the synagogue."[11] She spends much energy establishing (rightly) that the terms "Jew," "Jewish," and "Judaism" are very difficult to define for this period. But equally problematic is the term "Christian," which she employs several times through this section without definition. Obviously, Matthew does not use the term "Christian" as a self-designation, and one should be careful about assuming or imposing it. In its absence, the Matthean community and its Gospel can be regarded, at least in a first-century context, as a (largely) Jewish group within the breadth of diverse, vibrant, first-century Judaism.[12] It is not unfair to claim that such a historical location is by far the dominant view in contemporary Matthean scholarship.[13]

This recognition raises questions about how Levine stylizes the intent of this critique. She begins and ends this section on Hare's and Smiga's first category with the claim that interpreters often employ this category in such a way that it "absolves the evangelist from the charge of anti-Judaism."[14] But such a purpose need not be assigned to this approach. If one does not assume a "Christian" reading of a Gospel from an author/group separate from "Judaism," one can observe that this category might be employed not to absolve such a charge, but to identify the type/s of Judaism being attacked and type/s being advocated. Not all Jews are attacked. There is, as Levine observes, a distinction between the religious leaders (most often Pharisees and Sadducees) and various crowds. Some Jews follow Jesus.

This guiding principle of separation is evident again in the claim that Matthew does not attempt, as do the prophets, "to bring the people back to a proper relationship with the Deity. The focus of Matthew is not entirely on *tshuvah*, repentance, with turning back toward good

---

11. Ibid., 18.

12. The terms "Christian" and "Judaism" (for a distinctive religious phenomenon) are largely anachronisms until at least the mid-second century if not later. A. K. M. Adam summarizes a range of views stretching from mid-second century to the fourth century ("Matthew's Readers, Ideology, and Power," in *SBL 1994 Seminar Papers*, ed. E. H. Lovering Jr. [Atlanta: Scholars Press, 1994], 435–49, esp. 443). See also S. J. D. Cohen, " 'Anti-Semitism in Antiquity': The Problem of Definition," in Berger, ed., *History and Hate*, 43–47. The use of χριστιανός in Acts 11:26; 26:28 should be noted.

13. For a range of views, see W. Carter, *What Are They Saying about Matthew's Sermon on the Mount?* (New York and Mahwah, N.J.: Paulist Press, 1994), 56–77.

14. Levine, "Anti-Judaism," 16.

and away from evil. Matthew advocates a turn to something new."[15] Whether the relationship with the Deity that can be constructed from this Gospel is proper or not will have to be decided on other grounds. However, it does seem to me that Matthew is very interested in relationship with the Deity — the concern with saving from sin, the manifesting of presence, the use of familial metaphors for that relationship, the notions of reward and punishment, the call for commitment and obedience to the divine will, the use of covenant traditions, to name but a few indicators. He is also very much interested in repentance. It is not insignificant that the first words out of the mouths of John the Baptist and Jesus are "repent" (Matt. 3:2; 4:17).[16] Throughout, the Gospel is concerned with how one perceives and how one acts and lives.[17] It repeatedly calls Jews (and Gentiles) to do different things and to live differently.

The important question then becomes how new is this difference. Is Matthew really not interested in "turning back toward good and away from evil?" Is it the case that the Gospel "advocates a turn to something new," so new that any limits of internal critique are transcended?[18] It is quite possible to read its emphases as variations on familiar themes, as continuity and discontinuity. For example, it promises divine presence in Jesus Emmanuel (Matt. 1:23). But while the claim that divine presence is especially known in Jesus is new, the claim that the divine is present is not new, as Samuel Terrien, for instance, has shown.[19] Within this tradition the Gospel claims that divine presence is encountered in Jesus, just as others had claimed that presence in various kings (Isaiah 7–8), in the words of prophets, in wisdom, in the Temple. But the Gospel does not claim that God is present only in Jesus. God's workings through Israel's history are recognized, in the genealogy (Matt. 1:1–17), in speaking through the prophets (Matt. 1:22), in inspiring David (Matt. 22:43–45); even the sun and the rain that bless all indiscriminately testify to them (Matt. 5:45). A similar case could be made for "saving from sins." The claimed *locus* is new, but the reality is not.

Throughout, the Gospel is reticent in making claims about newness.

---

15. Ibid., 17.

16. The verb μετανο(έ)ω appears three more times, twice lamenting the cities that did not repent (Matt. 11:20, 21; 12:41), while its cognate noun appears twice (Matt. 3:8, 11).

17. J. D. Kingsbury, "The Rhetoric of Comprehension in the Gospel of Matthew," *NTS* 41 (1995): 358–77.

18. Levine, "Anti-Judaism," 17.

19. S. Terrien, *The Elusive Presence: Toward a New Biblical Theology* (San Francisco: Harper and Row, 1978).

Although it talks of new wine, it does not talk of a new covenant in
Matt. 26:28 and does not, as Levine notes, speak of a new or true Israel. It requires a good way of life marked by turning from evil and $+_\sigma$
the time-honored values of "justice, mercy, and faith" (Matt. 23:23).
It does, though, speak in Matt. 12:40–41 of something greater that
is present, greater than Solomon and the Temple. Such a claim can be
understood as subordination and/or abrogation, but need not be if it is
viewed as a part of, rather than apart from, a tradition.

Does new focus mean separation? We have come full circle. I agree
with Levine that mission to Jews has not ended. And the content of that
mission is a call to obey the will of God as manifested in Jesus' teaching
(Matt. 28:18–20). But while Jesus rather than Moses or Enoch or Solomon is the one who manifests the divine will, this does not add up to
separation, since this Gospel and the salvation it offers are not, in my
view, *primarily* christological but theological, as I have argued above.

In this theological context, it is significant that the christology is functional not ontological. One follows him only in so much as he acts
on behalf of the divine. I suspect that Levine might protest that it is
irrelevant whether the christology is functional not ontological; its exclusivism is what counts. And with this I partly agree, though claims
of exclusivism need to be qualified (see below). But I would suggest
that a functional christology serves to underline rather than undermine
continuity in salvation history. It places the emphasis on God, defining Jesus only in relation to God, as one of God's functionaries. The
God who has been active since the creation of the world through Israel's
people, kings, and prophets continues to be active in this Gospel also
through Jesus. This is another stage, not the only or final stage, in the
relationship of Israel and God. In the diversity of post-70 Jewish claims
about the knowability of God, the Gospel's community is not connected
to something other than or outside Judaism. There is no canon yet,
no Christianity. On this reading in this context, the Gospel is pro-a-
particular-type-of-Judaism and anti-various-other-types-of-Judaism.[20]

Levine rightly argues, however, that the socio-historical situation of
the Matthean community vis-à-vis the Jewish community is difficult
to reconstruct and that claims of the Jewishness of Matthew are difficult to sustain. But while there are difficulties, some reconstruction of
some Jewish context of origin has seemed possible to most scholars.

---

20. Adam, "Matthew's Readers," 443–44; cf. S. McKnight, "A Loyal Critic: Matthew's Polemic with Judaism in Theological Perspective," in *Anti-Semitism and Early
Christianity*, ed. C. A. Evans and D. A. Hagner (Minneapolis: Fortress, 1993), 55–79.

But removed from such "Jewish" contexts of origin, and assuming a context of Christian-Judaism separation, this material of course looks quite different. If one posits, as some have argued, a Gentile community, independent of a synagogue or Jewish community, that no longer engages in Jewish mission on the theological premise that Jews have been rejected from salvation history (Hare and Smiga's third option), the rhetoric sounds much more hateful, final, and much less familial than if one posits a (largely) Jewish group recently separated or separating from, or in conflict with, a synagogue or Jewish community. I emphasize this point not to argue that an in-house dispute cannot be anti-Judaic (I have argued above that it can be anti-some-type/s-of-Judaism), nor to privilege circumstances of origin as somehow normative or definitive for subsequent readings and thereby suggest that subsequent readings are misreadings (texts *are* polyvalent — capable of various readings in diverse social contexts), but to highlight (1) that the Gospel can be read as anti-/pro-types-of-Judaisms and (2) that the issue of the identity/location of the reader/s is crucial in the formulation and evaluation of readings.

HARE'S SECOND TYPE OF ANTI-JUDAISM: CHRISTIAN SOTERIOLOGICAL EXCLUSIVITY

Levine describes the Gospel's subordinating polemic as proclaiming that "any practice or belief that lacks such a christological center is contrary to the will of heaven."[21] This christocentric soteriology seems to be accurate for Matt. 1:21–23; 8:10–13; 10:32–33; 26:28, and so on. But while her emphasis on the overall picture is well placed, there are some qualifiers whose significance should not be overlooked.

There is debate about the Gospel's soteriology or soteriologies. Betz sees a separate one in the Sermon on the Mount, where salvation is not "based on Jesus' death and resurrection as salvation event,"[22] but on his teaching and interpretation of Torah.[23] D. Seeley reaches the same conclusion. If they are right, there are two ways of salvation: either through Jesus' redemptive death or through "conducting oneself properly" by following Jesus' teaching.[24] And perhaps there is a third in

---

21. Levine, "Anti-Judaism," 14.

22. H. D. Betz, *The Sermon on the Mount: A Commentary on the Sermon on the Mount, Including the Sermon on the Plain (Matthew 5:3–7:27 and Luke 6:20–49)* (Minneapolis: Fortress, 1995), 555.

23. Betz, *Sermon on the Mount*, 31–37.

24. D. Seeley, *Deconstructing the New Testament* (Leiden: E. J. Brill, 1994), 21–52, esp. 25, with a focus on Matt. 5:17–48.

which love for God and neighbor (Matt. 22:37–39) and the doing of mercy (Matt. 9:13; 12:7) are central elements.[25] These are, of course, traditional motifs concerning life in relation to the divine, revealed by Moses and Hosea. While they may also be part of following Jesus, one can know and live them in continuity with the tradition without having heard of Jesus or being part of his community.[26] Along with the Gospel's emphasis on right living rather than confession in the judgment (Matt. 7:21–23), it is not unreasonable to read this dimension as qualifying a christological soteriological exclusivism.

Nor can Matt. 23:39 be ignored. While most read that verse ("For I tell you, you will not see me again until you say, 'Blessed is he who comes in the name of the Lord.' ") as a statement of judgment, Graham Stanton offers some good reasons for reading it as an oracle promising future salvation.[27] The juxtaposition of an oracle of salvation immediately after statements of condemnation (so Matthew 23) is not unusual in the biblical tradition. The previous use of Ps. 117:25–26 LXX in Matt. 21:9 is positive and joyful (hence the term "blessed") as the crowds welcome Jesus to Jerusalem. Moreover, to read Matt. 23:39 as an oracle of salvation renders Matthew 23 consistent with the deuteronomic pattern of sin-exile or punishment-return. To these considerations could be added the observation that Psalm 118 is a psalm of thanksgiving that celebrates God's faithfulness in delivering the psalmist and people from "all the nations (that) surrounded me." If Stanton is right, the verse indicates continuing divine faithfulness to the covenant and ultimate salvation of Israel. Rejection of Jesus in his ministry or in the present mission of the Matthean community may not be the final and determining reality. Just how that salvation might come about is a perplexing question, and Stanton does not speculate.[28] While a precise reading seems difficult, the verse does not require a christological reading, though it does seem to affirm the yet future salvation of Is-

---

25. Some have appealed to Matt. 25:31–46 as support for judgment on the basis of deeds of mercy. Regrettably for the argument being sketched here, I do not find that reading of Matt. 25:31–46 convincing. As I indicated in note 5, I am more persuaded by those who see Matt. 25:31–46 outlining response to Christian mission.

26. I am not assuming that Betz and Seeley are correct, only that they formulate arguments worth considering. The Gospel's soteriology needs much more attention. I suspect that narrative or audience-oriented approaches may prove helpful.

27. Stanton, "Aspects of Early Christian-Jewish Polemic and Apologetic," in *Gospel for a New People*, 232–55, esp. 248–51.

28. D. Allison argues somewhat differently on the basis of contingent eschatology. He suggests that the verse indicates a condition for Israel's salvation, rather than promising it unconditionally. *If* Israel repents and blesses Jesus, then Jesus will deliver Israel ("Matt. 23:39=Luke 13:35b As a Conditional Prophecy," *JSNT* 18 [1983]: 75–84).

rael. These considerations of soteriologies do not negate Levine's focus on christocentric exclusivism. They do confirm her observation that the Gospel does not remove Israel's covenant status. And they also raise questions about its christocentricity and its exclusivism.

A PROPOSAL

Throughout these brief comments I have been emphasizing the roles and locations of readers in formulating anti-Judaic readings of this Gospel. Assumptions and/or decisions that readers make about aspects of this text shape the resultant reading, as the diverse and extensive scholarly debate demonstrates, and as the above discussion illustrates. This focus on the active role of readers in constructing meaning differs from the dominant text-centered approach that Levine utilizes in her paper. She, of course, recognizes the role of readers. Her discussion regularly employs phrases such as "in my reading" and she clearly acknowledges that not all readings of Matthew are anti-Jewish.[29] Yet her text-centered approach is evident in statements of her central thesis. She writes, "My fear is based in my conclusion that there is, on my reading, an anti-Jewish component *to the First Gospel.* My great joy results from my conclusion that there is less anti-Judaism *in Matthew's text* than has sometimes been suggested" (italics added).[30] Or, "*The Gospel* does suffer from the myopia of anti-Judaism, but the case is not as severe as one might think at first glance" (italics added).[31] I want to revise some aspects of these formulations in sustaining the claim that since the identities, locations, and assumptions of readers greatly impact readings, anti-Judaism exists not in the text, but may arise in the interaction between text and readers.

First, the unnuanced references to Matthew's Gospel. Even N. Beck, who has offered perhaps one of the most detailed source and redaction discussions of anti-Jewish passages in the Gospel does not include the whole Gospel.[32] Parts of the Gospel can be understood to be anti-Gentile (Matt. 6:2, 7; 20:25) and anti-disciple (Matt. 7:21–23; 22:1–14). Parts

---

29. Levine, "Anti-Judaism," 50.

30. Ibid., 9.

31. Ibid., 27. Despite the title of her fine essay, "Anti-Judaism *and* the Gospel of Matthew," and despite pausing to note some implications of the choice of "and" or "in" in the opening paragraphs, Levine's phrasing of her thesis indicates that she actually adopts the later text-centered position. For her, anti-Judaism inheres *in* the Gospel.

32. N. Beck, *Mature Christianity: The Recognition and Repudiation of the Anti-Jewish Polemic of the New Testament* (Selinsgrove, Pa.: Susquehanna University Press, 1985), 136–65.

of the Gospel present Jewish characters positively, as Levine notes. Parts
of the Gospel can be read as anti-Judaic.

Levine writes that the Gospel's anti-Judaism "is not as severe as one
might think at first glance."[33] Who is the "one"? It is certainly not
George Smiga who, even after much study, still thinks that the Gospel has a severe malady. In contrast, numerous other scholars do not
think it severe at first or last glance. In the Matthean community com-
prising mostly Jews and a few Gentiles (if Ulrich Luz is correct),[34] it
is possible to imagine different responses ranging from hostility to compassion. Multiple readings are not a modern phenomenon only. To move
to a popular contemporary level, I have encountered some readers who
recognize and are upset and embarrassed by anti-Judaic readings. But
I have known other readers — for example, some students in a protestant seminary context, and members of various "mainline" Protestant
churches — who neither at first or subsequent glances have thought
this Gospel to be severely, mildly, or even slightly anti-Judaic. They are
genuinely puzzled when I mention anti-Judaism.[35] These readers demonstrate that it is not true to claim, even with qualifiers, that "wherever
[Matthew] has been read, anti-Judaism erupts."[36] But I have been puzzled by their response. How is it that I can't read this Gospel without
being deeply disturbed by what I discern to be anti-Judaic passages while
others read it and don't notice any?

I am not suggesting that their reading is inadequate or not sufficiently
sophisticated if it is not the same as mine. It is a matter of reading or
interpretive communities. My questioning — and listening — concerns
identifying the various reading strategies that these readers adopt in in-
teracting with this Gospel and observing the readings that result. For
example, some see the Gospel as fundamentally a history of Jesus written by an eyewitness. Almost all the players are assumed to be Jews
involved in an internal family feud (a variation on Hare and Smiga's
first position) between those who do and those who do not believe. For
others, their reading strategy allows no place for ethnicity and religious

---

33. Levine, "Anti-Judaism," 27.

34. For his argument that the Gospel recognizes and legitimates a turning toward Gen-
tile mission, see U. Luz, *Matthew 1–7: A Commentary*, trans. W. C. Linss (Minneapolis:
Augsburg Fortress, 1989), 82–92. I do not agree, though, with his claim that mission to
Israel has finished.

35. Professor Levine, in a private communication, indicates from her work with synagogue adult education groups, that these readers of Matthew "overwhelmingly are
appalled."

36. Levine, "Anti-Judaism," 35.

allegiances. They have so internalized the story that all the characters —
including the religious leaders, Pilate, Judas, and Peter — are types of
disciples like them, disciples capable of noble and faithful as well as
faithless actions. For this reading community, ethnicity and different religious allegiances don't exist. Self-examination in and exhortation to
discipleship are the name of the game.

On the one hand these strategies raise for me disturbing questions
about rendering "the other" invisible, yet on the other hand they are not
hateful readings. Readers who produce hateful readings "know" that
all Jewish religious leaders and people are, without a doubt, faithless
hypocrites who oppose the divine purposes while preserving their own
positions of power and privilege. In my view, this strategy reinforces
prejudice and stereotypes, maintaining sinful readings that violate the
call of part (if not all) of this Gospel to love (Matt. 5:43–48; 9:13;
22:37–39).

Levine's formulation — that the Gospel's anti-Judaism is not as severe
as one might think at first glance — is somewhat monolithic. It does
not recognize and cannot embrace these diverse scholarly and popular
reading strategies and experiences.

I am impressed with, if ultimately unpersuaded by, some recent papers by S. Fowl[37] and A. K. M. Adam,[38] who argue that texts do not
have ideologies. Readers, impacted by their socio-historical locations,
construct meanings in their interaction with texts. From his demonstration of uses of the Abraham story, Fowl argues that all interpretations
are ideologically loaded, that the diverse ideologies do not derive from
the author but from readers who put texts to ideological use in various circumstances.[39] Ideologies are not uncovered in texts. Changing
situations mean new readings. Interpretation furthers and shapes the
particular social, political, and theological agenda of a community.[40]

Adam, building on Fowl, says it this way: "people who are already

---

37. S. Fowl, "Texts Don't Have Ideologies," *BibInt* 3, no. 1 (1995): 15–34; also "The
Ethics of Interpretation or What's Left Over after the Elimination of Meaning," in *The
Bible in Three Dimensions: Essays in Celebration of Forty Years of Biblical Studies in
the University of Sheffield*, ed. D. J. A. Clines, S. E. Fowl, and S. E. Porter, JSOTSup 87
(Sheffield: JSOT, 1990), 379–98.

38. Adam, "Matthew's Readers."

39. Fowl, "Texts Don't Have Ideologies," 28–33. He is particularly indebted to
J. Stout, "What is the Meaning of a Text?" *New Literary History* 14 (1982): 1–12. If one
privileges the ideology of an author, one "privileges one phase in the interpretive history of
a text," rendering "the vast majority of a text's interpretive history as a history of distor-
tion and violation of its original ideological aims" (Fowl, "Texts Don't Have Ideologies,"
30).

40. Fowl, "Texts Don't Have Ideologies," 31.

inclined to read a text as anti-Jewish find Matthew a useful document, and then 'find' in Matthew a warrant for their pre-existing attitude."[41] "Readers bring ideologically determined premises to their encounters with the text, and produce ideologically freighted interpretations."[42] Ideology inheres in the intersections of readers with colleagues, texts, and other institutional and social constraints on interpretation. One cannot say that Matthew is anti-Judaic. Rather, anti-Judaic readings arise in particular circumstances. Or, to nuance it so as to emphasize the interaction of text and reader more than Adam (and Fowl) do, readers recognize and construe textual conventions or markers in particular ideologically shaped ways.

Adam supports his claim with two further arguments, one historical and one pragmatic. His historical argument emphasizes the existence of Judaisms, identifies Matthew as "a polemical tract on behalf of one particular version of Judaism," and protests against the anachronistic use of Judaism as a distinctive religious phenomena before at least the second if not the fourth century C.E.[43] Any criticism of Judaism is not anti-Judaism. Matthew does not reject Judaism but promulgates "what he took to be the *correct sort* of Judaism."[44]

Adam's less successful pragmatic argument surveys the use of Matthew's Gospel in Second World War Germany, notes its diverse use by both Nazis and resisters, and argues rather inconsequentially that "Matthew's Gospel was more prominent in the arguments of those who defended Judaism than it was in National Socialist propaganda." He notes its "little use" among Nazi propagandists and its use by those "resisting the anti-Jewish activities of the Third Reich."[45] Adam's point is not to "minimize Christian responsibility in the abominable persecution of Jews over the centuries."[46] This he acknowledges.

> The critical problem is not that the text of Matthew is anti-Jewish . . . ; the problem is that we live under conditions which make anti-Jewish readings too real and too attractive a possibility. . . . The reason we find anti-Judaism in Matthew is that we live

---

41. Adam, "Matthew's Readers," 437.
42. Ibid., 438.
43. Ibid., 439–44, esp. 442.
44. Ibid., 444.
45. Ibid., 445.
46. Ibid., 447.

in a culture which has enacted just the sort of anti-Judaism we are claiming to discover."[47]

The response is to "live (converse, teach, interpret, preach) in ways which make anti-Judaism unthinkable.... When we are willing to live without anti-Judaism, beyond bigotry and scapegoating altogether, then Matthew will simply not be read as an anti-Jewish text."[48] He offers as an example the (Gentile) Chambonnais, who did not turn in their Jewish guests because they did not see an anti-Jewish reading of Matthew as plausible. "They constituted a reading formation which identified the relevant Matthean text not as 'His blood be on us and on our children,' but as 'Truly I tell you, just as you did it to one of the least of these of my family, you did it for me.' "[49]

Fowl and Adam helpfully highlight the contribution of readers and their social contexts in formulating acceptable and unacceptable interpretations. Yet I have several reservations about their approach, not the least of which is their overemphasis on the role of readers and their social circumstances at the expense of *interaction* with the text. I would argue that a reader employs textual markers or conventions to formulate readings, thereby recognizing a text's contribution to this interaction. Diverse readers, though, can and do construe the same markers in different ways to construct diverse readings.

Certainly a reader's circumstances will enable that reader to notice and give significance to some textual markers while ignoring others. Adam demonstrates this reality in his comments about the choice of Matthew 25 rather than Matthew 27. But readers can also notice and utilize markers or conventions in a text to formulate a reading to which they themselves are opposed. Readers then have the responsibility of being resisting readers. They can read against the grain, can refuse to join the authorial audience, can formulate alternative readings, can choose life-giving readings.[50] The attack on the religious leaders, for example, can be construed not as an attack on all Jews but an attack on mis-

---

47. Ibid.
48. Ibid., 448–49.
49. Ibid.
50. See W. Carter, *Matthew: Storyteller, Interpreter, Evangelist* (Peabody, Mass.: Hendrickson, 1996), 1–11, 259–71; A. Reinhartz, "The New Testament and Anti-Judaism: A Literary-Critical Approach," *JES* 25 (1988): 524–37. Fowl ("Texts Don't Have Ideologies," 32) suggests that "if we find that the conventional reading of a text helps to underwrite racism, we can offer a counter-reading which resists racism."

taken notions of authority and power,[51] Matt. 27:25 construed as a cry of blessing for reconciliation not a curse.[52] We can refuse to hate and exclude.

In the light of these concerns, especially this emphasis on the interaction between text and socially-located and constituted interpreters, I would like to propose a revision to Levine's thesis. Is the Gospel of Matthew anti-Judaic? *My fear is that parts of Matthew can be construed as anti-some-forms-of-Judaism by some readers at some times. My great joy is not all parts, not all Judaisms, and not by all readers.*

With this statement I want to acknowledge a history of some terrible and destructive readings of this text, but also to recognize, in hope and with Professor Levine, the possibility that our readings do not have to be of this kind, that we can live and interpret so as to make anti-Judaism impossible. Is this naive? I do not think so. Not all Christians, for example, have read this Gospel in an anti-Judaic way in the last two thousand years. To posit that it is impossible for Christians to do anything but offer anti-Judaic readings may be to maintain a bigotry that equals the one resisted in this discussion. Christians do not have to surrender their identity, though, to recognize that they do not have an exclusive monopoly on ways of knowing the divine or experiencing salvation, or to recognize that they are not the exclusive heirs and interpreters of this tradition. To choose not to draw conclusions about who is and who is not acceptable to the divine, to choose to refrain from making such judgments, may in fact render a faithful reading of at least parts of this Gospel (Matt. 7:1–5; 13:24–30, 47–50).

---

51. D. Patte, "Anti-Semitism in the New Testament: Confronting the Dark Side of Paul's and Matthew's Teaching," *CTSR* 78 (1988): 31–52, esp. 49–51.

52. D. Sullivan reads the notorious Matt. 27:24–25 in the context of Passover as a statement of Jewish folks including themselves in the covenant and seeking its forgiveness: "By voicing these words the Jewish people . . . are voicing a similar acceptance of the covenant in the blood of Jesus"; they express "the commitment of the whole people" ("New Insights into Matthew 27:24–25," *New Blackfriars* 73, no. 863 [1993]: 453–57, p. 456). In the later Gentile church the verses are understood not as statements of inclusion but exclusion. Who is reading where, matters. See also H. Kosmala, " 'His Blood on Us and on Our Children': The Background of Mat. 27,24–25," *ASTI* 7 (1970): 94–126.

Anti-Judaism and the Gospel of Luke

Daryl D. Schmidt

Definition of terms is often the most crucial stage of any structured argument. That was never more the case than with this topic. In one important sense, our primary goal here is to arrive at a definition of anti-Judaism in its relationship to the New Testament Gospels.

To describe our purpose this way suggests that the most important word we have to define is the "and" in the title. We are seeking to clarify how best to describe the relationship that exists between the phenomenon called anti-Judaism and each of the Gospels. Obviously, the term "anti-Judaism" is in some sense the real focus here. But we each begin with some sense of what it is that the term describes. To be sure, how narrowly or broadly we define it will effect, in large measure, how much of it we find in any given object of scrutiny.

But now I have introduced the word "in" to define this relationship. I do not want that taken as normative. After all, "in" defines a much more specific kind of relationship that does "and." I want "and" to include much more that "in," or "as seen in," or "as defined by." I will take the "and" to be an invitation to look inductively at the range of ways one can describe the phenomenon of anti-Judaism in relationship to the Gospel of Luke.

In this particular instance, the Gospel of Luke is the object of scrutiny. Even though we all have a rather solid sense of what the Gospel of Luke is, a careful study of its relationship to anti-Judaism must begin with some awareness of what *all* the Gospel of Luke includes.

First of all, the Gospel of Luke is the only Gospel we know of, canonical or extracanonical, that has an explicit sequel. The prologue to the Acts of the Apostles refers back to "the first book" the author dedicated to Theophilus. By scholarly consensus that first book is the Gospel of

Luke, also dedicated to Theophilus. A wealth of scholarship has established the many common features shared by these two books, to such
an extent that much of that scholarship is about "Luke-Acts." There is
no consensus, however, about how best to describe the relationship between the two books, either in terms of genre or composition history.
I use the term "sequel" to indicate no more than the loose relationship
suggested by the prologues themselves.

The existence of the sequel does mean that any study of the Gospel
of Luke must include awareness of Acts as well. The term "sequel" also
implies that each of the two books has its own literary integrity; they
are not to be treated simply as a single two-volume work. As a consequence, it is necessary in studying the Gospel of Luke also to give careful
attention to appropriate sections of Acts.

The Gospel of Luke itself can be read at several levels or from several
perspectives. In part that is merely an observation about how Luke has
been interpreted. But it is more than that; it is an important methodological consideration that can account for the range of interpretations
we will soon encounter. How the reader approaches the Gospel of Luke
makes a significant difference both in how the text is read and in how
that reading is described.

The first important difference is the extent to which the text is treated
seriously as a narrative. The current practice of narrative criticism goes
beyond the literary studies that first replaced redaction criticism.[1] As
welcome as those studies were at the time,[2] a different set of insights is
gained from more explicit narrative categories.

The most important insight of narrative criticism is the notion of the
"narrative world" of the text. No narrative provides a direct window to
some actual social-historical world. The reader must always discern the
degree of correspondence between the two. The first step in that process
is to focus on the world of the text itself, the presentation of its plot,
setting, and characters. A further crucial distinction is between the story
and the discourse, the "what" and the "how" of the narrative.[3] Any
summary of the "what" tends to overlook the "how," such features as
the point of view and the rhetoric of the narrator.

The story unfolds sequentially; its images are cumulative. Narrative

---

1. Mark A. Powell, *What is Narrative Criticism?* (Minneapolis: Fortress Press, 1990).

2. For example, Charles H. Talbert, *Reading Luke: A Literary and Theological Commentary on the Third Gospel* (New York: Crossroad, 1984).

3. See Seymour Chatman, *Story and Discourse: Narrative Structure in Fiction and Film* (Ithaca, N.Y.: Cornell University Press, 1978).

studies are thus different from literary thematic studies. The latter tend not to notice the narrative's sense of progression. A narrative study by nature must keep track of an expanding network of contexts when it isolates any one feature for particular attention. For example, first impressions established in the narrative have an ongoing effect throughout the rest of the narrative, even as they are modified and revised. Concrete observations about the unfolding story must also be described in terms that capture some of this nuance. Attending to both of these dimensions is probably the greatest challenge to the interpreter.

The "how" of the narrative's discourse is exceedingly important for the particular focus of this study. Our initial premise can be stated already: The amount of anti-Judaism found in a Gospel narrative hinges primarily on assessing the cumulative effect of the story's rhetoric. Crucial issues include, Does the (tone of the) speech within the narrative directly reflect the point of view of the narrator? Or does the implied author speak with a different (tone of) voice than the characters, either individually or collectively? The way the narrator frames the speech of the characters gives the implied reader clues about these issues.

The above description is framed entirely in categories about the text. One important ingredient is missing: the act of reading itself. All critics are themselves readers, and all interpretation begins with reading. To focus attention on the act of reading has become the goal of reader-response criticism.[4] It adds a second distinction important for the purposes of this essay. Narrative criticism taught us the importance of recognizing the difference between the "implied reader" projected by the text itself and any actual (set of) past readers that might be described. Reader-response criticism then reminds us that any and all distinctions about kinds of readers are in fact made by some specific reader and reflect a particular way of reading the text. We are thus cautioned never to forget that the critic is always also a reader, and "the reader is ultimately responsible for determining meaning."[5] Whatever meaning the

---

4. The notions of "implied reader" and "act of reading" derive from titles by Wolfgang Iser, *The Implied Reader: Patterns of Communication in Prose Fiction from Bunyan to Beckett* (Baltimore: Johns Hopkins University Press, 1974); *The Act of Reading: A Theory of Aesthetic Response* (Baltimore: Johns Hopkins University Press, 1978). I use these terms in the general sense in which they are described by Robert M. Fowler, "Reader-Response Criticism: Figuring Mark's Reader," in *Mark and Method: New Approaches in Biblical Studies*, ed. Janice Capel Anderson and Stephen D. Moore (Minneapolis: Fortress, 1992), 50–83. I thank my colleague David Gunn for his helpful comments on these matters.

5. Fowler, "Reader-Response Criticism," 51.

reader "finds" in a text reflects how the reader bridges the gaps that always exist in any narrative.

Readers who approach the text in this perspective are more likely to be interested in how the same text can produce conflicting readings. We will make use of these insights here, not as a lens through which to offer yet another reading of the text, but as a way to help us sort out disparate scholarly opinions about anti-Judaism in Luke-Acts. How can the same narrative be both "one of the most pro-Jewish and one of the most anti-Jewish writings in the New Testament"?[6] How can some past interpreters say this text shows "the cutting off of the Jews from redemptive history,"[7] while others find a contrasting focus on the restoration of Israel as the very basis of salvation for Gentiles?[8] How can one contemporary reader find a story that presents "the doomed condition of 'the Jews' "[9] and another see the story "confident of God's determined purpose to redeem Israel?"[10] Are these differences entirely in the eyes of the readers? If not, are there features of the text that can explain, at least in part, such divergent interpretations?

CURRENT STATE OF THE ISSUE

To facilitate our treatment of Luke, it is necessary to take a brief look at the current debate over anti-Judaism in Luke-Acts. This is not the context for any extended review of the recent scholarship, but only an indication of the current sense of the issue.

The present lack of consensus is well represented in the essays collected by Tyson in *Luke-Acts and the Jewish People: Eight Critical Perspectives*. Tyson's arrangement of the essays also provides us with a sense of cumulative insight about the narrative of Luke-Acts.[11]

---

6. Lloyd Gaston, "Anti-Judaism and the Passion Narrative in Luke and Acts," in *Anti-Judaism in Early Christianity*, vol. 1, *Paul and the Gospels*, ed. Peter Richardson and David Granskou (Waterloo, Ont.: Wilfrid Laurier University Press, 1986), 153.

7. Hans Conzelmann, *The Theology of St. Luke* (New York: Harper and Row, 1960), 145.

8. Jacob Jervell, *Luke and the People of God: A New Look at Luke-Acts* (Minneapolis: Augsburg, 1972), 68.

9. Jack T. Sanders, *The Jews in Luke-Acts* (Philadelphia: Fortress, 1987), 303.

10. David L. Tiede, " 'Glory to Thy People Israel': Luke-Acts and the Jews," in *The Social World of Formative Christianity and Judaism*, ed. Jacob Neusner et al. (Philadelphia: Fortress, 1988), 339; Tiede's essay is also found in *Luke-Acts and the Jewish People: Eight Critical Perspectives*, ed. Joseph B. Tyson (Minneapolis: Augsburg, 1988), 21–34.

11. In the preface to *Luke-Acts and the Jewish People*, Tyson (p. 7) intentionally seeks to present varied views on the treatment of Jewish people and institutions in Luke-Acts.

Jervell's close reading makes clear that Luke does not set up a simple contrast between Jews and Gentiles. Luke's interest is not in "pagan" (idolatrous) Gentiles, but in "Godfearers," those Gentiles who already have a relationship with the synagogue. Jervell further thinks that by the end of Acts they have become the sole focus for the church's future mission.[12]

Tiede addresses the overall narrative framework of the story and takes seriously the expression of Israel's hope in the first two chapters of Luke. Simeon's oracles, for example, "are still valid guides" at the end of Acts. Tiede then provides examples of the rhetoric of theodicy within Judaism that followed the destruction of the Second Temple. Despite the kind of strong prophetic language this literature shares with Luke-Acts, "God is never done with Israel." Thus Luke-Acts "remains a story of God's determined purpose to redeem Israel and even to restore Israel's glory of bringing the light of God's reign to the Gentiles."[13]

Moessner's response to Tiede provides the most explicit and succinct narrative-critical discussion available on Luke-Acts. By distinguishing the point of view of the omniscient narrator from the speech of characters within the narrative, Moessner demonstrates the ironic tension that results: "What certain characters believe and express as a hope or promise on one level is meant to be perceived by the readers on a different level." For Moessner, a pattern emerges in the narrative that is best explained as the pattern of the "Deuteronomistic view of Israel's history of the rejection of the prophets sent to them as God's mediators of redemption/salvation."[14]

Jack Sanders's reading of Luke-Acts sets up a relentless contrast. His main contribution is to note the difference between the view of "the Jews" in the speeches and in the narrative material. He finds evidence that supports the "blanket denunciation" in the speeches, "according to which Jews are by nature and congenitally obstreperous and opposed to the will and purposes of God and have been, as a group and as a nation, excluded from God's salvation." In the final analysis, "Luke has written the Jews off"; their "opposition to Christianity is now universal and endemic."[15]

---

12. Jacob Jervell, "The Church of Jews and Godfearers," in Tyson, ed., *Luke-Acts and the Jewish People*, 19.

13. Tiede, " 'Glory to Thy People Israel,' " 29, 33, 34.

14. David Moessner, "The Ironic Fulfillment of Israel's Glory," in Tyson, ed., *Luke-Acts and the Jewish People*, 38, 49.

15. Jack T. Sanders, "The Jewish People in Luke-Acts," in Tyson, ed., *Luke-Acts and the Jewish People*, 58, 66, 72.

Marilyn Salmon begins her response by wondering, "Could we really have read the same edition of the text?" Since she politely rejects much of Sanders's way of reading the text, she concludes that the primary difference is that Sanders "perceives Luke as an outsider." Her very helpful insight is that only an outsider's perspective could view the Jews that harshly. She rather calls attention to the variety of distinctions the author makes among types of Jews, and the attention given to Jewish piety: "His heroes are ... exemplary, pious, Torah-observant Jews."[16] That does not fit an outsider's sweeping condemnation.

Robert Tannehill focuses on the way Acts narrates Paul's "turning to the Gentiles." He calls attention to Paul's insistence on his "loyalty to Israel," especially as expressed through the theme of "the hope of Israel" found in the final speeches of Acts. Paul gives voice to the "tragic irony of Israel's situation" by taking on "the role of the prophet Isaiah." The final audience of Roman Jews in Acts 28 indicates Luke's persistent hope for the Jewish mission.[17]

In his response to Tannehill, Jewish scholar Michael Cook questions just this conclusion Tannehill reaches from his otherwise careful analysis. Part of the problem for Cook is that the more "natural inference by Luke's audience" would not arrive at that understanding. Rather, they would get "exactly the opposite impression" from the passages that are "abrasive toward Jews."[18] Cook cites the classic three speeches where Paul announces he is turning to the Gentiles (Acts 13:46; 18:6; 28:28). The third time sounds so definitive — "they will *never* understand" — that Cook endorses the conclusion reached by Tyson: "The failed mission to the Jews is terminated in favor of the mission to the Gentiles."[19] Cook finds especially convincing Tyson's argument that the portrayal of Paul's persistent return to the Jews is but part of Luke's literary pattern. The Jewish public always initially gives a favorable response, only to reverse itself suddenly and reject Paul. The literary pattern provides the mere context for what Paul says to the Jews. His "glaring, abrasive denunciations" are a much better indication of "Luke's actual intent."[20]

---

16. Marilyn Salmon, "Insider or Outsider? Luke's Relationship with Judaism," in Tyson, ed., *Luke-Acts and the Jewish People*, 76, 77, 81.

17. Robert C. Tannehill, "Rejection by Jews and Turning to Gentiles: The Pattern of Paul's Mission in Acts," in Tyson, ed., *Luke-Acts and the Jewish People*, 93, 94, 96–97, 101.

18. Michael J. Cook, "The Mission to the Jews in Acts: Unraveling Luke's 'Myth of the Myriads,'" in Tyson, ed., *Luke-Acts and the Jewish People*, 105, 104.

19. Joseph B. Tyson, "The Jewish Public in Luke-Acts," *NTS* 30 (1984): 582.

20. Cook, "Mission to the Jews," 107, 109.

For Cook, a different solution must be sought for the emphasis on the initial "myriads" of Jews who became believers. Cook's thesis is that "one of the predominant Lukan interests is to cast Christianity as the direct perpetuation of authentic Judaism." In Luke's portrayal, "Christianity has been brought into meticulous correspondence with what is symbolically central in Judaism." The result is that "Luke frequently implies that the fidelity of Jesus and his followers to Judaism sharply contrasts with the fidelity of Jews themselves!" Here Cook would modify only slightly Sanders's statement that Luke sets out to show the unbroken continuity of Christianity with the religion of ancient Israel. Christianity did not reject Judaism, it was *Jews* (rather than Judaism) who rejected Christianity. Toward this end, "Luke has driven a wedge between 'Judaism' and 'Jews.' "[21]

The "myriads" of Jewish believers is best explained as "a literary device" used by Luke to provide authentication for the Jewish roots of Christianity. The Godfearers are the "quasi-Jewish Gentiles" who act as the transition from the original Jewish Christians to the dominant Gentile church of Luke's day. Paul's persistent "overtures to the Jews" can now be seen as Luke's device to "assign responsibility for the underrepresentation of Jews, in Christian ranks, to Jewish intransigence." This device of past Jewish obstinacy allows Luke to maintain the claim that Christianity is "itself the extension of authentic Judaism," despite the reality that it is "severely underrepresented Jewishly."[22]

Cook thus cannot accept Tannehill's sense of "tragic irony" at the end of the Lukan narrative. Luke's narration does not seem "intended to elicit sympathy for the Jews." The Jews are pictured rather as "those unjustly opposing Christianity," who "receive only what they deserve and what retribution demands." The actual tragic irony is seen in the legacy of the genuine Paul, "a Jew deeply despairing and poignantly concerned with ... his fellow Jews." His "apprehension of Gentile attitudes toward Jews" expressed in Rom. 11:18ff. "ironically and tragically became fulfilled in the person of ... his unauthorized biographer, Luke." This is the irony that "became tragic for Jews — and for relations between Jews and Christians — throughout history."[23]

In his concluding essay, Tyson focuses on the final incident depicted at the end of Luke-Acts. In addition to its inherent significance as the scene that ends the narrative, Paul's final appearance before the Jews also

---

21. Ibid., 109, 110, 111, 116. For Sanders's judgment, see *The Jews in Luke-Acts*.
22. Cook, "Mission to the Jews," 120, 122.
23. Ibid., 122–23.

culminates the narrative's portrayal of the Jews. The presence of some believing Jews does not reduce the final impression that "the mission to the Jews was over."[24] Tyson then addresses three potential objections to this thesis.

One likely objection would be the oft-noted interest Luke-Acts displays in Jewish religious traditions. The author is clearly familiar with Jewish traditions and depicts major characters as practicing those traditions. Tyson attributes this to Luke's view of the "continuity between the Scriptures and the Christian message," even though it results in a "deep tension" with the final picture that "the Jews have rejected" that message. Secondly, the reader must account for the important role that Jewish believers have in the story, since "there are no leaders in Acts who are clearly designated as Gentiles." For Tyson these individual Jewish believers must be distinguished from the persistent role of "the Jews" as collective opponents. In Luke's literary pattern, Christian preaching regularly evokes opposition from "the Jews," despite the "acceptance of the Christian message by some Jews." The role of individual Jews thus "does not form an exception to the overwhelming phenomenon of Jewish rejection and does not diminish Luke's sense of the failure of the Jewish mission."[25]

A final objection to the view that the Jewish mission was now over is the importance attached to the Jewish Christians in Jerusalem. However, their relevance decreases in proportion to their role as opponents of the Gentile mission. Thus they do not "create an exception to the final failure of the Jewish mission and the Jewish rejection of the gospel." Tyson sees here such "deep ambivalence" about Jewish Christians that he suggests Acts could be retitled, "The Problem of Jewish Rejection."[26]

These eight essays point to the kinds of questions that must be faced in any attempt to assess anti-Judaism in Luke-Acts. The major differences in their perspectives raise important methodological issues. The final juxtaposition of Cook and Tyson in particular provokes the reader to wrestle with the overall issue of the narrator's point of view at the end of the two volumes. Tyson suggests that the controlling perspective is the problem of the Jewish rejection of the Christian message. Cook sees this as part of Luke's solution to a larger problem: how to make a

---

24. Tyson, "The Problem of Jewish Rejection in Acts," in idem, ed., *Luke-Acts and the Jewish People*, 127.
25. Ibid., 129, 130, 133.
26. Ibid., 137.

convincing case for Christianity as the heir of authentic Judaism when so few Jews were included in the new movement.

The ending of Luke-Acts has clearly become the decisive factor in interpreting the overall narrative. Each of the perspectives above amounts to a proposal for a plausible way to understand the ending. In that sense the ending becomes a starting point for the reader's final reflection on the cumulative effect of the narrative. Cook suggests that each narrative thread a reader follows is somewhat like tracing a fiber in a rope — not all fibers run continuously from one end to the other. In terms of narrative criticism this can be expressed as the reader's inclination to bridge the gaps left in the narrative. A critical reading attempts to point out the most important parts of the thread that should be accounted for. We will look more closely at some of the elements in the narrative that seem to be most crucial for assessing anti-Judaism in Luke-Acts. The prior step must be further methodological reflection on how a reader reads this kind of text.

Methodological Reflections on Assessing Anti-Judaism in Luke-Acts

A major amount of attention naturally gets focused on the ending of the second volume, or sequel, as I prefer to call it. The final impression left with the reader is indeed crucial, especially regarding this issue, since the final scene is Paul addressing Jews — one last time. As the reader would expect, the pattern of these encounters is repeated, but this time given a definitive sounding resolution with the quotation of Isa. 6:9–10. Interpreters frequently point out the emphatic, "you will *never* understand" (Acts 28:26, in most modern translations since the RSV), which sets up the contrast with the final statement, "the Gentiles will listen" (Acts 28:28).[27]

All the attention given the ending of Acts in the collection of essays surveyed above failed to provoke reflection on how it might relate to the opening — of either volume. This is surprising, methodologically, in an era of emphasis on narrative criticism. Beyond the general importance of first impressions, these two volumes are unique in having formal prefaces, which explicitly connect the two to each other. Both prefaces are part of the necessary context for evaluating the impact of the ending. And the first volume, the Gospel of Luke, has significant features about

---

27. The Greek has an aorist subjunctive verb with the double negative οὐ μή. This is an emphatic construction, but has no temporal component. Thus, "will never" is misleading. The emphasis could be expressed more idiomatically: "You just won't understand."

its ending that also affect the overall reading of these narratives. There are thus two sets of beginnings and endings that provide the narrative framework for assessing the cumulative impression about "the Jews" that the reader is given in Luke-Acts.

In the preliminary remarks we already noted some of the more general methodological features important for reading a narrative. An excellent overview of such categories is provided by William Kurz in *Reading Luke-Acts*. Several items in particular warrant our attention. The first is that narrative itself is the distinguishing feature of this literature. Valuable insights can be gained from narrative criticism "without first solving the dispute over what genre(s)" to call Luke and Acts.[28] We will develop the importance of this insight more fully below.

Kurz's observations derive from applying the categories of narration to Luke-Acts. Luke is the only Gospel that opens with first-person narration of the implied author in a prologue and then immediately begins the story with third-person narration, and very noticeably in the style of biblical narration. Acts follows a similar pattern, but goes further, using first-person ("we") narration in the second half of the book. Then there is the important amount of narration by the characters in the story. A careful reader, of course, is attentive to these changes of narration within the narrative. A few selected examples from Kurz will suffice here to indicate the potential value of noticing this literary feature of the text.

The narration of the (unnamed) implied author in the preface claims that the work is not an original narrative, but is based on a tradition of sources the author has investigated. The author's contribution is in the plotting of the traditional accounts, how they are put in sequence. An individual narratee, Theophilus, is named. The narrative is thus both personalized and professional, not anonymous community folklore. The narrator then claims community authentication by appealing to "us" who received these accounts and experienced them as accomplished.[29]

Within the narrative itself the omniscient narrator provides the implied reader with numerous clues about levels of meaning. The opening programmatic incident in Nazareth (Luke 4) establishes the use of literary features such as foreshadowing, irony, and intertextuality. Elsewhere the narrator effectively uses "behold" (ἰδού), from the tradition of biblical narrative, to "signal the abrupt arrival" of a character and to

---

28. William S. Kurz, *Reading Luke-Acts: Dynamics of Biblical Narrative* (Louisville: Westminster/John Knox Press, 1993), 2; see also Kurz's "Narrative Approaches to Luke-Acts," *Biblica* 68 (1987): 195–220.

29. Kurz, *Reading Luke-Acts*, 41–44.

"focalize the action from the perspective of the characters within the action, rather than from the narrator's usually more distanced viewpoint."[30] The example Kurz cites here is the sudden arrival of a crowd and Judas (Luke 22:47). Since this text is important in Tyson's reading of the "Jewish public" in Luke, it is worthwhile to reinforce Kurz's methodological insight here. Most instances of ἰδού are in characters' speech, making them sound "biblical." When this expression is used by the narrator, it always introduces the arrival of a new character.[31] The only instance when it is more than a countable number of individuals is here at Jesus' arrest, when it is a crowd (ὄχλος).

Tyson's analysis of the "Jewish public response" in Luke-Acts seems to assume that all references to people or crowd(s) describe the same Jewish public. Tyson finds a consistent literary pattern in the narrative that typically begins with a positive response that at some point suddenly turns to rejection. The predictability of the literary device then becomes a grid for reading this particular text. For Tyson, "the change in the role of the crowd seems to occur specifically at the scene of Jesus' arrest." Luke seems "very deliberate" when he sets the scene in Luke 22:6 (ἐζήτει εὐκαιρίαν τοῦ παραδοῦναι αὐτὸν ἄτερ ὄχλου αὐτοῖς): Judas seeks an opportunity "without a crowd," since it was "the people" who had provided Jesus' protection. When Jesus awakens his sleeping disciples, he is met by Judas, who now has a crowd: ἔτι αὐτοῦ λαλοῦντος ἰδοὺ ὄχλος καὶ ὁ λεγόμενος Ἰούδας εἷς τῶν δώδεκα προήρχετο αὐτούς (Luke 22:47). Tyson's description, "the crowd is now with Judas," is then clarified: "The crowd has deserted Jesus, and from now on it is part of the opposition." This constitutes "the shift in the function of the crowd" that Tyson expects from the literary pattern he discerns in Luke-Acts.[32]

Tyson's portrayal seems to picture the crowd as a stable entity that has now switched sides. However, there is nothing in Luke's text to suggest that. In fact, the rhetoric of the narrator suggests just the opposite. ἰδοὺ ὄχλος suggests the abrupt arrival of a new character: a crowd of persons not previously seen in the narrative. There may well also be some irony attached. The success of Judas depended on finding Jesus

---

30. Ibid., 62. This insight is based on Meir Sternberg, *The Poetics of Biblical Narrative: Ideological Literature and the Drama of Reading* (Bloomington, Ind.: Indiana University Press, 1987), 53.

31. Luke 2:25; 5:12, 18; 7:12, 37; 8:41; 9:30, 38, 39; 10:25; 13:11; 14:2; 19:2; 22:47; 23:50; 24:4, 13.

32. Tyson, "Jewish Public," 579.

ἄτερ ὄχλου, without a crowd. His success is announced by the narrator, ironically, ἰδού ὄχλος. When Jesus interacts with them, they are identi- fied: "chief priests, temple police, and elders" (Luke 22:52). The reader quickly recognizes these as the temple authorities who have been trying to catch Jesus without his own protective crowd. It would seem that the ὄχλος in these two instances describes two discrete groups that have no common members.

Robert Brawley directly challenges Tyson's methodology here. He asks, "Is the crowd always identical in Luke-Acts or does it wear dif- ferent masks?" Brawley is convinced: "The role of the crowds is fluid." He thus contends that Tyson "fails to distinguish the character of var- ious crowds."[33] The distinction Brawley sees significantly changes the outcome of Luke's view of the Jews. Tyson concludes that by the end of Acts, Luke pictures that "the entire Jewish population has turned against the gospel."[34] For Brawley, no such unified picture exists: "Nei- ther Luke's Gospel nor Acts ends on the final note of Jewish rejection."[35] The difference over this issue exemplifies a dividing line in the current interpretation of Luke-Acts.

Tyson has revisited this issue several times since. In *The Death of Jesus in Luke-Acts*, Tyson mostly repeats his arguments about the lit- erary pattern of initial acceptance and final rejection. He does add, however, a new awareness that "the treatment of crowds is exceed- ingly complex in Luke's trial narrative." Tyson notes that "two distinct groups" are involved, one "of people loyal to Jesus," the other "the crowd...that represents the Jewish public response to Jesus." He con- cludes from this that, although Luke pictures "a group of loyalists present at the time of Jesus's death, he was finally rejected by the Jewish public at large."[36]

Most recently, Tyson has approached this issue as part of a larger look at *Images of Judaism in Luke-Acts*. He approaches the big pic- ture this time from the explicit perspective of the implied reader. The descriptions are more fine-tuned, but the results are primarily the same. Tyson still sees a rather uniform picture of the Jews in Luke-Acts: "It was the Jewish people and their leaders who brought about the execu-

---

33. Robert L. Brawley, *Luke-Acts and the Jews: Conflict, Apology, and Conciliation,* SBLMS 33 (Atlanta: Scholars Press, 1987), 136, 139, 138.

34. Tyson, "Jewish Public," 582.

35. Brawley, *Luke-Acts and the Jews,* 144.

36. Joseph B. Tyson, *The Death of Jesus in Luke-Acts* (Columbia, S.C.: University of South Carolina Press, 1986), 34, 37.

tion" of Jesus. Although there are both positive and negative aspects about Luke's images of Jews, at the end "the reader is drawn to join in the condemnation of Jews for their rejection of the Christian message."[37] Tyson thus sets a firm challenge to the conclusion reached by Brawley: "rather than rejecting the Jews, Luke appeals to them."[38]

Adele Reinhartz has already demonstrated how the insights of narrative criticism can add precision to descriptions of anti-Judaism in the Gospels. Using the categories of reader-response criticism, she identifies three kinds of readers of the text. The *implied reader* is "reconstructed from the text as the one who is capable of understanding the text." Derived from this construct is the notion of the *ideal reader*, the one who perfectly understands the assumptions and values suggested by the text. These hypothetical readers are entirely constructed from clues within the text. The *real reader*, in contrast, is any actual historical person who reads the text in some real-world context. Such a person brings a concrete set of extrinsic assumptions and values to the text and thus fails or refuses to become the ideal reader.[39]

In terms of the values expressed by a text, the implied reader would notice the range of potential meanings in the text; the ideal reader would fully endorse all the claims implied by the text; only the real reader actualizes the text, either by acting on its claims or by challenging them. On the issue of anti-Judaism in the Gospels, the implied reader would notice both the villain role assigned to Jewish people, as well as the ironic ending that turns the hero's death into victory. The action of the opponents is deemed "a necessary aspect of God's plan for salvation," and the outcome is "cause for rejoicing." This scenario would not hold the opponents morally responsible for their action that contributed to this outcome.[40]

Each individual narrative, however, can give the reader signals that the villain should nonetheless be held responsible. Reinhartz finds such clues in each of the four Gospels. In Luke she points to Luke 20:20 without comment. A quick look at any synopsis makes it easy to surmise her case. The scribes and chief priests have failed to arrest Jesus, "so they watched him, and sent spies, who pretended to be sincere, that they

---

37. Joseph B. Tyson, *Images of Judaism in Luke-Acts* (Columbia: S.C.: University of South Carolina Press, 1992), 79, 188.

38. Brawley, *Luke-Acts and the Jews*, 159.

39. Adele Reinhartz, "The New Testament and Anti-Judaism: A Literary-Critical Approach." *JES* 25 (1988): 527, 528.

40. Ibid., 531.

might take hold of what he said, so as to deliver him up to the authority and jurisdiction of the governor." This editorializing is unique to Luke's version. The omniscient narrator tells the reader about religious authorities resorting to entrapment using insincere spies. Reinhartz surmises that "the implied reader would understand the plot...to be conveying a negative picture of the Jews and to be encouraging an attitude that can be described as anti-Jewish."[41]

The ideal reader, especially of Luke's preface, "regards the information presented as historically accurate: the Jews *are* guilty." There are "grave implications" of these views of the Jews. Yet it remains to the real reader to actualize these texts. History is indeed replete with examples of such readers. Nonetheless, historical criticism can assist real readers in assessing the intrinsic values of these texts and choosing "to refuse to enter totally into the belief-system and thought-world" of such narratives. Reinhartz thus concludes on an empowering note: "There is enough available data, of both an intrinsic and an extrinsic nature, to serve as a basis for criticizing [an] anti-Jewish reading" of the Gospels.[42]

SELECTIVE NARRATIVE READINGS FROM LUKE-ACTS

The methodology of narrative criticism noted above suggests a host of potential insights into the issue of anti-Judaism and the Gospels. A number of them seem particularly pertinent to Luke-Acts. Many hints have already been given. In what follows we will pursue several of the significant aspects of Luke-Acts that can shape our perspective on anti-Judaism in these writings.

Prologue and History

This is not the occasion to completely reconsider the nature of Luke's prologue. A brief summary of recent research on the rhetoric of ancient historiography will provide sufficient context for the issues under investigation here.[43] The preface identifies Luke's writing as διήγησις, "narrative." In its contemporary setting this put it in the category of

---

41. Ibid., 531–32.
42. Ibid., 532, 535–36, 537.
43. See David E. Aune, *The New Testament in Its Literary Environment* (Philadelphia: Westminster, 1987), 77–115; Daryl D. Schmidt, "Luke's Preface and the Rhetoric of Historiography in Luke-Acts," in *Luke the Interpreter of Israel,* ed. David P. Moessner (forthcoming).

rhetoric shared by biography and prose fiction.[44] "Historiography was itself primarily a form of epideictic" rhetoric; its goal was to persuade the audience to adopt a point of view, to praise or to blame someone.[45]

The preface to a historical narrative typically established the author's commitment to present the actuality/accuracy (ἀκρίβεια) of the events fairly and realistically, along with speeches that captured the gist of what was actually said.[46] In this regard, "The preface of Luke-Acts resembles the prefaces of histories more than those of biographies or any other ancient prose writings."[47]

The formation of the historical narratives in the biblical tradition developed parallel to ancient Greek historiography. Hellenistic Jewish historiography emerged from its biblical antecedents into the Maccabean literature, with its focus on martyrdom, and into the works of Josephus, both reflecting the influence of Greek historiography.[48] One important feature common to both Greek and Jewish historiography was the desire to show divine governance in history. For the Greeks, this was sometimes done in language that included *Tyche,* "Chance," and *Ananke,* "Necessity."[49] Biblical historiography more naturally used theological language, which Hellenistic authors, such as Josephus, tended to avoid.

The language of Luke's prologue makes its own historiographical claims. This narrative is based on traditional material that has been researched and made into an "accurate" sequence of the deeds "accomplished among us." The author expects the reader to view the entire narrative as reliable and trustworthy (Luke 1:1–4).

Endings and Hermeneutics

The last chapter of Luke expresses more explicitly the perspective for viewing the entire story. The reader is asked to picture two of the participants discussing "all this that had happened" (περὶ πάντων τῶν συμβεβηκότων τούτων [Luke 24:14]). They feel gloomy (σκυθρωποί

---

44. See A. J. Woodman, *Rhetoric in Classical Historiography: Four Studies* (London: Croom Helm, 1988).

45. George Kennedy, *New Testament Interpretation through Rhetorical Criticism* (Chapel Hill, N.C.: University of North Carolina Press, 1984), 19, 41.

46. Woodman, *Rhetoric in Classical Historiography*, 10.

47. Terrance Callan, "The Preface of Luke-Acts and Historiography," *NTS* 31 (1985): 576.

48. Arnaldo Momigliano, *The Classical Foundations of Modern Historiography* (Berkeley, Calif.: University of California Press, 1990), 24–27.

49. Charles W. Fornara, *The Nature of History in Ancient Greece and Rome* (Berkeley, Calif.: University of California Press, 1983), 78–81.

[Luke 24:17]) when they think about the crucifixion, because it dashed their hopes that they were about to experience someone "redeem Israel" (Luke 24:21). Their problem is lack of perspective (ἀνόητοι) and failure to trust what the prophets had said (πιστεύειν ἐπὶ πᾶσιν οἷς ἐλάλησαν οἱ προφῆται [Luke 24:25]). Contrary to appearances, all this was necessary (ταῦτα ἔδει [Luke 24:26]). Hindsight can provide the proper interpretation (διερμήνευσεν) of "Moses and all the prophets" (Luke 24:27). With an "open mind" one can understand all these events are the necessary fulfillment of everything in scripture (δεῖ πληρωθῆναι πάντα τὰ γεγραμμένα [Luke 24:44]; διήνοιξεν αὐτῶν τὸν νοῦν τοῦ συνιέναι τὰς γραφάς [Luke 24:45]).

Luke then provides glimpses of how this works in Acts. The very first words spoken to the initial community of believers are an appeal to this hermeneutical principle (ἔδει πληρωθῆναι τὴν γραφήν [Acts 1:16]) to authorize a replacement for Judas. Later, the text of Ps. 2:1–2 is called part of the "plan destined to take place" (ἡ βουλὴ προώρισεν γενέσθαι [Acts 4:28]) and then used to explain the roles of Herod and Pilate in the Passion narrative as representing the "kings and rulers" of that text. Since no other Gospel provides any suggestion about the role of Herod, it appears that for the author of Luke's Gospel, the "plan destined to take place" is not only a hermeneutic applied to Scripture, it also becomes a historiography with power to generate narrative incidents that "must happen."

In another incident Luke pictures an Ethiopian eunuch reading (aloud) from Isaiah 53 (Acts 8:28–30) on his way home from Jerusalem. When Philip is inspired to stop and ask if he understands what he is reading, the official dutifully requests that Philip guide him (Acts 8:31), and innocently asks him whether the text is about the author or someone else (Acts 8:34). Philip then "begins with that scripture," imitating the original scene of the post-Easter Jesus with his disciples (Luke 24:27), and uses it to "evangelize" him about Jesus (ἀρξάμενος ἀπὸ τῆς γραφῆς ταύτης εὐηγγελίσατο αὐτῷ τὸν Ἰησοῦν [Act 8:35]). For Luke the model is those who are "daily examining the scriptures" (καθ' ἡμέραν ἀνακρίνοντες τὰς γραφάς [Acts 17:11]).

The epitome of this hermeneutic is of course the closing scene of Acts. Paul one last time sets out to explain Jesus on the basis of Moses and the prophets. Some found it convincing, others not (οἱ μὲν ἐπείθοντο τοῖς λεγομένοις, οἱ δὲ ἠπίστουν [Acts 28:24]. The resulting disagreement ends with Paul having the last word: "It's just as the prophet said, 'You keep on listening, but y'all won't ever learn!' So you better understand (γνωστὸν οὖν ἔστω ὑμῖν): this message is now going to others; they'll listen" (Acts 28:25–28).

Echoes

The attentive reader will hear echoes from Paul's first speech. There too he had insisted, "You better understand: This is forgiveness you couldn't get through Moses. So beware not to have happen to you what the prophets said: 'I'm doing something y'all won't ever believe, even if someone tells you'" (Acts 13:38–41). The divided response Paul got the next week prodded him to speak out boldly: "It was necessary that God's word be spoken to you first. But since you refuse it, just watch; I'm turning to foreigners, for that's what the Lord ordered: 'I've made you a light for foreigners'" (Acts 13:46–47).

An even more important echo is back to Jesus' first public encounter (Luke 4:16–30). This text is regularly called "programmatic." But no description of that program has any scholarly consensus. The most discussed feature is the audience response. After Jesus reads from Isaiah 61 and pronounces it "fulfilled today in your hearing," the narrator declares that "everyone approved and seemed surprised" (ἐμαρτύρουν …καὶ ἐθαύμαζον [Luke 4:22]) at such words coming from Joseph's son. Jesus replies with two proverbs. One he suggests the audience is thinking: "Physician, heal yourself"; and the other one he offers: "No prophet is welcomed in his own homeland" (Luke 4:23–24).

Most of the focus on this text has been on interpreting the commentary Jesus then gives. He calls attention to Elijah and Elisha healing only Gentiles (Luke 4:25–27). Now everyone is enraged and they take him to the edge of town, where he escapes before they can hurl him down the hill. What makes this programmatic? One dominant tradition sees it in the sudden switch from acceptance to rejection that takes place after favor is given to non-Israelites. When the narrative continues, however, Jesus goes to another Jewish village and resumes teaching on the Sabbath and in a synagogue. The audience is astonished by his authority (Luke 4:32), reminiscent of Luke's opening summary that "everyone was giving him praise" (Luke 4:15). The narrative framework provided by these two summaries thus gives no support to the focus on audience reversal as the programmatic feature of this incident.

Brawley gives a more convincing reading of this text.[50] The careful reader would note the irony of the scene. Jesus first claims fulfillment

---

50. Brawley, *Luke-Acts and the Jews*, 39.

of a prophecy that announces the acceptable (δεκτόν) year of the Lord. Then he solemnly declares (ἀμὴν λέγω ὑμῖν): no prophet is δεκτός in his hometown. When he tells the truth (ἐπ᾽ ἀληθείας) about the great early prophets Elijah and Elisha, his hometown indeed finds him unacceptable. Their refusal to hear the message about the prophets only succeeds in proving that Jesus is truly a prophet.

Luke later will narrate two healing stories (Luke 7) that directly reflect the healings of Elijah and Elisha. The punch line of each story makes the connection clear. After the Elisha-like Gentile healing, Jesus lauds such faith "not found in Israel" (Luke 7:10), and the second healing provokes the acclamation, "What a great prophet has been raised among us!" (Luke 7:16), and they are all praising God. The people of Nain then declare, "God has visited his people" (Luke 7:16). This is not a Gentile healing, so Luke is not presenting a literal imitation of the Elijah-Elisha narrative. The careful reader must discern Luke's own hermeneutic at work here.

Luke uses an inquiry from John the Baptist to have Jesus reflect on the way prophets get treated (Luke 7:26–35). Their own generation disparages them regardless of what they do. The ascetic prophet is called "demonic" and the one who enjoys table fellowship is labeled "a glutton and a drunk" (Luke 7:33–34), the latter being a deuteronomic phrase for a disobedient Israelite. The prescribed remedy for such a one is to "purge the evil from your midst" and have "everyone in the town" participate in a public execution (Deut. 21:20–21). Over against that judgment by "this generation," Jesus and John are in fact "Wisdom's children" and they "do her proud" (Luke 7:35).

By word and by deed Jesus has now been established as a true prophet. But he is more, a "prophet raised" is what had been promised in Deut. 18:15 (a text quoted in Acts 7:37), a prophet like Moses whom God will raise "from among you."

It is important to note the deuteronomistic description of the prophet's role. His only task is to speak the words God puts in his mouth (Deut. 18:18). In typical deuteronomistic fashion there is judgment attached to these words: "Whoever does not listen to what the prophet says in the name of God" will receive God's vengeance (ἐγὼ ἐκδικήσω ἐξ αὐτοῦ [Deut. 18:19]). There immediately follows a warning: A prophet who speaks what God has not commanded will die (Deut. 18:20). The obvious question is, "How will we recognize a message that the Lord spoke?" (Πῶς γνωσόμεθα τὸ ῥῆμα ὃ οὐκ ἐλάλησεν κύριος; [Deut. 18:21]). The only sure answer is that if what the prophet says "does not happen and come to pass" (μὴ γένηται καὶ μὴ συμβῇ), the words are not authentic and "you should not spare that prophet" (οὐκ ἀφέξεσθε αὐτοῦ [Deut. 18:22]). The deuteronomic test for validity has no middle ground. The authenticity of a prophet's words is subject to historical testing. There are only two choices: a prophet who speaks authentic words and is not heeded will be avenged; or a prophet that speaks inauthentic words will perish.

This is all easier to assess in hindsight, of course, than when the words are first spoken. In fact, setting up the criterion this way makes it an obvious issue of historiography, not an "on the spot" reading. The historiographical challenge after the destruction of the First Temple was that the two options identified above now overlapped. For the deuteronomist, history proved Jeremiah had been right in speaking against the temple; his words went unheeded and justice was served on Jerusalem. But the rejection of Jeremiah's message included attempts to kill him. Thus a dead prophet could in fact have spoken the truth. From this emerged the prominent postexilic motif of the rejected prophet, most explicitly expressed in Neh. 9[LXX 2 Esdr. 19]:26–27:

τοὺς προφήτας σου ἀπέκτειναν, οἳ διεμαρτύραντο ἐν αὐτοῖς.... καὶ ἔδωκας αὐτοὺς ἐν χειρὶ θλιβόντων αὐτούς.

They killed your prophets who testified to them.... And you gave them to the hand of those who afflicted them.[51]

---

51. The motif of "killing the prophets" apparently began as a charge against Ahab and Jezebel (1 Kings 18:4, 19:1) to explain the demise of the northern monarchy, in words attributed to Elijah: the Israelites "killed your prophets with a sword" (1 Kings 19:10, 14 — quoted in Rom. 11:3). Similar language is used in Jeremiah's first speech in Jerusalem, "Your own sword devoured your prophets" (Jer. 2:30), a charge made without any evidence about Jerusalem. Similar echoes are heard in Heb. 11:37, in the list of faithful martyrs, including those "killed with a sword," and in Acts 7:52, Stephen's speech to the council in Jerusalem, which concludes with the charge that their ancestors killed the prophets and they murdered Jesus. A similar linking is found in 1 Thess. 2:14–15, but this passage was probably a later insertion (see Daryl D. Schmidt, "1 Thess. 2:13–16: Linguistic Evidence for an Interpolation," *JBL* 103 [1983]: 269–79). The only mention in the biblical tradition of a martyred prophet is Zechariah's stoning in 2 Chron. 24:21 (cf. Luke 11:51), which became legendary in later rabbinic tradition.

Michael Knowles traces this motif as it developed in ancient Jewish literature, including Josephus *Ant.* 10.38 (Manasseh "slaughtered prophets daily"), *Mart. Isa.* 5:1 (Manasseh "sawed Isaiah in half"; also in *Lives of the Prophets*, which includes other legendary violent deaths), and midrashic tradition (*Jeremiah in Matthew's Gospel: The Rejected Prophet Motif in Matthaean Redaction*, JSNTSup 68 [Sheffield: Sheffield Academic Press, 1993], 99–108; see also Betsy Halpern Amaru, "The Killing of the Prophets: Unraveling a Midrash," *HUCA* 54 [1983]: 153–80). Knowles cites Steck's conclusion: "This tradition is to be encountered in almost all writings that have survived from Palestinian Judaism between 200 B.C.E. and 100 C.E." (Odil H. Steck, *Israel und das gewaltsame Geschick der Propheten: Untersuchungen zur Überlieferung des deuteronomistischen Geschichtsbildes*

What is too often overlooked is the reassurance that is then given in Neh. 9[LXX 2 Esdr. 19]:31:

Καὶ σὺ ἐν οἰκτιρμοῖς σου…οὐκ ἐγκατέλιπες αὐτούς

Yet in your mercies you did not forsake them.

The destruction of Jerusalem was not interpreted as divine rejection. Just the opposite: In spite of appearances, God's mercy endures.

LUKE'S JESUS AS REJECTED PROPHET

The major section of Luke's narrative is Jesus' journey to Jerusalem. The deuteronomic motifs throughout the section have long been recognized. The section begins at Luke 9:51, "He set his face to go to Jerusalem." The language, αὐτὸς τὸ πρόσωπον ἐστήρισεν τοῦ πορεύεσθαι εἰς Ἰερουσαλήμ, directly echoes the words of divine judgment from Jer. 21:10, ἐστήρικα τὸ πρόσωπόν μου ἐπὶ τὴν πόλιν ταύτην εἰς κακὰ καὶ οὐκ εἰς ἀγαθά (I have set my face against this city for evil and not for good). As Jesus journeys to Jerusalem, "the Deuteronomistic depiction of the prophet's calling to Israel is a distinctive portrait for the Jesus of Luke's central section."[52] Moessner carefully documents the intertwining deuteronomistic themes that run through this section. We can note only a few of the more explicit texts.

Early in the journey Jesus calls attention to the fate of prophets. In a direct echo of Neh. 9:26, Luke has Jesus berate those who build memorials for the prophets "whom your ancestors killed" (Luke 11:47–48). Judgment is then pronounced on "this generation." They will have to answer for "the blood of all the prophets" (Luke 11:50–51).

As Jesus journeys on toward Jerusalem (Luke 13:22), he receives a warning from apparently friendly Pharisees that Herod wants to kill him. Jesus' message back to Herod is a reminder about the fate of a prophet: οὐκ ἐνδέχεται προφήτην ἀπολέσθαι ἔξω Ἰερουσαλήμ (Luke 13:33). That it is "not acceptable" to die outside Jerusalem also echoes the earlier proverb that a prophet is "not accepted" in his hometown.

---

im Alten Testament, Spätjudentum, und Urchristentum, WMANT 23 [Neukirchen-Vluyn: Neukirchener Verlag, 1967], 101). It was thus a readily available polemic after the destruction of the Second Temple.

52. David P. Moessner, *Lord of the Banquet: The Literary and Theological Significance of the Lukan Travel Narrative* (Minneapolis: Fortress, 1989), 130. See also David L. Tiede, *Prophecy and History in Luke-Acts* (Philadelphia: Fortress, 1980).

When a prophet mentions Jerusalem, Luke evokes the deuteronomic slogan, "Jerusalem, killer of prophets" (Luke 13:34). A prophetic judgment is then uttered: "This house is being abandoned" (ἰδοὺ ἀφίεται ὑμῖν ὁ οἶκος ὑμῶν [Luke 13:35]). Clear echoes can be heard here from Jeremiah:

Ἐγκαταλέλοιπα τὸν οἶκόν μου, ἀφῆκα τὴν κληρονομίαν μου, I have forsaken my house; I have abandoned my heritage (Jer. 12:7).

εἰς ἐρήμωσιν ἔσται ὁ οἶκος οὗτος, This house will became a desolation (Jer. 22:5).

The latter text is also echoed in Luke 21:20:

Ὅταν δὲ ἴδητε κυκλουμένην ὑπὸ στρατοπέδων Ἰερουσαλήμ, τότε γνῶτε ὅτι ἤγγικεν ἡ ἐρήμωσις αὐτῆς, When you see Jerusalem surrounded by armies, then you know that its desolation is near.[53]

The reader has heard enough words from Jesus already authenticated to know that this outcome is now inevitable.[54]

When Jesus gets within sight of Jerusalem he weeps in anticipation of its impending destruction, which he prophetically confirms, "because you did not know the time of your visitation" (ἐπισκοπή [Luke 9:44]). This judgment reminds the reader of the earlier affirmation in Nain following Jesus' prophet-like healing: God has visited (ἐπεσκέψατο) his people (Luke 7:16).

In the former scene, "everyone was praising God." The reader has come to recognize this feature of unanimous responses in the Lukan discourse. In the programmatic opening scene of Jesus' ministry, the response went from "all approved" (Luke 4:22), to "all were enraged" (Luke 4:28). This was framed on both sides by "all praised him" (Luke 4:15) and "all were amazed" (Luke 4:36). This discourse of consensus is featured throughout the narrative. John the Baptist was preaching a message destined for "all flesh" (Luke 3:6; cf. Isa. 40:5). In response, "all the people" were baptized (Luke 3:21). Jesus thus inherited the consensus support of John the Baptist.

---

53. This replaces the use of Dan. 9:27, "desolating sacrilege," in Matt. 24:15 and Mark 13:14.

54. In his response to my essay, Allan McNicol raises the question of whether the very use of this historiography borders on "anti-Judaism," and in fact goes beyond the rejected prophet motif. What Knowles has demonstrated for Matthew can as readily be shown for Luke. In neither case does the narrative imply that "all Israel" is the object of this judgment, although both are surely guilty of post-70 déjà vu about the destruction of Jerusalem.

When the narrative shifts to Jerusalem, Jesus has built his own consensus. He takes over the temple area for his teaching and "all the people" come to listen (Luke 19:48; 20:45; 21:38). Only at the moment of arrest is Jesus not protected by "the people." After he is arrested and sentenced, the crowds again returned. A "large number of people" followed him to Golgotha and stood watching (Luke 23:27,35), as did "all the crowds who gathered" and "all his acquaintances" (Luke 23:48–49).

Luke's narrator also pictures a consensus among the opposition. When the elders, priests, and scribes assemble their council to interrogate Jesus (Luke 22:66), their verdict sounds unanimous: "They all said, 'So then you are God's son?!'" (Luke 22:70). The reader, however, will later be told explicitly that Joseph of Arimathea was a council member who had not endorsed their action (Luke 23:50–51). This latter detail is unique to the Lukan narrative.

The exaggerated picture of group consensus needs to be recognized as a pervasive pattern of Luke's discourse.[55] How does the reader process these images? At one level this discourse is part of the intertextuality that is so strongly present in this text. One fitting example can be seen in the trial scene of Jeremiah 33 [26] LXX.

It begins with the word of the Lord to Jeremiah: Stand in the courtyard of the Lord's house and declare to "all the Jews" and to all those who come to worship there all the words I've commanded you (Jer. 33:2 LXX). The priests, the prophets, and "all the people" listened to all the words of Jeremiah and said, "You're going to die for prophesying like that against this house" (Jer. 33:9 LXX).

The rulers (ἄρχοντες, "princes") of Judah heard this and went up from the palace to the Temple, where all the people were assembled. The priests and (false) prophets addressed the rulers and all the people, "He deserves death" (Jer. 33:11 LXX). Jeremiah then spoke in defense to the rulers and all the people: "The Lord sent me to speak these words. I'm in your hands; do what's best for you. But you should know that if you slay me, you bring innocent blood on yourselves and this city. In truth, the Lord sent me to speak all these words" (Jer. 33:12–15 LXX). Then the rulers and all the people respond to the priests and prophets, "No judgment of death is due him" (Jer. 33:16 LXX). Some of the elders arose and reminded all the assembly about Micah. He had declared

---

55. When Pilate summons "priests, rulers, and people" to a hearing about the charges against Jesus, Codex Bezae again has "all the people" present (Luke 23:13).

to all the people of Judah that Zion would become a ploughed field, and they did not kill him. Another man, Uriah, then repeated Jeremiah's words, and when all the rulers heard all these words, they pursued him and he was killed.

We see here a highly stylized scene of a rejected prophet facing the rulers, the priests, and "all the people." They constitute "all the Jews," and they are assembled in the Temple courtyard. The role of "all the people" is never as instigators. They are at first present when the priests say he deserves death. When the rulers join the assembly, they and all the people now become the audience for the priests and declare the prophet not deserving death. The priests and (false) prophets are the only consistent "bad guys." The role of "all the people" hardly warrants making an assessment about their moral responsibility for any action taken in the scene described.

We have seen multiple ways in which the narrative of the deuteronomistic tradition echoes throughout Luke and Acts. Its influence is both historiographical (how it views history) and rhetorical (how the discourse of the narrative tells its story). This is nowhere clearer than in the Lukan Passion narrative.

The Lukan Passion Narrative

Gaston very pointedly lays the full burden of anti-Judaism in Luke on the Passion narrative. Prior to the Passion narrative the Jewish people "stand together" with Jesus "over against the wicked leaders." But that all changes so suddenly for Gaston that "the reversal of the role of the people in the passion narrative is astounding."[56] Gaston hangs all this on two slender threads of his reading of the narrative, neither of which is convincing.

The first crucial thread is the "crowd" with Judas at Jesus' arrest (Luke 22:47). We noted above that the text says, ἰδοὺ ὄχλος (codex D adds πολύς). By completely ignoring the discourse marker ἰδού as an introducing device, Gaston surmises that this "crowd" must be the same group of people as referred to in the previous use of the word in Luke 22:6 (ἄτερ ὄχλου, "without a crowd"). Therefore, it "seems to mean the people of Israel as such," and "not a crowd from the chief priests and the scribes and the elders, as in Mark."[57] But that in fact is exactly how Luke soon identifies them. Jesus addresses "the chief priests and officers

---

56. Gaston, "Anti-Judaism," 140, 144.
57. Ibid., 145.

~ of the temple and elders, who had come out against him" (Luke 22:52
, RSV; "the chief priests, the officers of the temple police, and the elders
who had come for him" [NRSV]).

Since this is such a crucial text, it must be examined more carefully. Jesus spoke πρὸς τοὺς παραγενομένους ἐπ᾽ αὐτὸν ἀρχιερεῖς καὶ
στρατηγοὺς τοῦ ἱεροῦ καὶ πρεσβυτέρους. The syntax of the construction
seems rather obvious, although the translations do not reflect it at all. A
definite article precedes the participle (τοὺς παραγενομένους ἐπ᾽ αὐτόν,
"those who came for him"), and then there are three separate nouns
(taking "temple officers" as a unit) connected by καί, none of which has
a separate article. The natural grammatical sense would be, "the priests,
temple officers, and elders who came for him," which would be a subgroup of the whole body of them. Of this group we next see "those
holding him" who rough him up (Luke 22:63). A (rump?) session of
the council is then convened by the body of elders (Luke 22:66) and
they "all" agree that they heard all they need (Luke 22:70–71), so the
"whole bunch of them" (ἅπαν τὸ πλῆθος αὐτῶν [Luke 23:1]) lead him
off to Pilate. Gaston calls this "deliberate vagueness" on Luke's part. He
avoids attaching "any official status" to this group's activity, in order to
"suggest that the whole people is responsible for Jesus' death."[58]

Pilate's exchange is then with "the priests and (their) crowds" (Luke
23:4). Gaston describes these "multitudes" as those "present from the
very beginning before Pilate, as indeed they have been ever since the
arrest and implicitly during the council." Gaston bases all this on his
reading of Luke 22:47, which "seems to mean the people of Israel as
such." From that slim thread he now gets, "Jesus' real trial is before the
Jewish people as part of the apologetic against the Jews of [Luke's] own
day." The only problem is that this reading makes nonsense out of what
- this group says: "He stirs up the people, teaching throughout all Judea,
from Galilee even to this place" (Luke 23:5). Gaston only can blame
bad editing — "an inconsistency that Luke has had to let stand" — for
momentarily allying the people with Jesus again.[59] This seems to be a
high price to pay for a particular reading of one word in the previous
chapter.

The second weak thread on which the whole people of Israel are hung
is based entirely on another single reading. This one is actually more
troublesome than the previous one. Pilate assembles "the priests and the

58. Ibid., 146, 145.
59. Ibid., 146, 147.

rulers and the people" (τὸν λαόν) and repeats the charge that presented
the previous problem: You say he "misleads the people" (Luke 23:13–
14). How can "the people" be on both sides? Gaston's solution again is
to blame bad editing and focus of the setting of the scene, which Luke
created. It makes "the people . . . both judge and executioner," because
they "provide the subjects for all of the impersonal verbs which follow."[60] The most crucial one follows immediately: "They all together
cried out, 'Away with this man,' " (Luke 23:18), and then they intensify
their shout, "Crucify, crucify him" (Luke 23:21). The clincher comes
when the narrative says that "their voices prevailed" and Pilate's judgment is to grant their request (Luke 23:23–24). Jesus is then turned over
"to their will" (Luke 23:25), rather than "to be crucified," as in the
other three Gospels.

The implications are quite clear for Gaston: "Here the Jews as such,
without qualification, are held responsible for Jesus' death, and as a
result are punished by the fall of Jerusalem." Since "no repentance
is possible" in this scenario, "the Jews as such have been irrevocably rejected." This then determines Gaston's reading of Luke 23:27,
ἠκολούθει δὲ αὐτῷ πολὺ πλῆθος τοῦ λαοῦ καὶ γυναικῶν αἳ ἐκόπτοντο
καὶ ἐθρήνουν αὐτόν, which he renders, " 'The great crowd of the people
and of women' who bewailed and lamented Jesus did so because they
surmised their fate."[61] Again Gaston has forced the text to support his
scenario. The clear sense of the Greek (put somewhat literally) is that
"a huge throng of the people follows him, and of women who mourned
and lamented." The only other πολὺ πλῆθος τοῦ λαοῦ in Luke is the
audience for the Sermon on the Plain (Luke 6:17), and the women in
Luke 23, we are soon told, are followers from Galilee (Luke 23:49, 55).
The reader is surely picturing this whole group as loyal followers from
Galilee. They are joined by "all his acquaintances" (Luke 23:49). These
are "the people" who stand watching while "the rulers" sneer (Luke
23:35).

Luke provides further evidence for this picture in the road to Emmaus story. Here, two of the participants give the reader an insider's
perspective. The Passion narrative has been about a prophet, "mighty
in word and deed before God and all the people," whom "our chief
priests and rulers handed over to a judgment of death and crucified him"
(Luke 24:19–20). This is the lasting impression the reader is given of

---

60. Ibid., 148.
61. Ibid., 150–51, 149.

Jesus' crucifixion. The motif of "rejected prophet" provides the set of images. The scene from Jeremiah brings together the same participants: the priests and the rulers and "all the people." Luke, at least, did not expect us to imagine "all" the people in this scene. Nonetheless, the image is still the same: all Israel is represented. Or maybe the emphasis should be that all Israel is affected by what happens here.

Gaston is especially helpful at the end in raising explicit questions about assessing how anti-Jewish this makes Luke. He is quick to point out "how much of this anti-Judaism is simply a matter of perspective!" Perspective includes both the reader/hearer and the time frame. When this kind of narrative is directed to Jews, its becomes anti-Jewish. But it might be used in a strictly Gentile Christian context and not be. The temporal setting also matters. When a deuteronomistic narrative describes the impending judgment, it is not anti-Judaic, "because of the call to repentance after disaster." What makes Luke-Acts "anti-Judaic" is that by the end of Acts the past of Israel is "irrevocably sealed as a part of history," meaning "that the Jews as such have been irrevocably rejected."[62]

Gaston has wrestled with the difficult texts and exposed what the harsh reading would be. The critique presented above has suggested that his reading goes beyond the evidence. A recent assessment of the entire matter of "the Jewish responsibility for the death of Jesus in Luke-Acts," reaches remarkably different conclusions than Gaston: "Luke-Acts gives no indication that its author regarded the entire nation of Israel as having rejected Jesus and the gospel."[63] Only the people and the leaders of Jerusalem bear the responsibility for Jesus' death. We saw earlier that Brawley also insists that Luke distinguishes between groups of Jews and that "it is symptomatic of the methodology" of some approaches that fail to do so.[64]

COROLLARY ISSUES

Space does not permit equal treatment of other issues that have received attention in this debate. Since at some level these issues are intertwined, we have already had glimpses of their relevance. Two in particular warrant mention here. The first is linguistic data. Studies that were typical

---

62. Ibid., 151
63. Jon A. Weatherly, *Jewish Responsibility for the Death of Jesus in Luke-Acts*, JSNTSup 106 (Sheffield: Sheffield Academic Press, 1994), 175.
64. Brawley, *Luke-Acts and the Jews*, 142.

prior to the advent of narrative criticism often had a strong lexical focus. For example, Luke's use of λαός and ὄχλος. The inclination to see each as having a constant referent and then making them equivalent surely seems misplaced (if Lewis Carroll's poem "Jabberwocky" taught us anything). Another instance is studies of Ἰουδαῖοι sometimes even insisting that the presence or absence of the article is irrelevant.[65] Sufficient examples have been discussed above to indicate the extent to which these are more than lexical matters. Whether the text is about some "Jews" or "all Jews" is initially a primary concern of the narrative.

A second major area, of course, is following these issues through in Acts. Again a number of pertinent features of Acts have already been brought into the discussion, but much more remains to be done.

ASSESSMENT

The assessment of anti-Judaism in Luke varies considerably upon the methodological perspective of the critic. The judgment of Gaston hinged on a few crucial editorial changes that contrasted Luke with his sources. The insights from redaction criticism of that era are limited especially in this one respect: They overemphasize changes in details from the presumed source documents.

The current trend in literary criticism is more comprehensive in its attempt to describe the whole "world" of the text. However, no consensus has yet emerged from this approach either. The differences can, at least in part, be explained by looking more closely at aspects of narrative criticism. Most of the attention thus far has been focused on narrative as story. The obvious primary feature is the plot and related matters such as characters.

Reflection on the nature of narrative has also yielded important results by discerning the point of view of the narrator/implied author and the expected reception by the narratee/implied reader. These distinctions can help sort out some of the disparate readings that the same text can produce. Is the story told from a point of view that seems to be pro-Jewish or anti-Jewish? There are clearly enough elements in Luke that seem anti-Jewish. Critics have identified literary patterns suggesting that aspects of the story are told at the expense of Jews and favorably to Christians. That would be difficult to deny.

---

65. For example, Augusto Barbi, "The Use and Meaning of (*Hoi*) *Ioudaioi* in Acts," in *Luke and Acts*, ed. Gerald O'Collins and Gilberto Marconi (New York: Paulist Press, 1993), 125.

Looked at from the other end, reader-response criticism tries to discern how much the reader is expected to notice. Here the results are more promising. In his recent work on "Images of Judaism" (and other unpublished articles), Tyson has made a strong case for the implied reader as exemplified by Luke's Godfearers. The narrative operates at a level that expects the reader to have "an attraction to Jewish religious life," and to be "familiar with the Hebrew Scriptures in their Greek translation" and accept "their authoritative status."[66] This image of the implied reader renders most unlikely the kind of reading given by Jack Sanders.[67]

Jack Sanders's view of Luke-Acts can serve to illustrate the distinction made by Reinhartz. It does exemplify one kind of actualization of the text. Sanders, Gaston, and others who find strong anti-Jewish elements in Luke-Acts remind us that this text has that potentiality. But Gaston, Tyson, and others call attention to the sympathetic treatment of Judaism as well. Thus Gaston's oft-quoted conclusion is that "Luke-Acts is one of the most pro-Jewish and one of the most anti-Jewish writings in the New Testament."[68] Rather than simply being a paradox — as Gaston sees it — it is also an unresolved tension. Current advancements are contributing to reduce that tension.[69]

Brawley concludes that "the evidence warrants a new reading of Luke-Acts as a product of a struggle for the legacy of Israel as the people of God."[70] The methodological suggestions we have made can contribute to this goal. It is at the discourse level of the narrative, its rhetoric, that such evidence is also found. This can best be illustrated in relationship to Tyson's conclusions in *Images of Judaism in Luke-Acts*. He first summarizes Luke's image of the Temple. The closing of its gates (Acts 21:30) "may be taken as Luke's description of the symbolic break between Judaism and Christianity...[which] serves to show that Judaism rejected Christianity, not vice versa."[71]

---

66. Tyson, *Images of Judaism*, 36.

67. The sympathetic reading of Luke-Acts by James Sanders seems much closer. For example, see his essays in Craig A. Evans and James A. Sanders, *Luke and Scripture: The Function of Sacred Tradition in Luke-Acts* (Minneapolis: Fortress, 1993). See also essays by others in Dennis D. Sylva, ed., *Reimaging the Death of the Lukan Jesus*, BBB 73 (Frankfurt: Anton Hain, 1990).

68. Gaston, "Anti-Judaism," 153.

69. Daniel Marguerat is especially interested in accounting for both dimensions of Luke-Acts. See, for example, "Juden und Christen im lukanischen Doppelwerk," *EvT* 54 (1994): 241–64; published also as "Juifs et chrétiens selon Luc-Actes: Surmonter le conflit des lectures," *Biblica* 75 (1994): 126–46.

70. Brawley, *Luke-Acts and the Jews*, 158.

71. Tyson, *Images of Judaism*, 185.

The implied reader, however, would picture the narrative activity of the Temple gates closing from the rhetorical perspective that dominates the second half of Acts in the speeches of Paul. The primary message is Paul's loyalty to Judaism, expressed in the rhetoric of public disputation. Paul's first public speech (Acts 13:16–41) concludes with "many Jews and devout converts" following Paul and Barnabas and urging them to make another speech. So on the next Sabbath "almost the whole city has gathered to hear the word of the Lord." When "the (other) Jews" see "the crowds," they are filled with jealousy and refute (ἀντέλεγον) what Paul says, "blaspheming" in the process. Paul and Barnabas boldly declare the necessity (ἀναγκαῖον) to speak first to those who then reject (ἀπωθεῖσθε) the word of God. The outcome is to turn to the Gentiles (ἰδοὺ στρεφόμεθα εἰς τὰ ἔθνη).

Paul is still harping on these themes in his final speech (Acts 28:17–28), this time to the leading Jews in Rome. He insists on his loyalty to both his people and their ancestral customs, despite his arrest. The Jews in Jerusalem had spoken against (ἀντιλεγόντων) his release, and Paul claims that the issue is "the hope of Israel," an echo from the end of the Gospel (ἠλπίζομεν) [Luke 24:21]). Predictably, they request another meeting to hear his response to the refutations (ἀντιλέγεται) against this new sect. Paul's tactic is to persuade them on the basis of Moses and the prophets. Some are convinced by this, others not (Acts 28:24), which leaves them disagreeing. Paul cites Isa. 6:9–10 and again says that the message is destined for Gentiles.

Any sense of complete separation between Jews and Christians is a projection beyond the end of the narrative. The language of rejection is limited to those Jews who refuse to be convinced by Paul's arguments. The statement is itself a direct echo of deuteronomistic language: The wise have rejected the word of the Lord (σοφοὶ ... τὸν λόγον κυρίου ἀπεδοκίμασαν [Jer. 8:9]). But Luke-Acts always stops short of the reverse deuteronomistic charge: and the Lord has rejected them (Jer. 6:30; 7:29). Rather, Paul claims to be as loyal to Judaism at the end of Acts as were the characters at the beginning of Luke.[72]

A second key item for Tyson is the image of Scripture in Luke-Acts. Tyson sees an unsolved tension between "Christian nonobservance of major parts" of Scripture and its use to support "the initiation of the Gentile mission." For Tyson, "Luke seems genuinely ambivalent on the

---

72. Paul's claims of Jewish loyalty in Acts compare favorably with his own words in Phil. 3:5–9. The key terms used there appear also in Luke-Acts.

question of the continuing authority of the scriptures." Its "eternal validity" requires "Christian interpretation."[73] The insight here needs to
be put more rhetorically. The end of Luke makes clear: It takes an "open
mind" to interpret the Scriptures the way Christians do. Paul's speeches
are filled with hermeneutical arguments. And of course, these disputes
only make sense among groups of Jews, who assume the validity of
Scripture. A Godfearer can only ask the right question: About whom
does the prophet speak? (Acts 8:34). The answer is what distinguishes
one "sect" of Judaism from another.

The scene Luke creates at Corinth (Acts 18), the middle of the
three times Paul declares his intention to go to Gentiles, captures
this succinctly: Paul is occupied testifying to Jews that the Messiah is
Jesus (διαμαρτυρόμενος τοῖς Ἰουδαίοις εἶναι τὸν Χριστόν Ἰησοῦν [Acts
18:5]). Paul meets with severe resistance (ἀντιτασσομένων...αὐτῶν καὶ
βλασφημούντων), and expresses his protest and intention to move on
(ἀπὸ τοῦ νῦν εἰς τὰ ἔθνη πορεύσομαι [Acts 18:6]). But he in fact does not
abandon his Jewish efforts. He goes right next door to the synagogue
and converts a synagogue official (Acts 18:7), among others.[74]

Paul next settles in Ephesus after the stay there of Apollos, an elo-
quent Jewish Scripture scholar from Alexandria (some stereotype!), who
had "received instruction" and already taught about Jesus "accurately"
(Acts 18:25, echoes from Luke 1:1–4). But he practices only "John's
baptism," so when Priscilla and Aquila hear him speaking boldly in the
synagogue, they expound to him "more accurately." We last see him dis-
puting publicly with Jews by expositing the Scriptures to show that "the
Messiah is Jesus" (τοῖς Ἰουδαίοις διακατηλέγχετο δημοσίᾳ ἐπιδεικνὺς
διὰ τῶν γραφῶν εἶναι τὸν Χριστὸν Ἰησοῦν [Acts 18:28]). Luke puts
forth a clear image of the role of Scripture in debates among groups of
Jews. Both Paul and Apollos, from their different locations within Diaspora Judaism, are pictured as sharing the same hermeneutic. It assumes
that all Jews are concerned about "the Messiah," so that the argument
is over applying messianic Scripture to Jesus (as in Luke 24 and Acts 8).

This is the hermeneutic that typifies the explicit use of Scripture in
the message of the characters in the narrative. We also need to identify
the separate hermeneutic that characterizes the implied author or point
of view of the narrator. That hermeneutic is historiographical, not christological. The deuteronomistic hermeneutic uses Scripture to interpret

---

73. Tyson, *Images of Judaism*, 186–87.
74. This surely indicates Luke's sense of humor; see Richard I. Pervo, *Profit with
Delight: The Literary Genre of the Acts of the Apostles* (Philadelphia: Fortress, 1987).

history in a particular way. The focus is on the present moment and how history got to this point. That can be viewed from either direction. The (divine) forces in history have brought us to the current moment. This same conviction allows tracing one's historical legitimacy to antiquity. Such historical writing was in vogue in the Hellenistic era. Gregory Sterling calls this "apologetic historiography," defined as "the story of a subgroup of people in an extended prose narrative written by a member of the group who follows the group's own traditions but Hellenizes them in an effort to establish the identity of the group within the setting of the larger world."[75] The methodology for Luke-Acts to accomplish new group identity within the traditions of the larger established Jewish groups was found in deuteronomistic historiography.[76]

Finally, Tyson directly addresses the issue of anti-Judaism in Luke-Acts. In light of his recent study he reformulates the issue: "Do the images that are embedded in Luke-Acts convey to the implied reader positive or negative impressions of Jewish religious life and the Jewish people? The answer, of course, is that they convey both." Tyson summarizes the evidence he has presented. The initial positive images are inevitably replaced for him by the powerful negative images.

> For the most part, the Jewish people are cast in the role of opponents of the Christian preachers. Not only do they reject the message that ostensibly was meant for them, but they frequently oppose the preachers in violent ways.... The negative images tend to increase as the narrative progresses, and the reader is drawn to join in condemnation of Jews for their rejection of the Christian message.[77]

That such images occur, especially in Acts, cannot be denied. It is not convincing, however, to generalize this whole set of images to be about "the Jewish people." My image of implied reader includes someone capable of making finer distinctions than that.

The last statement by Tyson is more troubling. In his own concluding comments, Tyson acknowledges that he finds the negative images

---

75. Gregory E. Sterling, *Historiography and Self-Definition: Josephos, Luke-Acts, and Apologetic Historiography,* NovTSup 64 (Leiden: Brill, 1992), 17.

76. David Balch's response to my essay puts this in the context of Greco-Roman rhetorical arguments for including outsiders. See also Balch's, "Paul in Acts: 'You Teach All the Jews...to Forsake Moses, Telling Them Not to...Observe the Customs' (Acts 21:21)," in *Panchaia: Festschrift für Klaus Thraede,* ed. Manfred Wacht (Münster: Aschendorffsche Verlagsbuchhandlung, 1995), 11–23.

77. Tyson, *Images of Judaism,* 187–88.

in Luke-Acts more powerful than the positive ones. He correctly notes
that these images have been used "as a justification for negative Christian attitudes toward Jewish people and their religious life. In this sense
these documents have played a role in a tragic history." The best Tyson
hopes for is that the tension in Luke-Acts between positive and negative images be preserved, not just for the sake of accuracy, but also to
"support more benign convictions about Jewish-Christian relationships
in our own time."[78]

While this modest goal is certainly laudable, I think an appeal can be
made for even more. Tyson connects the negative images in the text with
the reader "drawn to join in condemnation of Jews." For me, an important further distinction can be made here utilizing narrative criticism.
The images in the text are part of the story, the "what" of the narrative.
But it is not the images by themselves that compel a reader to action. It
is the rhetoric of the discourse, the "how" of the narrative, that directly
invites the reader to join in affirming images from within the text.

The dominant rhetoric in the latter part of Acts is about hermeneutics. Paul is engaged in public disputation. The language used is about
debate, refutation, persuasion, and *apologia*. What is pictured at stake
for Paul is the legitimacy of his claim to remain within authentic parameters of Judaism when he makes his hermeneutical claims about the
Jewish Scriptures. To be sure, wherever he goes, there are Jews who are
said to dispute his claims. But his arguments are never actually refuted.
The implied reader is someone who would find Paul's arguments convincing. The final scene may then suggest that it is no longer necessary
to continue those debates. "Going to Gentiles" now means "enough
debates over Scripture."

The image of Paul actually preaching to Gentiles is hardly reassuring.
The Areopagus speech is hardly overwhelming. Pagans can be counted
on to be curious about something new, but just as ready to scoff at it
(Acts 17: 22, 32). After modest success, Paul returns to turf he knows
better, arguing (διελέγετο) every sabbath in the synagogue at Corinth,
trying to convince (ἔπειθεν) Jews and Greeks (Acts 18:4). These are
Paul's kind of Greeks: They are already at the synagogue and he knows
how to debate with them. The pagan philosophers were a different
matter.

We end then back with the Godfearers. Tyson has made a convincing
case for the Godfearer as the model of Luke's implied reader. This is

---

78. Ibid., 88, 189.

a very different Greek from the skeptical agnostics in Athens. This is
the Greek Luke appeals to. Like Apollos, he already knows something
about "the way of the Lord" (Acts 18:25–26), which makes him open
to hearing about "the Way." This is especially appealing in the face of
Judeans who insist "all or nothing" — the custom of Moses requires
circumcision (Acts 15:1). That kind of Godfearer would be reassured by
Paul's rhetoric that loyalty to Judaism includes messianic claims about
Jesus. But would this message draw him to join in condemnation of Jews
for not accepting the same arguments? The rhetorical evidence would
make that seem unlikely.

When Paul himself makes similar arguments in Galatians, "he writes
as a Jew." Boyarin thus establishes Paul's identity as "a Jewish cultural
critic." When Boyarin, a Jew, then reads Paul's Jewish critique of Jews,
he concludes: "It is totally inappropriate to think of Paul's thought as
anti-Semitic, or even as anti-Judaic."[79] This judgment suggests that there
is nothing inherently anti-Jewish in the kinds of intra-Jewish arguments
Paul makes.

The problem for the historian is whether a similar judgment is appropriate for the image of Paul making such arguments in a narrative setting
such as Acts. The difference, of course, is in the very nature of narrative. The reader is not listening directly to Paul, but hears Paul from the
point of view of the narrator. Although this establishes additional layers
of rhetorical effect on the reader, each layer must be assessed separately
for its contribution to the total effect on the reader.

A FINAL REFLECTION

Discerning a narrative text to be in any sense anti-Jewish is a complex
matter. The narrative critic never stops being an actual reader. As I
attempt to reconstruct an (implied) reader from the text, I am simultaneously actualizing my own reading of the same text. The narrative
critic who is also a historical critic has an even more difficult task. Now
some image of an original reader comes into mind. As we reconstruct
the world of the late first century, what plausible readers existed for this
text? When we begin to have actual historical readers by the late second century and beyond, the task of historical criticism becomes more

---

79. Daniel Boyarin, *A Radical Jew: Paul and the Politics of Identity* (Berkeley, Calif.:
University of California Press, 1994), 137, 152.

concrete. I can readily discern which readings actualize the text in a way that invites condemnation of Judaism.[80]

Clearly then, these texts are potentially anti-Jewish. The task of the critic is to locate the source of that potential. In any narrative there are multiple possibilities. Luke-Acts is in many ways the most complex narrative in the New Testament. Among its diverse features is a set of characters that includes negative stereotypes. At times the accompanying rhetoric suggests that the reader should note the irony in a scene, or even the humor. That was likely the first aspect of the narrative to be lost when the text was read as Scripture. Then the hermeneutics applied to the text began to resemble the divisive hermeneutics practiced within the text. This is surely a less enjoyable form of irony.

---

80. One small example is the following digression in Tertullian's treatise "On Prayer" (chap. 14):

> Albeit Israel washed daily all his limbs over, yet is he never clean. His hands, at all events, are ever unclean, eternally dyed with the blood of the prophets, and of the Lord himself; and on that account, as being hereditary culprits from their privity to their fathers' crimes [Matt. 23:31; Luke11:48], they do not dare even to raise them unto the Lord, for fear some Isaiah should cry out [Isa. 1:15], for fear Christ should utterly shudder. We, however, not only raise, but even expand them; and taking our model from the Lord's passion, even in prayer we confess [or give praise] to Christ. (*ANF* 3, 685)

Response to Daryl D. Schmidt

Luke-Acts Is Catechesis for Christians, Not Kerygma to Jews

David L. Balch

PROFESSOR SCHMIDT AND I agree that the narrative of Luke-Acts has a close relationship to "apologetic historiography" as described by G. E. Sterling,[1] the rhetoric of which has an epideictic function; that is, its "goal was to persuade the audience to adopt a point of view, to praise or blame someone."[2] I add that Tcherikover has shown that such apologetic literature is often directed to *insiders*.[3]

There does seem to be some confusion between Schmidt's genre and literary criticism, between the epideictic function of the work and the discussion of implied readers, whom the author then is trying to persuade. Schmidt agrees with Tyson that the Godfearers are the model of Luke's implied reader. In Luke's literary world they are "quasi-Jewish Gentiles" who act as the transition from the original Jewish Christians to the dominant Gentile church of Luke's day.[4] They have an attraction to Jewish religious life and accept the authority of the Septuagint.[5]

Schmidt observes that the narrative world of the text is not a direct window to some actual social-historical world. I agree, but will make arguments about both. Historically, the term "Godfearers" is problematic and cannot be used without careful definition. Schürer collects the relevant literary texts and inscriptions, including book 4 of the *Sibylline*

---

1. Gregory E. Sterling, *Historiography and Self-Definition: Josephos, Luke-Acts and Apologetic Historiography* (Leiden: E. J. Brill, 1992).

2. Daryl D. Schmidt, "Anti-Judaism and the Gospel of Luke," in this volume, 77, quoting George Kennedy.

3. See Victor Tcherikover, "Jewish Apologetic Literature Reconsidered," *Eos* 48 (1956): 169–93.

4. Michael J. Cook, "The Mission to the Jews in Acts: Unraveling Luke's 'Myth of the Myriads,'" in *Luke-Acts and the Jewish People: Eight Critical Perspectives*, ed. Joseph B. Tyson (Minneapolis: Augsburg, 1988), 120.

5. Joseph B. Tyson, *Images of Judaism in Luke-Acts* (Columbia, S.C.: University of South Carolina Press, 1992), 36.

Oracles, a close reading of which suggests that there were different standards of observance of the Jewish law.[6] Collins emphasizes the lack of reference to circumcision by Diaspora Jewish writers, who never require Greeks to practice it.[7] Schürer concludes against Kraabel that "there were gentiles who judaised without becoming converts, and that in at least some places these 'God-fearers' formed a defined group."[8] The Sabbath commandment and the dietary laws were probably of first importance to them, but they must be distinguished from full proselytes who underwent circumcision and baptism.[9] Israel felt itself to be a teacher of the peoples of the world, as is clear from Justin Martyr's use of Isa. 49:6.[10] Dio Cassius (fl. 194–205 C.E.) writes of "Jews," a title that

> applies also to all the rest of mankind (ἄλλους ἀνθρώπους), although of alien race (ἀλλοεθνεῖς), who affect their customs (τὰ νόμιμα...ζηλοῦσι). This class exists even among the Romans, and though often repressed (κολουσθὲν) has increased (αὐξηθὲν) to a very great extent and has won its way to the right of freedom in its observances. They are distinguished from the rest of mankind in practically every detail of life, and especially by the fact that they do not honour any of the usual gods, but show extreme reverence for one particular divinity.[11]

This observation by Dio shows that Judaism in the Greco-Roman world was multiethnic (cf. Tacitus, *Hist.* 5.5). However, the term "Godfearer" can also be applied to observing Jews. Schmidt and Tyson are using a loaded English term that translates several Greek ones in the text of Luke-Acts and elsewhere. A confusion between historical and literary definitions is more than possible, and clear definition is necessary.

---

6. Emil Schürer, *The History of the Jewish People in the Age of Jesus Christ (175 B.C.–A.D. 135)*, ed. G. Vermes, F. Millar, and M. Goodman (Edinburgh: T. & T. Clark, 1973–87), vol. 3, 1:162–69. David L. Balch, "Attitudes toward Foreigners in 2 Maccabees, Eupolemus, Esther, Aristeas, and Luke-Acts," in *The Church in Its Context: Studies in Honor of Everett Ferguson*, ed. A. J. Malherbe, F. W. Norris, and J. W. Thompson NovTSup 90 (Leiden: Brill, 1998), 22–47.

7. John J. Collins, "A Symbol of Otherness: Circumcision and Salvation in the First Century," in *"To See Ourselves As Others See Us": Christians, Jews, and "Others" in Late Antiquity*, ed. J. Neusner and E. S. Frerichs (Chico, Calif.: Scholars Press, 1985), 166–69, 173–74, 178, 184.

8. Schürer, *History of the Jewish People*, vol. 3, 1:169.

9. Ibid., 169, 174, citing Epictetus (i.e., Arrian [fl. 134 C.E.]), Diss. 2.9.20–21.

10. Justin Martyr, *Dialogue with Trypho* 121–22, cited by Schürer, *History of the Jewish People*, vol. 3, 1:160.

11. Dio Cassius, *Roman History* 37.17.1, cited by Schürer, *History of the Jewish People*, vol. 3, 1:162.

The implied reader is rather Christian (Luke 1:1, "us"). Converts include orthopraxic Jews (the strict Pharisee Paul), some Africans/ Ethiopians (the eunuch, an official of Candace), Godfearers (Cornelius, who gives alms and prays), and pagans (a few Athenian Stoics). Because these Christians are diverse, I will refer to implied readers — the plural. Luke-Acts is not a missionary, but a catechetical (Luke 1:4) work. The implied author is not trying to persuade the implied Christian readers that the Christ is Jesus (Acts 18:5), but observes that the implied readers have heard many accounts of Christ (Luke 1:1), which according to the dominant modern scholarly theory include Mark and Q. Whichever accounts the implied readers have read, they are not outsiders. This raises two questions: Whom is the implied author trying to persuade, and of what? Who are the implied readers, and why does the author compose this narrative for them?

Schmidt discusses the current state of the question of anti-Judaism in the narrative by surveying articles edited in Tyson, *Luke-Acts and the Jewish People,* analyzing Michael Cook's and Tyson's own contributions at length. All discuss both the story and the discourse, the "what" and the "how" of the narrative. The story is sequential, and its images cumulative; narrative criticism stresses the story's sense of progression, first impressions that have ongoing effects. The "how" of the narrative's discourse involves the point of view of the narrator, the tone of voice that the implied author gives to the characters, the way the narrator frames characters' speeches, which gives the implied reader clues.

Cook agrees with Tyson that the story involves "the failed mission to the Jews [which] is terminated in favor of the mission to the Gentiles."[12] (It is ironic that a modern Jewish author would need to argue that cessation of mission to the Jews in Acts is anti-Judaic.) Both authors see a literary pattern: the "Jewish public" always initially gives a favorable response, but then reverses itself suddenly and rejects Jesus and Paul.[13] The character Paul's "glaring, abrasive denunciations" that he will turn to the Gentiles (in Acts 13:46, 18:6, and 28:28) are an indication of the implied author's intent.[14] Tyson himself sees the failure of the Jewish mission and the Jewish rejection of the gospel as so basic that he would retitle Acts "The Problem of Jewish Rejection."[15] The implied author's problem, ac-

---

12. Cook, "Mission to the Jews," 106.

13. Ibid., 107.

14. Ibid., 109.

15. Joseph B. Tyson, "The Problem of Jewish Rejection in Acts," in idem, ed., *Luke-Acts and the Jewish People,* 137.

cording to Cook, is how to convince the implied reader that Christianity is the heir of authentic Judaism, despite the fact that few Jews converted.

Tyson finds this literary pattern in the story of the change in the role of the crowd at Jesus' arrest (Luke 22): Their initial response is positive but suddenly turns to rejection. Reading the same story, Schmidt utilizes an insight of William Kurz: The narrator consistently (ten times) uses "behold" (ἰδού) "to signal the abrupt arrival" of a new character, to "focalize the action from the perspective of the characters within the action, rather than from the narrator's usually more distanced viewpoint."[16] The author sets the scene: Judas seeks Jesus "without a crowd" (Luke 22:6), since "the people" have provided Jesus protection. But when Jesus awakens his sleeping disciples, he is met by Judas. While Jesus is still speaking to them, "behold, a crowd (ἰδοὺ ὄχλος) and the one called Judas" appear (Luke 22:47). For Tyson this is the same Jewish crowd that earlier had responded to Jesus positively, but now has deserted him. For Schmidt, noting the discourse marker "behold," there are two crowds, the second one identified in Luke 22:52, as "chief priests, temple police, and elders."[17] Schmidt concludes that this story does not exhibit the pattern of acceptance followed by rejection, and his observation of the discourse marker "behold" is indeed acute. Neither does Luke 4 exhibit the pattern of initial acceptance followed by rejection. This is rather the story of a deuteronomic prophet who is rejected (cf. Deut. 18:18–19; Neh. 9:26, 31; Jer. 21:10; 12:7; 22:5; 33; 8:9; 6:30; 7:29).

The conclusion of the two volumes — the Gospel and its sequel — Acts 28, is crucial in all reconstructions of the narrative's meaning. Tyson focuses on this text, interpreting it to mean that the mission to the Jews was over; this is so even though many characters in the narrative practice Judaism, even though there are many "individual" Jews who accept the Christian message, and even though Jewish Christians in Jerusalem are important. Schmidt himself notes the definitive sounding resolution with the quotation of Isa. 6:9–10 (Acts 28:26–27) and compares this ending of Acts with the ending of the Gospel. All that had happened (Luke 24:14), including Jesus' crucifixion, is associated with the disciples feeling gloomy (Luke 24:21). But their problem is lack of perspective, a failure to trust the prophets, who had foretold the necessity of all this (Luke 24:25–26). All these events are the necessary

---

16. Schmidt, "Anti-Judaism and the Gospel of Luke," 73.

17. Cf. John T. Carroll and Joel B. Green, "Who Was Responsible for the Death of Jesus? The Cross and 'Anti-Judaism' in Early Christianity," in Neusner and Frerichs, eds., *"To See Ourselves As Others See Us,"* 197 n. 4.

fulfillment of everything in scripture (Luke 24:45). There are similar summary statements in Acts 1:16; 4:25–28, citing Ps. 2:1–2; and Acts 8:28–35, citing Isaiah 53. Just so in Acts 28, Paul explains Jesus one last time on the basis of Moses and the prophets, which some find convincing, others not (Acts 28:24). Schmidt's translation of Acts 28:27–28 is, "It's just as the prophet said, 'You keep on listening, but y'all won't ever learn!' So you better understand: This message is now going to others; they'll listen."[18] This concludes both volumes and particularly the second half of Acts, which has many Pauline speeches, the primary message of which concerns Paul's loyalty to Judaism. Acts does not then narrate a complete separation between Jews and Christians; the language of rejection is limited to those Jews who refuse to be convinced by Paul's arguments. Schmidt observes that this is an echo of deuteronomistic language that the wise have rejected the word of the Lord (Jer. 8:9), but also that the author of Luke-Acts always stops short of the reverse deuteronomistic charge, that the Lord had rejected them (Jer. 6:30; 7:29): "Neither Luke's Gospel nor Acts ends on the final note of Jewish rejection."[19]

Schmidt's conclusion is compelling. Nevertheless, I suggest that the initial question needs to be rephrased. Questions set up a possible range of answers, and when initial questions are nuanced, different answers follow. Michael Cook focuses first on whether Luke is signaling the church of the late first century to maintain the mission to the Jews as an ongoing concern, and second on Luke's understanding of Christianity as embodying authentic Judaism.[20] Is Luke's central problem that few Jews believed the Christian message, which Tyson observes is once summarized as worshiping "the God of our fathers, believing everything laid down by the law or written in the prophets, [and] having a hope in God which these themselves accept, that there will be a resurrection of both the just and the unjust" (Acts 24:14–15)?[21] Tannehill agrees that "the hope of Israel is a central theme in this cycle of speeches."[22]

What is the conflict in the plot in Luke-Acts? How do characters react

---

18. Schmidt, "Anti-Judaism and the Gospel of Luke," 78.
19. Ibid., 74, quoting Robert Brawley. David L. Balch, "Paul in Acts: '...You Teach all the Jews...to Forsake Moses, Telling Them Not to...Observe the Customs' (Acts, 21:21)," in *Panchaia: Festschrift für Klaus Thraede* (Jahrbuch für Antike und Christentum, Ergänzungsband 22: Münster: Aschendorffsche Verlagsbuchhandlung, 1995), 11–23.
20. Cook, "Mission to the Jews," 104, 109.
21. Tyson, "Problem of Jewish Rejection," 129
22. Robert C. Tannehill, "Rejection by Jews and Turning to Gentiles: The Pattern of Paul's Mission in Acts," in Tyson, ed., *Luke-Acts and the Jewish People,* 94.

to this conflict? If the speeches of Paul are written to persuade implied readers, who are Christians and not Godfearers, what would the author have them accept? To begin to find answers, we need more clarity about the content of the Christian message as formulated by the author of Luke-Acts as well as more content to our understanding of anti-Judaism in the Greco-Roman world. I will argue that the interpretation of Scripture by the characters Jesus and Paul is the content of their message, and this message engenders the conflict of the plot, which is not best stated by concluding that Jews rejected the Christian message. Rather, in the narrative world of Luke-Acts there is conflict *within* Judaism and *among* Christians (not primarily between Jews on the one hand and Christians on the other) over this interpretation of Scripture, over the proclamations of the observant Jesus and the strict Pharisee Paul.

Whatever the relation of dependence between them, Luke differs from Mark. In Mark the gospel is, "The Son of Man will be handed over to the chief priests and the scribes, and they will condemn him to death; then they will hand him over to the Gentiles; they will mock him, and spit upon him, and flog him, and kill him; and after three days he will rise again" (Mark 10:33–34; cf. 8:31, with δεῖ; 9:31). Luke reformulates this, reading Scripture as prophesying not one event but two, which then become the subject of not one volume but two. The resurrected Jesus holds a Bible study with the eleven, those with them, and the two disciples returned from Emmaus, repeating his teaching " 'while I was still with you — that everything written about me in the Law of Moses, the Prophets, and the Psalms must (δεῖ) be fulfilled.' Then he opened their minds to understand the Scriptures, and he said to them, 'Thus it is written [1] that the Messiah is to suffer and to rise from the dead on the third day, and [2] that repentance and forgiveness of sins is to be proclaimed in his name to all nations (εἰς πάντα τὰ ἔθνη), beginning from Jerusalem.' " (Luke 24:44–47).

The second item, concerning "all nations," is not only an interpretation of Scripture (e.g., Isa. 49:6 cited in Luke 2:32; Acts 13:47; 26:17–18; also Gen. 22:18 and 26:4, cited in Acts 3:25), but is a message of characters within the narrative world that generates conflict both among Jews and, as the story progresses, among Christians. In the *Temple* Simeon announces God's salvation "which you have prepared in the presence of all peoples, a light for revelation to the Gentiles" (Luke 2:31–32, alluding to Isa. 49:6), and he already foresees conflict: " 'This child is destined for the falling and the rising of many in Israel, and to be a sign that will be opposed.... And a sword will pierce your own soul too" (Luke 2:34–35). This conflict is realized after Jesus' first programmatic sermon in the synagogue in Nazareth, when his Scripture interpretation refers to a widow of Sidon and to Naaman the Syrian (Luke 4:26–27): "When they heard this, all in the synagogue were filled with rage" (Luke 4:28). In this narrative world, the conflict is not between Jews and Christians, but among Jews. Further, this literary conflict is historically realistic. The previous citations of Dio Cassius and Tacitus indicate that significant numbers of foreigners were becoming Jews and that Greeks and Romans resented it; such growth in a well-defined ethnic group could and did generate actual conflict.

Later among Christians this same scripture interpretation generates conflict, in the longest episode in these books (Acts 10–15). Peter, not simply as a Jew, but as an orthopraxic Jewish Christian, asserts that "it is unlawful for a Jew[ish Christian] to associate with or to visit a Gentile; but God has shown me that I should not call anyone profane or unclean" (Acts 10:28). Then Peter preaches a sermon, which Wilckens, against C. H. Dodd, has shown to be the author's own construction with a close relationship to the beginning and ending of the Gospel of Luke.[23] The sermon opens and closes, just as the Gospel does, with an emphasis on "in every nation anyone" (Acts 10:35) and "all the prophets testify...that everyone who believes" (Acts 10:43). This scriptural interpretation and sermon generate conflict within the Jerusalem church, just as it did in the Nazareth synagogue. In neither case is the conflict between Christians and Jews; in this narrative "the Jews" are not rejecting the Christian message.

Strikingly, two of the other passages that narrate conflict about Gentiles are precisely among the three problematic ones that Cook discusses. Paul preaches to "brothers" in the synagogue in Antioch in Pisidia (Acts 13:15), with echoes from Jesus' synagogue sermon in Nazareth. The leading idea in the speech is "the fulfillment of the promise to Israel of an heir to David's throne."[24] Just as Simeon had seen the "Lord's Messiah" (Luke 2:26) and then cited Isa. 49:6, so after Paul's sermon to "Israelites," which concerns "David their king" (Acts 13:16–41), Paul quotes the same prophecy, Isa. 49:6 (Acts 13:47). At the end of his sermon in Antioch in Pisidia, Paul concludes, "By this Jesus everyone (πᾶς) who believes is set free from all those sins from which you could not be freed by the law of Moses"; then he quotes Hab. 1:5,

---

23. Ulrich Wilckens, "Kerygma und Evangelium bei Lukas (Beobachtungen zu Acta 10 34–43)," *ZNTW* 49 (1958): 223–37.
24. Tannehill, "Rejection," 85, 88.

"you will never believe" (Acts 13:39, 41). After the resulting conflict, Paul quotes the Isaiah passage concerning Gentiles. (I will not take space to develop it, but this is at the heart of the conflict in the crucial chapter Acts 21 and Paul's apology in Acts 22, the chapters that introduce the final section of Acts.)[25] What conflict does the author who has constructed the plot expect the implied reader to perceive? Jews rejecting a vague Christian hope? No, in this narrative world conflict is generated rather by the inclusion of foreigners, the same problematic scriptural interpretation/proclamation announced in the infancy narrative, in Jesus' initial programmatic sermon, in his postresurrection Bible study, in the proclamations of Peter in the Pentecost sermon and to Cornelius, and of Paul in Antioch. The narrative setting for this conflict in Luke 2 and 4 is among Jews, and in Acts 13, the author sets the scene to present Paul in the synagogue among "brothers."

The final scene in the two-volume work is similar. But before interpreting it, two further questions are important. Does the author present us with "the" Jews and/or "the" Christians, unified but polarized and divided groups, as many discussions assume? And if there is diversity among Jews and among Christians, what is the intra-Jewish and intra-Christian conflict? In the following paragraphs I will argue that Luke mixes categories: Some Pharisees are Christians, and many believers in Jerusalem are "among the Jews." (My daughter, Christina, informs me that modern writers also problematize binary conceptions of race, arguing rather for "mixture").[26]

Beginning in Luke 5:17–21, Jesus is in conflict with the Pharisees, but his final conflict with them in the Gospel story is Luke 19:29–44, his triumphal entry into Jerusalem. In the following story he cleanses the Temple, and "the chief priests, the scribes, and the leaders of the people" look for a way to kill him, but cannot because the people are spellbound by his message (Luke 19:47–48). The author has constructed the story so that diverse Jewish groups play clearly differentiated roles; the Pharisees have no role in the Passion narrative. In a scene unique to Luke, Pharisees even warn him that Herod wants to kill him (Luke 13:31). Similarly, in Acts 5, when the high priest, the council, and all the elders want to kill the apostles, it is again a Pharisee, Gamaliel, who

25. David L. Balch, "Roman Ideology in Dionysius of Halicarnassus and Christian Ideology in Luke-Acts: A Comparison," in *The Book of Acts in Its First Century Setting*, vol. 6: *The Book of Acts in Its Theological Setting*, ed. B. W. Winter (Grand Rapids: Eerdmans, forthcoming).

26. See Elizabeth Martinez, "Beyond Black/White: The Racisms of Our Time," *Social Justice* 20, nos. 1–2 (1993): 22–34.

persuades them that they should not be found "fighting against God" (Acts 5:21–40). In this narrative it is hardly chance that the character Paul proclaims himself a student of Gamaliel, who educated him "strictly according to our ancestral law" (Acts 22:3; cf. 26:5). Some Pharisees become believers (Acts 15:5). Because the Pharisees believe the same things, Paul is able to elicit their support when he is on trial before the chief priests and the whole council (Acts 23:6–10). Pharisees, strict keepers of the Law, protect Jesus and Paul, and some of them tend to convert, including Paul, the central character in the second volume. This conflict in these books is not adequately summarized by concluding that the Jews reject Christian hope; neither the characters involved nor the content of the conflict is correctly described by this slogan.

Briefly observed, as the Pharisees protect Jesus and Paul in this narrative, so Jews "from Asia" are particularly eager for Paul's death (Acts 21:27; 24:19; cf. 6:9).

Sadducees are mentioned once in Luke (Luke 20:27); they do not believe in resurrection, as Jesus does. The priests, captain of the Temple, and Sadducees come to Peter and John, annoyed that they preach resurrection in Jesus, and arrest them (Acts 4:1–3). The narrator's parenthesis in Acts 5:17 is crucial: "Then the high priest took action; he and all who were with him (that is, the sect of the Sadducees), being filled with jealousy, arrested the apostles." This narrator's gloss identifies the high priest's opposition to Jesus in the Gospel Passion narrative with one sect differentiated from other Jews, the same sect that will oppose Paul in Acts 23. Despite the fact that the author of Acts frequently writes of "the Jews," there are crucial differences and tensions, unmistakably clear in the Pharisees' absence from the Passion narrative. As Schmidt observes (19–20), the author tends to use a "discourse of consensus"; "all" the people and "all" the opposition appear (as in Acts 5:17).[27] This sounds unanimous and is a pervasive pattern of Luke's discourse; but nevertheless, the author makes distinctions among the Jews that are central to the plot.

There are also tensions among Christians in Acts faced by both Peter and Paul. Peter believes it "unlawful to associate with or to visit a Gentile" (Acts 10:28). However, the word is ἀλλόφυλος not ἔθνος, and means "member of another tribe," "foreigner"; it is mistranslated as "Gentile," because it is not the opposite of "Jewish." Given the conflict sketched above around this hermeneutic/proclamation that God will

---

27. Daryl D. Schmidt, "Anti-Judaism and the Gospel of Luke," 83.

bless all nations and the six chapters (10–15) the author devotes to this particular episode, it must have something to do with the purpose of the whole two volumes. Would not some implied readers identify with Peter's assertion? Has not the author added this to Mark's Gospel, that is, woven conflict over this invitation to "all nations" into the plot in order to persuade *Christians* that neither Scripture nor Jesus was misanthropic?

Wilckens interprets Peter's sermon to Cornelius as a speech *to Christians:* "You know (ὑμεῖς οἴδατε) the message he sent to the people of Israel, preaching peace by *Jesus Christ* — he is Lord of *all*" (πάντων, v. 36), a proclamation that also begins and ends the sermon (Acts 10:34–35, 43), a scriptural interpretation that also begins and ends the Gospel of Luke (Luke 2:32; 24:47).[28] *Christians*, the implied readers of Luke 1:1, need to hear that Christ is Lord of *all.* This Lukan gospel is intra-Christian teaching, catechesis, not kerygma.[29] The characters rejecting this teaching in Acts 10–15 are more often Christians, not "the Jews." Peter must ask, "Can anyone withhold the water for baptizing these people?" (Acts 10:47). For this proclamation and act, "believers criticized" Peter when he arrived in Jerusalem (Acts 11:2), a story that continues for four more chapters, and that I do not have space here to interpret, except to emphasize that this story does not narrate "the Jews" rejecting Christian universalism. These are Christian believers criticizing catechetical instruction. The pagans to whom Peter is preaching have already been converted.[30]

Similarly in Acts 21, this time Paul, not Peter, arrives in Jerusalem to narrate what "God had done among the *Gentiles* through his ministry," and he is welcomed warmly as a "brother" (Acts 21:17–20). (Reading this as including intra-Christian conflict, would not many readers see hypocritical smiles on the brothers' faces?) There are myriads of believers among the Jews in Jerusalem, "but they have been told about you that you teach all the Jews living among the Gentiles to forsake Moses" (Acts 21:20–21). The brothers do not trust Paul! The orthopraxic Paul of Acts, however, insists that he has not forsaken Moses, which at this juncture of salvation history (cf. ἀπὸ τοῦ νῦν [Acts 18:6]) means that the one God is to be proclaimed to "all nations." Paul narrates that in the *Temple* he received the same revelation as Simeon had, that he

---

28. Ulrich Wilckens, "Kerygma und Evangelium bei Lukas (Beobachtungen zu Acta 10,34–43," *ZNW* 49 (1958): 223–37.

29. Ibid., 236.

30. Ibid., 237.

is to go to Gentiles (Acts 22:17–21; cf. Luke 2:25–32), which generates more conflict and cries for his death (Acts 22:22). But given the author's introduction to this episode, that there are "many thousands of believers... among the Jews" (ἐν τοῖς Ἰουδαίοις, [Acts 21:20]), the story implies that those calling for Paul's death include the Christian believers who had warmly received him. Similar is *1 Clem.* 5.2, 5: "Through jealousy and envy the greatest and most righteous pillars of the church were persecuted and contended unto death.... Through jealousy and strife Paul showed the way to the prize of endurance."

All this means that the author's final conclusion in Acts 28 does not exclude a whole group of people, the Jews. The narrator introduces the final scene observing that Paul "called together the local *leaders* of the Jews" (Acts 28:17; 28:23), which is already ominous. In the Passion narrative in the Gospel, the *leaders* oppose Jesus.[31] The author writes to persuade *Christians* who say they cannot associate with foreigners (Acts 10:28), to persuade them that Christ is Lord of *all*; so the conclusion does not exclude Jews, though it does criticize their leaders. The next-to-last verse of the two volumes proclaims that "[Paul] welcomed all (ἀπεδέχετο πάντας) who came to him," which the scribes of some manuscripts correctly interpret to mean, "welcomed all, both Jews and Greeks" (Ἰουδαίους τε καὶ Ἕλληνας) (Acts 28:30 [MSS 614, 2147, vg, sy]). A subtitle for Luke-Acts is not "the problem of Jewish rejection," but rather, "the problem of Christian misanthropy," or "Brothers, don't you know that Moses and Isaiah, Christ, Peter and Paul were philanthropic?" or "Theophilus, you are now to be called 'Philanthropos.'"

This concludes my response to Professor Schmidt. I want to add two matters, one shorter, one longer. First, we discuss anti-Judaism and the Gospels in the late twentieth century in light of the Holocaust. As a Christian theologian, more, as a Lutheran theologian, I confess and grieve with my church that many who called themselves Lutheran Christians murdered millions of Jews.[32] Some of them were "theologians for Hitler," among them Walter Grundmann, who studied in Tübingen four decades before I did. Virtually all European Christian theologians were

---

31. Schmidt, "Anti-Judaism and the Gospel of Luke," pp. 85ff.; see also Raymond Brown, *The Death of the Messiah: From Gethsemane to the Grave*, 2 vols. (New York: Doubleday, 1994), 1:340–57 (on the Sanhedrin), 1:389–91 (on Luke), 404–11 (on the chief priests); Carroll and Green, "Who Was Responsible for the Death of Jesus?" 195–98.

32. See "Declaration of the Evangelical Lutheran Church in America to the Jewish Community (April 18, 1994)," *Interfaith Focus* 2/1 (New York: Anti-Defamation League of B'nai B'rith, 1995), iii.

silent or, worse, cooperative in the face of this radical evil.[33] I reject Christian mission to the Jews, but for a qualitatively different reason than those interpreters who read a cessation of mission into Acts: Would Christians propose to teach Abraham Heschel about God, one who suffered the loss of his family in Treblinka and Auschwitz, but maintained his trust in God despite murderous, misanthropic Christians? With the author of Luke-Acts, I assume that Christians learn about God from Moses and Miriam, the Prophets, the Psalms, from the Jews Jesus, and Mary, and Paul, and from modern Abrahams and Sarahs.

Second, there were explicitly anti-Jewish writings in the Greco-Roman world, and our discussion of anti-Judaism and the Gospels should ask the question whether the Gospels are anti-Jewish by those Greco-Roman criteria, not making the error of evaluating the Gospels solely by modern standards. According to Clement of Alexandria (Strom. 1.21, 101), the Egyptian Apion, who taught in Rome under Tiberius and Claudius, wrote "against Jews" (κατὰ Ἰουδαίων), although that phrase describes the content of what he wrote, not the title of his work.[34] We have easiest access to these slanders in Josephus's response, Against Apion.[35] Cancik dates this work to 95–96 c.e. and observes that Josephus's patron was Epaphroditus, arguing that he was the same Roman who freed his slave Epictetus, the Stoic philosopher![36] Too briefly, one praised or slandered a people according to their antiquity, founder, similarity to the "civilized" Greeks, immigration, government, artistic contributions, virtues, piety, family laws, respect for the dead, treatment of foreigners, and penalties for crimes.[37]

Here follows a quick survey following the order listed above. With Josephus, Luke-Acts honors the antiquity of the Jews (Acts 15:21 [and

---

33. See Susannah Heschel, "Nazifying Christian Theology: Walter Grundmann and the Institute for the Study and Eradication of Jewish Influence on German Christian Life," Church History 63, no. 4 (1994): 587–605, a short version of "Theologen für Hitler: Walter Grundmann und das 'Institut zur Erforschung und Beseitigung des jüdischen Einflußes auf das deutsche kirchliche Leben,' " in Christlicher Antijudaismus und Antisemitismus: Theologische und kirchliche Programme Deutscher Christen, ed. Leonore Siegele-Wenschkewitz (Frankfurt: Haag und Herchen, 1994), 125–70

34. See Schürer, History of the Jewish People, vol. 3, 1:606; Hubert Cancik, "Theokratie und Priesterherrschaft: Die mosaische Verfassung bei Flavius Josephus, c. Apionem 2, 157–98," in Religionstheorie und Politische Theologie, vol. 3, Theokratie, ed. Jacob Taubes (Paderborn: Ferdinand Schöningh, 1987), 69 n. 35.

35. See David L. Balch, "Two Apologetic Encomia: Dionysius on Rome and Josephus on the Jews," JSJ 13, nos. 1–2 (1982): 102–22.

36. Cancik, "Theokratie und Priesterherrschaft," 68–69.

37. On Josephus's encomium of the Jews according to these topics, see Balch, "Two Apologetic Encomia," 115–20.

15.7?]; Luke 3:23 38; 9:8). Luke honors Moses as founder and law-giver throughout the work (esp. Acts 6:11, 14; 21:21; 26:22, related to the apologetic function of the whole work; also see Luke 2:22; 5:14; 9:30; 16:31; 20:37; 24:27, 44; Acts 3:22; 7:20–44; 15:5, 21; 28:23; contrast 13:49). The author appeals to Greek, that is, Stoic philosophy and theology in the Areopagus address, although our author has a problem with artistic contributions (as does Josephus), since this included statues for deities (Acts 14:15: 17:16, 24). Moses led the immigration, but the author repeats some problematic stories from Exodus, including the story of the ancestors who "offered a sacrifice to the idol," the golden calf (Acts 7:41; cf. 7:34, 38–42, echoing Exodus 32), idolatry so embarrassing that Josephus *never* narrates the story, not even in his *Antiquities*. Stephen airs the family's dirty laundry in public, so that the story functions as slander.[38] One aspect of Paul's speech in Acts 13 is praise of David's monarchy. Luke (1:6, 17; cf. 2:25; 23:47, 50; Acts 10:22) begins praising the first characters' justice/righteousness, and Paul inculcates the virtues and obedience to the government before the governors Felix and Festus (Acts 24:25; 25:8). (Contrast the anti-Jewish Apion, who "reviled the Jews" before Gaius Caligula, saying they neglect to honor the emperor; Caligula gave Philo no chance to offer a "defense against these accusations" [Josephus, *Ant.* 18.257–60].) But Acts 7:52 — Stephen's speech again — is polemic against the ancestors' justice (cf. Acts 15:7; 4:19, and so forth). Piety is valued (Acts 17:23). Moses' family laws are touched on only very lightly (Luke 16:17–18), since Luke promotes discipleship in the new, acquired family over against the hereditary family (cf. Luke 14:26; 20:34–35), in real tension with the family values typically eulogized in Greco-Roman society. Jesus fails the test of respect for the dead (Luke 9:60; very indirectly, cf. Acts 2:29). Neither this nor the critique of the family, however, is a slander of Moses; both rather are symbols of the cost of discipleship, which would have been very offensive. Jesus seems lax on penalties for crimes (Luke 6:27–38). In summary, Luke-Acts affirm many aspects of Judaism that Josephus eulogizes, beginning with the people's antiquity and the glory of the founder and lawgiver, Moses, although the function of Stephen's speech attacking the ancestors' piety and justice must be evaluated for its polemic.

My response essay has focused on one category crucial in Greco-

---

38. See E. Richard, *Acts 6:1–8:4: The Author's Method of Composition*, SBLDS 41 (Missoula, Mont.: Scholars Press, 1978).

Roman encomia and vituperation: the treatment of foreigners (cf. Josephus, *Ag. Ap.* 2.209–14). In response to many slanders against the Jews in Greco-Roman culture, Josephus claims that Jews "receive… foreigners" (ἀλλοφύλους…δέχεται, the same noun and verb we have seen in Acts).[39] Apollonius Molon, the teacher of Cicero and Caesar, wrote an "attack against Jews" (συσκευὴ κατὰ Ἰουδαίων) (cited by Eusebius, *Praep. Ev.* 9.19),[40] accusing them of being atheists and misanthropes (ἀθέους καὶ μισανθρώπους λοιδορεῖ) (Josephus, *Ag. Ap.* 2.148), of refusing to accept (ὅτι μὴ παραδεχόμεθα) persons with other preconceived notions about God, of declining to associate (μηδὲ κοινωνεῖν) with those who have a different mode of life (Josephus, *Ag. Ap.* 2.258); to which Josephus replies that Jews welcome (δεχόμεθα) those who wish to share their customs, a proof of their philanthropy (φιλανθρωπίας) (Josephus, *Ag. Ap.* 2.261). Luke *concludes* the whole two-volume work, in particular Paul's apology in Acts, using the same verb (ἀπεδέχετο πάντας [Acts 28:30]). Again, the passages cited previously from Dio Cassius and Tacitus show that Jews in the Greco-Roman world did attract many from other ethnic groups, and so became (or remained) multiethnic. Josephus and the author of Luke-Acts want, respectively, Jews and Christians to be seen as philanthropic in relation to foreigners, and Luke has written the resulting conflict into the plot (cf. Josephus, *J.W.* 2.409–15; *Ant.* 4.137–40). Josephus's apology eulogizes Jews for "receiving foreigners" over against slanders of the anti-Jewish writer Apollonius Molon; similarly Luke, quoting Moses and Jesus, narrates conflict among believers in Jerusalem who resist their leaders Peter and Paul, who call them to be an assembly "receiving all foreigners."

---

39. See Schürer, *History of the Jewish People*, vol. 3, 1:614, n. 141; Cancik, "Theokratie und Priesterherrschaft," 69 n. 35.

40. See Schürer, *History of the Jewish People*, vol. 3, 1:599.

RESPONSE TO
DARYL D. SCHMIDT

Allan J. McNicol

THE LITERATURE ON THIS TOPIC, even in the past decade, is immense and daunting. Yet it is fair to say that this has not intimidated Daryl Schmidt. He has engaged it in a serious and lively way and has supplemented it with a number of exegetical comments of his own, emerging mainly from the discipline of narrative criticism. Moreover, he has come to a definite conclusion on the topic at hand, which we will probe at some length in this response. It suffices now to say that this may be considered to be a judicious, well-conceived paper; and it certainly demands our serious attention.

Procedurally, I will focus first on several preliminary points of orientation toward the subject raised by Schmidt. Then I will turn to his analysis of the text, and enter into dialogue with him concerning several of his exegetical conclusions. I will finish by focusing on Schmidt's conclusions on determining whether there is anti-Judaism in Luke. My goal is to make an assessment as to whether he has made his case.

PRELIMINARY ISSUES

In his preface, Schmidt begins by reminding us of the current importance of both narrative and reader-response criticism for pursuit of the exegetical task. As presently conceived, these particular forms of literary criticism not only go beyond redaction criticism, but also constitute an advance over the literary thematic studies that initially supplemented and, in some quarters, supplanted it.

Later in the essay, Schmidt claims that reader-response criticism is particularly important because it furnishes a literary critical methodology that enables greater precision in describing anti-Judaism in the Gospels. He cites the work of Adele Reinhartz as important.[1] Schmidt

---

1. Adele Reinhartz, "The New Testament and Anti-Judaism: A Literary Critical Approach," *JES* 25 (1988): 524–37.

notes that Reinhartz sets forth three kinds of readers in the text: (1) the *implied reader* is our reconstruction of the preunderstandings of a hypothetical person who would have the facility to understand the text; (2) the *ideal reader* is one who not only can understand the text but also shares its values and assumptions; (3) the *real reader* is one who, based on personal pilgrimage, comes to the text with personal assumptions and actualizes its claims by either accepting or challenging them.

Given this particular description of the literary task, it makes a lot of difference as to which particular level of reader response one has in mind when the issue of anti-Judaism in Luke comes up. In the story line of Luke there are a number of texts in which representations of the Jews border on the malicious. Schmidt, quite appropriately, draws our attention to Luke 20:20. There the chief priests and scribes, clearly portrayed as acting out of a lack of sincerity, seek to entrap Jesus. Yet, instances of pejorative portrayals of some Jews in the story line do not necessarily indicate an expression of anti-Judaism. Any story has characters that range across the spectrum from the heroic to the infamous. Certainly, the implied reader and even the ideal reader would be capable of understanding that Luke is drawing attention to the treachery of a particular group of chief priests and scribes and not to all Jews. To me, the fundamental issue is whether the *real reader* of Luke is given such an image of the Jews in the story line that he or she is so drawn into this literary world that almost ineluctably he or she would perceive Judaism and its central symbolic ideas and rites as debased; and thus, given this reality, whether it would be reasonable to actualize one's attitudes toward Judaism in accordance with the direction mapped out in the story line. Then, without question, Luke could be considered to be anti-Jewish.[2] The issue before us is whether the *Tendenz* of the entire narrative world of the text leads us in that direction.

Yet, even with this set of clarifications, the task before us is still daunting. Schmidt throws icy water in our faces by reminding us of the well-traveled comment of Gaston, who asks how the same narrative can be both "one of the most pro-Jewish and one of the most anti-Jewish writings in the New Testament."[3] This seems to indicate that the answer

---

2. Schmidt readily agrees that there were plenty of people in the ancient world who, on the basis of their values and dispositions, were prepared to actualize the text of Luke so that it could serve as a vehicle for anti-Judaism. (One has only to think of Marcion and his successors.) But that is a far cry from viewing the text on the level of the implied reader, who could presumably easily differentiate between an unfavorable portrait of an individual or class of people and the integrity of a particular faith system as a whole.

3. Lloyd Gaston, "Anti-Judaism and the Passion Narrative in Luke and Acts," in

can only be found in the hermeneutical enterprise. In which direction (pro- or anti-Jewish) does the *Tendenz* of the text veer?[4] Inquiring minds want to know. Much is at stake in providing an adequate answer to this question. This brings us to an analysis of the narrative flow of the text of Luke.

SELECTED NARRATIVE ISSUES

At the heart of Schmidt's methodology is a plea to read the whole of the story line of Luke and not to concentrate on a few selected passages, such as the ending of Acts. Thus he seeks to attain this balance by rehearsing the story line of Luke-Acts paying special attention to certain key passages where he makes some selective probes in the general area of Luke's view of Israel. It is here that Schmidt gives us "solid meat" for making an assessment as to whether there is a tendency toward anti-Judaism in Luke.

Schmidt comes quickly to Luke 4:16–30. His analysis of the sermon at Nazareth allows him to dismiss a frequent reading that the rejection of Jesus takes place after favor is given to non-Israelites. Schmidt points out that in the next pericope Jesus immediately goes to another Jewish audience and *receives* favor (cf. Luke 4:32). Audience reversal is not the programmatic feature of the sermon at Nazareth. Instead, Schmidt champions Brawley's reading that turns on the word *dektos* ("acceptable")[5]. Early in the sermon Jesus announces the "acceptable" year of

---

Anti-Judaism in Early Christianity, vol. 1, *Paul and the Gospels*, ed. Peter Richardson and David Granskou (Waterloo, Ont.: Wilfrid Laurier University Press, 1986), 153.

4. Schmidt enters into dialogue with several works in the secondary literature and offers some methodological reflections. In his rehearsal of current literature on the subject, there are no real surprises. Central to his analysis is an evaluation of the interminable debate over the outcome of the narrative in Acts. Is the pattern of Paul turning to the Gentiles in Acts 13:46, 18:6, 28:26–28 an indicator that the early Christian community regarded its mission to Israel as a failure? Is the logical result of the turning to the Gentiles either a version of supersessionism or a sense of tragic irony? Or does the mission to Israel still remain open for the writer of Acts? This area of discussion has remained the central issue during the last decade. It continues to spawn various interpretations of Luke-Acts as being either pro- or anti-Jewish. I think Schmidt is correct in seeing this as a storm center in Lukan scholarship.

Carrying this concern into his methodological reflections, Schmidt rightly reminds us that recent scholarly preoccupation with the ending of Acts is unbalanced. Beginnings as well as endings have great significance in any literary work. Indeed, several examples are cited where the insights of narrative criticism can be used to show that the negative images assigned to the Jewish teachers at the conclusion of Acts are not as monolithic as some earlier literary approaches assumed. What seems to be called for here is a more balanced treatment of the entire literary complex of Luke-Acts as a whole.

5. Robert Brawley, *Luke-Acts and the Jews: Conflict, Apology, and Conciliation*, SBLMS 33 (Atlanta: Scholars Press, 1987), 6–27.

the Lord (Luke 4:19). Then comes the wordplay. Jesus declares that no prophet is "acceptable" in his home town (Luke 4:24). This gnomic statement is illustrated by the lives of the earlier prophets Elijah and Elisha, who were not always accepted by the homefolks (Luke 4:25–27). Yet, they meet the criteria for being true prophets. After the people are told that they do not take well to prophets, predictably, they find Jesus unacceptable (Luke 4:28–29). Ironically, the failure of the people to hear the truth about the prophets only confirms for the reader that Jesus is a prophet. But to repeat, the unit is not anticipating acceptance of Jesus' mission by the Gentiles rather than the Jews; it has to do with the issue of the reception of their own prophets by the people of Israel.

It seems to me that Schmidt is building a case for interpreting Luke as saying that the events involving Jesus and the formation of the early church stand in direct continuity with the earlier history of Israel. The emphasis is on continuity — similarity of a pattern of salvation-history. The same reception that the prophets received among their people was repeated in the life of Jesus of Nazareth. There is nothing new under the sun. Just as one can hardly conclude that Elijah and Elisha were anti-Jewish because some of the hard-hearted home folks did not receive them, neither is there anything in the way Jesus' story is related that should lead to a similar conclusion. The burden of Schmidt's essay is to suggest a reading of Luke that is congruent with this view. We need to ask, "Can this reading be validated?" According to Schmidt this reading is verified in Luke 7:2–17, where Luke has Jesus do two acts of power clearly imitative of those done by Elisha and Elijah. With respect to the latter action (the raising of the widow of Nain's son), the homefolks now cry out and attest that Jesus is a prophet and that God has visited his people. Here, Luke again is declaring that the ministry of Jesus is in direct continuity with the mission of the great constitutive prophets of Israel (Elijah and Elisha). But in this instance, there is acknowledgment of this point by some in Israel. Thus some in Israel hear and some do not. That point is made again and again with absolute clarity, later in Luke, and throughout Acts.

THE TRAVEL NARRATIVE

But in order for there to be continuity between the Jesus mission and the prophets of Israel, in Luke's mind (especially with respect to reception-history), another factor must now be brought into the equation. This brings us to Luke's "travel narrative" (here delimited as Luke 9:51–

19:27). At this point things start to get more troubling as Luke begins to explore the underside of the impact of Jesus' ministry by giving a negative portrayal of the leaders of Israel (e.g., Luke 15:1–2; 18:9–14, 31–33); although even here, we should not forget that this has to do with the theme of the rejected prophet — a frequent scriptural theme that is a central building block in Luke's literary artifact.

I believe that Moessner, Craig Evans, and others have overdone the supposed occurrences of deuteronomistic themes in the travel narrative.[6] I somewhat doubt whether the writer of Luke knew the term "deuteronomist," let alone developed a deliberate theology imitative of the supposed "deuteronomist school." But it is clear that the contours of the motif of the rejected prophet in the Scriptures of Israel are being used by Luke to give coherence to his description of the time of Jesus' later Galilean ministry until his entrance into the Holy City. The point is that there is nothing expressly untoward in this development. It already has precedent in the life of the prophets, especially Jeremiah. It is now being recapitulated in the life of Jesus. Schmidt is very convincing in laying bare the intertextual connections between Luke's account and the references to the rejected prophet in Jeremiah. In the reception of Jesus as he approaches Jerusalem, Schmidt shows how the deep opposition to Jesus stands in perfect continuity with analogues with the Jerusalem of Jeremiah five centuries earlier. And it should be underscored that this is no blanket condemnation of Israel, only of its leaders. The people still hang on Jesus' words (Luke 19:48).

The Portrayal of Israel's Leaders in the Passion Narrative

This brings us to the Passion narrative, which, as Schmidt rightly states, is the heart of the matter. So far, in my judgment, Schmidt has made a convincing case that there is little evidence of anti-Judaism in Luke. Can he maintain that position through the Passion narrative?

He opens his analysis with a dialogue with Gaston.[7] A critical issue arises as to whether Luke 22:47–53 can be made to carry the weight

---

6. David Moessner, *Lord of the Banquet: The Literary and Theological Significance of the Lukan Travel Narrative* (Minneapolis: Fortress Press, 1989); Craig A. Evans, "Luke 16:1–18 and the Deuteronomy Hypothesis," in *Luke and Scripture: The Function of Sacred Tradition in Luke-Acts*, ed. C. A. Evans and J. A. Sanders (Minneapolis: Fortress Press, 1993), 121–39.

7. Gaston, "Anti-Judaism in Early Christianity," 140–51.

of a shift *from* the somewhat diffident, even at times supportive, response to Jesus by the people (crowds) *to* their outright hostility. Clearly, Schmidt does not think so. Those who think otherwise will need to engage Schmidt's basic point, that the reference to the crowd in Luke 22:47 is only an instance of a scene constructed by the author to give dramatic intensity to Jesus' arrest. It refers to a selective group within the Jerusalem establishment. It is not a transparency of the entire Jewish people.

It must be admitted that those who see anti-Judaism here can begin to make a case if they connect Luke 22:47–53 with the narrative theme of intense opposition on the part of the Jerusalem leadership that emerges in Luke 23:13ff. Schmidt concedes an awareness of this point. It seems clear that with the reference to the people in Luke 23:13, Luke has worked them into some degree of complicity with the Jewish leadership in the death of Jesus (cf. Luke 23:35). Schmidt acknowledges this and ventures the explanation that it is more of the rejected prophet motif. But this may be something of a stretch. For me, Schmidt only touches on what is the real problem. That is found in the "daughters of Jerusalem" pericope which follows in Luke 23:27–31. Here Jesus addresses a large number of both the people and daughters of Jerusalem making a connection between his fate and the destruction of Jerusalem (cf. Luke 13:33–35; 19:41–44; 21:20–24). In contrast to Schmidt, given the presupposition that Luke was written post-70, it is difficult to escape the conclusion that Luke is drawing a direct connection between the destruction of the city, with its accompanying carnage, and the actions of those earlier who turned Jesus over to the Romans. And this, at least, implies that judgment was visited upon some of the people. Indeed, the direct accusation that they were complicit in the death of Jesus and would be held accountable is made explicit in Acts 2:22–23, 36; 3:12–13; 4:10; 5:30; 10:39; 13:27–28.

In my opinion, this is where Luke comes closest to this rather unstable compound that we call anti-Judaism. Luke does not contain the words of Matt. 27:25: "His [Jesus'] blood be on us and on our children." But is Luke that far away from Matthew here?[8] A wedge appears

---

8. An excellent case in point is Luke's version of the parables of the talents (Matt. 25:14–30) in Luke 19:11–27. Jesus is the nobleman who receives the kingdom (Luke 19:15). When he returns and begins to exercise his kingship by rewarding his servants (the disciples) (cf. Luke 22:29), he also exacts vengeance on his enemies (Luke 19:27). Is there much doubt that the enemies are those in Jerusalem who will shortly both reject Jesus' initial claim to kingship when he arrives in Jerusalem and the second offer to acknowledge his kingship when the gospel is proclaimed by the apostles?

to have been driven into the text at this point that led later generations of real readers, acclimatized in a culture of anti-Judaism, to use these texts in a destructive way.

Nevertheless, we need to be careful. I still think Schmidt is correct in his basic *Tendenz*. He notes that in the interpretation of the crucifixion of Jesus, the manner of his death brings remorse on the part of a good number of the crowd (Luke 23:48). And later in Acts, many within Israel are convinced that Jesus was treated unjustly and repented. It is in the context that it was the mysterious plan and purpose of God that Jesus, to fulfill the Scriptures, had to be handed over by his own people to be put to death and then vindicated through the resurrection, that Luke moves with ruthless consistency. It seems that this overarching concept takes us a bit beyond the theme of "the rejected prophet." But aside from denigrating the actions of certain leaders in Israel, Luke remains surprisingly positive in his treatment of the customs and traditions of Israel.[9]

CONCLUSION

In his conclusion, Schmidt comes back again to reassert his argument that close analysis of the rhetoric of the narrative in conjunction with reader-response criticism can advance understanding of the text. It gets us beyond the impasse of weighing the values of the positive and negative portrayals of the Jewish people and their religious life found in the text of Luke, to making some assessment. For Schmidt, the dominant feature of the rhetoric of the text, as it comes to a conclusion at the end of Acts, is about hermeneutics. Who is interpreting the Scriptures correctly — Paul the Jew or those Jews who do not believe Jesus is the Messiah?

Then Schmidt makes this critical point: "The final scene [Acts 28] may then suggest that it is no longer necessary to continue these debates. 'Going to Gentiles' now means 'enough debates over Scripture.' "[10] That is, the *apologia* is complete. Luke has given sufficient evidence that Paul is a legitimate expositor of the Scriptures within the various Judaisms of the time. One can still remain within the parameters of Judaism and

---

9. As is well known, throughout his narrative Luke retains the terminology of the Judaism of the first century by referring to Israel as a particular ethnic people (not the church) distinct from the Gentiles. Even when the Gentiles are incorporated into the people of God (restored Israel) through faith in Jesus as the Messiah, they retain their identity as Gentiles.

10. Daryl D. Schmidt, "Anti-Judaism and the Gospel of Luke," in this volume, 94.

accept Jesus. The case has been made that Christianity is a legitimate expression of Diaspora Judaism. To the *ideal reader,* perhaps a Godfearer, Luke's portrayal of Paul is fashioned rhetorically to make this case.

There is much in Schmidt's argument that makes good sense of the text. Indeed, there is no question, even as early as Luke 1:1 with its reference to "the things fulfilled among us," that Luke is going to rest his case on the interpretation of the Scriptures. But I would suggest that Schmidt's contention that the *ideal reader* of Luke would refuse to join in the condemnation of Jews for not accepting the argument of Paul, somewhat overstates the evidence. Luke is pro-Jewish, but in a mode that would cause a reader to be sharply critical of considerable segments of the expressions of Judaism of the first century of our era. It is hard for me not to see a sharp edge in all of this.

As I indicated earlier in my response, according to Luke, his narrative clearly indicates that there would be consequences for the leadership of Israel in their rejection of Jesus as the Messiah. Those consequences revolved around the destruction of the Temple and its replacement by another house: the restored community of the children of Abraham who obtained salvation in Jesus. As Stephen's speech in Acts 7:2–53 makes abundantly clear, the place (cf. Acts 7:7) of the fulfillment of the promise of 2 Sam. 7:10–14 was not a temple of masonry in Jerusalem, but a spiritual fellowship: the church founded in Jerusalem.

This explains Luke's stubborn insistence of the importance of the Jerusalem church, and his special interest in another of his heroes, James, the leader of the Jewish Christians. Even after the severe persecution of 41–43 C.E., the Jerusalem church continued to thrive (Acts 21:20). Indeed, as Richard Bauckham has demonstrated, at the Jerusalem council, James is the dominant figure in the ecumenical church; and the apostolic decree about the reception of the Gentiles constitutes an interpretation of Leviticus 17–18 that is well within the parameters of traditional Jewish exegesis.[11] What goes on in the Jerusalem church is a legitimate expression of Judaism!

This reality certainly undermines the widespread notion that a Gentile mission has superseded the mission to Israel. But at the same time, it aims a dagger at the heart of a number of branches of Judaism that had their vital center in various symbol systems such as the Temple and *kashrut* ("food laws"). For the *implied* reader of Luke, commencing

---

11. Richard Bauckham, "James and the Jerusalem Church," in *The Book of Acts in Its First-Century Setting,* vol. 4, ed. Richard Bauckham (Grand Rapids: Eerdmans/Paternoster, 1995), 452–67.

with the triumphal passages in Luke 1–2, the central focus is to hear the story as the account of the founding of the Jerusalem church and its sponsorship of a vital mission to the Gentiles as the fulfillment of God's plan for Israel. With respect to Israel, Luke's story is a continuation of what happened earlier in Scripture. It is not an account of tragic irony but a story of the triumph of God's promises attained through adversity.

Does Luke's making good on the pledge in Luke 1:1–4 portray traditional Judaism in such unfavorable terms that one is led to devalue it as debased? In other words, is Luke an expression of anti-Judaism? Both Schmidt and I agree that Luke considered the early Christian movement to be a legitimate form of Judaism. Therefore, by definition, Luke did not consider Judaism to be debased and the object of divine rejection. Consequently, Luke is not an expression of anti-Judaism.

However, the question of perspective is critical. To orthodox Christians, Mormonism, which appropriates most of the symbols central to Christianity and yet sees its own emergence and its central belief system as bringing Christianity to its purest form, is unacceptable. In the view of orthodox Christians, too many vital doctrines would have to be set aside. To Mormons, however, it is a very different matter. They view their faith as the true fulfillment of Christianity. They stand within its borders.

This is similar to the way certain Jews and Christians would have appropriated the point of view expressed in Luke-Acts at the end of the first century. An *ideal reader* of Luke-Acts would have viewed it as an expression of the purest form of the various Judaisms abroad during the first century. Some *ideal readers* may have made the additional step to supersessionism; but that is not abundantly clear. On the other hand, a devout attender at the synagogue, who belonged to another branch of Judaism, would have grave doubts about the legitimacy of Christianity as a valid expression of Judaism.[12]

At the end of the day can we say much more than that? For Luke-Acts, belief in Jesus as the Messiah is an enhancement of Judaism rather than a debasement. Adherents of some other expressions of Judaism were not so sure then nor would they be so sure today.

---

12. Michael J. Cook makes this point well ("The Mission to the Jews in Acts: Unraveling Luke's 'Myth of the Myriads,'" in *Luke-Acts and the Jewish People: Eight Critical Perspectives*, ed. Joseph B. Tyson [Minneapolis: Augsburg, 1988], 122).

❧ T • H • R • E • E ❧

ANTI-JUDAISM AND
THE GOSPEL OF JOHN

David Rensberger

I WANT TO ACKNOWLEDGE at the beginning that this essay has benefited greatly from the discussion of its original form at the conference in Dallas in October 1996. Not only the formal responses by Mark Goodwin and Thomas Lea but also the criticisms of other participants in the conference have helped me to refine my thinking in a number of ways. If my fundamental conclusions remain much the same, I hope that they are now more adequately nuanced, and take better account of John's historical position at the dividing point between Judaism and Christianity.[1]

For the purposes of this essay I accept the conference's working definition of Christian anti-Judaism as "an ideologically driven hostility toward Judaism and people presumed to be of the Jewish faith." I will use the term "anti-Judaism" in preference to "anti-Semitism," which carries overtones of modern-day racism. (However, when discussing the work of scholars who speak of anti-Semitism I will retain their terminology; and at some points it will be necessary to use both terms together.) I will also assume, as most scholars who approach this question do, that anti-Jewish hostility emanates from people who are not themselves Jewish.

The working definition raises the further question of what is meant by the term "Judaism" in this context. This question recurred frequently during the conference, and I will not attempt to answer it definitively

---

1. This essay is dedicated to Menahem Mansoor, Emeritus Professor of Hebrew and Semitic Languages at the University of Wisconsin in Madison, my first teacher in Jewish studies, a man of peace who has exemplified the possibilities of scholarship for transcending the barriers between Jew and Christian.

here. I will only say that I understand first-century Judaism as diverse rather than monolithic or homogeneous. Even after the destruction of the Temple in 70 C.E., consolidation around the Pharisaic position must have taken some time to come about. Certainly there were common traits that allow Pharisees, Sadducees, Essenes, Therapeutae, apocalyptists, John the Baptist, Judah of Galilee, Jesus of Nazareth, the Temple aristocracy, Philo, proto-Kabbalists, and perhaps even proto-Gnostics all to be gathered under the broad heading of "Judaism." But this list itself shows how very broad that heading is, and how difficult it may be to judge, from our remote vantage point, who might have considered themselves Jewish in antiquity. Some of the above-named entities may have been prepared to read some of the others out of the ranks of Judaism, to regard them as hopelessly apostate; but I do not consider that scholars today are in a position to do the same.

The question, then, is whether anti-Judaism so defined is to be found in the Gospel of John. On the surface, this is a question that almost seems to answer itself. There is no doubt that John contains some of the most repellent statements about Jews to be found in the New Testament. People identified as Jews are said to have neither the love nor the knowledge of God, to belong to this world rather than to heaven, to be children neither of Abraham nor of God, but of the devil (John 5:42; 8:19, 23, 39–44). Nor is it simply a matter of individual statements. The entire atmosphere of the Fourth Gospel is pervaded by hostility between these Jews and Jesus. Again and again they fail to understand what he says or what he does, the meaning of which is plain to the Christian reader (helped by the Gospel's narrator). They call him names; they want to kill him or arrest him, which in the end they succeed in doing; and he returns the favor by damning them to die in their sins (John 5:18; 7:1, 20, 25, 30, 32, 44–45; 8:24, 37, 40, 48, 52, 59; 10:20–21, 31–33, 39; 11:57; 18:1–12).

All this is exacerbated by John's status as one of the central documents of the Christian canon. It has been formative for the theology of every branch of Christianity, particularly in regard to Christian theological understanding of Jesus. Its influence on the Christian churches and on Christian people thus makes it a factor that must invariably be reckoned with. There is no way of pushing it to the fringes of Christian thinking; and there is hardly a passage in it, from the first chapter through the twelfth at any rate, that does not include these stigmatizing pronouncements about "the Jews." Thus Eldon Jay Epp has asserted that, because of both its harshness and its great popularity among Christians, John is more responsible for Christian anti-Semitism than any other New Testament writing.[2]

Yet in fact, the question of John's anti-Judaism is not self-answering, because John alone of the Gospels also makes the incomprehensible assertion that certain people, who in the narrative are obviously Jewish, are "afraid of the Jews" (John 7:13; 9:22; 19:38; 20:19). John's statements about "the Jews," like much else in this Gospel, are thus not transparent but require careful interpretation. In the absence of such interpretation, these statements will always tend to create anti-Jewish opinions, feelings, and perhaps also actions, in their Christian hearers. The identity of "the Jews" in John is both a more difficult question than it might seem, and a crucial one in addressing the problem of Christian anti-Judaism.

As we shall see, social location is an important factor in the interpretation of John, and this applies not only to the social location of the Gospel writer and the characters in the story, but to that of its modern readers as well. It is only right, then, that I begin with a word about my own location. I come to this Gospel as a Protestant Christian, and one for whom Johannine theology has come to have a great deal of meaning for my own understanding of Christianity, and increasingly for my own religious experience as well. I must therefore be aware of any inclination on my part to excuse and justify the Gospel and its author. I will try to set aside such inclinations for the sake of objectivity; but complete objectivity is not really possible, and blind spots may remain in my presentation. On the other hand, I also come to the task as one who has had Jewish friends since childhood, and whose first academic instruction in biblical languages and culture came from Jewish teachers. Denunciations of "the Jews" hurt me, and hurt me even more when they come from a source that I admire and respect.

THE PROBLEM: "THE JEWS" IN JOHN

The word Ἰουδαῖος occurs sixty-five times in the Gospel of John, primarily in the plural Ἰουδαῖοι (plus seven occurrences of Ἰουδαία, "Judea"), far more than in all the other Gospels combined, where it is almost entirely confined to the phrase "King of the Jews" in the Passion narratives. A number of these are simply descriptive, referring to Jew-

---

2. E. J. Epp, "Anti-Semitism and the Popularity of the Fourth Gospel in Christianity," *Journal of the Central Conference of American Rabbis* 22 (1975): 35–36, 40.

ish Holy Days and practices (John 2:6, 13; 5:1; 6:4; 7:2; 11:55; 19:40, 42). Others are relatively neutral references to the Jewish people, their leaders, and (as in the synoptics) to Jesus as their king (John 3:1, 25; 4:9; 11:19, 31, 33, 36; 12:9; 18:20, 33, 39; 19:3, 19, 20, 21). There are even some positive statements, such as that salvation is from the Jews (John 4:22). Indeed, some Jews, apart from his regular disciples, believe in Jesus (John 8:30–31; 11:45; 12:9–11; cf. 7:31, 40–43; 9:16; 10:19–21), producing a division that is no doubt reflective of John's historical setting (see below).[3]

It is often suggested that some or all of the uses of Ἰουδαῖοι in John have a geographical rather than an ethnic or religious sense, that is, that they refer to "Judeans" in distinction from Jesus and his Galilean disciples. Some would apply this to only neutral or positive uses,[4] others to almost every use.[5] In the latter case, the ground of John's controversy would shift dramatically, from Christian versus Jew to Galilean versus Judean, and the appearance of anti-Judaism would largely be eliminated. There are points at which a geographical sense is plausible, especially in John 11 (note also John 7:1). Yet the Galilean Jesus understands himself as a Ἰουδαῖος, at least in distinction from Samaritans (John 4:9, 22), and there are Ἰουδαῖοι who fall afoul of him in Galilee (John 6:41, 52). It is especially hard to see what sense it could make to speak of "the Passover of the Judeans" and other "festivals of the Judeans" (John 2:13; 5:1; 6:4; 7:2; 11:55; 19:42) or "purification rites of the Judeans" (John 2:6, in Cana of Galilee!); Malcolm Lowe's arguments here are unconvincing.[6] One may point out that in antiquity Ἰουδαῖοι referred to a group with specific customs whose origin was in Judea, and that the problem is really one of English translation, since Ἰουδαῖος covers both of our terms "Judean" and "Jew."[7] But this is as much as to admit that the originally geographical term was, by John's day, no longer limited to that meaning, but encompassed what we would call ethnicity and religion: There were Ἰουδαῖοι who practiced the customs of the Ἰουδαῖοι, but who did not live in, and had perhaps never been to, Judea.[8] Partic-

3. R. A. Culpepper, "The Gospel of John and the Jews," *RevExp* 84 (1987): 276–80.

4. U. C. von Wahlde, "The Johannine 'Jews': A Critical Survey," *NTS* 28 (1982): 46, 51–53.

5. M. Lowe, "Who Were the Ἰουδαῖοι?" *NovT* 18 (1976): 101–30.

6. Ibid., 115–17.

7. J. Ashton, "The Identity and Function of the Ἰουδαῖοι in the Fourth Gospel," *NovT* 27 (1985): 43–46.

8. W. A. Meeks, " 'Am I a Jew?': Johannine Christianity and Judaism," in *Christianity, Judaism and Other Graeco-Roman Cults: Studies for Morton Smith at Sixty* 1 SJLA 12, ed. J. Neusner (Leiden: E. J. Brill, 1975), 182.

ularly in a work coming from the Diaspora, as John most likely does, one expects to see Ἰουδαῖοι used in this ethnic and religious sense.[9] To propose that anomalies are the work of a later redactor[10] or an earlier source,[11] or should simply be left out of account,[12] is to reduce the Gospel's intentional complexity by artificial means.

Responding to such difficulties, Jouette M. Bassler proposed that the dichotomy is not between two geographical regions, Judea and Galilee, but between two groups of people, Ἰουδαῖοι and "Galileans," and that the former stand for those who reject Jesus and the latter for those who accept him.[13] If correct, this would again mean that John does not intend Ἰουδαῖοι to refer to Jews as an ethnic or religious entity at all. There is something to this more nuanced understanding, given the belief of Galileans in John 1:43–51; 2:1–11; 4:45–54. Unfortunately, however, it still does not account for *Jesus'* identity as a Ἰουδαῖος; nor for Ἰουδαῖοι who do believe in him, however suspect the faith of some of them may be (see the passages listed above, and John 2:23–3:2); nor for one group of Galileans that rejects him: his own brothers (John 7:1–5). No attempt to limit the meaning of Ἰουδαῖοι in John to "Judeans," whether literal or symbolic, seems likely to succeed. Rather, Ἰουδαῖοι generally seems to have as its basic meaning the "ethnic" sense of "Jews."

As noted above, however, there are several passages in which Jews are said to be "afraid of the Jews" (John 7:13; 9:22; 19:38; 20:19). In such cases, "the Jews" can hardly mean "the Jewish people" in general (nor could it mean "the Judeans" in general); and these cases seem closely related to the bulk of the negative, hostile occurrences of Ἰουδαῖοι, the "characteristically Johannine" usage that is of most concern. What is meant by "the Jews" in this usage? Note first that in one place this sort of intimidation is said to come not from "the Jews" but from "the Pharisees" (John 12:42). On other occasions, "the Jews" seem to be simply interchangeable with "the Pharisees" (John 1:19, 24; 8:13, 22; 9:13–23, 40; 18:3, 12; and compare John 11:46–52 with 18:14); and at a

---

9. K. G. Kuhn, "Ἰσραήλ, Ἰουδαῖος, Ἑβραῖος in Jewish Literature after the OT," *TDNT* 3:359–69.

10. Lowe, "Who Were the Ἰουδαῖοι?" 117, 120; von Wahlde, "The Johannine 'Jews,'" 42–44, 50–51; Ashton, "The Identity and Function of the Ἰουδαῖοι," 62.

11. J. Ashton, "The Identity and Function of the Ἰουδαῖοι," 49–52.

12. Ibid., 55.

13. J. M. Bassler, "The Galileans: A Neglected Factor in Johannine Community Research," *CBQ* 43 (1981): 243–57; following W. A. Meeks, "Galilee and Judea in the Fourth Gospel," *JBL* 85 (1966): 159–69.

number of points it is clear that "the Jews" means people in positions of religious authority (besides the passages just listed, note John 5:10, 15–18). Thus the proposal that makes sense for most of the hostile usages of Ἰουδαῖοι is that the term is used to refer, not to Jews in general or as a people, but specifically to Jewish religious authorities, possibly identical with the Pharisees.[14] It should also be observed that the debates between Jesus and these opponents all center on christology, that is, on Jesus' divine identity, unlike the arguments over Torah and other matters in the synoptic Gospels. This suggestion and observation bring us to the question of the historical background of the Gospel of John.

Taken as a whole, then, John most characteristically uses the plural Ἰουδαῖοι, "Jews," to refer to Jewish authorities, who are evidently Pharisees and hostile to Jesus and to those who believe in him. How the author came to use the sweeping designation "the Jews" in this narrowly limited way will be considered below. Here I will note that, on the one hand, this language has the effect of distancing Jesus and his disciples from "the Jews" in an extraordinary way. Throughout much of the Gospel, it is hardly possible to think of them as Jews. Yet on the other hand, Jewish Holy Days and customs are mentioned with no overt antipathy; salvation has its origin in the Ἰουδαῖοι; Jesus is identified as a Ἰουδαῖος; there are some Ἰουδαῖοι who believe in him to some extent; and his disciples, if never called Ἰουδαῖοι, are at any rate Israelites, and Israel remains a positive term (see below). If we suppose, as most scholars do, that there are various "senses" or "uses" of Ἰουδαῖοι in John, then we must ask how the author could have expected his readers to distinguish among them. If there is no simple clue to tell the reader when the sense of Ἰουδαῖοι shifts, then the massively negative usage is bound to color the neutral and positive ones, so that the distancing effect carries over to them as well. Whether this also was part of John's intention is difficult to say; but there can be no doubt that it has been part of the book's effect.

JOHN'S SETTING IN HISTORY

Our understanding of John's historical setting is much different from what it was a generation or two ago. Once regarded as the most Hellenistic of the New Testament Gospels, breathing the same air as

---

14. See further von Wahlde, "The Johannine 'Jews,'" 41–46, and the earlier studies cited there.

Gnosticism and the mystery religions, written for Gentile believers far removed from the issues of Christianity's Jewish origins, John has undergone a remarkable facelift. The entire history of this process need not be rehearsed here.[15] Partly as a result of study of the Dead Sea Scrolls, more largely as a result of applying form-critical, historical-critical, and sociological methods to the Fourth Gospel, a number of scholars have reconstructed a plausible set of historical circumstances that go far to explain John's idiosyncrasies, including its statements about "the Jews."[16] Rather than being a Gospel for Gentile Christians (as was suggested in the initial working statement for the conference), John is now understood to have arisen out of a conflict between a group of Jewish Christians and their fellow Jews, and to be addressed primarily to those Jewish Christians.

It is sometimes suggested that John's explanations of Jewish customs reflect a Gentile readership, if not indeed a Gentile author.[17] But in fact the opposite is true. Jewish Holy Days, and traditions associated with them, are mentioned with such *minimal* explanation that readers unconversant with Judaism would be left largely in the dark. Note, for instance, the abrupt mentions of Passover in John 2:13; 6:4; Preparation for Passover in John 19:14, 31, 42; and Sukkoth in John 7:2; and the association of manna with Passover in John 6:31 and water and light with Sukkoth in John 7:37–38; 8:12. John's readership likely did include some Gentile Christians, and for them Passover and Sukkoth are

---

15. See D. Rensberger, *Johannine Faith and Liberating Community* (Philadelphia: Westminster Press, 1988), 15–36.

16. J. L. Martyn, *History and Theology in the Fourth Gospel*, 2d rev. ed. (Nashville: Abingdon Press, 1979); R. E. Brown, *The Gospel According to John*, 2 vols., AB 29, 29A (Garden City, N.Y.: Doubleday, 1966–1970); idem, "The Relationship to the Fourth Gospel Shared by the Author of 1 John and by His Opponents," in *Text and Interpretation*, ed. E. Best and R. McL. Wilson (Cambridge: Cambridge University Press, 1979), 57–68; W. A. Meeks, "The Man from Heaven in Johannine Sectarianism," *JBL* 91 (1972): 44–72; K. Wengst, *Bedrängte Gemeinde und verherrlichter Christus: Der historische Ort des Johannesevangeliums als Schlüssel zu seiner Interpretation*, BTS 5, 2d ed. (Neukirchen-Vluyn: Neukirchener Verlag, 1983); D. M. Smith, "Johannine Christianity," original title, "Johannine Christianity: Some Reflections on Its Character and Delineation," in *Johannine Christianity: Essays on Its Setting, Sources, and Theology* (Columbia, S.C.: University of South Carolina Press, 1984), 1–36; B. J. Malina, *The Gospel of John in Sociolinguistic Perspective*, Protocol of the Colloquy of the Center for Hermeneutical Studies in Hellenistic and Modern Culture 48, ed. H. C. Waetjen (Berkeley, Calif.: The Center for Hermeneutical Studies in Hellenistic and Modern Culture, 1985); J. H. Neyrey, *An Ideology of Revolt: John's Christology in Social-Science Perspective* (Philadelphia: Fortress Press, 1988).

17. J. T. Townsend, "The Gospel of John and the Jews: The Story of a Religious Divorce," in *Antisemitism and the Foundations of Christianity*, ed. A. T. Davies (New York: Paulist Press, 1979), 80–81; M. J. Cook, "The Gospel of John and the Jews," *RevExp* 84 (1987): 265.

simply identified as Jewish festivals; but any detailed information about these festivals they would have had to obtain elsewhere than in this text.

What are the indications that this Gospel speaks to a conflict among Jews? For one thing, John, for all its negative characterization of "the Jews," unhesitatingly affirms the Jewish origin of its Christian faith — "salvation is from the Jews" (John 4:22). More importantly, on three occasions characters in the story are said to be under the threat of being "put out of the synagogue" (ἀποσυνάγωγος γενέσθαι) if they confess Jesus to be the Messiah (John 9:22; 12:42; 16:2). John says nothing about how this would be done, or why a messianic confession of Jesus should bring about this punishment, or whether the expulsion would be permanent or temporary, or how wide a territory such an order would cover. It may not be possible to reconcile this expulsion with what is known of Jewish practice from other ancient sources;[18] but those sources are far from complete for the first century, and there is no reason to think that the writer of John is indulging in paranoid fantasy. Clearly this was a serious matter for the author and readers of this Gospel. The three mentions of expulsion in John are the only ones in the New Testament. That John uses a fixed terminology of which there is no other mention in early Christian or Jewish literature suggests that the phenomenon was probably limited to a particular place and time. It is quite clearly out of place in the lifetime of Jesus himself; even the book of Acts represents Christians as being disciplined within the synagogue, not expelled from it. It seems most likely that the references to expulsion refer to events decades after Jesus' time, in the experience of the Gospel writer's own Christian community.

Such a threat could have such dire meaning only for Jews. All the people to whom it is addressed are Jewish, and there is no indication that it has anything to do with the entry of Gentiles into the Christian community (the references to Greeks in John 7:35; 12:20 have no connection with the synagogue threats). It should be noted that in two of the three relevant passages (John 9:22; 12:42) people's actions are conditioned by the threat of expulsion. The Gospel does not seem so much concerned with what believers should do after they are expelled (as if this had already happened) as with what they should do or not do with the prospect of expulsion before them. This suggests that these passages are not an etiology from a later vantage point, explaining how the

---

18. Despite K. L. Carroll, "The Fourth Gospel and the Exclusion of Christians from the Synagogues," *BJRL* 40 (1957): 19–32.

Christian community had come to be separated from the synagogue,[19] but rather that they come from a time when expulsion of confessing Christians had begun but had not been completely carried out.

There is also the phenomenon already noted of Jews who are "afraid of the Jews." As suggested above, and commonly recognized, "the Jews" who inspire such fear must be a particular group within Jewish society, evidently an authoritative group closely related to if not identical with the Pharisees. It should be noted that the Pharisees are a much more powerful and pervasive presence in John than in Mark or Luke, or even Matthew. This is not only because they seem to be in a more authoritative position than in the synoptic Gospels, but also because the other groups mentioned there, such as the scribes and the Sadducees, disappear entirely in John. Even the chief priests, who take official action against Jesus, are associated with the Pharisees until the Passion narrative (John 7:32, 45; 11:47, 57; 18:3). All opposition to Jesus is thus concentrated in this one group, whom the writer often calls simply "the Jews."

John thus evidently portrays on the canvas of the mission of Jesus a conflict that in fact took place between synagogue authorities and Christians of Jewish origin at a much later time. This fundamental realization by J. Louis Martyn, and the significance that he rightly attributed to it, are responsible for the predominant current understanding of the historical background of John in general, and of its relation to Judaism in particular. The fact that the Pharisees are the dominant, indeed almost the only, factor in the opposition to Jesus suggests that the conflict in question took place at a time and in a location where they were the most powerful group in the synagogue community. It is now widely recognized that their dominance was not universal prior to 70 C.E., and was not achieved everywhere and at once after 70. Thus it seems likely that the Gospel of John was composed after 70, perhaps ten or twenty years after 70, in response to a controversy that may have been taking place in only one particular city or district. Though there are traditions in John that show evidence of being rooted in Palestine in the time of Jesus, the location of this controversy was probably in the Diaspora, perhaps in Syria or in western Asia Minor.

A word should be said about the position of those whom the Fourth Gospel speaks of as the "rulers" or "authorities" (ἄρχοντες) of the Jew-

---

19. A. Reinhartz, "The Johannine Community and Its Jewish Neighbors: A Reappraisal," in *"What Is John?"* vol. 2: *Literary and Social Readings of the Fourth Gospel*, ed. F. F. Segovia, SBLSymS 7 (Atlanta: Scholars Press, 1998), 135.

ish community. Whatever group these may be supposed to represent in the narratives about Jesus, for the Gospel writer they most likely stand for traditional Jewish authorities in his locale. What is especially noteworthy is that these authorities are not identical with the Pharisees. Wherever the two are mentioned together they are clearly distinguished from each other. Indeed, in John 12:42 some "authorities" are said to believe in Jesus but to be unwilling to confess it because they were afraid that the Pharisees would put them out of the synagogue (see also John 3:1; 7:48). The term ἄρχοντες was widely used in the Greek-speaking Diaspora for synagogue officials who, though their duties are not clear to us, were of high honor and responsibility.[20] That such people could be intimidated by the Pharisees suggests that in John the ἄρχοντες are not the rulers de facto (despite John 7:26), but members of a traditional authority class, while real power is coming to be held by the Pharisees. Nicodemus (John 3:1–21; 7:45–52; 19:38–42) seems to represent secret believers of this ruling class, whose open confession could have been of real help to the Christian group as a whole.[21] It is possible that one of the significant aims in the writing of John was to encourage these and other secret Christians to bring their faith out into the open.[22]

In some manner, then, in the synagogue or synagogues of this specific locale, authorities who belonged to the Pharisees were putting those who openly asserted that Jesus was the Messiah out of the synagogue. The mechanism used for this expulsion is not clear. Martyn thought of the *birkat ha-minim*, the twelfth of the Eighteen Benedictions,[23] but this is now generally considered disproven.[24] The Gospel of John represents a strident response from the Christian side. Its intentions and its theological meaning are not limited to this; it presents a solution in many respects greater than the difficulty to which it was addressed. Yet this response is also highly problematic with regard to its treatment of the

---

20. D. Rensberger, "Oppression and Identity in the Gospel of John," in *The Recovery of Black Presence: An Interdisciplinary Exploration: Essays in Honor of Dr. Charles B. Copher,* ed. R. C. Bailey and J. Grant (Nashville: Abingdon Press, 1995), 88–89.

21. D. Rensberger, *Johannine Faith and Liberating Community,* 37–41, 54–59.

22. S. J. Tanzer, "Salvation is *for* the Jews: Secret Christian Jews in the Gospel of John," in *The Future of Early Christianity: Essays in Honor of Helmut Koester,* ed. B. A. Pearson, A. T. Kraabel, G. W. E. Nickelsburg, and N. R. Petersen (Minneapolis: Fortress Press, 1991), 285–300.

23. Martyn, *History and Theology in the Fourth Gospel,* 37–62.

24. R. Kimelman, "*Birkat Ha-Minim* and the Lack of Evidence for an Anti-Christian Jewish Prayer in Late Antiquity," in *Jewish and Christian Self-Definition,* vol. 2: *Aspects of Judaism in the Greco-Roman Period,* ed. E. P. Sanders (Philadelphia: Fortress, 1981), 226–44; S. T. Katz, "Issues in the Separation of Judaism and Christianity After 70 C.E.: A Reconsideration," *JBL* 103 (1984): 48–53, 63–76.

people whom it calls "the Jews." Neither the greatness nor the problems of John can be understood apart from its historical context. The Gospel's high christology and love commandment, its dualism and its sectarianism, all are affected by this context. The same is certainly true of what it says about "the Jews."

Because it was the confession of Jesus as Messiah that was the crucial point at issue between the Christian group and the synagogue authorities, christology and the acceptance or rejection of a particular kind of christology is at the heart of the Fourth Gospel, in its narratives and in its dialogues and discourses. However exalted the Christian community's claims about Jesus at the beginning, they seem to have grown higher and more firmly held as a result of the conflict. Certainly that is the development that the Gospel writer wanted to encourage, as can be seen, for instance, in the story of the blind man in John 9, who is healed by Jesus but only comes to a full understanding of his identity as a result of his struggle with the authorities. Thus there seems to have been a kind of dialectic between the Christians' confession of faith and their rejection by the synagogue authorities (and, most likely, by the majority of their fellow Jews). The higher their claims about Jesus, the more firmly they were rejected; and the more forceful the rejection, the more radically the claims were asserted.

Thus the current, and I believe correct, scholarly majority view of the origin of the Fourth Gospel is that it arose out of the persecution of a group of Jewish-born Christians by the local synagogue authorities, and that its author responded to this persecution in part by viciously demonizing those authorities, whom he calls simply "the Jews." This is a set of circumstances that neither Jews nor Christians can regard happily today. One of the most difficult aspects of the interpreter's task is to prevent our discomfort about the actions of long-dead members of our religious communities, some of which have had terrible consequences through the centuries, from hindering our acknowledgement of the reality of ancient events in a way that may bring the chain of evil consequences to an end.

SCHOLARLY APPROACHES TO ANTI-JUDAISM IN JOHN

I will identify and briefly discuss three approaches that scholars have taken to the problem of John's treatment of "the Jews." One of these approaches is essentially theological. The second seeks to understand the data in John in relation to the context of the Gospel in antiquity, and in general does not see the Gospel writer as having anti-Jewish intentions. The third type of approach includes those who have been more strongly critical of the writer and the Gospel.

Theological Interpretation

Part of the way in which John's solution is greater than the problem it addresses is its extension of vision beyond the immediate crisis to profound issues of divine relationship to the human world. It has long been recognized that the opposition to Jesus in the Fourth Gospel represents not just Jewish rejection of Christian claims, but a fundamental human rejection of the divine initiative for salvation. The usual way of putting this is that "the Jews" in John stand for "the world" in its resistance to God. Rudolf Bultmann, for instance, produced a penetrating interpretation of the Fourth Gospel in which this understanding featured prominently.[25] In support of this interpretation, John Ashton notes that in the Farewell Discourses of John 14–17, "the Jews" no longer appear, but are replaced by "the world."[26] For Michael J. Cook, John's polemic against "the Jews" is subsidiary to his overarching theological aim, in which he needed role models for his readers to emulate. Jesus' disciples are these positive models, and "the Jews" simply contrast with them as those who fail to believe.[27]

Some may find such approaches helpful in pointing away from negative assertions about Jews and Judaism toward a more universal critique of human attitudes. In Bultmann's interpretation, which in general pursues a theological line that tends toward the ahistorical, "the Jews" as Jews take on a less central importance for understanding John. Yet this is hardly adequate as a solution to the problem. As Werner Kelber has pointed out, it only magnifies the potential or actual anti-Judaism to cosmic proportions.[28] "The Jews" in John now become a symbol for all human unbelief and opposition to God ("Οι Ἰουδαῖοι does not relate to the empirical state of the Jewish people, but to its very nature"),[29] the very type of demonization that has led to some of the most vio-

---

25. E.g., R. Bultmann, *The Gospel of John*, trans. and ed. G. R. Beasley-Murray; trans. R. W. N. Hoare and J. K. Riches (Philadelphia: Westminster Press, 1971), 86.

26. Ashton, "The Identity and Function of the Ἰουδαῖοι," 65–68.

27. Cook, "The Gospel of John and the Jews," 267–68.

28. W. H. Kelber, "Metaphysics and Marginality in John," in *"What Is John?": Readers and Readings of the Fourth Gospel*, SBLSymS 3, ed. F. F. Segovia (Atlanta: Scholars Press, 1996), 131–32.

29. Bultmann, *The Gospel of John*, 87.

lent anti-Semitic outrages of Christian Europe.[30] While John may well take Jewish opposition to Christian claims about Jesus as indicative of a general human tendency to hold out against divine love, this in itself needs a theological and ethical interpretation that is sensitive both to the Gospel's historical situation and to the later history of Christian anti-Semitism.[31]

Contextual Interpretations

There have been a number of studies in recent years by scholars who take more serious account of John's historical context while reflecting on its portrayal of "the Jews." Many, like the present essay, have been part of larger projects devoted to the problem of anti-Semitism or anti-Judaism in early Christianity. John T. Townsend, for instance, observed the presence of both anti-Jewish elements and relatively positive statements about Jews in John, and concluded that the latter must belong to literary strata that come from the early stages in the Johannine community's development and the former to those from the subsequent period of expulsion from the synagogue, when the community no longer considered itself Jewish.[32] Some such development in the community's language and sense of itself seems plausible, though whether it can be linked to literary inconsistencies in the Gospel seems to me more questionable. A few years later, D. Moody Smith examined the data in John and laid out a historical reconstruction similar to the one I have given above, concluding that despite initial appearances, John is not anti-Semitic or anti-Jewish but "a response to a specific crisis in Jewish-Christian relations" that had begun within the synagogue. This crisis and the persecution that it threatened makes John's apparently gratuitous anti-Judaism historically understandable.[33] More recently still, Robert Kysar, after similarly surveying the Gospel for the impression it makes on the reader with regard to anti-Semitism and presenting the

---

30. See also S. Sandmel, *Anti-Semitism in the New Testament?* (Philadelphia: Fortress, 1978) 117–18; R. R. Ruether, *Faith and Fratricide: The Theological Roots of Anti-Semitism* (New York: Seabury, 1974), 116.

31. Cook's specific form of this theological amelioration of John's anti-Judaism underplays both the significance for John's readers of expulsion from the synagogue and the extent to which *Jesus*, not the disciples, is the reader's true role model (e.g., John 12:26; 13:34; 14:12; 15:9–12, 18–21).

32. Townsend, "The Gospel of John and the Jews"; cf. Ashton, "The Identity and Function of the Ἰουδαῖοι," 49, 62.

33. D. M. Smith, "Judaism and the Gospel of John," in *Jews and Christians: Exploring the Past, Present, and Future,* Shared Ground among Jews and Christians 1, ed. J. H. Charlesworth (New York: Crossroad, 1990), 87–88.

historical context, pointed out the literary necessity for an antagonist in any effective narrative and concluded, "The puzzling and perplexing portrayal of the Jews as the opponents of Jesus in the Gospel of John, therefore, owes its existence to a literary necessity and a historical accident."[34] A more popular presentation along similar lines has been made by Urban C. von Wahlde.[35]

Both Smith and Kysar offer further reflections on the significance of their conclusions. Smith recognizes that the adequacy of John's dualistic response to its historical circumstances might be questioned and that, given John's place in the Christian canon, the Gospel makes Christian-Jewish dialogue necessary while offering little basis for a positive outcome from such a process.[36] The integrity of such a dialogue requires honoring the reality of both sets of mutually exclusive claims, those of Johannine Christianity and those of Pharisaic Judaism, remembering that they represent opposite possibilities coming out of the same tradition. The tension between them, according to Smith, is not proper to Judaism and Christianity as separate religions, but arises *within* religions that claim both that God has spoken and that God continues to speak.[37] Kysar goes somewhat further, noting that historical reconstruction by itself is not enough to safeguard the ordinary Christian reading of John from anti-Semitic consequences, which result from the transformation of an occasional writing into canonical Scripture read in isolation from its historical context. Kysar therefore calls for those charged with the interpretation of John within the church to distinguish the normative from the merely contingent, a risky task that must be carried out in congregations and classrooms, not just scholarly discussions.[38]

Luke T. Johnson has taken a somewhat different approach, observing not only John's historical context but its context within ancient rhetorical practice. After noting the minority status of Christianity within Judaism, and emphasizing the diversity within both of them, Johnson proposes to interpret the rhetoric of Judaism and Christianity within the

---

34. R. Kysar, "Anti-Semitism and the Gospel of John," in *Anti-Semitism and Early Christianity: Issues of Polemic and Faith*, ed. C. A. Evans and D. A. Hagner (Minneapolis: Fortress Press, 1993), 124.

35. U. C. von Wahlde, "The Gospel of John and the Presentation of Jews and Judaism," in *Within Context: Essays on Jews and Judaism in the New Testament*, ed. D. P. Efroymson, E. J. Fisher, and L. Klenicki (Collegeville, Minn.: Liturgical Press, 1993), 67–84.

36. Smith, "Judaism and the Gospel of John," 91–93.

37. Ibid., 95–96.

38. R. Kysar, "Anti-Semitism and the Gospel of John," 124–27.

context of that of ancient philosophical schools.[39] In competition with
one another, representatives of such schools often uttered what to us
seems violently abusive slander. The point of this was not factual accusation but standardized depictions of opponents for internal consumption
within a school, and secondarily the provision of a negative counter-
image in order to promote one's own positive ideal of the philosopher.[40]
He also finds numerous examples of Jewish use of such polemic, both
against outsiders and against other Jews.[41] He concludes that, in a context where opponents were commonly spoken of as hypocrites, blind,
and in the service of demons, the language of New Testament Christians
about other Jews hardly stands out. Recognizing it as the convention of
its time, and shared on all sides, robs it of its capacity for mischief.[42] A
similar point is made by Craig A. Evans.[43] The Dead Sea Scrolls provide
some sterling examples of this kind of rhetoric, and no one would regard
them as anti-Jewish. As partial parallels within the New Testament, note
the intra-Christian demonization in 2 Cor. 11:13–15 and 1 John 4:1–6.

I have indicated already my belief that placing John within its historical and literary context is indispensable for any accurate understanding
of it. Yet this must not be done simply as a superficial apologetic to defend the Gospel from charges of anti-Judaism. Townsend, Smith, and
Kysar in different ways all recognize that John remains and will always
remain problematic in the context of Christian-Jewish relations, and for
that reason within the Christian environment itself. Others have asked,
however, whether the question has been posed trenchantly enough in
such studies.[44] I turn next to scholars who have raised much sharper
questions about the viability of the Johannine treatment of "the Jews."

Stronger Critiques of John

Samuel Sandmel has pointed out that, even when one recognizes that
"the Jews" in John may sometimes have a geographical reference, or
that the term refers to Jewish leaders and not to the people as a whole,
the problem of this language is not solved. By using this designation for

---

39. L. T. Johnson, "The New Testament's Anti-Jewish Slander and the Conventions of
Ancient Polemic," *JBL* 108 (1989): 423–30.

40. Ibid., 430–33.

41. Ibid., 434–40.

42. Ibid., 440–41.

43. C. A. Evans, "Faith and Polemic: The New Testament and First-Century Judaism,"
in *Anti-Semitism and Early Christianity: Issues of Polemic and Faith*, ed. C. A. Evans and
D. A. Hagner (Minneapolis: Fortress Press, 1993), 1–8.

44. Culpepper, "The Gospel of John and the Jews," 283–84.

Jesus' opponents, John creates a sense of fundamental opposition that makes Jesus appear not to be a Jew at all. Unlike the synoptics, in John it appears that the movement of Jesus and his disciples has few if any Jews within it, so that "the Jews" are outsiders and opponents.[45] The bitterness of John may reflect one side of an animosity that was two-sided; but though one may explain its historical circumstances, "one cannot deny the existence of a written compilation of clearly expressed anti-Jewish sentiments."[46]

Norman Beck, in an unusually radical project, proposes actually to "repudiate portions of our scriptural traditions" that are injurious to other people. His rationale for this is that, while certain polemic utterances may be natural during the "adolescence" of a religion as it seeks to establish its own identity over against its "parent," they are no longer appropriate once the religion has become "mature."[47] Not surprisingly, Beck finds a good deal of such polemic in John, deriving from the historical circumstances of the Johannine community, and from its "exclusivism" and frustration over its inability to convert Jews.[48] Because Beck's work is primarily concerned with the practical outcome of this repudiation in translation and liturgy, I will return to it in my concluding section.

Rosemary Radford Ruether has taken the critique to a deeper level. For her, the problem is not just John's language but the christological interpretation of Scripture in the service of which that language is used. By identifying "the Jews" with a false principle of existence that refuses to know God in the only legitimate way, namely through Jesus, John sets them up as the embodiment of alienation from the divine. It is thus the christological hermeneutic as such, the insistence that in Jesus and only in him the ultimate divine revelation has taken place, that leads to the demonizing of Jews and Judaism by John and, taking its cue from this Gospel above all, by Christianity as a whole.[49]

---

45. Sandmel, *Anti-Semitism in the New Testament?* 101–2.

46. Ibid., 119.

47. N. A. Beck, *Mature Christianity in the 21st Century: The Recognition and Repudiation of the Anti-Jewish Polemic of the New Testament*, rev. ed. (New York: Crossroad, 1994), 57, 71–72, 322–23, 328.

48. Ibid., 286–87, 326.

49. R. R. Ruether, *Faith and Fratricide*, 111–16. For responses to Ruether, see T. A. Idinopulos and R. B. Ward, "Is Christology Inherently Anti-Semitic? A Critical Review of Rosemary Ruether's *Faith and Fratricide*," *JAAR* 45 (1977): 193–214; J. G. Gager, *The Origins of Anti-Semitism: Attitudes toward Judaism in Pagan and Christian Antiquity* (Oxford: Oxford University Press, 1983), 24–34.

Werner Kelber takes a similarly fundamental line.[50] After surveying and criticizing a number of approaches to the anti-Judaism of John, including some of those I have mentioned in the preceding two sections,[51] Kelber goes on to make a literary analysis of what he calls the Gospel's "principal project," its "metaphysical agenda." This agenda he sees as a longing for transcendence and unified identity, the overcoming of difference and otherness. Thus in spite of Jesus' appearance in the world of flesh, John portrays him as consistently maintaining his heavenly identity. In carrying out this agenda through its language of irony and double entendre, John places on "the Jews" the burden of the difference that it yearns to transcend, marginalizing and even demonizing them. The anti-Judaism of John is thus for Kelber the direct and apparently inevitable implication of its transcendental metaphysics, which require an other to repudiate and exclude. It is the consequences for these "others" that Kelber believes historical, sociological, and even literary criticism have not yet adequately addressed.[52]

In studies such as these we have the issue of anti-Judaism in John put with all possible force and directness. Yet it must be asked whether it has really been considered in all its dimensions even here, since these studies neglect the historical conditions in which the utterances they deplore arose. To be sure, all of those just mentioned recognize, at least in passing, the situation of conflict with the synagogue authorities that characterizes the Fourth Gospel. But (with the possible exception of Beck) they seem to treat it as a matter of methodological and hermeneutical indifference. That is, the question of historical context is not allowed to affect the *interpretation* of John's "anti-Judaism" at all.

Only Kelber makes an attempt to justify this procedure. His critiques of historical and other approaches, including literary criticism itself, are clear-sighted and valuable. I will not attempt a response to his understanding of John's metaphysics within the scope of this paper. His treatment of Johannine irony will be considered below. Here I will note that, in an area where definitions are significant, he assumes a meaning for anti-Judaism without saying what it is. More importantly, by dismissing what he calls the "external causality" invoked by historical critics as a hermeneutical criterion (external to the text, that is; in

---

50. I am grateful to Professor Kelber and to R. Alan Culpepper for providing drafts of their essays that have now appeared in *"What Is John?"* and to Fernando F. Segovia, the editor of that volume, for sharing page proofs of them with me.

51. Kelber, "Metaphysics and Marginality in John," 131–36.

52. Ibid., 136–54.

other words, the actual lives of the Gospel's writer, first readers, and their contemporaries), Kelber makes it impossible to understand either John's "metaphysical agenda" or its demonization of the Jews. Rightly recognizing the importance of social location for modern readers,[53] he implicitly denies it any significance for ancient ones. Thus even Kelber has not done all that needs to be done in addressing the issue of anti-Judaism in the Gospel of John.

A MORE COMPREHENSIVE APPROACH

As is no doubt apparent, my own sense of how John's treatment of "the Jews" should be understood falls somewhere between the contextual approach and those of Kelber, Ruether, et al. Literary critics have justifiably faulted historical criticism for narrowing the range of meanings to be sought in and derived from the biblical texts. Here is a case, however, where historical criticism is vitally needed to redress misinterpretations and the misdeeds, past and present, that result from them. Literary criticism alone will not do the job. Without a sense of the historical context in which John was written, we may be able to identify the way in which it led later Christians into acts of oppression and violence, but we will not be able to assess the Gospel itself accurately.

Kelber is right, however, to insist that historical criticism by itself also fails to address the issue adequately. The recognition of historical realities, whatever they may be, is essential in exegesis, but historical exegesis alone cannot meet the responsibilities of those who interpret the Bible in this or any other age. It is at this point that biblical scholarship in the second half of the twentieth century has suffered a major failure of nerve. The gap between critical exegesis and theological and ethical interpretation, let alone the translation of these into responsible Christian preaching and teaching, is well known, and movement can be seen here and there in the scholarly community to reconnect with the larger issues facing both churches and contemporary societies. With regard to the Gospel of John and anti-Judaism, both Kelber and R. Alan Culpepper rightly assert that recognizing John's historical context without recognizing the later effect that John has had on Christian anti-Judaism and anti-Semitism cannot meet these contemporary needs.[54] Culpepper

---

53. Kelber, "Metaphysics and Marginality in John," 133.
54. R. A. Culpepper, "The Gospel of John as a Document of Faith in a Pluralistic Culture," in *What Is John? Readers and Readings of the Fourth Gospel*, SBLSymS 3, ed. F. F. Segovia (Atlanta: Scholars Press, 1996), 112–14.

proposes a "hermeneutics of ethical accountability," leading to interpretation that is both faithful to the text and ethically responsible, including a responsibility to those who have suffered as a result of oppressive elements in biblical texts. Not only theological and historical but also ethical concerns must inform interpretation.[55]

What I would like to attempt here, then, is a reading of John's language about Jews and Judaism that both sets it in its historical context and evaluates its implications beyond that context. In this reading, social location, of both text and readers, will be of crucial significance. Whether John offers liberation or oppression, inclusion or exclusion, depends a great deal on who is reading it and how they relate to other people in their own social environment. Recognizing the location of the Gospel's original author and readers provides a vital clue to later readers in other locations about what this language meant once, and, given an accountable hermeneutic, that meaning can be an important aid in avoiding harmful interpretations now.

JOHN AND ANTI-JUDAISM

The point at issue in this essay is whether the Gospel of John is anti-Jewish. Given its social and historical context, I believe that the answer must be a qualified no, as will be made clearer below. But, as must also be made clear, this answer is not complete without some ethical reflection on the adequacy of John's response to its context.

John does not, in my judgment, represent an outsider's hostility toward Judaism or toward people of the Jewish faith, the definition of anti-Judaism with which I began this essay. The primary reason for this assertion is that the fourth evangelist, like other early Christians, did not yet regard his Christianity as a new or separate religion, but considered it to *be* Judaism. In a modern context, of course, and indeed throughout the history of Jewish-Christian relationships since the second century, this assertion must seem both absurd and hugely offensive to most Jews. But, as Craig A. Evans reminds us, John and the other New Testament writings were not produced in the context of later relationships but in the very different and unreproducible environment of first-century Judaism, which was not monolithic but composed of a wide variety of competing groups, theologies, and ideologies. In its beginnings Christianity was one of these, and Evans suggests that the kind

---

55. Ibid., 126–27.

of polemic we find in the New Testament should be seen as part of an ancient and widespread practice of internal critique within Israel.[56] Johannine Christianity was a subtype of this Christianity, and if its Jewish members had not still felt themselves to be Jewish, it is hard to understand why they would have been so concerned about their exclusion from the synagogue. The hostility that John expresses is fundamentally that of one group toward others within the same religious/ethnic entity. It is not a rejection of Judaism, its Scriptures, practices, institutions, and people, *in toto*, but an interpretation of them in conflict with competing interpretations.

As became evident at the conference on which this volume is based, the crucial point in whether one agrees or disagrees with the preceding assessment is whether the Johannine Christian community, including the author of the Fourth Gospel, can in fact still be considered Jewish. If so, then the Gospel's violent invective remains a Jewish sectarian response to discipline by local religious authorities. If not, then it must represent the anti-Jewish malice of hostile outsiders. It must be granted that, however one decides this question, the decision may well seem an irrelevant exercise in labeling, given the harshness of John's language and the severity of its historical effects. Let me therefore state clearly that whether John is judged to be anti-Jewish or not, and however understandable its rhetoric might be within its historical context, I do not consider the branding of the Gospel's opponents as "children of the devil" to be morally justified. Nevertheless, in my opinion issues of power and relative social location do matter. It does matter whether exclusionary language is used by those in a position to do harm, whether invective and castigation come from the margin or the seat of power. That is part of what is bound up with the question of whether John is or is not still "Jewish," whether it represents sectarian Judaism or hostile anti-Judaism.

If John is not Jewish, then most would agree that its language must be considered anti-Jewish. On the other hand, "There can be by definition no anti-Jewish polemic by early Christians and in early Christian documents until there is a separate, self-conscious, early Christian existence."[57] At what point, then, do we draw this dividing line? When did someone born a Jew cease to be one by becoming and remaining a Christian? Though this question must be posed, it is virtually impossi-

---

56. Evans, "Faith and Polemic," 1–11.
57. N. A. Beck, *Mature Christianity in the 21st Century*, 287.

ble to answer given the information available to us, and all the more so
since it would probably have been answered in different ways in antiquity depending on the standpoint of the person doing the answering. A
Christian, a Pharisee, a Jew of some other persuasion or no particular
persuasion, and a pagan might each have given a different answer. Most
Jews and many Christians today would say that anyone who becomes a
Christian is from that moment no longer a Jew; but the matter was by
no means so clearcut in the first century.

Does John's christology, in which Jesus is "equal to God," *ipso facto*
render it non-Jewish? It would seem only reasonable to say so. But
"equal to God" (John 5:18) is only one statement in a diverse complex of christological assertions. Elsewhere we read that Jesus is one
with God (John 10:30; 17:11, 21–23), that God is greater than he (John
14:28) and is his God (John 20:17), that Jesus is perfectly obedient to
God (e.g., John 5:19, 30; 10:18; 12:49–50; 15:10). The simple equation "Jesus=God" does not really seem to express what John wants to
say. The incarnational christology of the Fourth Gospel is not an obvious step to take from a Jewish starting point; but then it is not a very
obvious step from any other starting point either. Intermediary divine
principles were known in various Jewish theologies,[58] precedents that
formed fundamental building blocks in the construction of Christian
belief. While the christology developed in John was obviously beyond
what was acceptable to most other Jews, there is no reason to suppose
that the Gospel's author thought of it as ditheistic.

It is evident that the fourth evangelist considered his faith a revelation of the same God to the same people, not the cornerstone of a new
religion. John does not dispute the continuing legitimacy of Passover,
Sabbath, and other Jewish observances, though it offers new, christocentric interpretations of them (see below). John 2:19–22; 4:19–24 may
deny the ongoing value of the Temple, but by the time this Gospel was
written the Temple had been destroyed.[59] The food laws are not mentioned in John one way or the other, while circumcision seems to be
regarded positively in John 7:22–23. To be sure, the Christians have a
new initiation rite, one that is part of their claim to a new birth "from
above"; yet John expects that a Pharisee, a "teacher of Israel," ought to

---

58. R. Schnackenburg, *The Gospel According to St. John*, 3 vols. (New York: Crossroad Publishing, 1968–1982), 1:481–87; C. H. Dodd, *The Interpretation of the Fourth
Gospel* (London: Cambridge University Press, 1953), 263–85.
59. J. T. Townsend, "The Gospel of John and the Jews," 75.

find such things comprehensible (John 3:1 10), that is, that such things are within the realm of Jewish understanding.

Even granted all this, how can a writing that says such hateful things about "the Jews" be considered in any sense Jewish? Doesn't this author, by using "the Jews" as a negative, outsider term thereby overtly define himself as non-Jewish? He does not indeed seem to consider himself a Ἰουδαῖος; yet he continues to assert that Jesus was a Ἰουδαῖος, that in fact he was and is the King of the Ἰουδαῖοι, and that salvation comes from the Ἰουδαῖοι. Moreover, Ἰουδαῖος was not the only self-identifying label for a Jew in antiquity. The writer of John evidently still considers himself a member of *Israel,* not a new Israel but "the nation" for whom Jesus died (as will be discussed below). For all the acrimony of the debates in John 5–10, the question still seems to be, "Who has the right interpretation of our *common* heritage?" That may be precisely why the debates are so acrimonious.

The most serious breach with Jewish identity in John seems to me to be the designation of the Torah as "your law" or "their law" ("our law" on the lips of "the Jews"; see John 7:19, 51; 8:17; 10:34; 15:25; 18:31; 19:7; and note 1:17). (Something similar could be said about the labeling of Passover and other Holy Days as festivals "of the Jews." This is generally considered one of the "neutral" uses of Ἰουδαῖοι, but, as noted earlier, it cannot help but share somewhat in the distancing effect of the hostile uses.) Here we do seem to see a new identity being created, one that centers not on Torah but on Jesus. Of course, not every mention of "the law" in John is negative, nor does John disparage the keeping of Torah. However, the primary function of the Law, and of Moses through whom it was given, is to bear witness to Jesus. It is those who refuse to take the new step indicated (in John's view) by the Law itself that the Gospel criticizes (John 1:17, 45; 3:14; 5:39–47; 7:42; 9:28–29; 10:34–36; 12:34). This move away from a life defined and given meaning by Torah to one centered on Jesus, to whom the Law bears witness, clearly implies the creation of a new self-understanding different from the one inherited from Judaism. Yet even here the breach is defined largely in terms of the rejection of the Johannine message by their fellow Jews. If a phrase like "the Passover of the Jews" has any negative connotations, it is as a festival whose communal celebration is under the control of the religious authorities who oppose the Johannine group. It is those same authorities whose official interpretation of Torah rejects and is rejected by the Johannine claims concerning Jesus. "The law" is now "their law" in part because "they" no longer admit the Johannine Christians to the discussion of its meaning.

This leads us to the question why John chose οἱ Ἰουδαῖοι in the first place as a term to designate the hostile religious authorities. It is this more than anything else that causes John's hostility to seem directed against Jews in general, and causes the Gospel writer to seem non-Jewish and therefore anti-Jewish. John Ashton is one of the few scholars who raise this question explicitly. Unfortunately, his rather cloudy suggestion that somehow Ἰουδαῖοι were already distinguished from sectarian groups within which the Johannine community may have originated does not provide a satisfactory answer.[60] It is certainly possible that the term Ἰουδαῖοι had some prehistory for John's author that caused him to use it in this way. For example, the original opponents of Johannine Christianity could have been perceived as geographical "Judeans," though this approach to the problem still seems unlikely to me. Perhaps Ἰουδαῖοι was the Jewish self-designation favored by the authorities themselves, and John simply allowed them to keep it, preferring "Israel" for the Jewish Christian group (see below). The most obvious explanation to many readers, however, is that the author of this Gospel simply wanted nothing more to do with Jews and Judaism. Yet if this were so, it is hard to understand why he depicts the debates about Jesus in such thoroughly Jewish terms: obedience to God, knowledge of God, Moses, the meaning of the Scriptures, the interpretation of Jewish traditions. A new identity is being formed, but not without an anguished look back at what has been and what might yet be. For the way in which John refers to expulsion from the synagogue makes it clear that the writer did not view this expulsion as the inevitable outcome of Jewish-Christian history; nor, to judge by the highly ambivalent portrayal of Nicodemus, did he preclude the possibility of "rulers of the Jews" and even Pharisees joining the Christian group.

Earlier I described my conclusion that John is not anti-Jewish as only a qualified one. From the preceding discussion, the reasons for this qualification should be apparent. John comes from a unique, transitional period that belongs neither to the purely intra-Jewish sectarianism of Christianity's earliest days, when it might have seemed that the new group would either remain within or come to dominate Judaism, nor yet to the fully separate religion that Christianity became. Instead, John shares aspects of both. Kysar, Smith, Evans, and others accentuate the

---

60. Ashton, "The Identity and Function of the Ἰουδαῖοι," 70–75.

inner-Jewish characteristics, while Sandmel, Beck, Ruether, Kelber, and others stress the separateness. The notion of John as internal prophetic critique within Judaism does not do full justice to the estrangement from Torah and synagogue that, whatever its origin, so strongly characterizes this Gospel.[61] The choice of "the Jews" to designate the hostile authorities may indicate a willingness to undergo the complete break with Judaism that was imminent. Yet to treat John as the product of a religious community already alien to Judaism and bent on overthrowing it fails to recognize the lingering status of the Christian body as a minority group within the Jewish community and subject to discipline by Jewish authorities. It is still *as Jews* that believers are "afraid of the Jews," and it is as Jews that the Gospel writer encourages them to show the fearlessness of the blind man in John 9.

John is at the point of separation between Christianity and Judaism. This means that it is still Jewish enough for its language to be viewed as sectarian protest, but no longer Jewish enough to remain in this category for long. If Johannine Christianity is already a separate religion, the fourth evangelist does not yet seem fully aware of this fact; if it is not yet separate, the evangelist has nonetheless contributed to making the breach inevitable. The Jewish author of John certainly meant to say that the Jewish religious authorities in his locale were failing to acknowledge a divine revelation, indeed the ultimate divine revelation, and he meant to censure them harshly for this. He did not mean, however, to claim that Jews in general were demonic haters of God. This is what I mean by answering a qualified no to the question of John's anti-Judaism. And yet John's language is so hateful and its consequences have been so abhorrent that the answer to this question almost seems irrelevant. I do not believe that the fourth evangelist intended to slander other Jews in a way that would endanger Jewish lives and the Jewish religion itself for centuries to come; but that has nevertheless been the result of his writing.

Specific Themes in John

Certain themes in John of special significance for the question of anti-Judaism still need to be examined. These include the use of the designation "Israel," John's reinterpretation of Jewish traditions, the Passion narrative, and the issue of John's marginalization of "the Jews" as it has been raised by Werner Kelber.

---

61. Culpepper, "The Gospel of John and the Jews," 284.

Israel

Earlier I noted that, even as "the Jews" are presented so very negatively
in the Gospel of John, "Israel" remains a positive term. Early in the Gospel, John the Baptist declares that the reason for his own mission was
that Jesus might be revealed to Israel (John 1:31). Accordingly, Jesus is
soon acclaimed "King of Israel" by his disciple Nathanael, whom Jesus
had already designated as "an Israelite without guile" (John 1:47). The
same acclamation is used by the crowd at the "triumphal entry" (John
12:13), forming a notable contrast with the expression "King of the
Jews" that dominates the trial narrative. (In the synoptics, "King of Israel" is used only in mockery during the crucifixion scene: Mark 15:32;
Matt. 27:42.) Only once is "Israel" used in what might seem a negative
context, where Jesus seems surprised that the Pharisee Nicodemus, the
"teacher of Israel," does not understand him (John 3:10). Even here,
however, the disparagement is not of Israel but of Nicodemus.

"Israel," unlike "the Jews," thus generally refers positively to those
to whom Jesus is revealed, some of whom accept his revelation. He
is Israel's true king and teacher, and even if "king" and "teacher" are
among the titles that John finds only partially adequate for him, they
express authentic components of his relation to Israel as the object of
divine redemption. This is in accord with the unconscious "prophecy"
by the chief priest Caiaphas that Jesus would die for the people or nation (λαός, ἔθνος; see John 11:47–52). There is no hint in all this of
a "new" or "true" Israel consisting of the (Gentile) church. The "nation" is distinguished from God's other scattered children in John 11,
and throughout John "Israel" refers only to Jews. It is clear, therefore,
that the Johannine Jewish Christians still considered themselves to be Israel, not a new nation or religion, and that, like other Jewish sectarian
movements, they regarded themselves as the heirs of God's promises to
Israel. It is possible that they used "Israel" as a designation for those
among the Jewish people who had accepted the revelation of Jesus as
the Messiah; but John 3:10 and 11:47–52 suggest that they still considered all Israel potentially within this group, with only its leadership
standing in the way.

The Reinterpretation of Jewish Traditions

It is widely recognized that in John, Jesus takes to himself a wide variety
of Jewish symbols, values, beliefs, and institutions. In this process he
not only fulfills their traditional meaning but also brings them a new

meaning. He is thus made not only the realization but the transcendence of Jewish traditions and expectations, all of which become concentrated in him. It is not so much that they are abolished or rendered obsolete (though some of them may be) as that their meanings are taken up into his meaning, where they are given a new relevance.

Only a few examples will be given here. Any reader of John who is knowledgeable about Judaism will easily find more. As noted above, John claims that Moses, and the Scriptures in general, testify to Jesus. When Jesus speaks of the Temple, he is talking about his own body (John 2:19–22). It was not Moses who gave bread from heaven, in the form of manna; rather, God gives the true bread from heaven, which is Jesus himself (John 6:30–35). Thus Jesus is the fulfillment and transcendence of Exodus and Passover. Other Jewish festivals similarly take on new meaning in him, as when at the feast of Sukkoth, celebrated in ancient times with ceremonies of lamp lighting and water drawing, Jesus offers drink to all who are thirsty and declares himself to be the light of the world (John 7:37–39; 8:12). When Martha affirms the traditional faith that her brother Lazarus will be raised on the last day, Jesus replies, "I am the resurrection and the life" (John 11:23–27). Overarching the Gospel as a whole is the christology that sees in Jesus the incarnation of the *Logos,* which is evidently the equivalent of the Wisdom that had been God's helper and agent in creation (John 1:1–18). It is as this *Logos* that Jesus can say, when compared with the patriarch, "Before Abraham was, I am" — thus taking to himself the divine self-designation revealed to Moses at the burning bush (John 8:58; cf. 8:23–29; 13:19; 18:4–9).

It is not hard to see in such declarations the roots of Christian supersessionism, the claim that Christianity and the church have superseded Judaism and the Jews as the religion and the people of God. Townsend, for instance, speaks of John's "replacement theology,"[62] and Beck of the replacement of the "superseded" Jews by "a new religion."[63] Offensive as such a claim is to Jews, it had consequences that went beyond mere insult. If the Jews had been superseded, they were in danger of becoming superfluous. By the third or fourth century, Christian theology was having a hard time understanding their continued existence, and it is at least arguable that many acts of violence committed against Jews in the

---

62. Townsend, "The Gospel of John and the Jews," 72–74.
63. Beck, *Mature Christianity in the 21st Century,* 288.

name of Christianity stem from this embarrassment.[64] To the extent that
John laid the groundwork for the claim of supersession, it also prepared
the way for the later violence.

It makes all the difference in the world, however, whether this "replacement" is viewed from the standpoint of triumph or of defeat. In
its own context and not in that of later centuries, John's gathering up
of Jewish values into Jesus served much more a defensive than an offensive purpose. The Jews in the Johannine Christian community were
themselves suffering dispossession from their heritage. Whatever "being
put out of the synagogue" meant, it undoubtedly meant being excluded
from the official and corporate worship of Judaism in that locale. The
celebration of the festivals and the interpretation of the Scriptures were
in the hands of their adversaries, who were apparently willing to deny
them access to these things because of their insistent confession of Jesus.
A major part of what John is doing is constructing a new world for
its Christian Jewish readers, rebuilding the belief system that had given
meaning to their universe. And it is characteristic of the Fourth Gospel
that the new system centers on Jesus. If Sabbath and Passover and the
ancient revelation of God were being taken from them, John promises
them something new, the same only better, in Jesus. Whatever the ultimate outcome of this procedure, John's intention was not to rob the
Jews in order to give their sacred possessions to others. It was rather
to sustain a group of Jewish sectarians by newly interpreting for them
what still seemed their common inheritance as Jews.

Here as elsewhere, we see the different appearances taken on by
Johannine phenomena when they are considered from different perspectives. In its historical context, the Fourth Gospel did little more by its
reinterpretation of Jewish traditions than other Jewish movements had
done, such as the Qumran covenanters or even the Pharisees themselves.
At this relatively early stage of Christian history, the "replacement"
was still an expression more of continuity than of discontinuity, of the
consciousness of a new religious subgroup rather than that of a separate religion. The evil consequences were unintended from the Gospel
writer's point of view. Yet unintended consequences remain real consequences, and a sense of why the Gospel writer did what he did does not
give us permission to overlook the ultimate results.

---

64. I am indebted to my friend Daniel Kohanski for sharing with me his research on
this point.

The Passion Narrative

In every Gospel, the Passion narrative — the story of Jesus' arrest, trial, and execution — presents themes of central importance for relations between Christians and Jews. This is not the place to go into the much-debated question of the relative involvement of Jewish and Roman authorities in the historical death of Jesus. Suffice it to say that as time went on, Christians came to lay far more of the blame and the guilt for his death on Jewish leaders and far less of it on the Roman government than reason requires, and then beyond all reason came to extend that guilt to Jews of later ages. My interest here, however, is solely in the Passion narrative of the Gospel of John.

A curious ambiguity of interpretation has arisen around the Johannine Passion. Most commentators find in John the same exculpation of Pontius Pilate, and implicit indictment of the Jewish authorities, as in the synoptic Gospels.[65] It is often noted that the wording of John 19:15–16 gives the impression that Pilate hands Jesus over to the Jewish chief priests to be crucified, as if they rather than the Romans carried out his execution. Thus for Ruether, "John goes the farthest of all the Gospels in depicting Jesus as actually being crucified *by the Jews.*"[66] This is probably not the Gospel writer's intent (given John 18:31; 19:19–24); but the phrasing certainly allows that impression. Culpepper even considers John "the first document to draw a connection between the authorities who condemned Jesus and the Jews known to the Christian community at a later time";[67] and Epp ascribes to John major responsibility for the libeling of Jews as "Christ-killers" by many Christians.[68]

Yet others have found in John's narrative much less of a false burdening of Jews with the guilt of Jesus' death.[69] Philip S Kaufman, in a short work aimed at correcting the anti-Semitism produced by the church's liturgical preference for the Passion narratives of Mark and Matthew, found John's account to be much less anti-Semitic than theirs. He points out, for instance, that only in John are there Roman soldiers present at Jesus' arrest, while the only Jewish representatives are some Temple officers, not an entire "crowd." John does not have the improbable night trial by the Sanhedrin found in Mark and Matthew, but only a prelimi-

---

65. E.g., Brown, *The Gospel According to John*, 2:794–95, 860.
66. Ruether, *Faith and Fratricide*, 114.
67. Culpepper, "The Gospel of John as a Document of Faith," 114; similarly Kysar, "Anti-Semitism and the Gospel of John," 123–24.
68. Epp, "Anti-Semitism and the Popularity of the Fourth Gospel," 35, 42.
69. E.g., Townsend, "The Gospel of John and the Jews," 76–78.

nary Jewish interrogation, with no verdict given. Whereas the synoptics have the Jewish people or crowd calling for Jesus' death, in John it is only the chief priests and officers (John 18:12–13, 24, 28–30; 19:6, 15 specify the identity of "the Jews," that is, the authorities, in John 18:31, 38; 19:7, 12, 14). At the cross, there is no Jewish mockery.[70] Kaufman finds the Johannine Passion narrative to be "minimally anti-Jewish," ascribing responsibility only to elements of the leadership in Jerusalem, not to the people as a whole. He finds this same lack of bias throughout John.[71]

Kaufman is far too optimistic about the historical reliability of John's account as a whole, but the Roman presence at Jesus' arrest and the lack of a Sanhedrin trial at least show John's independence from unhistorical efforts to increase Jewish responsibility. Yet one reason that John can refrain from showing condemnation of Jesus by Jewish authorities in the Passion narrative is that he has already placed this condemnation at earlier points in his story (John 5:16–18; 7:1, 19–20, 25, 30–32; 8:37, 40, 59; 10:31–39; 11:47–53, 57). The Fourth Gospel still insists that the guilt of those who handed Jesus over to Pilate is greater than Pilate's own (John 19:11). David Granskou, while acknowledging that the Johannine Passion is less harsh toward the Jewish people than that of the synoptics, sees the use of "the Jews" in the trial scenes as widening the scope from the chief priests alone and thus increasing the anti-Judaism of the narrative.[72] Granskou exemplifies the ambiguity mentioned above by suggesting that John's Passion narrative can be read either way, as hostile only to the Temple authorities or as negative toward Judaism as a whole.[73]

Yet Kaufman is probably fundamentally correct that John's Passion narrative as such shows little interest in heaping blame on the Jewish authorities, let alone on the entire Jewish people. Instead, John pursues a different and quite remarkable Jewish political agenda, promoting the sovereignty of Jesus over against both that of Caesar and that sought by Jewish revolutionary movements. So, far from being the good-hearted but easily manipulated figure of the synoptic Gospels, Pilate skillfully

---

70. P. S Kaufman, *The Beloved Disciple: Witness against Anti-Semitism* (Collegeville, Minn.: Liturgical Press, 1991), 44–53.

71. Ibid., 61.

72. D. Granskou, "Anti-Judaism in the Passion Accounts of the Fourth Gospel," in *Paul and the Gospels*, vol. 1 of *Anti-Judaism in Early Christianity*, SCJ 2, ed. P. Richardson and D. Granskou (Waterloo, Ont.: Wilfrid Laurier University Press, 1986), 212–15.

73. Ibid., 216.

maneuvers the chief priests into betraying all hope for liberation from Caesar (John 19:15), while himself failing utterly to grasp the significance of the man who stands unawed before Roman might. The title "King of the Jews," so prominently featured in John's ironic trial scenes, is a true appellation of Jesus, indicating his fulfillment of Jewish political aspirations, albeit in a way surprising to all around him.[74] A bit unexpectedly, then, John's narrative of the death of Jesus actually presents a somewhat less antagonistic picture of Judaism than do those of the synoptics.

Marginalization of "the Jews"

Werner Kelber in particular has raised the issue of John's marginalization of "the Jews": "The narratological, linguistic, and theological dramatization of the Johannine agenda thrives on the marginalization, indeed demonization, of the Jews."[75] Jews are indeed literally demonized in John 8:44, when Jesus is made to tell a group of them, "You are from your father the devil, and you choose to do your father's desires," which are then specified as murder and lying. It should be noted that this group does not consist of the leadership, but of "Jews who had believed in him" (John 8:31). Thus the harshest dialogue between Jesus and "the Jews" is reserved for putative believers, perhaps representing people in the Johannine environment who not only hoped to remain in the synagogue, but who regarded Jesus only as an authentic teacher, not as the incarnate *Logos* who brought the ultimate revelation of God. There can be little doubt, however, that the author of the Gospel would have found this demonizing abuse to be equally applicable to all who failed to acknowledge Jesus in this way.

But is it accurate to say that John *marginalizes* "the Jews"? Marginalization implies oppression, a dominant group driving a weaker group into a corner, refusing to allow them a voice and access to power. What sense does it make to speak of marginalization in regard to the Gospel of John? Kelber uses this term purely in reference to John's language and theology, that is, as an ethical evaluation of literary phenomena, and in this usage it makes some sense. As Kelber goes on to demonstrate, marginalization occurs throughout the dialogues and misunderstandings in John, as "the Jews" are continually shown failing to understand Jesus

---

74. Rensberger, *Johannine Faith and Liberating Community*, 87–106; originally published as "The Politics of John: The Trial of Jesus in the Fourth Gospel," *JBL* 103 (1984) 395–411.

75. Kelber, "Metaphysics and Marginality in John," 147.

and depicted as people with no place in the theological coordinates that define his ministry.[76] But this is a marginalization on paper only. If we do not accept Kelber's narrow perspective, a different perspective once more appears.

John is, in sociological terms, a sectarian document, which means that it portrays a conflict over sectarian heresy from the *heretics'* point of view. Its strictures are not in defense of an established orthodoxy against heretical innovation; they represent a heretical offensive *against* orthodoxy. The theology and language of the Fourth Gospel are in the service of dissent and innovation, and already on purely literary grounds this suggests quite a different interpretation of its ironic rhetoric. Citing Kierkegaard's view of irony as a tool of limitation and destruction, and Kierkegaard's reference to Socrates as a user of irony against the pretensions of classical Hellenism, Kelber concludes that irony can be "the perpetrator of negativity, of cruelty even."[77] The example of Socrates is most instructive, however; it shows exactly where Kelber's disregard for social location goes wrong. Socratic irony worked to undermine established views, and that is the case with Johannine irony as well. It is a tool not of cruelty but of resistance. Irony from below is not an instrument of marginalization but a defense against marginalization.[78]

Social location does matter in the reading of John, not only the location of the modern reader but that of its author and original reading community. If we want to read and interpret John with regard to situations of conflict between majority and minority, the established and the marginal, we must bear in mind which end of these polarities the Gospel represents: It was written from the standpoint of the marginal. Its development into a central document for an established church that wielded power against Jews and other minorities is a significant factor in the history of its interpretation, to which I shall turn shortly. But there is no reason for this *later* use by established authorities to determine how we assess the import of its language *in its own time and place*. Kelber's eschewing of "external causality" in reading John risks worse than arriving at an erroneous interpretation. It risks an unjust interpretation. Care for a true understanding of the historical circumstances of a document's origin is not only a matter of accurate scholarship, but also a matter of justice, and I would include it in the "hermeneutics of ethical accountability" that Culpepper proposes. It is unjust to misrepresent the

---

76. Ibid., 147–52.
77. Ibid., 146.
78. Cf. Malina, *The Gospel of John in Sociolinguistic Perspective,* 11–17.

voice of the oppressed as that of the oppressor, even when that voice comes to us from the past. Yet that is what is done when the Gospel of John is read as a deliberately marginalizing document.

I would insist, then, that John cannot be said to marginalize "the Jews," since it speaks *from* the margin against the authorities whom it calls "the Jews." I have no interest in affixing blame here. It is not hard to see why a local group of Pharisees, vitally concerned for the survival of their people in the aftermath of the First Revolt, would exercise reasonable discipline against a disruptive group promoting a questionable theology. My only point is that John's literary "marginalizing" of these authorities within its text was an act of protest by a group that had utterly no power to marginalize anyone in reality. Indeed, this fact is one reason for John's extraordinary creation of a new reality, an ironic counterreality, in which the tables are turned, the outsiders are inside, the "ignorant rabble" (John 7:49) know the secret, the blind see and the sighted are blind (John 9:39–41). John's literary "marginalization" of "the Jews" is a sectarian response to the actual marginalization of a dissenting community.

But what happens when the revolution succeeds? Was Johannine language still ironic when it came to be wielded by a dominant, established church? Or had it become a language of literal inside and outside, above and below, triumph and powerlessness? When the heirs of marginal language become the establishment, the legitimacy of the language itself is lost if it is used in defense of an authoritarian position. If the now-established group continues to repeat the demonizing insider-versus-outsider language, the result will be new oppression, as the once rhetorical outsider is now a real outsider and placed in real jeopardy. Similarly, while Luke Johnson may be right about the context of Johannine and other early Christian slander within ancient rhetoric, the context changed when the new group became dominant over the old and sought to put its rhetoric into practice. At that point the polemic ceased to be merely the culturally standard abuse of one's opponents and came to be taken literally, as expressing salvation-historical and theological truth — a truth that the church was now in a position to enforce. The result was centuries of libel, racism, and genocide.

Thus while it is wrong to regard John as marginalizing "the Jews" in any meaningful sense in its own context, the ethical question about its language remains. As read by later Christians, John became a stimulus and an instrument of anti-Judaism and anti-Semitism. Its rhetorical counterreality left the written page and became the historical reality of dominant politics and power. I do not believe that this should lead us to condemn a Gospel emanating from an oppressed group as if it were oppressive, nor that it necessarily overwhelms the elements in John that are liberative. Nevertheless it must be asked whether John is an ethically adequate response to its situation of oppression.

The Fourth Gospel could be used as a tool of anti-Judaism only because its author had drenched it in demonizing invective. Kelber is right to call attention to the harm done to characters in John's story,[79] because these characters later came to be identified with people whose welfare was thereby put at risk. In seeking to preserve its own historical community by literarily demonizing others, John took a path whose end was, if unforeseen, nonetheless largely determined by these beginnings. The fact that its author was operating within the normal parameters of the sociology of sectarianism and the rhetoric of polemical abuse, and could not envision a Christian church empowered to use his words to wreak such destruction, may lessen his guilt. Even so, however, John serves as a very sobering reminder that words once written leave their writer's control, and that no one can expect to utter violent words without facing a violent consequence. The fourth evangelist's use of such violent language is, in the long view, difficult to defend, however much Christians may be inspired by his theology or scholars may be able to understand his historical reasons.

CONCLUSION

John and Anti-Judaism

The Gospel of John is not anti-Jewish in the sense of intending hostility toward Jewish people in general. This is because it comes from a time when its Christian author and readers did not yet consider themselves and their beliefs distinct from the Jewish people or Judaism, though John itself probably reflects that breach in the making. Its language, though unconscionably harsh to our ears, was not an instrument of oppression, since its speakers and hearers lacked the power to oppress anyone. Instead, this language was the response of a minority group to its own perceived oppression, feeling itself pushed to the outside and alienated from its own spiritual heritage. It is still fundamentally the language of a Jewish sect employed against other Jews in positions of authority. For this reason, I do not consider John's language anti-Jewish,

---

79. Kelber, "Metaphysics and Marginality in John," 153–54.

though there can be no doubt about its subsequent anti-Jewish effects. Striving to preserve and re-create the identity of a Jewish Christian community, the Fourth Gospel showed that community a way of retaining its heritage by relocating the meaning of that heritage in Jesus. In spite of its hostility toward the Pharisees — the authorities to whom the disparaging use of the phrase "the Jews" primarily refers — the Gospel represents a community that still regards itself as Israel, the same Israel that the Pharisees claimed to teach, "the people" for whom Jesus himself had first and foremost died.

I find little cause for Christian self-congratulation in this assessment, however. The brutal effects of this writer's drastic solution to his problem are all too plain for us to see. His vituperation against "the Jews" produces a distancing effect that must not be underestimated. The Johannine community may still consider themselves Israelites, and the Scriptures, Holy Days, and institutions of Judaism may still be so valued that they must be given new meaning in Jesus; but the fourth evangelist has set this community on a path toward the place where "the Jews" as such, and not just the religious authorities, will be thought of as the enemy. The move to complete separation, on both sides, is not far off now, when the new community of Jews, Samaritans, and Gentiles really does begin to think of itself apart from all connection with its community of origin. The result, however, will be not only the separate existence of Christianity as a new religion, but a grim history of anti-Judaism and anti-Semitism. That history, to the extent that it drew its impetus from John, resulted from misinterpretation of the Gospel in two senses. It was a misinterpretation because John in its original context was not meant to be destructive toward the Jewish people as a people; and it was a misinterpretation because it took a document intended to encourage an oppressed community and used it to foster oppression. The fact that John's language was used in ways not intended by its author does not excuse the author from responsibility for the harmful outcome, however; for violent deeds always need violent words to justify them.

What Shall We Do?

Christians are not going to stop reading and valuing the Gospel of John. What can be done, then, to bring this Gospel's violent consequences to an end? How can continued, authentic Christian use of this Gospel be prevented from arousing renewed storms of anti-Jewish behavior? This is a question often raised by scholars who have studied the question of

John and anti-Judaism,[80] and I do not claim much originality for what follows.

One solution sometimes proposed is to limit or modify the use of John in public worship, by altering the lectionaries and even the liturgies that Christian churches use, perhaps especially around Good Friday and Easter.[81] This approach has several drawbacks, however. It would require the cooperation and approval of a number of authorities in the various Christian communions. If carried through thoroughly, it could seriously restrict the use of a major text of the Christian Scriptures, since the problem is so pervasive in this Gospel. It would also be no help to Christians reading John privately. On the whole, though this might be a partial solution to the problem in some ways, in other ways it is merely an avoidance of it.

The fundamental difficulty is the constant designation of Jesus' opponents as οἱ Ἰουδαῖοι in John. For English readers and hearers to be presented constantly with "the Jews" as the adversaries of Jesus inevitably raises the possibility of misunderstanding him and his disciples as non-Jews, rejected and harassed by an entire uncomprehending people. Therefore one common suggestion is that the translation of this phrase be given more accurate nuance. In some places it might be rendered "Judeans," in others adjectivally ("Jewish festival" rather than "festival of the Jews"), in most as "Jewish leaders," or simply "the leaders" or "the authorities."[82] Norman Beck has made the most thoroughly worked-out proposals to date along these lines. Beck would render not only Ἰουδαῖοι but also "Pharisees" and "chief priests" by such terms as "some of the religious leaders," "many people," "Jesus' enemies," "those who opposed him," or often simply "they."[83]

There is certainly much to be said for this approach, particularly to the extent that it attempts to represent in English more accurately what John was actually saying. It also preserves the Johannine double reference to leaders or authorities, that is, to those of Jesus' day on the narrative level and to those of the Christian community's day

80. E.g., Epp, "Anti-Semitism and the Popularity of the Fourth Gospel," 55; Kysar, "Anti-Semitism and the Gospel of John," 124–27; von Wahlde, "The Gospel of John and the Presentation of Jews and Judaism," 83; Culpepper, "The Gospel of John as a Document of Faith," 115–16; see also Rensberger, *Johannine Faith and Liberating Community*, 139–40.

81. Beck, *Mature Christianity in the 21st Century*, 298, 300, 302, 308, 324.

82. D. G. Burke, "Translating *Hoi Ioudaioi* in the New Testament," *Explorations* 9, no. 2 (1995): 1–3.

83. Beck, *Mature Christianity in the 21st Century*, 290–309 passim.

on the level of the original readers. Yet it has the disadvantage of re-moving some of the power of interpretation from the modern reader. More seriously, it risks concealing how John's use of language distances the Johannine Christian community from people whom the Gospel does designate as "the Jews." The separation from Judaism that has begun to take place here ought not to be covered up by the translation. Indeed, if Beck's suggestions were carried out consistently, the Fourth Gospel, already considered abstract and "spiritual" by many, might lose its an-choring in history altogether. "What religion is it exactly," the puzzled reader might well ask, "of which these unpleasant people are the 'lead-ers'?" Some proposed revisions might even make matters worse, for example, rendering οἱ Ἰουδαῖοι "Jesus' own people."[84] The rejection of Jesus by "his own" (John 1:11) is one of the aspects of this Gospel that has done the most to create antipathy toward Jews among many Chris-tians, who ask whether "his own people" shouldn't have recognized the Messiah. Worse yet is the proposed transformation of the antagonistic "your law" (John 8:17; 10:34; cf. 15:25; 19:7) into "our law,"[85] which utterly misrepresents what the Gospel writer means to say.

Rendering Ἰουδαῖοι by "Jewish authorities" or the like may be the best of a bad set of choices in translating John, where one must decide between perpetuating a tradition of violence based on a false impres-sion and falsifying the violence that really is in the text.[86] What is meant by an "accurate" translation in such circumstances is a very difficult question. Precision with words is of the utmost importance in these complex and sensitive questions; yet we cannot possibly hope that even the most precisely nuanced translation will communicate John's mean-ing perfectly to everyone, or overcome the potential for anti-Judaism in this Gospel.

The most important task to be undertaken, I believe, is the clear and consistent explanation of what it is that John is saying and why it is say-ing this. That is, it must simply become common knowledge, especially among Christian readers, that John's negative portrayal of "the Jews" refers only to religious authorities of a certain place and time, under the specific historical conditions of a particular conflict. This explana-tion must also frankly acknowledge the ethically questionable nature of

---

84. Cook, "The Gospel of John and the Jews," 269; cf. Beck, *Mature Christianity in the 21st Century,* 305.

85. Cook, "The Gospel of John and the Jews," 269.

86. T. Pippin, "'For Fear of the Jews': Lying and Truth Telling in Translating the Gospel of John," *Semeia* 76 (1996): 81–97.

the Gospel's demonizing of its opponents. Such efforts are already going on at some levels, and should and no doubt will increase in the coming years. Christian biblical scholars, theologians, and ethicists have little problem making this adjustment, though we may sometimes need to remind ourselves that we too need to make it. For meaningful change to come about, however, the explanation must be put into the hands of Christians in general. Scholars who write for popular publications such as religious periodicals, Christian education materials, study Bibles, and Bible dictionaries have the opportunity to do this directly, as do those who teach college religion and religious studies classes. But perhaps the most important undertaking, although it will be accomplished more slowly, is the education of Christian pastors and teachers, who in turn have the responsibility of educating their congregations. This can be encouraged by instructions and guidelines coming from church officials, but will primarily take place in seminary classrooms and textbooks, and in the commentaries and lectionary guides to which preachers turn for information "on the fly." Here is one of the more important places where critical scholarship can and must begin breaking through the wall that has grown up between itself and the church at large, not as condescending to enlighten the benighted but as sincerely offering honest information to those in search of it.

What is needed most basically, however, is not a revision of Christian theology, liturgy, or biblical translation, or even an improved historical reading of John, but a movement of the will.[87] Christians must *want* to purge themselves and their churches of anti-Judaism and anti-Semitism; or, to put it more pointedly, we must *stop wanting* to be anti-Jewish or anti-Semitic. Scapegoating, triumphalism, and the general need for an enemy must be faced in ourselves and rooted out. There may be some reason to feel encouraged about the prospects for this movement.[88] I recently heard a colleague mention that when he teaches Christian laypeople, they seem able to understand John's christology well enough, but are puzzled and offended by the Gospel's hostile references to "the Jews." It will be such shifts in the Christian will and ethos, away from a sense of anti-Judaism as a natural component of Christianity, that will make it possible for better theological and historical explanations to be effective.

---

87. Cf. Idinopulos and Ward, "Is Christology Inherently Anti-Semitic?" 204–5, 209–10.

88. Beck, *Mature Christianity in the 21st Century,* 325–28.

In the end, Gentile, especially European, Christians must shoulder the responsibility for our own acts of oppression and ideologies of racism, rather than trying to saddle the *Jewish* founders of our religion with them. As long as the rhetoric of critique, dissent, and controversy remained internal to Judaism, however far short it may have fallen of the biblical ideal of mutual love, it had no power to defame and destroy an entire people, especially when those who wielded it were a relatively powerless minority themselves. Only when *we* acquired the rhetoric, made it canonical, and failed to exercise even the historical sense culturally available at the time did *we* turn it into something not only potentially evil but actually so. It is therefore up to us to right the wrong, not by reading it back into texts that still knew nothing of it (even though the seeds of it are there), but by contemplating our own historical need for enemies and scapegoats and the way it has twisted disputes within Judaism into an anti-Judaism made to serve ourselves.

Response to David Rensberger

Questions about a Jewish Johannine Community

Mark Goodwin

Professor David Rensberger, in his "Anti-Judaism and the Gospel of John," has made a valuable contribution to our understanding of John and its anti-Jewish effects upon later Christian readers. He has done so by making the claim that John was not anti-Jewish in its first-century setting and yet ended up contributing to the development of Christian anti-Judaism. In this claim, Rensberger has offered a fresh approach to thinking about anti-Judaism and John, one that will be given attention in the first section of the following discussion. The discussion will also examine Rensberger's social-historical argument in favor of a Jewish Johannine group, beginning, in the second section, with a review of critical evidence used in supporting this claim and concluding, in the third section, with an assessment of the strengths and weaknesses of the historical argument. While the evidence in favor of a Jewish Johannine community is strong, there remain some nagging questions about the "Jewish" character of this community in its late first-century setting.

Anti-Judaism As a Problem of John's Violent Language and Christian Misreading

In Rensberger's view, John is closely associated with the problem of Christian anti-Judaism, since "John contains some of the most repellent statements about Jews to be found in the New Testament"; further, "There can be no doubt about its subsequent anti-Jewish effects."[1] Despite this problem of John's language, however, John cannot be viewed as anti-Jewish in its setting, because the Johannine community existed as a first-century Jewish group that did not perceive itself as a separate

---

1. David Rensberger, "Anti-Judaism and the Gospel of John," in this volume, 121, 153.

"Christian" entity. According to Rensberger, the fourth evangelist "did not yet regard his Christianity as a new or separate religion, but considered it to be Judaism."[2] John's polemic, then, in its first-century setting, should be viewed as part of an intra-Jewish debate that arose after the lifetime of Jesus in the late first century.

In clarifying the social setting of this Jewish Johannine community, Rensberger makes use of his own liberationist approach, developed from his earlier work in *Johannine Faith and Liberating Community*.[3] He observes that the Johannine community was a persecuted and oppressed Jewish minority that had no power to harm those who persecuted them. Johannine polemic against "the Jews" should therefore be read as the dissenting voice of a marginalized group that had no intent of persecuting adversaries; the polemic of the Gospel "was an act of protest by a group that had utterly no power to marginalize anyone in reality."[4] Thus the Gospel's violent polemic, directed against "the Jews," is language used in the service of dissent and innovation, but not in the service of fostering physical violence against the synagogue.

According to Rensberger, then, the problem of anti-Judaism in the Fourth Gospel is not the problem of the Jewish Johannine community perpetrating physical violence against its Jewish opponents; rather, it is a problem of the Gospel's violent language, which arose in response to the community's experience of hostility and persecution by synagogue authorities. More specifically, the problem concerns the vicious demonizing of opponents, which has had implications beyond its original historical context. As Rensberger observes, "John serves as a very sobering reminder that words once written leave their writer's control."[5]

Therefore, although the Fourth Gospel is not anti-Jewish in its original outlook, the group's response to its experience of persecution, nonetheless, remains ethically questionable. As a response to persecution, the demonizing rhetoric of the Fourth Gospel was part of a solution that went far beyond the historical problem, and so the author of the Fourth Gospel has to assume some of the responsibility for the brutal effects of this rhetoric: "In seeking to preserve its own historical community by literally demonizing others, John took a path whose end was, if unforeseen, nonetheless largely determined by these

---

2. Ibid., 138.
3. *Johannine Faith and Liberating Community* (Philadelphia: Westminster, 1988); see esp. pp. 109–13.
4. Rensberger, "Anti-Judaism and the Gospel of John," 151.
5. Ibid., 152.

beginnings."[6] The consequences of Johannine polemic may have been unintended, but they are, nonetheless, real.

A good example of this ethically questionable Johannine language producing unintended (anti-Jewish) consequences is found in the Gospel's many references to "the Jews." Although many occurrences of "the Jews" are neutral and not overtly negative, those references that are negative tend to color the overall impression of the term for later readers. Rensberger maintains that "the negative usage of Ἰουδαῖοι is bound to color the neutral and positive ones, so that the distancing effect carries over to them as well."[7] This distancing effect is seen in specific instances in the Fourth Gospel; for example, following Kelber's insight, "the Jews" can be taken as indicative of a false principle of reality, serving to magnify the potential or actual anti-Judaism to cosmic proportions. This negative effect also creates the impression of a non-Jewish Jesus set in stark contrast to "the Jews": "By using this designation [the Jews] for Jesus' opponents, John creates a fundamental opposition that makes Jesus appear not to be a Jew at all."[8]

In Rensberger's view, however, John's violent language is not the sole factor leading to anti-Judaism. The problem of John's language has to be understood in tandem with later Christian readers who were willing to read in anti-Jewish ways. More precisely, Rensberger speaks of the reader's social location as a significant factor in later misreadings of the Gospel: "Social location is an important factor in the interpretation of John, and this applies not only to the social location of the Gospel writer and the characters in the story, but to that of its modern readers as well."[9] Rensberger here is concerned not so much with a literary hermeneutic as with a liberationist hermeneutic in which readers are influenced by unconscious ideological factors that significantly shape their preunderstanding.[10] In other words, John's readers, modern or otherwise, are significantly influenced by the social location from which they read, a social location that has been radically changed with respect to the original social location of the Gospel.

---

6. Ibid., 152.

7. Ibid., 125.

8. Ibid., 134.

9. Ibid., 122.

10. For assessments of Rensberger's position as "liberationist," see Jeffrey L. Staley, "Reading Myself, Reading the Text: The Johannine Passion Narrative in Postmodern Perspective," and R. Alan Culpepper, "The Gospel of John as a Document of Faith in a Pluralistic Culture," in *"What Is John?": Readers and Readings of the Fourth Gospel*, SBLSymS 3, ed. Fernando F. Segovia (Atlanta: Scholars Press, 1996), 64–65 and 119–21, respectively.

This point about social location affecting the reader is easy to accept if one thinks of postbiblical Christian readers who were predominantly Gentile in character and who read the Fourth Gospel anachronistically, assuming that Judaism and Christianity were separate religious entities when John was written. This anachronistic Gentile perspective would have predominated by the second century and thus affected the reading of the Fourth Gospel in significant ways. Eldon Epp makes the point, asking us to imagine "the impression made upon Gentile Christians from the second century on by a gospel that speaks repeatedly of 'the Jews' as the persecutors and murderers of Jesus Christ the Lord of the Church!"[11] Christian anti-Judaism, then, is abetted, in part, by a process of postbiblical Christian readers misreading the Fourth Gospel from their own Gentile social locations, the result being that the original intra-Jewish polemic of John is mistaken as something directed against "the Jews."

Further, Rensberger understands social location in terms of the political status of the reading community. If the Johannine community found itself to be an oppressed Jewish minority in the first century, this certainly was not the status of later Gentile Christians, who became part of an increasingly dominant religious group in the Roman empire. By the time of Constantine, for example, Christian readers of John found themselves as a politically empowered group, a status that significantly affected how the Fourth Gospel was interpreted. In a process of ironic reversal, the original social location of the marginalized Johannine group was lost and misread from the social location of a later dominant Christianity. The polemic of an originally marginalized Johannine group is misread in support of later programs of political domination and oppression. In other words, John ends up being misread from the perspective of the empowered, rather than being viewed from its original perspective of the marginalized and oppressed.

In summary, then, Rensberger has advanced the discussion of John and anti-Judaism by focusing attention on key factors that make the Fourth Gospel anti-Jewish. Although John cannot be considered anti-Jewish in its original historical setting, it is nonetheless implicated in the development of Christian anti-Judaism through its ethically questionable use of polemic against Jewish opponents. The language of the Fourth Gospel had, as it were, anti-Jewish potential in its violent

---

11. Eldon J. Epp, "Anti-Semitism and the Popularity of the Fourth Gospel in Christianity," *CCARJ* 22 (1975): 42.

polemic against "the Jews," and this potential was eventually actualized in later Christian reception.

However, in Rensberger's view it is also clear that anti-Judaism cannot be understood apart from postbiblical readers who were willing to misread in anti-Jewish ways, and here the factor of social location plays a significant role. From a later Gentile perspective, the original Jewish sectarian protest of the Gospel was misread as literal opposition to "the Jews," who were understood as a different ethnic-religious group. In other words, anti-Judaism involves a process in which later Christian readers lost sight of the original Jewish setting of John and ironically mistook the Gospel's intra-Jewish polemic as something anti-Jewish. It is therefore John's ethically questionable language in combination with the changed social location of later readers that contributed to the development of Christian anti-Judaism.

One implication of this assessment is worth noting. It would seem that a crucial factor in Christian anti-Judaism is found in the postbiblical period, from the second century on, when Christian readers were reading John in anti-Jewish ways. This would mean that the issue of John and anti-Judaism necessarily extends beyond the study of John's original historical setting and includes a study of the later Christian reception of the Gospel. The issue of John and anti-Judaism necessarily entails some insight into the effect of the Gospel's language upon later Christian readers and the process by which these readers came to misread. Subsequent treatments of John and anti-Judaism would thus do well to consider the effect of the Fourth Gospel in postbiblical Christian tradition, perhaps through an examination of its reception history *(Wirkungsgeschichte)*.

In terms of some minor criticisms a few points in Rensberger's discussion need clarification, especially the point concerning the hermeneutical process of misreading which remain largely undiscussed and unexplained. What exactly is "social location" as a hermeneutical factor in Rensberger's thinking, and how does it influence the reading process? How determinative is social location in affecting the reading process?

Further, Rensberger's discussion could have been sharpened by offering some concrete illustrations of Christian readers misreading John in anti-Jewish ways. Where exactly in later Christian interpretation of the Gospel do we find John being misread in anti-Jewish ways? Do patristic authors, for example, in their handling of John, confirm Rensberger's claims? Are there examples in the *Adversus Judaeos* tradition that demonstrate John as a factor in anti-Jewish polemic? Does the use of John in later Christian liturgy somehow influence readers to read in anti-Jewish ways?

Despite these minor criticisms, Rensberger has furnished a fresh way of thinking about how anti-Judaism developed in post-biblical Christian communities.

THE HISTORICAL CASE FOR A JEWISH JOHANNINE COMMUNITY

In Rensberger's assessment of John and anti-Judaism, he accords fundamental significance to the use of historical exegesis. The value of historical exegesis is evident in several respects, including its function as a corrective to the ahistorical interpretations of exclusively literary approaches, where historical conditions are not allowed to affect the interpretation. Further, the use of historical exegesis is not only a matter of accuracy, but also a matter of justice: "Care for a true understanding of the historical circumstances of a document's origin is not only a matter of accurate scholarship, but also a matter of justice.... It is unjust to misrepresent the voice of the oppressed as that of the oppressor, even when that voice comes to us from the past."[12]

The real benefit of historical exegesis for Rensberger, however, is found in its wider function of providing a criterion by which later anti-Jewish misreading can be recognized. Anti-Jewish misreadings of John become clear only against the background of the Gospel's original (historical) significance. As he notes, "Recognizing the location of the Gospel's original author and readers provides a vital clue to later readers in other locations about what this language meant once, and, given an accountable hermeneutic, that meaning can be an important aid in avoiding harmful interpretations now."[13] In other words, the original historical meaning of the Fourth Gospel provides the crucial corrective to an anti-Jewish misreading of John by providing a point of reference against which later anti-Jewish readings become recognizable.

Given this important function of historical exegesis in Rensberger's approach, it will be helpful to take a close look at his historical reconstruction of the Johannine community, in particular, his claims in favor of a Jewish Johannine group. What is the evidence that supports his conclusion of a Jewish Johannine group? In supporting his claims Rens-

---

12. Ibid., 150; cf. 130.
13. Ibid., 138.

berger has drawn upon three kinds of evidence from the Gospel: the three references to expulsion from the synagogue; the Gospel's familiarity with Jewish traditions and beliefs; and sociological evidence that marks John as the product of a Jewish sectarian group.[14]

Taking up the first type of evidence, Rensberger reconstructs John's setting in history based on references to expulsion from the synagogue (John 9:22; 12:42; 16:2), and Rensberger here follows a consensus portrait established by J. Louis Martyn and others, who read the Gospel as a two level drama consisting of events from the life of Jesus and from the later setting of the Johannine community.[15] It is the latter level that provides the context for understanding the expulsion reports: "The references to expulsion refer to events decades after Jesus' time, in the experience of the Gospel writer's own Christian community."[16]

For Rensberger, as for many scholars, expulsion from the synagogue is "the determinative factor in the milieu of the Johannine Christian community."[17] This event of exclusion from the synagogue was the result of conflict between the Johannine group and the synagogue over certain christological claims made about Jesus: "Authorities who belonged to the Pharisees were putting those who openly asserted that Jesus was the Messiah out of the synagogue."[18] The conflict erupted not only in expulsion, but also in the persecution of Johannine Christians, as is suggested in John 16:2: "They will put you out of synagogues. Indeed, an hour is coming when those who kill you will think that by doing so they are offering worship to God." The significance of these expulsion reports in John is clear for Rensberger: they suggest the Jewish roots of the Johannine community. The threat of expulsion could have such dire meaning only for Jews: If members of the Johannine community "had not still felt themselves to be Jewish, it is hard to understand why they would have been so concerned about their exclusion from the synagogue."[19]

Rensberger further maintains that the expulsion references offer critical hints about the Gospel's chronological relation to the expulsion

---

14. Rensberger (*Johannine Faith and Liberating Community*, 25–30) furnishes a review of the recent scholarly views on the Johannine community.

15. Rensberger, *Johannine Faith and Liberating Community*, 22, 26. Robert Kysar has a good summary of Martyn's positions and the consensus that has developed around it (*The Fourth Evangelist and His Gospel: An Examination of Contemporary Scholarship* [Minneapolis: Augsburg, 1975], 149–56).

16. Rensberger, "Anti-Judaism and the Gospel of John," 127.

17. Rensberger, *Johannine Faith and Liberating Community*, 25.

18. Rensberger, "Anti-Judaism and the Gospel of John," 129.

19. Ibid., 139.

event. According to Rensberger, the expulsion event reflects a conflict
that was just beginning when John was written, rather than a conflict
that has already occurred:

> The Gospel does not seem to be so much concerned with what
> believers should do after they are expelled (as if this has already
> happened). . . . This suggests that these passages are not an etiology
> from a later vantage point, explaining how the Christian commu-
> nity had come to be separated from the synagogue, but rather that
> they come from a time when expulsion of confessing Christians
> had begun but had not been completely carried out."[20]

The implication is clear for Rensberger: If the expulsion is not viewed as
a past event, then it reflects a Johannine group that is still part of and in
close connection with the synagogue.

The second type of evidence favoring a Jewish Johannine community concerns the Jewish character of the Gospel, an observation that
has been widely made in New Testament scholarship.[21] Major ideas and
symbols in the Fourth Gospel are undeniably derived from Judaism, not
to mention the Johannine style of using scripture, which is reminiscent
of Jewish exegetical tradition.[22] Rensberger notes that "Jewish Holy
Days, and traditions associated with them, are mentioned with such
minimal explanation that readers unconversant with Judaism would be
largely in the dark," and that "John does not dispute the continuing
legitimacy of Passover, Sabbath, and other Jewish observances."[23] Further, the debates over Jesus' identity in the Gospel are expressed in
Jewish terms: obedience to God, knowledge of God, Moses, the meaning of the Scriptures, and so forth. Even Johannine christology, in all
its uniqueness, can be understood in connection with Jewish roots. For
example, John's assertions about Jesus' divinity, that is, being equal to

---

20. Ibid., 127.

21. C. H. Dodd, *The Interpretation of the Fourth Gospel* (Cambridge: Cambridge University Press, 1953), 74–96; Wayne Meeks, " 'Am I a Jew?' — Johannine Christianity and
Judaism," in *Christianity, Judaism, and Other Greco-Roman Cults: Studies For Morton
Smith at Sixty*, ed. J. Neusner (Leiden: E. J. Brill, 1975), 163–86, esp. 167–79; Urban C.
von Wahlde, "The Gospel of John and the Presentation of Jews and Judaism," in *Within
Context: Essays on Jews and Judaism in the New Testament*, ed. D. Efroymson, E. Fisher,
and L. Klenicki (Collegeville, Minn.: Liturgical Press, 1993), 68–69.

22. Meeks (" 'Am I a Jew?' " 175–76) discusses similarities of style between John and
Jewish exegetical traditions. Detailed study of this similarity can be found in Peder Borgen,
*Bread from Heaven: An Exegetical Study of the Concept of Manna in the Gospel of John
and the Writings of Philo*, NovTSup 10 (Leiden: E. J. Brill, 1965).

23. Rensberger, "Anti-Judaism and the Gospel of John," 126, 140.

God (John 5:18; 10:33), have precedent among certain Jewish groups that promoted the teaching of "two powers in heaven"[24]

Finally, Rensberger incorporates a third kind of evidence into his discussion: "John is, in sociological terms, a sectarian document, which means that it portrays a conflict over sectarian heresy from the *heretics'* point of view."[25] Viewing the Johannine group as a sect is significant for Rensberger because a sect, sociologically speaking, would still be part of the dominant Jewish culture as one of a variety of competing groups within first century Judaism.

While not delving into an explicit discussion of the Johannine group as Jewish sect, Rensberger repeatedly makes mention of sectarian features that characterize the group, drawing upon the work of other scholars.[26] Thus the Johannine community is a group of Johannine sectarians and their language is sectarian protest. Rensberger provides a fuller treatment of this issue in his earlier work *Johannine Faith and Liberating Community,* concluding that "it seems unavoidable that we regard the Johannine community as a sect, at least in relation to Judaism."[27] The Johannine group is a Jewish sect that has turned inward on itself, renounced the world, and established a separate community.

Sectarian character is also evident in the Gospel's reinterpretation of Jewish symbols in subordination to Jesus. This reinterpretation of Jewish symbols attests to the struggle of the Johannine group to retain possession of its Jewish heritage in conflict with other Jews. According to Rensberger, John's gathering up of Jewish values into Jesus had a more defensive than offensive purpose, since the Johannine community had suffered dispossession from its Jewish heritage. This reinterpretation of the Jewish heritage served to "sustain a group of Jewish sectarians by newly interpreting for them what still seemed their common inheritance as Jews."[28]

Summarizing Rensberger's results: He has marshaled a formidable array of evidence in favor of a Jewish Johannine group. In assessing the

---

24. Alan F. Segal, *Two Powers in Heaven: Early Rabbinic Reports about Christianity and Gnosticism* (Leiden: E. J. Brill, 1977). Segal infers from rabbinic literature the existence of Jewish sects that violated the essential premise of Jewish monotheism by speaking of angelic mediator figures in close association with God.

25. Rensberger, "Anti-Judaism and the Gospel of John," 150.

26. For example, Wayne A. Meeks, "The Man From Heaven in Johannine Sectarianism," in *The Interpretation of John,* ed. John Ashton (Philadelphia: Fortress, 1986), 160–65; Raymond Brown, *The Community of the Beloved Disciple* (New York: Paulist Press, 1979), 14–17.

27. Rensberger, *Johannine Faith and Liberating Community,* 28.

28. Rensberger, "Anti-Judaism and the Gospel of John," 146.

three types of evidence, it is clear that the first two types are the most compelling. The expulsion reports in the Gospel undeniably reflect the community's origins in a local synagogue; the Gospel's familiarity with Jewish beliefs and symbols confirms the Jewish character of the Johannine group. Rensberger is thus successful in showing that the Johannine group, at the earliest stages in its history, perceived itself from within a Jewish perspective. When all is said and done, the Gospel of John "unhesitatingly affirms the Jewish origin of its Christian faith: 'salvation is from the Jews,' " and "comes from a time when its Christian author and readers did not yet consider themselves and their beliefs distinct from the Jewish people or Judaism, though John itself probably reflects that breach in the making."[29]

ASSESSMENT OF THE JOHANNINE GROUP IN ITS LATE FIRST-CENTURY SETTING

While Rensberger has made a compelling case in favor of a Jewish Johannine community, some nagging questions remain. There are certain elements in the Gospel that do not square with the reality of a Jewish Johannine group, and Rensberger, to his credit, recognizes these problematic elements. He notes, for example, several references made by Jesus to the Torah as "your law" or "their law," indicating a possible breach with Jewish identity (John 7:19, 51; 8:17; 10:34; 15:25; 18:31; 19:7). Commenting on these points, Rensberger admits that "here we do seem to see a new identity being created, one that centers not on Torah, but on Jesus."[30]

This kind of evidence calls into question Rensberger's claim of a Jewish Johannine community, a claim that can be maintained only in a qualified sense. Rensberger himself recognizes the need for qualification, explaining that

John comes from a unique, transitional period that belonged neither to the purely inner-Jewish sectarianism of Christianity's earliest days ... nor yet to the fully separate religion that Christian-

---

29. Ibid., 127, 152.
30. Ibid., 141. Many scholars cite these references to the Law as evidence of an emerging Christian consciousness (for example, Raymond Brown, *The Gospel According to John I–XII*, AB 29 [New York: Doubleday, 1966], lxxii). Brown (*The Community of the Beloved Disciple*, 41) observes that "the Jesus who speaks of 'the Jews' (13:33) and of what is written in 'their law' (15:25; see 10:34) is speaking the language of the Johannine Christian for whom the Law is no longer his own but is the hallmark of another religion."

ity became.... The notion of John as internal prophetic critique
within Judaism does not do full justice to the estrangement from
Torah and synagogue that, whatever its origin, so strongly characterizes this Gospel.... John is at the point of separation between
Christianity and Judaism.[31]

In Rensberger's view, then, the evidence points to a Jewish Johannine
group that is in the process of transition.

    In response to this claim, however, one may ask whether this group
has not already separated from Judaism. John Townsend is one of several scholars who conclude that the Johannine group had transcended
its Jewish roots by the time of the final form of the Gospel:[32]

> Jesus and his earliest followers were Jews; yet... by the time that
> the Gospel of John had reached its present form, the Johannine
> community no longer considered itself Jewish. Since the movement
> of the community was away from Judaism, the Gospel's relatively
> pro-Jewish elements must belong to the earlier stages of its devel-
> opment, while the more anti-Jewish aspects would have entered
> the text with later editing.[33]

Townsend is not alone in this conclusion. Alan Culpepper observes that
"the 'prophetic critique' or 'intra-Jewish' debate positions do not recognize the extent of the breach with Judaism that is already reflected
in John"; Paula Fredriksen perceives that "this Gospel... is written by
someone who consciously placed himself outside, if not against Judaism" (although she adds that this does not necessarily mean that the
author was not Jewish); and John Gager, referring to Jews in the Gospel who believe in Jesus, concludes that "within the total framework of
the Gospel this [belief in Jesus] surely means that such individuals cease
thereby to be Jews."[34]

---

31. Rensberger, "Anti-Judaism and the Gospel of John," 142.
32. John T. Townsend, "The Gospel of John and the Jews: The Story of a Religious Divorce," in *Antisemitism and the Foundation of Christianity*, ed. A. T. Davies (New York:
Paulist Press, 1979), 72–97.
33. Ibid., 83.
34. R. Alan Culpepper, "The Gospel of John as Threat to Jewish-Christian Relations,"
in *Overcoming Fear between Jews and Christians*, ed. J. H. Charlesworth (New York:
Crossroad, 1992), 40; John Gager, *The Origins of Anti-Semitism: Attitudes toward Judaism in Pagan and Christian Antiquity* (Oxford: Oxford University Press, 1983), 153; Paula
Fredriksen, *From Jesus to Christ: The Origins of the New Testament Images of Jesus* (New
Haven: Yale University Press, 1988), 25.

Townsend's comments also remind us that the question of the Johannine group's identity is closely bound up with the complex literary character of the Fourth Gospel itself. It has been observed that the composition of the Fourth Gospel is characterized by different editorial stages, reflecting different periods in the history of the Johannine community, even if these periods cannot be reconstructed with any certainty.[35] The question, then, of a Jewish Johannine community, is considerably complicated when viewed in this light, since we are likely dealing with a first-century community that was not static in its identity, but that underwent changes and developments.

One such development in the life of the Johannine community came as the result of expulsion from the synagogue, as noted above. But the problem here is that the expulsion reports in John do not furnish details about the event, thus leaving us in the dark as to its precise significance. For example, what is the chronological relation between the event of expulsion and the composition of the Gospel? Does the Gospel in its final form look back on expulsion as a past event from a vantage point outside of the synagogue, or was it written, as Rensberger claims, just as the expulsion was about to begin (that is, from within the synagogue)? How pivotal was the expulsion in defining a new sense of identity in the Johannine community?

Admittedly, there are no conclusive answers to these questions, but it is possible to take the expulsion reports as indicative of a final break between the Johannine community and Judaism (against Rensberger). For example, Raymond Brown has concluded that, at the time of the writing of the Gospel (ca. 90), "the expulsion from the synagogue is now past but persecution (16:2–3) continues and there are deep scars in the Johannine psyche regarding 'the Jews.' "[36] Further, the recurring themes of division and alienation in John 5–12 would seem to support a Johannine perspective that is rooted in a painful past experience of displacement from the synagogue.

The latter view has been given its classic expression by Wayne Meeks, who understands the Gospel as an etiology of the Johannine group following its painful dislocation from the synagogue, and who interprets the figure of Jesus in the Gospel as a cipher for the community's own

---

35. Urban C. von Wahlde ("Presentation of Jews and Judaism," 67–72) discusses the Gospel's editorial history as essential in understanding the relation of the Gospel to anti Judaism. According to von Wahlde, the final edition of the Gospel was composed after expulsion from the synagogue, leading to the formation of "a separate, independent group apart from Judaism."

36. R. Brown, *Community of the Beloved Disciple*, 23.

sense of alienation from its synagogal home.[37] Meeks observes in John the story of

> the progressive alienation of Jesus from the Jews. But something else is happening, for there are some few who respond to Jesus' signs and words, and these... are progressively enlightened and drawn into intense intimacy with Jesus, until they, like him, are not "of this world." Now their becoming detached from the world is, in the Gospel, identical with their being detached from Judaism. Those figures who want to believe in Jesus but to remain within the Jewish community and the Jewish piety are damned with the most devastatingly dualistic epithets.... Coming to faith in Jesus is for the Johannine group a change in social location. Mere belief without joining the Johannine community, without making the decisive break with "the world," particularly the world of Judaism, is a diabolical "lie."[38]

The Gospel, in other words, reflects the experience, already past, of being displaced from participation in Jewish life; and separation from the synagogue was traumatic and pivotal, forcing the Johannine community into a process of redefinition, a process that involved a radical reinterpretation of its Jewish roots.

In reading the Fourth Gospel, then, we are, it seems, faced with a community whose identity is in the process of a redefinition that will eventually move it beyond its Jewish past. The problem facing modern interpreters, however, is in understanding the exact nature of this transformation and at what point Johannine identity ceased perceiving itself in relation to the synagogue. What does it mean to call such a group "Jewish" during this unique process of transformation? Unfortunately, conclusive answers are not possible, given the paucity and ambiguity of evidence in John. Bound up with this issue is the more fundamental problem of defining what was meant by "Jewish" and "Christian" in the unique and unreproducible environment of the late first century.

Nonetheless, David Rensberger has made a compelling case that the Fourth Gospel is the product of a Jewish group whose polemic was anti-Jewish in its effects upon later Christian readers. However, his conclusions that this group remained Jewish in the late first century are less certain and open to further discussion. One wonders what it means to

---

37. Wayne A. Meeks, "The Man From Heaven," 141–73, esp. 163.
38. Ibid., 162–63.

call this Johannine group "Jewish" in its late first-century setting. What kind of Jewish group stands displaced from the synagogue and estranged from Torah? What kind of Jewish group makes christological claims that are blasphemous to Jewish ears (e.g., John 8:58–59; 10:33)? Unless these questions can be addressed, it will be difficult to arrive at any definite conclusions on the issue of John and anti-Judaism.

RESPONSE TO
DAVID RENSBERGER

Thomas D. Lea

THE 8 JULY 1996 issue of *Time* contained a political commentary explaining why Bill Clinton has been impervious to numerous charges of scandal during his term in office. Entitled "Your Own Man Says So!" the commentary explained that "every incumbent 20th-century president who has been seriously challenged for renomination winds up either losing or retiring."[1] The commentator pointed out that most of the charges against Clinton have come from Republicans. He added, "If some of his [Clinton's] own men begin to make that case, however, it's a whole new ball game."[2] The author's point is that external criticism of a political leader may be nasty and vicious, but it is not damaging. Although the author does not specifically say so, he implies that the public expects external criticism to be unbalanced. Using the American political experience as a paradigm, we might say that criticism of Democrats by Republicans would be anti-Democratic. We may view criticism of Democrats by Democrats as an internal feud, but not necessarily as anti-Democratic.

In discussing the presence of anti-Judaism in the Gospel of John, Professor Rensberger declines to name the criticism of the Jews in the Gospel as anti-Judaism. His basic reason is that "the hostility that John expresses is fundamentally that of one group toward others within the same religious/ethnic entity."[3] He points out that the author and readers did not yet regard Christianity as a new or separate religion, but considered it to *be* Judaism. He views the critique of Judaism within the Fourth Gospel as an in-house squabble, but not a bashing of Judaism by an external enemy. If we adopt the definition of anti-Judaism suggested for contributors to this volume, his views are correct.

---

1. Jeff Greenfield, "Your Own Man Says So!" *Time,* 8 July 1996, 27.
2. Ibid.
3. David Rensberger, "Anti-Judaism and the Gospel of John," in this volume, 139.

Rensberger comes to his conclusions after a well thought out survey of potential anti-Jewish elements in the Fourth Gospel. He admits that John contains some of the most repellent statements about Jews to be found in the New Testament. As evidence for this, he discusses the use of the term "the Jews" in the Fourth Gospel. Admitting that the term is used with more than one sense, he nevertheless observes that many of the usages show hostility by the writer toward "the Jews." He explains this as primarily due to John's setting in history. He believes that John's Gospel was not accurately describing Jewish opposition to Jesus in Jesus' lifetime, but was portraying events occurring decades after Jesus' time in the experience of the writer's own Christian community. Thus he perceives that John wrote with a two-level view, one view reflecting incidents in Jesus' lifetime and the other reflecting incidents in the lifetime of the writer.

Rensberger's concluding statements emphasize that John's Gospel "comes from a time when its Christian author and readers did not yet consider themselves and their beliefs distinct from the Jewish people or Judaism, though John itself probably reflects that breach in the making. Its language, though unconscionably harsh to our ears, was not an instrument of oppression, since its speakers and hearers lacked the power to oppress anyone."[4] He laments the language of John's Gospel having been used in ways not intended by its author to contribute to anti-Semitism. But he will not excuse the author from all responsibility for that outcome, because "violent deeds always need violent words to justify them."[5]

I agree enthusiastically with Rensberger that the Fourth Gospel is not anti-Jewish, but for different reasons. I find Rensberger's hesitancy to endorse the historical reliability of John's Gospel unwarranted. John's Gospel gives, I believe, a historically reliable picture of the opposition to Jesus: *Ioudaioi* ("Jews") as groups of leaders and as groups of commoners; John also has an ethnic use of *Ioudaios* (as opposed, for example, to "Samaritan") and the geographical term *Ioudaia* ("Judea"). All appearances of the term "the Jews" in the Fourth Gospel can be understood within these four classifications. The writer of the Fourth Gospel did not have a theologically driven antipathy toward the Jews, but he did disagree with their religious teaching. He has also portrayed, accurately,

---

4. Ibid., 152.
5. Ibid., 153.

I believe, that various groups of the Jewish people disagreed with the teaching of Jesus.

I also question Rensberger's use of the two-level reading proposal of J. L. Martyn. He suggests that in some manner the authorities who belonged to the Pharisees were expelling from the synagogue those who asserted that Jesus was the Messiah. He hints that this occurred at a time later than the lifetime of Jesus. But the process of expelling heretics from the synagogue need not be relegated only to the lifetime of the writer; it may also have occurred during the life of Jesus.

W. Horbury argues that a benediction against heretics had long been in existence in the synagogues.[6] And other scholars are much more cautious about dating the synagogal disciplinary action in John to a time later than the life of Jesus.[7] If the expulsion occurred during Jesus' life, then we may have more confidence that the writer was accurately picturing a response of Jews to Jesus.

With Rensberger, I reject erroneous interpretations of John's text by those who would find in the language of the Gospel a basis to justify racial hatred of the Jews (see, e.g., John 8:44). Only a perverted hermeneutic could find in the language of John a basis for contempt toward the Jews.

Rensberger wants the writer of John's Gospel to share the blame for some of the anti-Judaic actions that have occurred in history. He feels that some of John's language has been used to foment hatred of the Jews, and he credits the author of John with some responsibility for the later misuse of his more "extreme" statements. I do not deny that some people have used the language of John to justify racial hatred of the Jews. I lament this unfortunate state of affairs. What I disagree with is holding the author of John accountable for their actions.

Rensberger's words suggest that a writer should be held accountable for using terms that unbalanced people later take to justify their actions. Abolitionist John Brown used the words of Heb. 9:22 ("without the shedding of blood there is no forgiveness") to justify his urging the murder of five Kansans in the Pottawatomie Massacres in 1856.[8] Might a principle of authorial accountability for nonauthorial action compel us

---

6. William Horbury, "The Benediction of the *Minim* and Early Jewish-Christian Controversy," *JTS* 33 (1982): 19–61.

7. D. A. Carson, *The Gospel According to John* (Grand Rapids: Eerdmans, 1991), 369–72; G. R. Beasley-Murray, *John,* Word Biblical Commentary (Waco, Tex.: Word, 1987), lxxvi–lxxviii.

8. Alan Nevins, *Ordeal of the Union,* vol. 2, *A House Dividing, 1852–57* (New York: Charles Scribner's Sons, 1947), 475.

to excise Heb. 9:22 from Scripture because an unbalanced person later used it to justify homicide? It is not necessary to blame the author of Hebrews for the Pottawatomie Massacres, and it is not necessary to blame the writer of the Fourth Gospel for the Holocaust.

I agree with Rensberger that the writer of the Fourth Gospel did not practice anti-Judaism in the sense of a theologically driven attitude toward the Jews. But I do believe that the writer of the Fourth Gospel disagreed with the beliefs and practices of some Jews in his day and in Jesus' day, and that he designated some of those who differed with him as "the Jews." His purpose was not to show contempt toward these people, but to demonstrate a theological difference between Christians and those Jews who opposed the burgeoning Christian movement.

❦ F • O • U • R ❦

SOMETHING GREATER THAN
THE TEMPLE
Robert Louis Wilken

F OR TWO GENERATIONS Christian theology has been engaged in a fundamental rethinking of Christianity's relation to Judaism and to the
Jewish people. This work has been carried out by biblical scholars, by
historians of Christian thought, by theologians, by Christian educators,
and by bishops and other leaders of the various Christian communions.
It has dealt with technical points of biblical exegesis, profound questions of dogmatic theology, and, not least, with how words and images
and ideas influence the attitudes of the faithful.[1] Whether one thinks of
the "Nostra Aetate" decree of Vatican Council II and other Catholic
statements over the last two decades.[2] the various declarations of the
World Council of Churches and Protestant denominations,[3] or more recently the historic meeting of Orthodox Christians and Jews in Athens
in 1993,[4] the depth and seriousness of Christian engagement with the
Jews is unprecedented in Christian history. Something very new and
extraordinary has taken place in our lifetimes.

We must not, however, forget that this new movement of the Spirit
was born out of Jewish suffering and of the struggles of the Jewish

---

1. See Eugene J. Fisher, *Faith without Prejudice: Rebuilding Christian Attitudes toward Judaism* (New York, 1993). For discussion of the theological issues, see Bruce D.
Marshall, "The Jewish People and Christian Theology," in *The Cambridge Companion
to Christian Doctrine*, ed. Colin Gunton (Cambridge: Cambridge University Press, 1997),
81–100.

2. "Declaration on the Relationship of the Church to Non-Christian Religions (Nostra Aetate)," in *The Documents of Vatican II*, ed. Walter M. Abbott (New York: America
Press, 1966), 660–68.

3. See *The Theology of the Churches and the Jewish People* (Geneva, 1988).

4. See *Orthodox Christians and Jews on Continuity and Renewal*, Third Academic
Meeting between Orthodoxy and Judaism, ed. Malcolm Lowe (Jerusalem: Ecumenical
Theological Research Fraternity in Israel, 1994).

people. The occasion for the church's reconsideration of her relation to the Jews was the Holocaust.[5] The first books and articles that laid the foundation for what followed were written in the late 1940s. To be sure, there were some earlier voices, Christian thinkers who had begun to write about Christianity's relation to the Jewish people in the decade before the war — notably John Oesterreicher, Erik Peterson, Jacques Maritain, and Henri deLubac.[6] But the great outpouring of Christian reflection did not begin until after the destruction of six million Jews.

The other factor that awakened Christian thinking was the establishment of the State of Israel. For the first time since antiquity the Jews were able to reestablish Jewish life and institutions under Jewish rule in the Land of Israel. Jews, as it were, returned to history, and Christians began to look at the Jewish people, as well as the Bible and Christian theology, with fresh eyes. Jacques Maritain thought it providential that Vatican Council II was convened so shortly after the return of the Jews to the Land of Israel: "It seems to me very significant that these two events of such great bearing — on the Jewish side the return of a portion of the people to the Promised Land, on the Christian side the Second Council of the Vatican — took place at almost the same time, the first in 1948, the second in 1962–1965. They mark, each in its own way a reorientation of history."[7]

Today, Christian discussion of the Jews and study of the New Testament and early Christian interpretation of the New Testament do not take place in a vacuum. What we have to say will be formed by the events of our century and by what others have said in response to these events. I am not thinking primarily of the work of historical scholarship but the sense of sadness and shame that has come over Christian thinkers as they have studied the history of relations between Christians and Jews, and of the need for repentance. I am thinking also of symbolic

---

5. This point was recognized by Cardinal Bea in the introduction to his commentary on the "Nostra Aetate" decree. See *The Church and the Jewish People* (New York, 1966), 7.

6. Oesterreicher's periodical, *Die Erfüllung*, was begun in the early 1930s and had as its purpose to communicate to Christians a vision of Jewish existence, trying to break down the walls of ignorance and discord. In 1939 he began to broadcast radio addresses in German from Paris to oppose with all his strength "Hitler's lies and hate." See Johannes Oesterreicher, *Wider die Tyrannei des Rassenwahns: Rundfunkansprachen aus dem ersten Jahr von Hitlers Krieg* (Salzburg, 1986); Erik Peterson, *Die Kirche aus Juden und Heiden* (Salzburg, 1933); for Maritain, see Robert Royal, ed., *Jacques Maritain and the Jews* (Notre Dame, 1994), with Maritain bibliography; for deLubac, see his *Christian Resistance to Anti-Semitism: Memories from 1940–1944* (San Francisco, 1990).

7. Jacques Maritain, *On the Church of Christ,* trans. Joseph W. Evans (Notre Dame, 1973), 174.

gestures: the visit of John Paul II to Auschwitz in 1979, his visit to the Jewish synagogue of Rome in 1986, his remarks to the Jews of Germany in 1980 in which he said that the covenant with the people of God of the "old covenant" is "never revoked by God." If I were to single out one sentence from among the many things that have been spoken in the last two generations, it would be these words from "Nostra Aetate": "The Jews still remain most dear to God because of their fathers, for he does not repent of the gifts he makes nor of the calls he issues."[8] This must be the starting point for all discussion.

The continuing existence of the Jewish people is of profound hermeneutical significance for contemporary Christian understanding of what the Gospels have to say about the Jews. More than anything else this historical *and* spiritual fact sets us apart from the world of the church fathers. It is not that early Christians did not know flourishing Jewish communities firsthand — they did. And one of the results of historical scholarship of the last two generations has been to discover this world anew, to make Jewish social and religious life *after* the beginning of Christianity part of the foreground of early Christian history. We no longer speak of *Spätjudentum*, "late Judaism," as though Judaism were simply the background of Christianity.

In the early church the Jews were perceived differently. Because of the unhappy course of Jewish history in the first and early second centuries of the common era, Christian thinkers opined that the Jews would cease to exist as a distinct people. The destruction of the city of Jerusalem, the end of Temple worship and the priesthood, the subjugation of the Land of Israel to the Romans, all of which seemed permanent, made a deep impression on Christians living in the third, fourth, and fifth centuries and beyond. We live at a different time and have witnessed new things, and it is to be expected that our thinking, because we believe in a God who is disclosed in history, should be formed by what we have seen.

It is also evident that the formulation of this volume's topic — anti-Judaism and the Gospels — grows out of the events and debates of the last forty years. The term "anti-Judaism," like Jules Isaac's memorable phrase "teaching of contempt," has become a way of acknowledging that words and theological ideas found in the Bible and in Christian tradition have been a factor in shaping hostile, malevolent attitudes and — let it not be forgotten — behavior toward the

---

8. *Documents of Vatican II*, 664. The reference is to Rom. 11:28–29.

Jews. Of course the term "anti-Judaism" must be seen in relation to another term, "anti-Semitism." On occasion "anti-Semitism" is used in scholarly literature on our topic, but in general the preferred term is "anti-Judaism." "Anti-Judaism" accents religious and theological factors, "anti-Semitism" racial aspects of antipathy to the Jews.[9] In dealing with the early church, racial factors play no part in Christian understanding of Judaism.

Yet if one is not sensitive to the distinction between anti-Judaism and anti-Semitism or privy to the scholarly literature on the topic, the term "anti-Judaism" is ill-chosen.[10] Like a magnet, it has drawn certain texts into the discussion while excluding others. There is of course debate about its meaning,[11] and there may be writers for whom it is appropriate. But in dealing with the early church, I cannot bring myself to use it. In trying to say something true, namely, that Christian thinking was formed in part by opposing Judaism, the term "anti-Judaism" accents only one side of the relation of Christianity to the Jews.

A more serious objection to the term "anti-Judaism" is that it has Marcionite overtones. Indeed, one might say that in calling early Christianity anti-Jewish, we make Christianity into the very thing that it struggled valiantly to overcome. Anti-Judaism, like Marcionism, collapses the dialectic that is built into Christianity's relation to Judaism. One of the first tasks facing early Christian thinkers was how to hold on to what had been received from Israel while embracing the new that was revealed in Jesus Christ. That is another way of saying that in the second century (by which I mean the period up through Origen of Alexandria), when Christian teachers expounded texts from the Gospels dealing with the Jews, there were thinking as much about Marcion (and the Gnostics) as they were about the Jews. With these thoughts in mind let us turn to the sources.

---

9. On this point, see John Gager, *The Origins of Anti-Semitism: Attitudes toward Judaism in Pagan and Christian Antiquity* (New York, 1985), 8.

10. Discussion of anti-Judaism in early Christianity is extensive. See the following studies: Rosemary Ruether, *Faith and Fratricide: The Theological Roots of Anti-Semitism* (New York, 1974); *Anti-Judaism in Early Christianity*, vol. 1, *Paul and the Gospels*, ed. Peter Richardson and David Granskou (Waterloo, Ont., 1986); *Anti-Judaism in Early Christianity*, vol. 2, *Separation and Polemic*, ed. Stephen G. Wilson (Waterloo, Ont., 1986); *Anti-Semitism and Early Christianity*, ed. Craig A. Evans and Donald A. Hagner (Minneapolis, 1993); *Anti-Semitism and the Foundations of Christianity*, ed. Alan Davies (New York, 1979).

11. For discussion of different meanings of anti-Judaism, see Miriam S. Taylor, *Anti-Judaism and Early Christian Identity: A Critique of the Scholarly Consensus* (Leiden, 1995).

Disputes over the Law

I begin with Irenaeus of Lyons, who is the first Christian thinker to expound at length texts of the Gospels concerning the Jews. Irenaeus's great work *Adversus Haereses* was written to help the faithful in his church meet the objections of Gnostics (and Marcionites) to Catholic teaching about the one God and the revelation in Jesus Christ. His book is largely a work of biblical exegesis. Gnostics and Marcion set the God of the Jews, the God of the Old Testament, in opposition to the Father of the Lord Jesus Christ. For Irenaeus, the Old Testament and the apostolic writings were considered one book with a central theme: the self-disclosure of the one God in history. The God who created the world, called Israel, gave the Law through Moses, and spoke through the prophets is the God who appeared in Jesus at the end of the age.[12]

Marcion taught that the God of Abraham is a different God than the God of Jesus Christ, and hence Abraham would not share in the salvation offered by Christ. To answer Marcion's argument, Irenaeus launches into a detailed exegesis of a series of texts from the Gospels. All deal in some fashion with whether Jesus transgressed the Law of Moses. One passage is Luke 13:10–17, the story of the ruler of the synagogue who was indignant because Jesus had healed on the Sabbath: "Then the Lord answered him, 'You hypocrites! Does not each of you on the Sabbath untie his ox or his ass from the manger and lead it away to water it? And ought not this woman, a daughter of Abraham whom Satan bound for eighteen years, be loosed from this bond on the Sabbath day?' " (Luke 13:15–16).

For Irenaeus, the key question here is whether Jesus, by healing on the Sabbath, did something contrary to the Law. The Law, he says, prohibited work on the Sabbath and forbade carrying on any business activities; but it also encouraged people to attend to "matters of the soul," which include actions beneficial to one's neighbor. Hence it is permissible to do good for others on the Sabbath by healing. In this way Jesus "fulfilled" the law "by carrying out the office of the high priest, praying to God on behalf of others, cleansing the lepers, healing the sick."[13] The point to notice here is that Irenaeus's exegesis is designed to establish continuity between what Jesus did and what was done by the ancient Israelites *without* reference to actual precepts of the Law, that is,

---

12. *Adversus Haereses* 4, preface.
13. Ibid., 4.8.1.

to legislation found in the Pentateuch.[14] To accomplish this, he appeals to actions that are parallel to what Jesus did, for example, cleansing lepers, healing the sick.

Irenaeus turns next to Luke 6:1–11, the story of the disciples who were censured by the Pharisees for picking grain on the Sabbath. Here he makes a similar argument, this time drawing directly on the words of Jesus: "Have you not read what David did when he was hungry, he and those who were with him: how he entered the house of God, and took and ate the bread of the Presence, which it is not lawful for any but the priests to eat, and also gave it to those with him?" Jesus, says Irenaeus, defends the disciples by "words of the law," by which he means passages from the Old Testament.[15]

Next he cites Matt. 13:52, the saying about the householder "who brings out of his treasure what is new and what is old." Jesus here teaches that what is old and what is new come from the same source. "Old" and "new" refer to the "two covenants," the old to "the giving of the law which took place in former times," and the new to "the way of life according to the gospel." Again his point is that the God of Jesus Christ was not a new God. The same God who gave the law to Moses and called the people of Israel through Abraham became flesh in Jesus.[16]

From here he moves to Matt. 12:6: "There is here something greater than the temple." Irenaeus thinks that the use of the term "greater" is significant, because it puts the emphasis on that which two things have in common. The words "greater" and "less" are not applied to things that are dissimilar, opposite, or contradictory. Rather they are used for things that have properties in common but differ in number and size. In the present discussion this means that what was given in Jesus is similar to what was given by Moses, but it is *greater*. It is similar in that its source is "one and the same Lord," but it is more in that Jesus is "greater than the temple, greater than Solomon, greater than Jonah" because the gift that he confers is "his own presence and the resurrection from the dead."[17]

For Irenaeus, everything turns on the confession that there is one

---

14. By Law here I mean what later came to be called *halakah*, that is, laws ordering individual and communal actions drawn from the Torah. The term "Law" can be used in a more general sense to refer to biblical tradition, as in the phrase "the Law and Prophets" (Rom. 3:21). With respect to this sense of Law, Irenaeus thought that what Jesus did was faithful to the Law.

15. *Adversus Haereses* 4.8.3.

16. Ibid., 4.9.1.

17. Ibid., 4.9.2.

true God who has been revealed at two different times in history: in ancient Israel, and at the end of the age in Jesus Christ. The God worshiped by Abraham, Isaac, and Jacob, the God of Moses, the God of Solomon, is the Father of Jesus Christ and the God worshiped by Christians. Without the revelation to Israel, the revelation in Jesus would not have been recognized. Tertullian, in *Adversus Marcionem*, deems it risible that Jesus could have been the emissary of a God who was formerly unknown.[18] It is the same God who spoke in ancient times that speaks now, as in the opening words of the Epistle to the Hebrews: "In many and various ways God spoke of old to our fathers by the prophets; but in these last days he has spoken to us by a Son." (Heb. 1:1)

But Irenaeus does more than defend the continuity between the new and the old. He says that Jesus is more than Abraham, more than Moses, more than Solomon, who built the First Temple. He is, in the words of Matthew, "greater than the temple." Although the continuity between God's self-disclosure to Israel and in Jesus is apparent, the Scriptures also accent the discontinuity. In Jesus, God was known more fully than previously: "For the law was given through Moses; grace and truth came through Jesus Christ" (John 1:17). It is this "more" that is the source of tension and conflict between Christianity and Judaism.

In his arguments against Marcion, Irenaeus turns next to Matt. 15:3–4: "Why do you transgress the commandment of God for the sake of your tradition? For God commanded, 'Honor your father and your mother,' and 'He who speaks evil of father or mother, surely let him die.' " Jesus did not reject what was given in the Law and the Prophets. The Pharisees and scribes had asked, "Why do your disciples transgress the tradition of the elders?" The disciples were being accused of failing to engage in the ritual washing of their hands, according to Jewish Law, before eating. To which Jesus responds, "And why do you transgress the commandment of God for the sake of your tradition?" What this means, says Irenaeus, is that the Pharisees had introduced traditions of their own devising, "their own law in opposition to the [commandment of God]." Even to this day, he says, these traditions are called "pharisaical," that is, they belong to a rabbinic tradition that is supplementary to what is written in the Scriptures.[19]

If Irenaeus's discussion is read as a debate between Christians and Jews, it is unintelligible. Jews would have found his arguments puzzling.

---

18. *Adversus Marcionem* 4.6.
19. *Adversus Haereses* 4.9.3.

His opponents are Marcion and the Gnostics. Against their cavalier assertion that the God of the Jews is alien to Jesus, he wants to show that the Jesus who disputes with Jews in the Gospels was sent by the God who gave the Law to Moses. Hence he cites John 5:39–40: "You search the Scriptures, because you think that in them you have eternal life; and it is they that bear witness to me. You refuse to come to me that you may have life." His interpretation of this text is explicitly anti-Marcionite. How could the Scriptures bear witness to Jesus "if they did not come from one and the same Father, instructing men before the coming of his son"?[20] "If you believed Moses, you would believe me, for he *wrote of me*" (John 5:46). This means that the "Son of God is everywhere implanted in Moses' writings." The reason that Jesus is found in the writings of Moses is that the God of Moses is the same God who was the Father of Jesus. "It is evident that the Father is the same one who was proclaimed by the prophets, and the Son who came to us did not bring knowledge of another father, but of the same one who was preached from the beginning."[21]

Within this discussion Irenaeus inserts several polemical passages against Jewish observance of the Law, for example, that they added or deleted matters given in the Law of Moses. His intention is to show that Jesus' teaching is continuous with the teaching of Moses. This comes out clearly when he says that the meaning of the commandments is the "love of God." He has in mind, of course, the words of Jesus in Matthew (22:37), "You shall love the Lord your God with all your heart and with all your soul and with all your mind," but he knows that these words come directly from Deuteronomy (6:5). Jesus, he says, did not hand on a "commandment greater than this one, but renewed this same one." The words of Jesus are confirmed by Paul: "Love is the fulfillment of the Law" (Rom. 13:10).[22] Hence Irenaeus concludes, "Since the first and greatest commandment in the Law as well as in the Gospel is to love the Lord God with all your heart, and the second is similar, to love your neighbor as yourself, the author of the Law and the Gospel is shown to be one and the same."[23]

The chief texts, then, that provide the framework of Irenaeus's discussion are the following: Jesus healing on the Sabbath (Luke 13); the disciples picking grain on the Sabbath (Luke 6); the householder who

---

20. Ibid., 4.10.1.
21. Ibid., 4.11.4.
22. Ibid., 4.12.1–2. (He also cites 1 Cor. 13:13.)
23. Ibid., 4.12.3.

brings out of his treasure what is old and new (Matthew 13); there is something greater than the temple (Matthew 12); you transgress the commandment of God for the sake of your tradition (Matthew 15); Moses wrote of me (John 5); you shall love the Lord your God (Matthew 22). They provide a useful dossier of early Christian exegesis of texts from the Gospels dealing with the Jews.

Now some observations; first the obvious. Texts from the Gospels play a small part in disputes with the Jews and in the *Adversus Judaeos* literature. In those writings (e.g., Justin Martyr's *Dialogue with Trypho*) the debate centers on texts from the Old Testament.[24] It is largely in polemical works against Marcion and the Gnostics (e.g., Irenaeus's *Adversus Haereses*, Tertullian's *Adversus Marcionem*) or in commentaries and homilies on the Gospels that Gospel texts dealing with the Jews are discussed in any detail. Yet even though the controversy with Marcion and the Gnostics sets the terms for the debate, the larger issue is Christianity's relation to Judaism. For Marcion challenged Christians to think through the relation of the church to Israel. What the discussions with Marcion and the Gnostics show is that the Gospel texts under dispute centered mainly on the Law.

Second, the texts from the Gospels are interpreted in relation to other parts of the Bible. Here, patristic exegesis differs from modern approaches that focus on individual books or traditions. Irenaeus cites passages from Paul, the Pentateuch, and the Prophets, to guide his interpretation of passages from the Gospels. Individual texts are always interpreted in light of the Scriptures as a whole. The Bible is not a random collection of individual works; it is a unified book with a central theme, a single *skopos* that "God is one." For this reason, one cannot really ask whether the interpretation of the *Gospels* in the early church was anti-Jewish. The Gospels did not stand alone; they were part of a unified interpretation of the Bible as a whole. What is said in one place is illuminated and often modified by what is said elsewhere. As a Christian biblical interpreter, Irenaeus's primary assignment was to show that what was disclosed in the Scriptures about Jesus completed and perfected what had been revealed to Israel. It was inevitable that Jews who did not see this continuity between Israel and Jesus would be subject to criticism. To Jews, Jesus appeared to be a transgressor of the Law, but Irenaeus argues that what appeared to be a transgression — for example,

---

24. On Justin's *Dialogue with Trypho* and the Jews, see Harold Remus, "Justin Martyr's Argument with Judaism," in Richardson and Granskou, eds., *Anti-Judaism in Early Christianity,* vol. 2, *Separation and Polemic,* 59–80.

healing on the Sabbath — was in fact a deeper form of obedience, an obedience to the command recorded in Deut. 6:5: "Love the Lord your God with all your heart, with all your soul, and with all your might."

Tertullian had to deal with the same challenge. In his large work *Adversus Marcionem* he devotes most of book four to an exposition of the Gospel according to Luke. He wished to show that even in Marcion's expunged version of Luke it was possible to demonstrate that Marcion misunderstood the Gospel. He held that "there is one Christ who in the time of Tiberius was revealed by a god formerly unknown, for the salvation of all the nations; and another Christ who is destined by God the creator to come at some time still future for the reestablishment of the Jewish kingdom. Between these he sets up a great and absolute opposition, such as that between justice and kindness, between law and gospel, between Judaism and Christianity."[25] Notice that the phrase *magnam et omnem differentiam scindit... inter Iudaismum et Christianismum* (italics added) might be understood to mean that Marcion claims that Christianity is anti-Jewish.

When Tertullian comes to Luke 6:1–11, the picking of grain on the Sabbath, he accents the same features of the text as did Irenaeus. Citing the words of Jesus in Luke 6:5, Tertullian says that Jesus "presented himself as Lord of the Sabbath." In his typically acerbic way, Tertullian shows the absurdity of Marcion's view that Jesus was deliberately breaking the Sabbath because he had no allegiance to the God who gave authority to the Sabbath. How could a question have arisen as to why he broke the Sabbath if "it was his duty to break the Sabbath"? For if he had belonged to another God, he would have been expected to disregard the Sabbath. The dispute arose because it was assumed that the laws of the Sabbath were to be obeyed. If Jesus were the emissary of a new and different God, the discussion would have been pointless. "The only reason why discussion arose about the novelty of any of his teaching was that nothing had ever yet been said about any new deity, nor had there been any discussion of it."[26]

Like Irenaeus, Tertullian argues that the Jewish Scriptures allow for exceptions in observing the Sabbath, for example, "healing" or "deliverance," which, says Tertullian, is not properly human work but divine.[27] Hence he cites Matt. 5:17, where Jesus claims not to destroy but to fulfill (*adimplere*) the Law, and explains its meaning as follows: "He fulfilled

---

25. *Adversus Marcionem* 4.6.
26. Ibid., 6:1– 11.
27. Ibid., 4.12.

the law by explaining the circumstances which condition it, by throw-
ing light upon different kinds of works, by doing the things which the
law exempts from the restraints of the Sabbath, by making even more
holy by his own kind deeds that Sabbath day which since the beginning had been holy by the Father's kind words." To fulfill the Law, then,
means that Jesus "introduced nothing new, nothing which was not in
line with the example, the gentleness, the mercy, even the prophecies of
the Creator."[28]

The same issues arise in Origen's exegesis of texts from the Gospels.
Consider Matt. 19:3: "And Pharisees came up to him and tested him
by asking, 'Is it lawful to divorce one's wife for any cause?'" Here, says
Origen, the Pharisees put a question to Jesus in order to "censure him
for what he might say." If, for example, Jesus had said that it is lawful,
they would have accused him of dissolving marriages for trifles; if he had
said that it was not lawful, they would have accused him of permitting
a man to dwell with a woman who had sinned.

In his answer, Jesus cites the words of Gen. 2:24, that in marriage
a man and woman become "one flesh," and concludes that what God
joins together humans must not pull apart. Jesus wants to show that
"not any cause is justifiable as a basis for dissolving a marriage, and
that the husband must dwell with the wife as the weaker vessel and
honoring her."[29] Marriage, says Origen, is a gift of God to be nurtured
by those who enter into it. If one approaches it solely as a matter of
Law (as the Pharisees did), it will never be understood. According to
Origen, this exchange between Jesus and the Pharisees poses the question of whether we are to inquire only about "things according to the
law" or whether we are to seek what is "beyond the letter." Again the
dispute between Christians and Jews centers on the Law. As Origen puts
it elsewhere, "The reason why we do not live like the Jews is that we
think the literal interpretation of the laws does not contain the meaning
of the legislation."[30]

In their exposition of passages from the Gospels relating to the Jews,
early Christian exegetes forged a distinctive Christian understanding of
the Law. As Gregory the Great put it centuries later, Christians are urged
to "live according to the Law without the Law" (*sine lege legaliter
vivere*).[31] At each point where the question of the Law arises in the

---

28. Ibid., 4.12.
29. *Commentary on Matthew* 14.16 (on Matt. 19:3).
30. *Contra Celsum* 5.60.
31. Gregory the Great, *Moralia*, preface 2.4.

Gospels, early Christian writers subordinate the Law to something else:
gentleness and mercy, healing or deliverance, love. Christianity is not
anti-Jewish, but it is anti-halachic; it does not believe that Christian life
is to be ordered by the legislation in the Torah and the institutions associated with the Temple. Christians found in Jesus "something greater
than the temple." Here is the source of conflict between Jews and Christians. It is not that Jews had no place for mercy, justice, or love, or that
Christians did not in time develop a body of law to regulate the church's
life, but that each started at a different point, subordinating the one to
the other. Once Christians dispensed with the authority of the Law, it
was inevitable that Jews, who continued to live by the law, would be
the object of criticism. By insisting on obedience to the "letter" of the
Law, Jews, so Christians claimed, did not discern the deeper meaning
of the Law.

THE DEATH OF JESUS

The Gospels include not only sayings of Jesus but also events. The
key events include Jesus' birth and baptism, arrest, interrogation, and
flogging, death and resurrection. For our topic, the events surrounding
Jesus' death are the most illuminating because they raise questions about
who was responsible.[32]

The words "his blood be on us and on our children," spoken by the
Jews in the Gospel of Matthew (Matt. 27:25) are seldom cited in the
second century, and when they are cited, the interpretation is not consistent.[33] In his commentary on Matthew, Origen understands "his blood
be on us and our children" to mean that the culpability of the Jews of
Jesus' generation will be extended to later generations. Citing Isa. 1:15,
"your hands full of blood," Origen explains that the blood of Jesus was
not only on those who wanted him to be crucified, but "on all generations of Jews in the following generations even to the consummation
of all things. For this reason their house is even now abandoned and
deserted."[34] Elsewhere, however, he expounds the story of the release of

---

32. See Robert Wilde, *The Treatment of the Jews in the Greek Christian Writers of the
First Three Centuries* (Washington, 1949), 184–89; M. Simonetti, "La morte di Gesù in
Origene," *Rivista di Storia e Letteratura Religiosa* 8 (1972): 3–41; also Giuseppe Sgherri,
Chiesa e Sinagoga nelle opere di Origene (Milan, 1982), 78–92.

33. On Matt. 27:25, see E. Talos, *"Sein Blut über uns und unsere Kinder": Eine Unter-
suchung zu Mt. 27.24–25* (Vienna, 1969); Rainer Kampling, *Das Blut Christi und die
Juden* (Münster, 1984).

34. *Commentary on Matthew*, ser. 124.

Barabbas and says nothing about "his blood be on us and our children."
He is interested only in Pilate's handwashing.[35] Similarly, Tertullian can
explain "his blood be on us and our children" without mentioning the
Jews as such, referring instead in a general way to "the people."[36]

The most striking text on the death of Jesus from the second century
is "On Pascha," a homily by Melito of Sardis.[37] Melito's sermon is a
skillfully crafted rhetorical piece delivered at the festival celebrating the
death and resurrection of Jesus, what Melito called "the mystery of the
Pascha." A significant portion of the homily is devoted to Israel's culpability in the death of Jesus, and might be construed as a commentary on
the words spoken by the Jews to Pilate in Matt. 27:22, "Let him be crucified." Melito writes, "He [Jesus] is the lamb being slain. . . . It is he that
has been murdered. And where has he been murdered? In the middle of
Jerusalem. By whom? By Israel."[38] And "What have you done, Israel?
Or is it not written for you, 'You shall not shed innocent blood,' so that
you may not die an evil death? 'I did,' says Israel, 'kill the Lord. Why?
Because he had to die.' You are mistaken, Israel, to use such subtle eva-
sions about the slaying of the Lord. He had to suffer, but not by you;
he had to be dishonored, but not by you."[39] And "You killed your Lord
at the great feast."[40] Finally, Melito depicts the death of Jesus as the
killing of God. "He who hung the earth is hanging . . . the Sovereign has
been insulted; God has been murdered; the King of Israel has been put
to death by an Israelite right hand."[41]

Melito stands at the beginning of a long tradition of paschal preaching. The stylized rhetoric of early paschal homilies developed into
liturgical hymns in the east, and in the west into the *improperia*, the re-
proaches. Melito's language is emotive and flamboyant, and the exegesis
rigorously typological: "Old is the law, but new the world, temporary
the model, but eternal the grace. . . . Instead of the lamb there was a
Son, and instead of the sheep a Man."[42] His theology is supersessionist:

---

35. *Homilies on Leviticus* 10.2. For other interpretations of Matt. 27:25 by Origen,
see *Commentary on Matthew* 14.19; *Homilies on Joshua* 3.5; 26.3; *Homilies on Leviticus*
3.1.

36. *Adversus Marcionem* 2.15. Interestingly, translator Ernest Evans, usually scrupu-
lously accurate, consistently renders the word *populus* in Tertullian's text as "Israel."

37. Text with English translation in *Melito of Sardis: On Pascha and Fragments*, ed.
Stuart George Hall (Oxford, 1979).

38. "On Pascha," 71–72.

39. Ibid., 74–75.

40. Ibid., 79.

41. Ibid., 96.

42. Ibid., 1, 5.

"When the church arose, and the gospel took precedence, the model was made void, conceding its power to the reality, and the law was fulfilled, conceding its power to the gospel." And "this people was made void when the church arose."[43]

More than any other early text, Melito's homily embodies elements that are conventionally associated with anti-Judaism. In part this is a function of Melito's style. He employs a rhetorical technique that uses short parallel contrasting statements, for example, "The law has become word, and the old new, and the commandment grace, and the model reality, and the lamb a Son, and the sheep a Man, and the Man God."[44] The homily is based on a contrast between Israel and the church. Yet Melito was not a Marcionite; like Irenaeus and Tertullian, he was a critic of Marcion.[45] The new is not wholly new; it is always the new in the form of the old. Events in the life of Jesus are presented as a deeper enactment of what happened in ancient Israel. The slaughter of the paschal lamb foreshadows the "mystery of the Lord."[46]

Melito's approach to the events of the Old Testament has roots in Paul. The key passage is in 1 Corinthians 10, where Paul writes, "I want you to know, brethren, that our fathers were all under the cloud and all passed through the sea, and all were baptized into Moses in the cloud and in the sea, all ate the same supernatural food and all drank the same supernatural drink. For they drank from the supernatural rock which followed them, and the rock was Christ" (1 Cor. 10:1–4). But Melito goes much further and makes Paul's suggestion into a strict parallelism: "Therefore if you wish to see the mystery of the Lord, look at Abel who is similarly murdered, at Isaac who is similarly bound, at Joseph who is similarly sold, at Moses who is similarly exposed, at David who is similarly persecuted.... Look also at the sheep which is slain in the land of Egypt, which struck Egypt and saved Israel by its blood."[47]

For Melito of Sardis, typology is not simply one strategy for relating what happened in Jesus to the history of Israel, that is, to the people and events of the Old Testament; it is the only way. The rigor of his exegetical scheme is without precedent in this early period. When this typological exegesis is set within a rhetorical scheme of alternating lines,

---

43. Ibid., 42–43.
44. Ibid., 7.
45. See J. Blank, *Meliton von Sardes VOM PASSAH: Die älteste christliche Oesterpredigt* (Freiburg, 1963), 15–17.
46. "On Pascha," 33.
47. Ibid., 59–60.

the contrast between Judaism and Christianity is drawn with unusual starkness. However, it should be noted that Melito makes no mention of "Judaism," nor of the "Jews." In reading through the homily in preparation for this essay, I noticed that Melito never uses the terms "Jews" or "Hebrews," the words normally used by the church fathers to designate Jews of their own time. He always uses the term "Israel," as in his rhetorical question, "What have you done, Israel?" In the homily, Israel is a type, a paradigmatic instance of unfaithful people, as is sometimes the case in the prophets. For example, Isaiah writes, "The ox knows its owner, and the ass its master's crib; but Israel does not know, my people do not understand. Ah, sinful nation, a people laden with iniquity" (Isa. 1:3–4).[48]

The difference between Melito and Isaiah, however, is that Isaiah wrote from within Israel; for Melito, "Israel" is "other." Israel has become a foil and a stereotype, not unlike the Canaanites in the Hebrew Bible. In Exodus, God commends to Moses the intention "to blot out utterly the remembrance of Amalek from under heaven," and Moses builds an altar as a sign of remembrance, saying, "The Lord will have war with Amalek from generation to generation" (Exod. 17:14–16; Deut. 25:17–19). Commenting on these texts, Jon Levenson says, "Like the Jews in some New Testament and much patristic literature, the Canaanites in the Hebrew Bible are, without exception, wicked in the worst of ways. It is their wickedness, inter alia, which justifies their loss of the land to Israel and which condemns them eternally in the sight of God, who has graciously and mysteriously (Deut. 7:6–8) chosen Israel to supplant them." Something of the same logic and historical dynamic comes into play in Melito's depiction of Israel in this homily.[49]

Melito's paschal homily, then, is a significant text for our discussion. It provides a rhetorical and theological interpretation of the death of Jesus that will influence later Christian exegesis and thought. Its most striking features are the strict typological exegesis and the consequent depiction of Israel in contrast to Christianity, that is, as a negative type. Though the language is highly charged and emotive, the theology and

---

48. Ibid., 72.

49. Melito's theology also gives his language a pungency that is uncommon in this period. He identifies Jesus wholly with God, and in places even uses the term "father" to refer to Jesus. Everything that is said of Jesus is unreflectively attributed to God. In several places he addresses doxologies to Jesus; for example, "This is Jesus the Christ, to whom be glory for ever and ever" ("On Pascha," 10). It is in this context that his statement "God is murdered" ("On Pascha," 96) is to be interpreted. To say that "God is murdered" means that Jesus, who is God, was crucified.

exegesis of the homily are controlled by a relentless logic that excludes other ideas and biblical texts. In this scheme Israel loses any sense of historical reality, even though we know that Melito lived in a city with a flourishing Jewish community. That may well have been his intention.[50] His is an obdurate legacy.

In contrast to Melito's idealized presentation of Israel, Origen thinks much more concretely about the death of Jesus and the Jews.[51] A good example is his commentary on Matt. 26:3–5, the account of the chief priests and elders taking counsel to kill Jesus. In the words "lest there be a tumult among the people," Origen is careful to distinguish different groups among the people who were in Jerusalem at the time of Jesus. All had heard of Jesus' signs and wonders, and this was what was troubling the chief priests and elders. Because of Jesus' wonders, "there were many among the people who were *for him,* who would perhaps have said, 'A great prophet has arisen in Israel.' Others, however, were against him, and they said, 'No one casts out demons unless by Beelzebub the prince of demons.' It was unavoidable that there be an uproar among the people when Jesus was arrested because of the different feelings of the people; some loved Christ and listened to him, some believed and others did not believe in him."[52]

Origen provides another perspective on the death of Jesus in his commentary on the Gospel of John 11:47–48: "So the chief priests and the Pharisees gathered the council and said, 'What are we to do? For this man performs many signs. If we let him go on thus, everyone will believe in him, and the Romans will come and destroy both our holy place and our nation.'" Origen comments,

> The Pharisees and the high priests understand that because the miracles performed by Jesus were so impressive, it was possible that the entire people of the Jews would be brought to faith in him and that once they believed they would think little of the levitical and priestly worship in the holy place, the temple. Since the Jews no longer respected the place, this would encourage the Romans to think the place considered holy by the Jews and indeed the entire nation of the Jews were under the Savior and that they no longer wanted to hold on to their Jewish way of life. But since the high

---

50. See Robert L. Wilken, "Melito, the Jewish Community at Sardis, and the Sacrifice of Isaac," *TS* 37 (1976): 53–69.

51. See in particular Sgherri, *Chiesa e Sinagoga,* 78ff.

52. *Commentary on Matthew,* ser. 76 (italics added).

priests and Pharisees preferred their form of worship in the temple
and the preservation of the Jewish nation above everything else
they conspired against Jesus so that he would not live.[53]

In this passage the death of Jesus is linked to the future of the Jewish people and the Jewish way of life. Though Origen is speaking about
the Pharisees at the time of Jesus' death, the way he puts things suggests
he is not speaking solely about the first century. The situation he describes (which he imagines to be in the minds of the Pharisees and high
priests) is not dissimilar to what actually happened in the centuries following Jesus' death, viewed from the Christian perspective. In the wake
of Jesus' death, the things Jews considered holy came under the control
of the Romans, and Jewish worship in the Temple ceased. Furthermore,
the future of the Jewish people was in jeopardy because Jerusalem had
been replaced by a new Roman city, Aelia Capitolina. Looking back, it
appeared that the death of Jesus and the misfortunes of the Jews were
somehow linked to each other.

The destruction of the Temple by the Romans in 70 C.E. occurred
some forty years after the death of Jesus. Consequently the Gospels
make no mention of the actual destruction of the Temple. But all three
synoptic Gospels include Jesus' prophecies about the destruction of the
Temple: "Jesus left the Temple and was going away when his disciples
came to point out to him the buildings of the Temple. But he answered
them, 'You see all these, do you not? Truly, I say to you, there will not
be left here one stone upon another that will not be thrown down.'"
(Matt. 24:1–2 and pars.). These words belong to Jesus' last discourses
and were spoken shortly before his suffering and death. Furthermore,
the writers of the Gospels interpret the impending destruction of Jerusalem in the light of the prophecy of Dan. 9:27 about the "desolating
sacrilege" that will stand in the Holy Place (Matt. 24:15). Unlike other
prophecies that spoke in general terms about future events, Daniel mentioned specific times when things would occur (see, for example, the
cryptic "seventy weeks of years" in Dan. 9:24–27.). By setting forth
a historical scheme in which a series of kingdoms succeed each other,
Daniel offers an implicit historical framework in which coming events
could be placed.

The proximity of Jesus' prediction about the destruction of Jerusalem to the Passion accounts and the citation of Daniel invited Christian
thinkers to reflect on the relation between the two events. The most

---

53. *Commentary on John* 28.86 (on John 11:47–48).

detailed discussion occurs in Origen's commentary on the "desolating sacrilege" (Matt. 24:15). With the help of ancient historians (e.g., Phlegon), Origen worked out in detail the chronology of Daniel's prophecy so that the death of Jesus and the destruction of the Temple fall within the same "week" of seventy years. The "prince" and "anointed one" of Dan. 9:25 refer to Jesus; hence the words of Matt. 24:15 concerning the desolating sacrilege are to be taken to refer to his death. A great tribulation, Origen says, came upon the people because "they dared to lay hands on the Christ of God."[54] Commenting on the report in Matt. 26:3–5 that the chief priests and elders "took counsel together in order to arrest Jesus by stealth and kill him," Origen says, "It was necessary that the city which had accused the founder of the entire world, which had formerly killed the prophets, and later the Lord of the prophets — it was necessary that this city cease to exist."[55]

Although Origen is scrupulous in working out the chronological details to link the death of Jesus and the destruction of the Temple, it should also be noted that he lived two hundred years after the death of Jesus and the destruction of Jerusalem. As the years passed and people looked back on the two events, the gap between them seemed to diminish. The two events were separated by forty years, but two centuries later it became easier to see the earlier event as the "cause" of the other.[56] Origen here follows a pattern he learned from Josephus, who had interpreted the destruction of Herod's army as an act of "divine vengeance... for his treatment of John, surnamed the Baptist."[57]

For Christian thinking, it was significant that the misfortunes of the Jews in the first century were not reversed in the second century and the years following. After the unsuccessful Bar Kochba revolt, the Romans had plowed over the Jewish city and built a new Roman *colonia*, Aelia Capitolina, in the place where the Jewish city once stood. To non-Jewish observers, the Jewish city was a thing of the past. The apparent conjunction of the two events — the death of Jesus and the demise of Jewish Jerusalem — worked together to forge a new Christian interpretation, as can be seen in the following passage from Origen:

---

54. *Commentary on Matthew*, ser. 41.

55. Ibid., ser. 76; see also *Homilies on Luke* 38.3.

56. See Origen, *Commentary on Matthew* 10.17; also *Contra Celsum* 1.47; 2.13.

57. Josephus, *Antiquities* 18.116–17. Origen claims that Josephus thought that the death of Jesus was the cause of the destruction of Jerusalem and the fall of the Temple, but our present text of Josephus does not say this. On this problem, see the discussion by Robert Girod, *Origène: Commentaire sur l'Évangile selon Matthieu*, SC 162 (Paris, 1970), 1:112–17.

I challenge anyone to prove my statement untrue if I say that the
entire Jewish nation was destroyed less than one whole generation later on account of these sufferings which they inflicted upon
Jesus. For it was, I believe, forty-two years from the time when
they crucified Jesus to the destruction of Jerusalem. Indeed, ever
since the Jews existed, it has not been recorded in history that
they were ejected for so long a time from their sacred ritual and
worship, after they had been conquered by some more powerful
people.... One of the facts which show that Jesus was some divine
and sacred person is just that on his account such great and fearful
calamities have now for a long time befallen the Jews. We will go
so far as to say that they will not be restored again. [Origen has
in mind Jesus' prophecy that "no stone will be left standing upon
another."] For they committed the most impious crime of all when
they conspired against the Savior of mankind in the city where
they performed to God the customary rites which were symbols of
profound mysteries. Therefore that city where Jesus suffered these
indignities had to be utterly destroyed. The Jewish nation had to
be overthrown, and God's invitation to blessedness transferred to
others, I mean the Christians, to whom came the teaching about
the simple and pure worship of God. And they received new laws
which fit in with the order established everywhere. Those which
had previously been given were intended for a single nation ruled
by men of the same nationality and customs, so that it would be
impossible for everyone to keep them now.[58]

In my darker moments I am grateful that it was Origen — never can-
onized — who wrote these words, not Augustine. But what Origen says
is not merely private opinion. His views took root in Christian thinking
and can be found in other, more orthodox writers.[59] His interpretation
is only possible because of events that had taken place since the Bible
was written. What he says is very much conditioned by what had happened to the Jews during the first and second centuries. Because the
Temple was destroyed (making Jewish worship impossible) and the city
laid waste (depriving the Jews of their capital city), it appeared not only
that the Jewish way of life had come to an end, but that the Jewish
people would have no continuing existence.

---

58. *Contra Celsum* 4.23.
59. See H. J. Schoeps, "Die Tempelzerstörung des Jahres 70 in der jüdischen Religions-
geschichte," in *Aus Frühchristlicher Zeit* (Tübingen, 1950), 144–83.

Origen's argument is speculative. He has taken two events, linked them to each other, and concluded that the one caused the other. Of course, as we have already seen in a passage cited above, Josephus had linked the misfortunes of Herod's army to divine vengeance. Also, in the Old Testament the calamities that come upon the Jewish people are never random events without a cause. Again and again the Scriptures attribute the misfortunes of the Israelites to their disobedience, their sin, their unbelief. There is nothing pernicious or malevolent as such about what Origen says here. But Origen was not a biblical prophet who was granted a vision of the divine plan. What he says is a deduction from the text based on later events, an interpretation imposed on the Gospels, not one that is drawn from the Scriptures. Here it may be appropriate to quote the words of "Nostra Aetate": "True, authorities of the Jews and those who followed their lead pressed for the death of Christ; still, what happened in his Passion cannot be blamed upon all the Jews then living, nor upon the Jews of today. Although the Church is the new people of God, the Jews should not be presented as repudiated or cursed by God, *as if such views followed from the holy Scriptures.*"[60] Origen, uncharacteristically, has abandoned his biblicism.

Origen knew another way of reading texts depicting Jewish hostility to Jesus. Take, for example, Matt. 23:13–14: "Woe to you scribes and Pharisees, hypocrites! because you shut the kingdom of heaven against men; for you neither enter yourselves, nor allow those who would enter to go in." Origen first presents the plain meaning of this text: "First this text is to be understood simply as referring to the scribes and Pharisees of the Jews. These were content not only that they did not believe in the Lord, but they belittled his doctrine, and undermined every prophecy that was written about him, and ridiculed everything he did as false and dreamed up by the devil, when they said, 'It is only by Beelzebub that this one casts out demons'" (Matt. 12:24).[61]

But then he gives another interpretation. These words apply equally to "those who sin among us, since all who conduct themselves in evil ways give the people an example of sinning and cause harm to those who are weak and immature, robbing them of life and scandalizing them, closing off the kingdom of heaven to men, and not only themselves not entering but not allowing others to enter." This text applies particularly to teachers, who are supposed to teach according to the jus-

---

60. *Documents of Vatican II*, 666 (italics added).
61. *Commentary on Matthew*, ser. 14.

tice of the Gospels, but "do not live according to that which they teach" because they are evil shepherds. They do not care for the welfare of their flock, but think only of their own gain. In particular the text applies to "bishops, presbyters, and deacons." When they live upstanding lives they open the door to the kingdom of heaven, but when they live evil lives they close the door of the kingdom.[62]

In this passage the Jewish leaders become an example of a malady that was as much evident among Christian clergy in Origen's day as it was among Pharisees at the time of Jesus.[63] The Jews are no longer singled out as a distinct group; they become paradigmatic figures of shortcomings found in others. Cardinal Bea defended this kind of exegesis as thoroughly biblical, arguing that interpreters should relate passages that speak of the behavior of certain Jews at the time of Jesus to passages that speak of the universality of human sin. Thus Bea invokes Paul: "We have already shown that all people, both Jews and Gentiles, are under the power of sin; as it is written: 'None is righteous, no, not one.' " (Rom. 3:9–10).[64] And contemporary biblical scholars have defended this reading of the Gospels. Speaking of the Gospel of John, Raymond Brown observes that the term "the Jews" has nothing to do with "ethnic, geographical, or religious differentiation." "The Jews" is a theological category used to refer to anyone who is opposed to Jesus.[65]

SALVATION COMES FROM THE JEWS

Finally, I wish to discuss the well-known words of 4:21, "The hour is coming when neither on this mountain nor in Jerusalem will you worship the Father." Origen first explains the background of the text, that the Samaritans consider Mount Gerizim holy and the Jews consider Jerusalem (on Mount Zion) holy, citing the appropriate biblical texts (Deut. 27:11–13 for Gerizim, Ps. 132:13 for Zion). He gives an allegorical interpretation of the Samaritans as representing false teach-

---

62. Ibid.

63. Similarly, in regard to the scribes and Pharisees attending to the tithe of herbs while neglecting the weightier matters of the Law (Matt. 23:23), Origen says that such things are to be found "not only among the Jews, but also among us, who commit such sins and 'swallow a camel' " (*Commentary on Matthew*, ser. 19).

64. Augustine Cardinal Bea, *The Church and the Jewish People: A Commentary on the Second Vatican Council's Declaration on the Relation of the Church to Non-Christian Religions*, trans. Philip Loretz (New York, 1966), 18–19.

65. Raymond Brown, *The Gospel According to John I-XII*, AB 29 (New York: Doubleday, 1966), lxxi. For a discussion of this matter, see Eugene Fisher, *Faith without Prejudice: Rebuilding Christian Attitudes toward Judaism* (New York, 1993), pp. 59–61.

ing and the Jews as an "image of those who have the sound teaching —
for salvation comes from them" (John 4:22). But, says Origen, since
the hour had not yet come when one would worship God in Spirit and
in truth, one should flee the mountain of the Samaritans and "worship
God in Zion...for Christ said that Jerusalem is the city of the great
king" (Matt. 5:35). Zion itself, however, represents the "church built
with living rocks and stones...where spiritual sacrifices are offered to
God." Thus when the fullness of time comes, then "perfect worship"
will no longer be celebrated in this Jerusalem, for then worship will be
wholly spiritual, not according to a type but in truth, when there will be
a perfect likeness between God and those who worship him.[66]

John 4 points to a form of worship that is "more elevated" than
that offered at Jerusalem, an observation, Origen notes, with which the
"Jews would agree."[67] Then Origen asks to whom the "you" and "we"
refer when the text says, "you adore what you do not know," and "we
adore what we know, for salvation comes from the Jews." The plain
sense of "you" is of course the Samaritans, while its symbolic meaning is the heretics. The plain sense of "we" is the Jews; symbolically,
however, it refers to "me" (that is, the "Word"), and those "formed according to me [the Word] possess salvation as coming from the Jewish
teaching. For the mystery made known now had been made known by
the writings of the prophet and by the appearance of our Savior Jesus
Christ."[68]

Heracleon, a Gnostic interpreter of the Gospel of John with whom
Origen is in continuous dialogue throughout his commentary, took the
"you" to refer to Jews and pagans. Like Marcion, his intention was to
oppose the revelation to the Jews (the Old Testament) to the revelation
in Jesus Christ. In his view, it made no difference whether one was Jewish or pagan; in either case God's revelation in Jesus Christ was wholly
new. But Origen wants to distinguish Jews and pagans. The pagans worship material objects, venerating pieces of wood or stones. The Jews, on
the other hand, even though they worshiped God with material offerings
(sacrifices), knew that they were offering their sacrifices to the "Creator
of the universe." Origen cannot understand why the heretics deny "the
God of Abraham, Isaac and Jacob, the fathers of the Jews" when the
Savior says clearly that "salvation comes from the Jews."[69]

---

66. *Commentary on John* 13.77–85.
67. Ibid., 13.99.
68. Ibid., 13.101.
69. Ibid., 13.104–108.

Origen's exegesis of John 4 is provocative and unexpected. This passage, with its contrast between worship in particular places and worship "in spirit and in truth," came to be understood as a key text to set Christianity off against Judaism.[70] And there is some support for that view in Origen.[71] Yet, faced with the challenge of Heracleon's exegesis, he takes the text in a different direction. Heracleon argued that the revelation in Jesus Christ is to be contrasted to everything that had gone before, whether Jewish or pagan. The contrast Origen draws, however, is not between Christianity and Judaism, but between Christianity and Judaism on the one hand, and idolatry or paganism on the other. Both Jews and Christians are capable of recognizing the higher form of worship in spirit and in truth, because Jews and Christians worship the same God. Thus Jesus can say that "salvation comes from the Jews"; that is, it was through the Jews that other nations came to know the one God.

In *Contra Celsum*, Origen explains what it means to say that "salvation comes from the Jews." There he argues that the Jews were unique among ancient peoples, because they were the only society that "displayed a shadow of the heavenly life on earth." "No other God but the one supreme God was venerated" by the Jews, and idol makers were banished from Jewish society. As support for this view Origen cites Deut. 4:15–18, prohibitions against making graven images, and he praises the keeping of the Sabbath and the celebration of Jewish festivals because they provided leisure "to listen to the reading of the divine laws."[72] From childhood Jews were taught to rise up beyond "sensible" things and to think of God "not as existing in the sensible world but to seek him beyond material things." Jewish society was unlike any other society. In fact, says Origen, if one would compare the Jews to any other nation, "he would admire none more, since as far as it is humanly possible they removed everything not of advantage to mankind, and accepted only what is good."[73]

Origen goes one step further. After describing the society of the Jews, he says that it is because of the way they lived that they deserve to be called God's "portion" or "elect portion."[74] That is, the uniqueness of the Jewish people is based on divine election. This is one of the few passages

---

70. See Robert L. Wilken, *Judaism and the Early Christian Mind* (New Haven, 1971), 69–92.
71. See, for example, *Contra Celsum* 6.70.
72. *Contra Celsum* 4.31.
73. Ibid., 5.42.
74. Ibid., 5.42. The phrase is from Deut. 32:9. He also applies to the Jews the phrase from 1 Pet. 2:9, "chosen race and royal priesthood" (*Contra Celsum* 4.32).

in early Christian literature that discusses the election of the Jews, and that presents election, not as a theological idea but as a historical fact, as the basis for the kind of society developed by the Jews in antiquity.[75]

Origen, of course, also says that there came a time when the Jewish way of life, which was confined to one people and one place, had to give way to a way of life that was adequate to other peoples and other lands.[76] Yet even as he draws a contrast between the Jews and the Christians, he steadfastly maintains that the Jews are not to be placed in the same category as the idolaters, the pagans. In defending the worship of the one God — the chief goal of early Christian apologetics — Christian thinkers consider the Jews allies. This is a point of no little importance, for it suggests that even after the coming of Jesus, on the matter of central importance, worship of the one God, Jews and Christians belong together.

Early Christian exegesis of the Gospels is as varied and kaleidoscopic as the biblical text itself. Seldom does the interpretation of the text conform to a predetermined scheme. In concluding this section, I offer one more example dealing with the death of Jesus. The text is from Matt. 26:39: "If it be possible, let this cup pass from me." First Origen explains that the text shows that Jesus was fully human. No one wants to suffer pain, especially pain that leads to death. But then, Origen offers another interpretation. Because he was the Son of God, Jesus loved those from the Gentiles who would come to faith; "The Jews, however, as seed of the holy fathers, from whom is adoption and glory and the covenant and the promises, he loved as branches of the good olive tree. Because he loved them, he saw those things they were to undergo if they asked that he be put to death and chose to give life to Barabbas. For this reason he said, 'Father, if it is possible, let this cup pass from me.'" But when he realized the good that would come to the whole world, he said, "Not what I will but what you will." He did not want the Jews to suffer on account of his death, which would bring salvation to the whole world.[77]

Here again Origen argues, as with John 4, that the relation of Christians to Jews is different from their relation to other peoples. Origen's exposition of this passage is controlled by his understanding of the relation between the death of Jesus and the difficulties that would come upon the Jews when the city of Jerusalem was destroyed. Yet, in his

---

75. For other texts, see Robert L. Wilken, "Cyril of Alexandria's *Contra Julianum*" in a forthcoming *Festschrift* for Robert Markus, edited by M. Vessey and published by the University of Michigan Press.

76. *Contra Celsum* 4.32.

77. *Commentary of Matthew*, ser. 92; see also Sgherri, *Chiesa et Sinagoga*, 90–92.

actual exposition of the text, something else breaks in. Jesus loved the Jews as his own people; hence, when he was facing his own death, he thought first of the Jewish people, not of what his death would mean for the nations. When he prayed, "Let this cup pass from me," he was thinking not of his own suffering, but of the people he loved. He did not want them to suffer. Thus he prayed that God might bring about the salvation of the world in some other way than by his own death.

CONCLUSION

Let me conclude with a personal story. Some years back when I visited Jerusalem, it was my privilege to go to the synagogue with my friend Rabbi Pinchas Peli — may he rest in peace. One semester Peli came to the University of Notre Dame to teach, and he said that he wanted to visit my church. So one Sunday morning, when his wife Penina was in South Bend visiting him, they joined our family for the eucharist. It was a beautiful May morning, as we took our places in the pew, with warm spring sunlight streaming in the windows. I was delighted to have Pinchas and Penina sitting next to us, and eager to have them share in our worship.

It happened to be the fifth Sunday of Easter, and the first lesson was from the book of Acts, chapter 13. That morning the lector was a talented young woman, an actress, who was a skilled and effective reader. The text was the account of the visit of Paul and Barnabas to the synagogue in Pisidian Antioch, and she read the passage with power and enthusiasm. The text says that on the Sabbath almost the whole city gathered to hear the word of God, "but when the Jews saw the multitudes, they were filled with jealousy, and contradicted what was spoken by Paul, and reviled him." When the lector reached the final sentences of the passage, she raised her voice to highlight the dramatic ending: "And Paul and Barnabas spoke out boldly, saying, 'It was necessary that the word of God should be spoken first to you. Since you thrust it from you, and judge yourselves unworthy of eternal life, behold, we turn to the Gentiles.'" To which she responded, "This is the word of God." And the congregation in return replied, "Thanks be to God."

It was as though Pinchas and Penina had been hit over the head by a sledgehammer. Penina began to cry, and Pinchas was visibly agitated. But they stayed in their places and endured the rest of the service, which went on longer than usual because it included confirmation. After the service the Pelis were invited to our home for brunch and of course the chief topic of conversation was the reading from Acts. Penina was outraged and kept asking, "How can you continue to read such a passage after the Holocaust?" Pinchas, with what seemed to me a keener spiritual insight and religious sensibility, had something quite different to say: "It is a hard saying. But it is part of the Bible, and one cannot, after all, take scissors to the pages of the Scriptures. The only way to deal with such a text is through interpretation."

Interpretation has always been a matter of relating what is said in one part of the Bible to what is said in other parts of the Bible, and relating that in turn to the faith of the community that lives out of the Bible, the church. The Bible is not primarily a book from the past; it is a "carried book," in the words of Paul van Buren. What any given passage or book meant in its original setting is not the goal of interpretation. The historical task is only one aspect of the work of exegesis, and not the most important. It is introductory, propaedeutic, and must be completed by relating the text to the rest of the Bible, to the church's faith and life, and to what has taken place since the Bible was written.

If we view interpretation in this light, as a perennial task of the Christian community as it reads, studies, prays, and lives the Bible, we will be in a better position to give meaning to the passages in the Scriptures dealing with the Jews. Biblical exegesis is an art of discovery, of invention, if you will, of finding what the text discloses, and the best exegetes have always been those able to show that what is newly found was always there. What one finds will depend in large measure on what one is looking for. Paradoxical as that may seem, it states a profound truth, one that is known to every good expositor. The interpreter knows beforehand what to look for. What we have discovered in the Scriptures concerning the Jews differs from that of earlier generations; yet what they saw was more nuanced than is often recognized, and, even with its limitations, helps our generation discern the unique relation between Christians and Jews.

Early Christian thinkers knew that what set the Jews apart from others was that they worshiped God by observing the Law of Moses. When everything is stripped away, Christians, though critics of the Jews, understood the Jews in terms the Jews themselves could recognize. Only Christians are capable of this, for they grasp, as others cannot, what makes Judaism distinctive. As the contemporary Jewish theologian David Novak has written, "It is the Torah that makes Judaism stand out from anything in the human background."[78] For Christianity, however,

---

78. Novak cites Saadyah Gaon, "Our nation is only a nation by virtue of its laws." See *Jewish-Christian Dialogue: A Jewish Justification.* (New York, 1989), 129.

the Law is not the key to the Bible; Jesus Christ is, and for that reason Christian thinkers were critical of the central place of the Law in Jewish life. This is the great debate between Christians and Jews, a quarrel within the biblical tradition quite unlike debates with the Greeks and Romans, or later with Islam or, more far afield, with Buddhism.

Yet, even while saying that there was something better than the Law, Christians recognized that the Law was a gift of God (Rom. 9:4), and that the new way revealed in Jesus Christ was irrevocably bound to what had been revealed earlier. What John called "worship in spirit and in truth" was not simply a new spiritual worship (as Marcion had claimed), it was, in Origen's phrase, a "spiritual worship *of the Law*" (italics added). Christians did not dispense with the books of the Law; they preserved them and interpreted them anew.

Christianity cannot be indifferent to the people of God who continue to observe the Law, even though their existence is an abiding spiritual challenge to Christianity. For if there is no worship according to the Law, if there is no Jewish community that observes the Law as an act of covenantal obedience to the one God, what does it mean to say that there is a "spiritual worship of the Law"? In the most profound sense, this was what was at issue in the rejection of Marcion, as well as in Paul's words in Rom. 11:17 cited in "Nostra Aetate": "If some of the branches were broken off, and you, a wild olive shoot, were grafted in their place to share the richness of the olive tree, do not boast over the branches. If you do boast, remember it is not you that support the root, but the root that supports you."

When Paul wrote these words he used the present tense — the root that *supports* you. At Vatican II, it would have been easy to transpose the word "supports" into the past tense, "supported." Hence it is of some theological significance that when "Nostra Aetate" paraphrases Paul's words in Romans, it retains the present tense. The church received the revelation of the Old Testament from the Jewish people, and "cannot forget that she *draws* sustenance from the root of that good olive tree onto which have been engrafted the wild olive branches of the Gentiles."[79] One might have expected, two thousand years later, to read "*drew* sustenance" from the Jewish people. But the decree says, "draws sustenance from the root of that good olive tree." This is the mystery at the heart of Christianity's relation to the Jewish people.

---

79. *Documents of Vatican II*, 664 (italics added).

RESPONSE TO
ROBERT L. WILKEN

Everett Ferguson

ROBERT WILKEN'S ESSAY "Something Greater Than the Temple" sets the topic of anti-Judaism and the Gospels in the context of Christian rethinking in the aftermath of the Holocaust and the establishment of the State of Israel. Historical scholarship, no less than theology, is influenced by societal attitudes and cultural issues.

It is good that at the outset he distinguishes between the terms "anti-Judaism" and "anti-Semitism," the latter being a term that was never well chosen. As a friend of mine who lived for a number of years in the Arab world once observed: "I am not anti-Semitic; I like the Arabs." Well, I like the Jews whom I have been privileged to know; but our topic is not about racial matters.

Wilken focuses his essay on interpretations in the second century (expanded to include Origen) of selected passages in the Gospels. These interpretations are sufficient to surface three principal issues between Christians and Jews in the early history of Christianity and today.

The first is the status of the Law. Wilken is surely right that the anti-Law perspective of Christians is the important distinction. This different starting point determined the Christian stance. "Christianity," says Wilken, "is not anti-Jewish, but it is anti-halachic."[1]

A second issue is the meaning of the death of Jesus. Wilken here develops the correlation that later Christian writers (represented by Origen) made between the death of Jesus and the destruction of the Jerusalem temple some forty years later.

A third issue is raised by the destruction of the Temple: the meaning of worship. Here, Wilken finds in Origen positive assessments of the Jewish heritage: "Salvation comes from the Jews." Indeed, on many Christian attitudes, there were significant antecedents in Judaism.

---

1. Robert L. Wilken, "Something Greater Than the Temple," in this volume, 187.

Among the many things Christians inherited from the Jews were precedents for the very attitudes now found to be objectionable or problematic. Wilken's paper provides striking examples. For instance, I found very instructive the parallel that Jon Levenson drew between the characterization of the Canaanites in the Hebrew Bible and the characterization of the Jews in patristic literature. Likewise, Josephus's correlation of the execution of John the Baptist with the defeat of Herod (as well as the prophets' interpretations of the misfortunes of the people) is parallel to Origen's treatment of the relation between the death of Jesus and the destruction of Jerusalem. In a positive vein, Origen recognized what Second Temple Jewish literature attests, that Jews too exalted a spiritual worship.

There are two ways, broadly speaking, in which Christian scholars have sought to deflect, or at least to ameliorate, the charge of anti-Judaism against early Christian literature. One approach is to argue, accurately I think, that the negative statements in the early period of the church about Jews and Jewish institutions represent a family quarrel. Similar, if not worse, negative judgments were given by Jews about Samaritans, by Pharisees about Sadducees, by Essenes about Pharisees, and so on. In our human families we say things about other family members that would infuriate us if an outsider said them. For Jewish believers in Jesus to say certain things about their compatriots was different from Gentiles later saying these same things. Also, it is pointed out that these negative words sounded one way when Christians were a minority struggling for survival and recognition, and another way when said many years later in a context of Christianity as the dominant religion. This is well illustrated in the reaction of the wife in the personal story with which Wilken led into his conclusion. The situation of an intrafamily quarrel has a bearing on what Wilken has described as "the dialectic that is built into Christianity's relation to Judaism"[2] (about which more in a moment).

A second approach to the "anti-Jewish" texts in early Christian literature is to present them as theological constructs. They were part of early Christianity's efforts at self-definition. It was not so much contemporary Jews and contemporary Jewish institutions that were described negatively, as it was a certain interpretation of the biblical materials. Again, at a later period, these negative judgments could reinforce nega-

---

2. Ibid., 179

tive personal feelings with unfortunate consequences, but that was not the purpose of these texts originally.

The first approach is more relevant to the New Testament period, before the separation between church and synagogue became definitive; the second approach is more applicable, although not exclusively, to the development in the second century and beyond. This second approach, the theological construct, is particularly pertinent to Wilken's discussion of Irenaeus, who was not discussing Judaism directly but Gnostics and Marcionites. Melito's sermon "On Pascha" in particular is an example of a theological construct, as Wilken portrays it. I think he is right, but it is appropriate to note, as he does, that there was a large and influential Jewish community in Sardis, a fact that surely has something to do with Melito's rhetoric.[3]

Wilken, rejecting the term "anti-Judaism" as at best a one-sided way of describing the situation, offers a third way of looking at the texts that are troublesome to modern readers within the recent historical climate. His approach is to recognize the "dialectic" inherent in the Christian position. The most that can be said for "anti-Judaism" is that it is only one part of the dialectic. Christians could never give up the Old Testament, and with it the Jews, who were its recipients and preservers. It was at once the answer to the pagan charge of novelty and the verification (through its prophecies) of the Christian truth claims. The presence of living, practicing Jews, however, was an embarrassment. If the Scriptures were given to the Jews, why didn't the Jews understand them the way Christians did? The Jew Trypho could ask Justin why Christians, "professing to be pious...do not obey [the] commandments" pertaining to festivals, Sabbaths, and circumcision.[4] Similarly, the pagan Celsus assumes the role of a Jew to press the charge that Jewish converts to Christianity "have forsaken the law of their fathers." How is it that Christians take the beginning of their system from Judaism and then treat it with disrespect?[5] Christians were both "for" and "against" Judaism, and to dissolve the dialectic in either direction was to cease to be what they were. As Wilken's essay reminds us, everything comes down to an interpretation of Scripture. And this interpretation must be done, as Irenaeus did it, in the light of the whole of Scripture.

---

3. For another interpretation, Marianne Palmer Bonz, "The Jewish Community of Ancient Sardis: A Reassessment of Its Rise to Prominence," *HSCP* 93 (1990): 343–58; Lynn Cohick, "Melito of Sardis's *Peri Pascha* and Its 'Israel,'" *HTR* 91 (1998): 351–72.

4. Justin Martyr, *Dialogue with Trypho* 10.

5. Origen, *Against Celsus* 2.1, 4.

Wilken notes, "Once Christians dispensed with the authority of the Law, it was inevitable that Jews, who continued to live by the Law, would be the object of criticism."[6] It worked the other way too: It was inevitable that Law-observant Jews would be hostile to Christians. We should remember that in the pre-Constantinian period we have to reckon with a Jewish "anti-Christianity."[7] However, Wilken has rendered a valuable service to our discussion by lifting up the positive assessments of Jews and Judaism in Origen's comments.

The literature of the second century for the most part does not permit us to look behind the literary polemics to glimpse the actual living contact between individual Christians and individual Jews. There may have been more of this than we are explicitly told. It seems to me that the *Epistle of Barnabas* reflects real contacts and discussions.[8] Likewise, although Justin's *Dialogue with Trypho* is a literary construct, Justin's familiarity with Judaism and Jewish arguments suggests more than a bookish knowledge, so that the literary work probably reflects some actual discussions.[9] Origen had many contacts with Jews, including a "Hebrew teacher,"[10] something that may explain his favorable notices of Judaism. The theological constructs of "Judaism" may not have corresponded to what the living contacts were. My personal example comes from growing up in a strongly Catholic community in southern Texas. The teaching I got in my church was strongly anti-Catholic. Yet many of my best friends in childhood were Catholic. It was as if the theological teachings and the personal relationships were two different compartments that seldom if ever met. There may have been some of that in the experience of Christians in the second century.

If we broaden our subject from the explicit exegesis of Gospel texts, we see that there were various options considered by Christians in the

---

6. Wilken, "Something Greater Than the Temple," 187.

7. *Martyrdom of Polycarp* 13, 17; Tertullian, *Scorpiace* 10. A cautionary word on the latter is offered by David M. Scholer, "Tertullian on Jewish Persecution of Christians," *SP* 17, no. 2 (1982): 821–28.

8. See S. Lowy, "The Confutation of Judaism in the Epistle of Barnabas," *JJS* 11 (1960): 1–33; reprinted in E. Ferguson, *Studies in Early Christianity* (New York: Garland, 1993), vol. 6, *Early Christianity and Judaism*, 303–35.

9. See A. Lukyn Williams, *Adversus Judaeos: A Bird's-Eye View of Christian Apologiae until the Renaissance* (Cambridge: Cambridge University Press, 1935), book 1, iv.

10. See N. R. M. Lange, *Origen and the Jews: Studies in Jewish-Christian Relations in Third-Century Palestine* (Cambridge: Cambridge University Press, 1976); Paul M. Blowers, "Origen, the Rabbis, and the Bible: Toward a Picture of Judaism and Christianity in Third-Century Caesarea," in *Origen of Alexandria: His World and His Legacy,* ed. Charles Kannengiesser and William L. Petersen (Notre Dame: University of Notre Dame Press, 1988), 96–116.

second century concerning their relationship to the Jewish heritage.[11] Wilken has reminded us of Marcion's total rejection of that heritage. On the opposite extreme, but with a similar result, was the *Epistle of Barnabas*'s total appropriation of the Bible and its covenant for Christians with the consequence of disinheriting the Jews. Other thinkers made various distinctions within the Bible. Thus the Valentinian Gnostic Ptolemy distinguished those parts of the Law coming from God, from Moses, and from the elders.[12] The Jewish Christians known as Ebionites remained the closest to Judaism, but they claimed there were "false pericopes" that had been introduced into the Scriptures; in this way they maintained their loyalty to a Jewish way of life while rejecting large parts of the Old Testament.[13] The third-century Syriac *Didascalia*, contemporary with Origen, addressed a community in close contact with Jews. The author, perhaps himself of a Jewish background, argued that the moral law (the Decalogue) is eternal, but the ceremonial law (the "second law," in his terminology) was temporary.[14] Irenaeus developed more fully the perspective of Justin Martyr, that there were successive covenants in God's dealings with humanity, so the eternal covenant in Jesus Christ has replaced the "old covenant" given through Moses.[15] This view is perhaps represented in Ignatius and drew on the statements of Paul and the author of the Epistle to the Hebrews.

As Christian self-consciousness became more sharply defined in the second century, several apologists spoke of three or four "races" of people. Their analysis closely corresponds to Origen's distinction between pagans, who worship material objects, Jews, who worship the one God with material offerings, and Christians, who worship God spiritually. The *Preaching of Peter* says, "Worship God, not as the Greeks.... Neither shall you worship as do the Jews.... Worship God in a new way through Christ.... We after a new manner, as a third race, worship God as Christians."[16] In a similar manner, the *Epistle to Diognetus* rejects the gods of the Greeks, credits the Jews with worshiping the one God but rejects their "superstitions" — material sacrifices, Sabbath observance,

---

11. My article "Justin Martyr on Jews, Christians, and the Covenant" discusses the topic in terms of the treatment of the Jewish Bible (in *Early Christianity in Context: Monuments and Documents*, ed. F. Manns and E. Alliata [Jerusalem: Franciscan Press, 1993], 395–405; see pp. 398–402).

12. Epiphanius, *Panarion* 33.3–7.

13. Pseudo-Clement, *Homilies* 2.38; 3.52; *Recognitions* 1.35ff.

14. *Didascalia* 26.

15. Irenaeus, *Adversus Haereses* 4.32–34.

16. Clement of Alexandria, *Stromateis* 6.5.30, 41.

circumcision, fasts, and feasts — and praises the manner of life of Christians, who have learned the truth. The *Apology* of Aristides (Syriac) says that there are four classes of people in this world: Barbarians, Greeks, Jews, and Christians. The detailed description of each gives superiority over Barbarians and Greeks to Jews for their confession of one God and their imitation of him in philanthropy, but faults them in comparison to Christians for their observance of Sabbaths, the feast of unleavened bread, a great fast, circumcision, and distinction of meats.[17] These similar arguments from second-century apologists accord with what Wilken has presented from a different group of texts: The superiority of Judaism over paganism but its inferiority to Christianity. That, historically speaking, is the "anti-Judaism" of the second-century understanding of Christianity.

---

17. *Epistle to Diognetus* 1–4; Aristides, *Apology* 2–14.

RESPONSE TO
ROBERT L. WILKEN

D. Jeffrey Bingham

T HE TASK ASSIGNED ME in this response to Professor Wilken's essay "Something Greater Than the Temple" is to focus attention upon what I regard as its most important issues. Four issues should, I believe, be the concern of our discussion.

First is the nature of the dialectic that characterized early Christianity's understanding of the Law. Wilken has described that dialectic in a manner that moves away from seeing it as reflective of anti-Judaism. His description prompts us to consider what should be regarded as anti-Jewish. Is something anti-Jewish if it confesses continuity with essential features of Judaism yet restructures and reinterprets some of those features? Does Marcion provide us a paradigm from which to frame our own understanding of what is anti-Jewish?

On the one hand, Irenaeus argues that the God of the Law and Moses is the same God and Father of Jesus Christ (cf. Matt. 13:52; John 5:39–40). Furthermore, Jesus is found in Moses' Law (John 5:39–40); he uses Moses' Law to defend his disciples (Luke 6:3–4); he teaches the same love as did Moses' Law (Matt. 22:37); and he reacts not against Moses' Law but against the devised tradition of the Pharisees (Matt. 15:3). Here is the continuity between Christianity and the Law. On the other hand, Irenaeus can justify the actions of Jesus, when he is challenged with transgression of the Law, without giving warrant from the Pentateuch's precise legislation (Luke 13:15–16). In Irenaeus's mind, the Old Testament Scriptures allow exceptions to the Law. Therefore, rather than quote the legislation, he sets forth the harmony between Jesus' actions and those of ancient Jews by appealing to the perennial practice of the enduring virtues of mercy, compassion, and service already revealed in the Old Testament. He also interprets Jesus as not affirming uncritical continuity with the Jewish perspective of the Law when he explains that Jesus believed the gospel to be similar to the Law, but also greater (Matt.

12:6). Here is Christian distancing from the Law, a perspective that sees perfection and ultimate authority in Christ. And yet, even in this distancing, some of the "greater" is already in the Scriptures of the Old Testament. In particular, Jesus' practice is already in the love command of Deuteronomy.

Tertullian has the same tension as Irenaeus (cf. Luke 6:5; Matt. 5:17). He affirms that Jesus belongs to the God of the Law and did not come in rebellion against the Law. But there are exceptions — things outside the Law yet within the Jewish Scriptures given by the Creator. Occasions that call for some kind of healing or deliverance meet the criteria for exceptions.

For Origen, the question of marriage and divorce cannot be viewed merely as a legal issue stipulated by the Law (Matt. 19:3). When Jesus was challenged on this matter, he went outside the legislation to Gen. 2:24 in order to show the supportive, nurturing, forbearing nature of marriage. This nature of marriage, resident in the meaning of the Law, is lost in the strictly legal, literal, Pharisaic interpretation of the Law.

From their exegesis of the Gospels, then, it can be gathered that these early Christians were not dispensing with the Law, but setting forth a Christian interpretation of the Law. In this interpretation, Law (*halakah* — see Wilken's definition in his notes) is subordinated to the (scriptural) virtues of gentleness and mercy, healing or deliverance, love.[1] Our early exegetes of the Gospels retained the Law, but in conflict with the Jews, dispensed with its preeminent authority, ceased insisting on the sufficient meaning of the legislation through its "letter," and subordinated it to the one who showed and was "something greater than the Temple." The Law was not renounced but reread, and therefore Christians engaged in, as Origen says, "spiritual worship of the Law."

There is a dialectic here, but it is a dialectic that results in a carefully defined synthesis rather than utter opposition. It is not ultimately an invalidation of Jewish Law or an anthropological valuation that judges the Jews as inferior. Rather there is a view of revelation that sees continuity with expansion of the prior, lesser revelation into the greater revelation. And there is a hermeneutic that sees the greater already present and anticipated in the lesser, and therefore values the lesser by interpreting it rather than invalidating it.

It is this perspective of the Law in early Christianity, a perspective so far from the complete "anti-Jewish" opposition of Marcion (a tar-

---

1. Robert L. Wilken, "Something Greater Than the Temple," in this volume, 181.

get of Irenaeus and Tertullian) that prevents Wilken from using the term "anti-Judaism" to characterize the stance of second-century (orthodox) Christianity. For him, the term is "ill-chosen,"[2] inequitable. Early Christianity was, yes, "anti-halachic";[3] life was not governed by the Jews' religious, communal legislation. But no, it was not anti-Jewish; it embraced the Jews' God and the enduring virtues revealed by their God in their book.

The second issue upon which I would like to focus our attention is found in Wilken's treatment of Melito's paschal homily. Here he shows us that the rhetorical style of an early Christian exegete can sometimes explain that exegete's extreme language and demonstrate that no actual anti-Jewish sentiments exist.

Melito develops at length the culpability of the Jews in Jesus' death. Melito's homily perhaps forms a commentary on the Jews' words en couraging Pilate to crucify Jesus (Matt. 27:22). His language is "emotive and flamboyant," his exegesis is "rigorously typological," and his "theology is supersessionist."[4] And though his text may seem to fit a pattern associated with "anti-Judaism," he — like Irenaeus, Tertullian, and Origen — was no Marcionite.

We understand Melito best when we take into account his exegetical method and his theology. Wilken shows him to be a thoroughgoing typologist: Jesus' life is a deeper enactment of events in Israel's history; Abel, Isaac, Joseph, Moses, David, and the lamb of the Passover in Egypt all foreshadow the Lord's Passion; and "Israel" (Melito never uses "Judaism" or "Jews") is a negative type, a paradigmatic instance of unfaithful people.[5] Furthermore, theologically, Melito so closely identifies Jesus with God the Father that his reference to God's murder on the tree must be seen as naive modalism.

Although Melito's interpretation of Jesus' Passion will impact later Christian formulation of the Jewish culpability, we must read him with full attention to his typological references to Israel. There, Wilken notes, "Israel loses any sense of historical reality,"[6] existing only as an image, an archetype of the unfaithful.

This careful reading of Melito by Wilken and Miriam Taylor's recent thesis encourage me to ask if other "anti-Jewish" Christian writings

---

2. Ibid., 179.
3. Ibid., 187.
4. Ibid., 188.
5. Ibid., 190.
6. Ibid., 191.

might not be as "anti-Jewish" as once thought. Taylor argues that early anti-Judaism is a product of Christian theologizing that sees the Jews not as actual adversaries, but as a figurative entity.[7] Wilken's insight came through repeated reading of Melito's text. Several other texts may be due this same respect.

Third, there is the issue of diversity in the early Christian exegesis of the Gospels. Presented to us particularly through the writings of Origen, Wilken shows us a mind that can both criticize and honor the Jews. It is not a mind predicted by our century, it is not a mind ultimately hostile to Judaism or the Jews.

Origen is more concrete on the Jews and Jesus' death than Melito. When Origen interprets "the people" of Matt. 26:3–5, he doesn't idealize them, but classifies groups within them: many were followers of Jesus, though others were adversaries. Origen was unwilling to stereotype the Jews.

Origen's comments on the Jewish leaders' conference leading to the plot to kill Jesus, however, are not as balanced. In John 11:47–48 the leaders worry that allowing Jesus to continue would lead to the people's conversion to him and thence the fall of the Temple at the hands of the Romans. Origen's interpretation suggests to Wilken that he is looking back after the fall of the Temple and the cessation of Jewish worship under Roman domination, and connecting the misfortune of the Jewish people with the death of Jesus. This connection in Origen is most developed in his comments upon a phrase in Matt. 24:15, "the desolating sacrilege." Influenced by the close proximity between Jesus' Passion and Jesus' prediction of the destruction of Jerusalem in the Gospels, Origen reads the phrase as referring to Jesus' death, which brought upon the Jews a great tribulation. Later, commenting on Matt. 26:3–5, he reiterates the point. In retrospect, the two events became so closely linked that he saw them as cause and effect. This linkage formed an interpretive paradigm for Origen, one that denied any future restoration for the Jews and saw the Jews cursed for Jesus' death.

Wilken critiques this paradigm and faults it for being speculative, a model constructed by one who was not an inspired prophet with the

---

7. Miriam Taylor, *Anti-Judaism and Early Christian Identity: A Critique of the Scholarly Consensus* (Leiden: E. J. Brill, 1995), 140–43. Lynn H. Cohick has also suggested a typological sense to Melito's "Israel" in her paper, "Melito of Sardis' *Peri Pascha* and Its 'Israel'" (paper presented at the annual meeting of the Society of Biblical Literature, New Orleans, La., 23–26 November 1996). The paper was taken from her doctoral thesis, "Reassessing the Use of Scriptural Material and Interpretation in the *Peri Pascha* Attributed to Melito of Sardis" (Ph.D. diss., University of Pennsylvania, 1996).

capability to interpret the meaning of events within history. He reminds us of the impact of historical setting upon the early Christian interpreter of the Gospels. Though one eye of the interpreter may have been on the text, the other gazed at past and contemporary events that seemed inextricably linked to the text's meaning. In that way, what began as the reading of a Gospel text quickly became the interpretation of an event imposed upon the text. Event had usurped Scripture.

This, however, was not the only way Origen read those texts that described the hostility of the Jews toward Jesus. He interprets the scribes and Pharisees of Matthew 23 as paradigmatic of Christian leaders who live evil lives.

The same pattern is present in Origen's exegesis of John 4:19–24 and Matt. 26:39. The Johannine passage has Jesus, in dialogue with the woman at the well, describing true worship with, among other things, a contrast between Samaritans and Jews. Origen can interpret this passage to put Christianity in conflict with the Jews. But, in polemic against the Gnostic Heracleon, who did not distinguish between Jews and pagans, Origen gives a "provocative and unexpected" interpretation.[8] The Samaritans are symbolically the heretics, pagans. The Jews are symbolically the Word, the Savior who is from the Jews. For Origen, the Jews and Christians are aligned together against the heretics and pagans, because they worship the one, same God.

Further evidence of his high estimation of the Jews can be seen in *Contra Celsum*, where Origen praises them for their spirituality, ethics, morals, and their identity as the elect. And it can be seen in his exegesis of the word of Jesus, "If it be possible let this cup pass from me" (Matt. 26:39). Jesus' initial thoughts, Origen believes, with his death looming before him, were for the protection of the Jews from the suffering they would incur by participating in his death. Thus he prays for the passing of his death for the sake of the Jews. He thinks first of the welfare of the Jews, not of the wider blessing his death would bring. Jesus' love for the Jews comes through in an interpretation that sees them as the ones judged for their guilt in his death.

Wilken has presented us with a variety of interpretations, particularly of the Passion of Jesus. Melito condemns Israel, but as a paradigm of all who are unfaithful. Origen links the fall of Jerusalem to the Jews' culpability for Jesus' death, but he refuses to stereotype most of the people as Jesus' adversaries; he sees the scribes and Pharisees as paradigmatic

---

8. Wilken, "Something Greater Than the Temple," 198.

of evil Christian leaders; and he believes that Jesus' first prayer at Gethsemane was for his beloved Jews. Even a passage that can be read as
distancing Christianity from Judaism can also be read as aligning the
two together by their common faith in the same God.

This "varied and kaleidoscopic" exegesis of the Gospels demonstrates
that "seldom does the interpretation of the text conform to a predetermined scheme."[9] Wilken's method in presenting this demonstration
reminds me of a passage in Jaroslav Pelikan's *Historical Theology:*

> As historical research, by showing that the exegetical tradition is .
> by no means as homogeneous as it may seem, refutes the claims
> of hegemony for any one interpretation, so it may also liberate
> the biblical scholar from the exegetical fashions of the moment by
> giving him a perspective on the text that seems new because it is
> very old.[10]

Hegemony, Wilken shows, cannot be claimed for an exegetical paradigm in early Christianity that is exclusively condemnatory of the Jews,
their actions, and their Law. And he shows a spectrum of "old" models
that could liberate contemporary exegetes from their own paradigms.
Early Christian exegetes of the Gospels were not anti-Jewish Marcionites. Their reading of the Gospels did not lead them to see either Jesus
or the evangelists in this light. Their exegesis shows them struggling
with a tension that often embraces extremes. Many of these extremes
can be explained as unprecedented rhetorical force or dominance of historical setting. Neither their language nor their hermeneutic represented
the second-century Christian mind. That mind inevitably, by matching
Scripture with Scripture, embraced a newness in Christ "irrevocably
bound to what had been revealed earlier."[11] The early approach to reading the Scriptures by forming intertextual, intertestamental networks of
biblical passages that explained each other guided Christian thought to
such a conclusion. This relationship between the new and the old is the
understanding of the early Christian mind on the issue of the Law and
Jesus' practice, and the issue of the Jews and Jesus' death.

Finally, I consider Wilken's comments about the role of contemporary history in our own hermeneutic worthy of mention. They remind
us of the historical, cultural character of any interpretive lens and of the

---

9. Ibid., 199.
10. J. Pelikan, *Historical Theology: Continuity and Change in Christian Doctrine,*
ThRes (Philadelphia: Westminster Press, 1971), 137.
11. Wilken, "Something Greater Than the Temple," 202.

negative or positive value that character renders. Pious reflection upon the sacred text can be both aided and hindered through the influence of contemporary events. Origen's hermeneutic of event that sees the Scripture teaching God's cursing of the Jews for the death of Jesus and sees no restoration for Israel cannot have a place in our time. The events of our century coupled with the testimony of Scripture ignored by Origen's hermeneutic do not allow its use. The establishment and existence of the State of Israel joined with Paul's words seen anew in the light of our historical moment distance us from Origen's paradigm and call us to ultimately understand the texts of Scripture with an eye to Israel's existence rather than Israel's demise. History has opened our eyes to the biblical texts, which were already written in Origen's day, but which had been cast in a shadow by the pressing force of his moment. In our time history has helped illumine, not usurp, the text. Christians do well when they are informed by history and the Church's faith and practice to see in a new way what was always there; when these sources aid in the development of intertextual, intertestamental networks of biblical material that complement each other and help us understand the mind of the one God. The sober lesson, of course, is how easily the Christian can use history and the church to pervert the text's meaning.

❧ F • I • V • E ❧

ANTI-JUDAISM IN THE CRITICAL STUDY OF THE GOSPELS

Joseph B. Tyson

IN HIS EXCELLENT STUDY of the treatment of Judaism in Christian scholarship, Karl Hoheisel claims that the year 1947 marked a significant change in the ways in which Christian scholars looked at Judaism in the time of Jesus.[1] By 1947 we knew the horrors of the Holocaust and were beginning to become more sensitive to the implications of Christian anti-Judaism. But also in 1947 the Dead Sea Scrolls were discovered, and we gradually became aware of the multiplicity of Jewish groups and the diversity of religious viewpoints and practices among Jews at the time of Jesus. The term by which we began to designate this first-century phenomenon changed. We ceased to call it "late Judaism," which implied something that had come out of the Hebrew Bible, had become moribund at the time of Jesus, and had no genuine future. We began to call it "early Judaism," by which we meant to signify a phenomenon that had a new beginning, coming out of the history of ancient Israel and making use of the writings of the Hebrew Bible, of course, but with a vital future, pointing toward the developments that led to the Mishnah, the Talmuds, and modern Judaism.

These developments sometimes brought with them fundamental changes in the ways in which Judaism was portrayed. In some cases, rabbinic writings began to be perceived more positively. The change may be illustrated by reference to two editions of Emil Schürer's *History of the Jewish People in the Time of Jesus Christ*. The English edition of 1897, in a short chapter entitled "Life under the Law," refers to several early Jewish writers, including Antigonus of Socho. The reference to Antigonus says, "The saying of Antigonus of Socho: 'Be not like ser-

Parts of this chapter appear in Joseph B. Tyson, *Luke, Judaism, and the Scholars: Critical Approaches to Luke-Acts* (Columbia: University of South Carolina Press, 2000), and are used here by permission.

1. Karl Hoheisel, *Das Antike Judentum in christlicher Sicht: Ein Beitrag zur neueren Forschungsgeschichte*, SOR 2 (Wiesbaden: Otto Harrassowitz, 1978).

vants who serve their master for the sake of reward, but be like those who do service without respect to reward,' is by no means a correct expression of the keynote of Pharisaic Judaism, which was in fact like the servants who serve for the sake of recompense."[2] In the 1979 edition, revised by Geza Vermes and others, the chapter is retitled "Life and the Law," and at the comparable place we have the following: "The saying of Antigonus of Sokho, 'Be not like servants who serve their master for the sake of reward, but be like those who do service without consideration of reward,' foreshadows many similar counsels preserved in rabbinic literature."[3] In 1897 Schürer, implicitly applauding the saying of Antigonus, confidently labeled it an exception to the rule. In 1979 Vermes maintained that it is not untypical of rabbinic teaching.

Despite positive movements in some quarters, Hoheisel is not optimistic about Christian scholarship. He contrasts general studies of Jewish religious history and studies that concentrate on the connection between early Judaism and early Christianity. Among the former, "there is a long line of relevant representations of Jewish religious history at the beginning of the Christian era. The understanding of the Torah is given proper assessment in them."[4] In the latter, however, which I take to include studies by New Testament scholars, "the historically incorrect view of 'the late Jewish religion of law' has persisted."[5]

Hoheisel's judgment of the significance of 1947 in the history of New Testament scholarship is debatable. I intend to return to it at the end of this essay. But before doing so, it will be useful to take a serious look at this history, with the issue of the treatment of Judaism in mind. I intend first to provide a brief introduction to the topic by calling attention to the major participants and the most important issues in the history of nineteenth- and twentieth-century critical scholarship on the New Testament and then to engage in greater depth with the works of two scholars, one who wrote well before 1947 and one not long after.

At this point, however, it is appropriate to clarify what, for me, constitutes anti-Judaism. This is particularly important since there exists no scholarly consensus on the meaning of this term. I take the term "anti-Judaism" to mean a specifically Christian, theologically driven attitude

---

2. Emil Schürer, *A History of the Jewish People in the Time of Jesus Christ,* trans. Sophia Taylor and Peter Christie (Edinburgh: T. & T. Clark, 1897), div. 2, 2:93.

3. Emil Schürer, *The History of the Jewish People in the Age of Jesus Christ (175 B.C.-A.D. 135),* rev. and ed. Geza Vermes, Fergus Millar, and Matthew Black (Edinburgh: T. & T. Clark, 1979), 2:466.

4. Hoheisel, *Antike Judentum,* 215.

5. Ibid.

toward Jews, including concepts of the divine rejection and punishment of Jews, as well as Christian supersessionism and triumphalism. Since others in this volume address the question of anti-Judaism and the Gospels, I refrain here from making a judgment on this controversial issue. In scholarship on the Gospels, I understand anti-Judaism to be the tendency to stress negative aspects of Jewish religious life and thought in the first century and to neglect or de-emphasize more positive aspects, and to this topic I now turn.

JUDAISM IN NEW TESTAMENT SCHOLARSHIP

There are a number of excellent essays on the treatment of Judaism in Christian New Testament scholarship. The book by Karl Hoheisel has already been mentioned. George Foot Moore's 1921 article is still important, especially in its contrast of scholarship in the nineteenth century with that in previous times.[6] Although the focus is on Pauline studies rather than on the Gospels, a section of E. P. Sanders's *Paul and Palestinian Judaism* cannot be overlooked.[7] In a section entitled "The Persistence of the View of Rabbinic Religion as One of Legalistic Works-Righteousness," Sanders clearly shows how this anti-Jewish tradition developed. Geza Vermes has also provided important insights on some of the most significant scholarship.[8] In a recent article, Susannah Heschel shows how the work of Abraham Geiger, a leader of Reform Judaism in the middle of the nineteenth century, had the potential of providing an alternative view of Jesus in his relationship to the Pharisees.[9] Heschel maintains that Christian scholars knew but intentionally ignored Geiger's work.

Drawing on the studies cited above, I want to survey the work of those scholars who made important contributions to the development of anti-Judaism in critical biblical scholarship. Professor Heschel has pointed out that many of the concepts that we will find expressed by these scholars were not really new. They had become familiar and popular through centuries of Christian teaching. She writes, "One wonders

---

6. George Foot Moore, "Christian Writers on Judaism," *HTR* 14 (1921): 197–254.

7. E. P. Sanders, *Paul and Palestinian Judaism: A Comparison of Patterns of Religion* (Philadelphia: Fortress Press, 1977), esp. 33–59.

8. Geza Vermes, "Jewish Studies and New Testament Interpretation," *JJS* 31 (1980): 1–17.

9. Susannah Heschel, "The Image of Judaism in Nineteenth-Century Christian New Testament Scholarship in Germany," in *Jewish-Christian Encounters over the Centuries: Symbiosis, Prejudice, Holocaust, Dialogue*, ed. Marvin Perry and Frederick M. Schweitzer (New York: Peter Lang, 1994), 215–40.

how much difference there really was between the attitudes toward Judaism of a village pastor in nineteenth-century Germany and those of Schürer or Harnack, other than the idiom in which they were expressed.... These historians apparently did not try to free themselves from traditional Christian biases toward Judaism, even when alternative historical models and interpretive modes had been developed by Jewish historians such as Geiger."[10]

Curiously, one of the earliest of the nineteenth-century scholars had become familiar with early Jewish literature, and he came away with relatively positive views of Judaism. George Foot Moore claims that August Friedrich Gförer (1803–1861) represents the beginning of the modern period in Christian studies of Judaism. Moore found a major change in Christian scholarship beginning in the mid-eighteenth century. "The seventeenth century was the great age of Hebrew learning among Christian scholars; it lasted on till toward the middle of the eighteenth and then abruptly ended."[11] Nineteenth-century scholars claimed to be writing history, but "for this purpose they employed chiefly the material that came down from their predecessors, without giving sufficient consideration to the fact that it had been gathered for every conceivable motive except to serve as material for the historian."[12] Moore adds, "A delectus of quotations made for a polemic purpose is the last kind of a source to which a historian would go to get a just notion of what a religion really was to its adherents."[13] Indeed, the opening sentence of Moore's article claimed that "Christian interest in Jewish literature has always been apologetic or polemic rather than historical."[14] And Moore has adequately shown this statement to be true. But Gförer appears to be an exception. His "was the first time that the attempt had been made to portray Judaism as it was, from its own literature, without apologetic, polemic, or dogmatic prepossessions or intentions."[15] And Moore claims that "it is to this day [1921] the most adequate presentation of the subject from the hand of a Christian scholar."[16]

---

10. Ibid., 233.
11. Moore, "Christian Writers," 221.
12. Ibid.
13. Ibid., 221–22.
14. Ibid., 197.
15. Ibid., 225.
16. Ibid., 226. Hoheisel (*Antike Judentum*, 11) agrees that Gförer opened a new epoch in scholarship. He writes that Gförer's studies have made him a "forerunner of that modern teaching that highly esteems rabbinic literature for knowledge about Judaism in the early Tannaitic period."

Heschel notes that Gförer made the then popular association between Jesus on the one hand and Essenic and Philonic ideas on the other. Even so, "Gförer's conclusions are particularly significant because of the weight of research behind them."[17] She adds, "His presentation of Jewish thought draws extensively on the collections of rabbinic, midrashic, and kabbalistic texts prepared by earlier Christian scholars, from Raymund Martini (thirteenth century) onward, as well as on his own readings of Talmudic texts."[18]

Heschel laments that, for the most part, Christian scholars ignored the work of Gförer. Of far greater influence was Ferdinand Weber (1836–1879). Although some scholars find the origin of anti-Judaism in Christian scholarship with earlier writers, Moore and Sanders agree that it began with Weber. Moore says that he was the chief resource of Christian writers for forty years. He served the needs of Christian writers by providing a system of theology for Judaism at the time of Jesus, but it was a modern German system that he used, not an ancient Jewish one. For him, legalism was the sum and substance of Jewish religion. Actually, Moore questions Weber's originality: "Most of his quotations come out of the common stock which had been accumulated by the labors of many generations, not all of them even verified. Confiding successors have appropriated these errors, and not always given Weber the credit of them."[19] Although he notes Weber's characterization of Judaism as legalism, he says that what Weber calls "transcendentism" is on his part a fundamental misunderstanding. "Weber's original contribution to the misunderstanding of Judaism was what he calls 'transcendentism,' the inaccessibility of God, wherein he finds the characteristic difference of the Jewish idea of God, and its immense inferiority to the Christian idea."[20]

Sanders has a fairly full summary of Weber's most important concepts, beginning with the story of the universal fall of humankind, which resulted in human estrangement from God. Weber understands that, in Jewish thought, a divine account is kept of sins and fulfillments, and that we have two ways to overcome our estrangement: repentance, understood as a work, and obedience to the Law. In regard to Israel, Weber believes that the Mosaic covenant restored Israel to a pre-Adamic position, but this was short-lived. "Because of the incident of the golden

---

17. Heschel, "Image of Judaism," 218.
18. Ibid., 219.
19. Moore, "Christian Writers," 232.
20. Ibid., 233.

calf, Israel loses its restored status: as Adam's fall resulted in the separation of mankind from God, 'es ist Israels Sündenfall.' . . . Thereafter it becomes the goal of the individual Israelite to regain what had been lost through the fall of Israel."[21] The individual Israelite does this through meticulous obedience to Torah, through the sacrificial system, through good works, and through the treasury of merit. According to Weber, "Judaism is a religion in which one must *earn* salvation by compiling more good works ('merits'), whether on his own or from the excess of someone else, than he has transgressions."[22]

Hoheisel also recognizes Weber's importance. He notes that today we know there is nothing that may be called the talmudic system. But he writes that "Weber found not just the 'tenor' or the 'central complex of ideas' in these writings, but he also thoroughly systematized them, not by using representatively selected material, but by means of the system of Lutheran theology."[23] Hoheisel claims that Weber invented the theory of legalism as a pejorative description of Jewish religion, and Moore also implicitly confirms this assertion. Near the end of his essay, in commenting on Christian scholarship before Weber, Moore says that legalism "is not a topic of the older polemic; indeed, I do not recall a place where it is even mentioned. Concretely, Jewish observances are censured or ridiculed, but 'legalism' as a system of religion, not to say as the essence of Judaism, no one seems to have discovered."[24]

Although his major interest was not in New Testament studies, Julius Wellhausen (1844–1918) is clearly a contributor to the tradition of anti-Judaism in critical scholarship. Commenting on his source criticism of the Pentateuch, Hoheisel says that Wellhausen was romantically attracted to origins and primitive times. He tended to look upon Israel's preexilic period as a time of freedom and spontaneity, without Mosaic Law. The postexilic period, by contrast, was one of degeneration, in which the priestly cult became a substitute for what Wellhausen regarded as genuine religion. Hoheisel points out that "with the religious liberalism of his time, Wellhausen was filled with a deep mistrust of law and statutes."[25] Geza Vermes also shows how Wellhausen's religious leanings influenced his scholarship: "Liberal Protestantism — represented, say, by Wellhausen — promoted a sort of academic anti-Judaism

---

21. Sanders, *Paul and Palestinian Judaism*, 37.
22. Ibid., 38.
23. Hoheisel, *Antike Judentum*, 12.
24. Moore, "Christian Writers," 252.
25. Hoheisel, *Antike Judentum*, 19.

which, in an oversimplified way, may be summed up thus. Authentic Judaism — i.e., all that a nineteenth-century enlightened Christian found acceptable in the Old Testament — was propounded by the prophets before the Babylonian exile. After the return of the Jews to Palestine, came the Law which completely suffocated the free impulses of a living religion."[26]

The relationship between Wellhausen and Weber may be shown by reference to the fact that the latter adopted the former's historical construction. Weber wrote in his introduction, "Something new arose with Ezra's return to the Jewish community. Through him the law of Moses became the exclusive means of religious thought and the life of all the people's piety. The influence of the prophetic words retreated behind the law; indeed, the law became the sole religious principle."[27]

Wellhausen also wrote on the Sadducees and Pharisees, explicitly intending to counter the claims of Abraham Geiger. He pictured the Pharisees as "characterized by their 'religious materialism.... The Pharisees killed nature through the commandments, 613 written commandments and 1000 other laws and they leave no room for conscience. One forgot God and the way to him in the Torah.' "[28] Thus in Wellhausen's view, Jesus could not have been a Pharisee, as Geiger had claimed.

In a recent appraisal of the work of E. P. Sanders, Martin Hengel and Roland Deines write about Paul Billerbeck (1853–1952), "who was himself — as was his teacher H. L. Strack — a decided opponent of anti-Semitism, and who in our opinion did more to spread the knowledge of rabbinic texts in academic theology than any other Christian theologian, including Sanders."[29] Sanders's judgment about Billerbeck is, however, decidedly negative: "Billerbeck, who carefully compiled countless 'parallels' to New Testament passages from Rabbinic literature, more than any other passed on Weber's soteriological scheme to the present generation."[30] Sanders notes that many New Testament scholars do not perceive a theory at work in the selection of passages in the *Kommentar zum neuen Testament aus Talmud und Midrasch*, but he insists that Billerbeck nevertheless distorted the clear meaning of some texts and by his selections prejudiced the questions addressed to them. In his own

---

26. Vermes, "Jewish Studies," 7.

27. Ferdinand Weber, *Jüdische Theologie auf Grund des Talmud und verwandter Schriften*, 2d ed. (Leipzig: Dörffling und Franke, 1897), xiii.

28. Heschel, "Image of Judaism," 228.

29. Martin Hengel and Roland Deines, "E. P. Sanders' 'Common Judaism,' Jesus, and the Pharisees," *JTS* 46 (1995): 68–69.

30. Sanders, *Paul and Palestinian Judaism*, 42.

statement of soteriology, Billerbeck talks of Torah as providing an occasion for individuals to earn merit and reward, of God as bookkeeper, and of the merits of the fathers. "Billerbeck summarizes: 'the old Jewish religion is thus a religion of the most complete self-redemption (*Selbsterlösung*); it has no room for a redeemer-saviour who dies for the sins of the world.'...The last clause indicates what is *really* wrong with Judaism."[31] Later in the same volume, Sanders' comments on Billerbeck's *Kommentar* are even more devastating: "Billerbeck may retain some usefulness as a collection of passages on individual points, with several provisions: that the user be able to look up the passages and read them in context, that he disregard as much as possible Billerbeck's own summaries and syntheses, and that he be able to imagine how to find passages on the topic not cited by Billerbeck."[32] In other words, "Billerbeck's *Kommentar* should not be used by those it was designed to serve: New Testament scholars who have no ready independent access to Rabbinic material."[33] Hoheisel would agree, and he says that Billerbeck "developed the Pharisaic teaching on righteousness as the pure negation of the magnificent evangelical teaching of justification, which Jesus is supposed to have brought into the world."[34] He adds that Billerbeck's portrayal is so totally dark that no one can make use of it to claim that Judaism was a preliminary stage of the gospel.[35]

Moore reserves some of his most negatively critical comments for Wilhelm Bousset (1865–1920). He claims that Bousset's knowledge about Judaism was only negligible. He was only twenty-seven years old when he wrote his *Religion des Judentums*. "What Bousset lacked in knowledge, he made up, however, in the positiveness and confidence of his opinions and for the failure to present evidence, by an effective use of what psychologists call suggestion — unsupported assertion coming by force of sheer reiteration to appear to the reader self-evident or something he had always known."[36] Jewish scholars have censured Bousset for his exclusive use of the Apocrypha and Pseudepigrapha, especially apocalypses, and his secondary use of "the writings which represent the

---

31. Ibid., 43.
32. Ibid., 234–35.
33. Ibid., 235.
34. Hoheisel, *Antike Judentum*, 43.
35. Ibid. Vermes ("Jewish Studies," 7) points out that Billerbeck depended heavily on Weber: "Very often the choice of the illustrative material in the famous *Commentary to the New Testament from Talmud and Midrash* is governed by Weber's understanding of Judaism."
36. Moore, "Christian Writers," 242.

acknowledged and authoritative teachings of the school and the more popular instruction of the synagogue."[37] Bousset would defend himself by saying that he used works that appeared before the first century, not afterward. But Moore writes, "The relative age of the writings is of much less importance than their relation to the main line of development which can be followed from the canonical Scriptures through many of the postcanonic writings, including the Synoptic Gospels and the liturgy of the synagogue, to the Midrash and Halakah of the second century."[38]

Hoheisel also notes the criticism about Bousset's limited use of sources, but he argues that the sources were pre-Christian and that, while rabbinic literature might show us the religion of the scribes, the literature Bousset used was that of popular piety. Nevertheless, Hoheisel claims that a "detailed source analysis confirms that Bousset did not write a history, but painted a dark background for the proclamation of Jesus."[39]

One of Bousset's basic emphases is on the contrast between the Jewish idea of God and that of Jesus. He conceives of the Jewish God as distant and estranged. Moore explains that Bousset's concept comes from his pre-occupation with apocalyptic literature, which characteristically pictures God as remote and approachable only through intermediaries. Sanders, however, traces Bousset's concept of Jewish theology to Weber, and he judges that for this reason the idea of the remoteness and inaccessibility of God dominated Bousset's work.[40]

Heschel notes that Bousset was heavily dependent on Geiger in his characterization of the relationship between Sadducees and Pharisees, but that he presented the Pharisees in a way very different from that of Geiger. She writes that, according to Bousset, "Although the Pharisees were originally the representatives of progress in Judaism, 'piety in their hands soon became stiff and lifeless,' and the Pharisees, once they attained power, 'very quickly developed into the conservatives, the representatives of a hard and rigid piety, a new aristocracy which forcibly displaced the old.' Ultimately, he concludes, Judaism is a religion of external observance lacking sincerity."[41]

Bousset stressed the legalistic aspects of what he called "late Ju-

---

37. Ibid., 243.
38. Ibid., 244–45.
39. Hoheisel, *Antike Judentum*, 26.
40. See Sanders, *Paul and Palestinian Judaism*, 39.
41. Heschel, "Images of Judaism," 230.

daism"; Jewish piety means a divine demand of righteousness and countless requirements for good works. Life is thus an account book or a balance sheet.[42] He wrote, "If we should ask about the foundation of the late Jewish religious community, there can be no doubt that only one answer can be given: that foundation is the law."[43] He calls attention to the fact that a number of tractates in the Mishnah are concerned, in the smallest detail, with sacrifice, observances, and the Temple cult. The civil law, he says, covers almost everything — marriage, rights of elders and children, relations of masters and slaves, trials and punishments. Moral law also covers every conceivable detail, but it is limited. Obligations of Jews to fellow Jews is of a different order from their obligations to Samaritans and the ʿam haʾaretz. So, "Judaism knows nothing of the interest and unconditional good will of persons to other persons."[44] Nevertheless, the rigid demands of the Law called on the people to bear astounding and almost impossible burdens.[45] And, as Sanders points out, Bousset rejected the concept of the treasury of merit, found in Weber's theology, and this had a profound effect on his description: "Thus, in Bousset's view, the one hope of Jews — the transfer of the merits of the fathers — was doomed to frustration, and Judaism was consequently judged to be an inadequate and non-functional religion."[46] There is also the character of casuistry. Next to each other are ritual, cult, civil law, important and unimportant matters, large and small details.[47] Bousset's judgment is similar to that of Harnack, as we shall see: "Judaism knows so many higher and more excellent demands of ethical culture, but it knows so much more besides."[48] Over against all this stands Jesus' Sermon on the Mount, which is a great polemic against the legalistic character of Jewish religion. It is intended to replace the many individual commands with a way of thinking.[49]

Hoheisel claims that Emil Schürer (1844–1910) wrote his history in the spirit of Wellhausen. It has a great deal of important data on the three-hundred-year period that is covered, but only two chapters specifically on religion. "His choice of the topics, 'Messianic Hope,'

---

42. See Hoheisel, *Antike Judentum*, 31.
43. D. Wilhelm Bousset, *Die Religion des Judentums im neutestamentlichen Zeitalter*, 2d ed. (Berlin: Reuther und Reichard, 1906), 136.
44. Ibid., 156.
45. See ibid., 151.
46. Sanders, *Paul and Palestinian Judaism*, 39–40.
47. See Bousset, *Religion des Judentums*, 158.
48. Ibid., 158.
49. See ibid., 153.

and 'Life under the Law,' shows his apologetic Christian interest."[50] Schürer added his own authority to the equation that he did not discover, namely, "Judaism=Legalism," which "plays a dominating role in theological teaching and research up to the present day."[51] Heschel claims that Schürer's purpose in painting such a negative picture of Judaism is to provide a contrast with Christianity. She also points out that, although he had argued against the use of rabbinic literature "for reconstructing political developments within Second Temple Judaism, he nonetheless uses rabbinic texts for his reconstruction of the alleged legalism and religious sterility of first-century Jewish life."[52]

Schürer's brief treatment of "Life under the Law" is a prime example of the negative portrayal of Judaism in Christian scholarship. The Law, he says, was intended to govern all of life, and Jews were enthusiastic about it because they had total belief in divine retribution, "a retribution in the strictest juristic sense."[53] In the Law all commands, large and small, are on the same level. "Not the doing of the good as such, but merely formal accuracy in fulfilling the letter of the law is the aim."[54] "All law is necessarily casuistic, for it lays down a multiplicity of individual statutes. All casuistry is by its nature endless."[55] And so Schürer concludes, "Life was a continual torment to the earnest man, who felt at every moment that he was in danger of transgressing the law; and where so much depended on the external form, he was often left in uncertainty whether he had really fulfilled its requirements."[56]

Sanders claims that Rudolf Bultmann (1884–1976) continued the practice of picturing Judaism negatively and lent enormous prestige to the tradition of Weber, Billerbeck, Bousset, and Schürer. Sanders is convinced that Bultmann had no independent access to the rabbinic literature but depended on Schürer, whom he commended for his work on both history and religion. But, writes Sanders, "It is a testimony to Bultmann's mental prowess and theological sophistication that his presentation of Judaism, though derivative, is often more acute and better nuanced than the works of those from whom he derived his information."[57] Bultmann believed that Second Temple Judaism no longer

50. Hoheisel, *Antike Judentum*, 19–20.
51. Ibid., 20.
52. Heschel, "Images of Judaism," 229–30.
53. Schürer, *History of the Jewish People* (1897 edition), div. 2, 2:91.
54. Ibid., div. 2, 2:95.
55. Ibid.
56. Ibid., div. 2, 2:125.
57. Sanders, *Paul and Palestinian Judaism*, 44.

regarded God as an important factor. He had acted in the past but does not in the present. Ritual observances were elaborated in Judaism "to the point of absurdity." Bultmann thus emphasized legalism in Judaism, referred to the laws as complex and often unintelligible, and believed that, in Jewish thought, one could do an excess of good works, which could balance transgressions. This legalism could lead either to "an unhealthy anxiety" or to "smug self-righteousness."[58] Even repentance and faith are counted as good works. Sanders shows that alternative views were available to Bultmann in the works of George Foot Moore and Erik Sjöberg, but that Bultmann chose to ignore them in favor of the view of Weber, which "is simply repeated."[59] Hoheisel underscores this judgment and alludes to the reason for Bultmann's acceptance of the negative picture. He writes, "With Bultmann as well as with the research on late Judaism that preceded him, questions about work, reward, and retribution are so exclusively oriented toward the Protestant understanding of justification that the significance of the law for collective salvation . . . is generally not perceived."[60]

In Bultmann's *Primitive Christianity,* the first section in the chapter on "Synagogue and Law" is entitled "Jewish Legalism."[61] There is little difference here between Bultmann and Weber. The Bible, Bultmann affirms, "was no longer primarily a historical record of God's dealings with his people, but a book of divine Law."[62] Bultmann acknowledges that "life under the Law was still worship and service of God."[63] But the Pharisees imposed harsh and restrictive laws on the people. "These regulations went into detail to the point of absurdity."[64] The emphases on honesty and marital fidelity were still upheld, and in these matters Judaism was exemplary. But "most important of all, no distinction was drawn between the moral and ritual law in respect of their divine authority."[65] A failing of this religion is that it is something other than "radical obedience," which is what Jesus taught. "What was required was specific actions, or specific abstentions from action. Once these had been got through, a man was free to do what he liked."[66] "Where the motive of

---

58. Ibid., 45.
59. Ibid., 47.
60. Hoheisel, *Antike Judentum,* 58–59.
61. Rudolf Bultmann, *Primitive Christianity in Its Contemporary Setting,* trans. R. H. Fuller (New York: Meridian Books, 1957), 59.
62. Ibid., 62.
63. Ibid., 65.
64. Ibid.
65. Ibid., 67.
66. Ibid., 69.

obedience is simply that a certain course of action is prescribed, there is no personal assent to the requirements of the Law. Radical obedience is possible only where the Law is understood and answered by personal assent."[67]

A review of the critical scholarship treated here shows that there is no exaggeration in speaking of a dominant anti-Jewish tradition in Christian biblical scholarship. From Weber to Bultmann, critical scholarship has created a foil against which the teachings of Jesus and Paul may be seen as clearly superior. The Judaism of the time of Jesus, which does not go back to the earliest strata of the Hebrew Bible but only to the time of Ezra, is a legalism that emphasizes the individual's efforts at self-salvation, concepts of merit, reward, and punishment. Almost as a caricature, God is pictured as an accountant making entries in each individual's balance sheet. But God is not directly accessible, as God had been accessible in early Israelite times. The Judaism of Jesus' time nevertheless emphasizes a special relationship of Jews to God, and this particularism and nationalism add to the shortcomings of this religion. To be sure, some of our scholars recognized that there were brilliant insights and commendable ethical teachings among the Rabbis, but, they said, there was so much trivia that the brilliance was hidden. Although individual scholars provided different emphases of this portrait and wrote with different nuances, the above description emerges as a consensus of scholarship. There were demurrals, mostly from Jewish scholars, and it is clear that these did not go unnoticed. But they were largely ignored in the effort to paint the dark portrait of first-century Judaism that we have observed.

I turn now from this general tracing of a tradition in critical scholarship to look in depth at the work of two major scholars who have significantly influenced the study of the Gospels. In doing so, I have three things in mind. First, I want to examine the ways in which questions about the Gospels and contemporary Judaism have informed the work of specific scholars and thus to determine the strength of the anti-Jewish tradition that I have just traced. Second, I have chosen two scholars who have worked on the same text, so that I might make meaningful and fairly specific comparisons. The text in question is Luke-Acts. Third, I have chosen one scholar of the late nineteenth and early twentieth century and one postwar scholar, so that, if possible, I might determine important differences in their approaches vis-à-vis first-

---

67. Ibid.

century Judaism. This, of course, cannot be seen as a definitive test of Karl Hoheisel's theory that 1947 made a significant difference in the character of New Testament scholarship, but it makes a step in that direction. The two scholars are Adolf von Harnack (1851–1930) and Hans Conzelmann (1915–1989).

Adolf von Harnack

In a discussion of the distinctiveness of the teaching of Jesus in the third lecture of his *Das Wesen des Christentums*, Adolf von Harnack raises the question of the relationship of this teaching to Judaism, and he makes an oblique reference to nineteenth-century Jewish scholarship, perhaps that of Abraham Geiger.

> "What do you want with your Christ," we are asked, principally by Jewish scholars; "he introduced nothing new." I answer with Wellhausen: It is quite true that what Jesus proclaimed, what John the Baptist expressed before him in his exhortations to repentance, was also to be found in the prophets, and even in the Jewish tradition of their time. The Pharisees themselves were in possession of it; but unfortunately they were in possession of much else besides. With them it was weighted, darkened, distorted, rendered ineffective and deprived of its force, by a thousand things which they also held to be religious and every whit as important as mercy and judgment. They reduced everything to one dead level [*Fläche*], wove everything into one fabric; the good and holy was only one woof in a broad earthly warp.[68]

Even if the German, *Fläche* does not carry quite the same negative quality as the English "dead level," there is no doubt about the force of this statement.[69] Harnack continues with similar imagery to speak of the purity and strength of the gospel, and he uses the metaphor of a spring to signify the holiness of truth: "As regards purity, the spring of holiness had, indeed, long been opened; but it was choked with sand and dirt,

---

68. Adolf von Harnack, *What is Christianity?* trans. Thomas Bailey Saunders (New York: Harper and Row, 1957), 47. The original, taken from sixteen lectures delivered by Harnack in 1899–1900, was published as *Das Wesen des Christentums* (Leipzig: J. C. Hinrichs, 1905).

69. *Fläche* is a generally neutral term for area or surface. A better translation of the phrase in question might be, "For them everything was on one level...."

and its water was polluted."[70] With Jesus this truth burst forth in pure clarity, without the pollution of priests and Rabbis.

Harnack's judgment about Judaism is in the first instance a product of his conviction about the distinctiveness of Jesus. This distinctiveness could not be allowed, however, to play itself out in absolute terms, for Harnack fully recognized the weight of Jewish objections. It was possible to cite parallels in the Hebrew Bible and later Jewish literature to many of the sayings of Jesus. So the distinctiveness must be established in a different way, by emphasizing the purity of the teaching of Jesus, and this required Harnack to characterize the Jewish tradition as a kernel of truth hidden within a husk that threatened to obscure whatever truth it contained.

Harnack was, however, less than explicit when it came to describing the character of first-century Judaism. The reader is left to fill in the negative characterization with whatever content might seem appropriate, and Harnack only hints at what the appropriate content might be. The essential distinction appears to be between matters such as justice and mercy, which may be characterized as inward dispositions, and ritual and worship, which are characterized as external acts. Later, in *What is Christianity?* Harnack includes what appears to be a carefully nuanced statement about Pharisees:

> To judge the moral ideas of the Pharisees solely by their childish and casuistical aspects is not fair. By being bound up with religious worship and petrified in ritual observance, the morality of holiness had, indeed, been transformed into something that was the clean opposite of it. But all was not yet hard and dead; there was some life left in the deeper parts of the system.[71]

In this light, Harnack points out that Jesus' contribution was a breaking of the connection between ethics and ritual. "He [Jesus] would have absolutely nothing to do with the purposeful and self-seeking pursuit of 'good works' in combination with the ritual of worship."[72]

In *The Expansion of Christianity in the First Three Centuries*, Harnack concedes that there was a kind of *preparatio evangelium* in Jewish proselytism. He notes that the Jewish missionaries found it necessary to de-emphasize ritualistic elements in order to call attention to the signifi-

---

70. Harnack, *What is Christianity?* 48.
71. Ibid., 70–71.
72. Ibid., 71.

cance of monotheism.[73] But this alteration in Jewish concepts appears to be motivated only by political and rhetorical considerations and is not a matter of principle. Besides, says Harnack, there was a vital omission in Jewish proselytism, namely, that "no Gentile, in the first generation at least, could become a real son of Abraham. His rank before God remained inferior. Thus it also remained very doubtful how far any proselyte — to say nothing of the 'God-fearing' — had a share in the glorious promises of the future. The religion which will repair this omission will drive Judaism from the field."[74]

Although Harnack displays a modicum of appreciation for the contribution of Jewish missionary preaching as a preparation for Christian preaching to Gentiles, he insists that there is no essential connection between Jewish and Christian theology. His *History of Dogma* begins without a treatment of the Jewish ideology that might have formed a context for Jesus and the early church. Indeed, Harnack is convinced that Christianity is new, despite its relation to Jewish history, concepts, and practices. As a fundamental presupposition to his history of dogma, Harnack maintains that "the Gospel presents itself as an apocalyptic message on the soil of the Old Testament, and as the fulfillment of the law and the prophets, and yet is a new thing, the creation of a universal religion on the basis of that of the Old Testament."[75] This principle would appear to cause trouble for a consideration of Jesus, whom Harnack is careful to associate, though loosely, with Judaism but not at all with Hellenism. He admits that Jesus "did not withdraw from the religious and political communion of his people, nor did he induce his disciples to leave that communion. On the contrary, he described the Kingdom of God as the fulfillment of the promises given to the nation, and himself as the Messiah whom that nation expected."[76] But this connection to Judaism appears to be a political strategy on Jesus' part to secure "for his new message, and with it his own person, a place in the system of religious ideas and hopes, which by means of the Old Testament were then, in diverse forms, current in the Jewish nation."[77] There seems to be little emphasis on either cultural context or religious conviction in this analysis of Jesus' intentions. The Hebrew Bible, transformed

---

73. See Adolf von Harnack, *The Expansion of Christianity in the First Three Centuries*, trans. James Moffatt (London: Williams and Norgate, 1904), 1:1–18.

74. Harnack, *Expansion of Christianity*, 1:15.

75. Adolf von Harnack, *History of Dogma*, trans. Neil Buchanan (Boston: Little, Brown and Company, 1905), 1:41.

76. Ibid., 1:42.

77. Ibid.

by the message of Jesus, provided the believer a sense of comfort and strength, and it supplied a firm footing that preserved the gospel "from dissolving in the glow of enthusiasm, or melting away in the ensnaring dream of antiquity."[78] Even so, the result of Jesus' preaching "was not only the illumination of the Old Testament by the Gospel and the confirmation of the Gospel by the Old Testament, but not less, though indirectly, the detachment of believers from the religious community of the Jews from the Jewish Church."[79] The movement of Christian believers away from Judaism and toward Hellenism is not surprising, for the latter exercised a powerful attraction: "Israel, no doubt, had a sacred treasure which was of greater value than all the treasures of the Greeks — the living God; but in what miserable vessels was this treasure preserved, and how much inferior was all else possessed by this nation in comparison with the riches, the power, the delicacy and freedom of the Greek spirit and its intellectual possessions."[80]

Negative appraisal of Judaism in the *History of Dogma* becomes radical rejection in Harnack's study of Marcion.[81] His emphasis on the newness of Christianity is a reflection of his fascination with Marcion, and his explanation of Marcion's motivation appears to reflect his own. For example, Harnack states that Marcion's point of departure is "provided *in the Pauline contrast of law and gospel, on the one side malicious, petty and cruel punitive correctness, and on the other side merciful love.*[82] Harnack finds no basis for disagreeing with Marcion in this characterization. For him, Marcion's theology is an extension of Paulinism, and this recognition led Harnack to sympathize with Marcion's attitude toward the Hebrew Bible.

> If one carefully thinks through with Paul and Marcion the contrast between "the righteousness that is by faith" and "the righteousness that is by works" and is persuaded also of the inadequacy of the means by which Paul thought that he could maintain the *canonical* recognition of the Old Testament, consistent thinking will not

---

78. Ibid.
79. Ibid., 1:43.
80. Ibid., 1:47.
81. Adolf von Harnack, *Marcion, Das Evangelium vom fremden Gott: Eine Monographie zur Geschichte der Grundlegung der katholischen Kirche* (Leipzig: J. C. Hinrichs, 1921); English translation, *Marcion: The Gospel of the Alien God*, trans. John E. Steely and Lyle D. Bierma (Durham, N.C.: Labyrinth Press, 1990). Unless otherwise noted, quotations here are from the English translation.
82. Harnack, *Marcion*, 21 (italics original).

be able to tolerate the validity of the Old Testament as canonical documents in the Christian church.[83]

Later in the same chapter, Harnack states the following thesis, for which he argues:

> The rejection of the Old Testament in the second century was a mistake which the great church rightly avoided; to maintain it in the sixteenth century was a fate from which the Reformation was not yet able to escape; but still to preserve it in Protestantism as a canonical document since the nineteenth century is the consequence of a religious and ecclesiastical crippling.[84]

Harnack recommends that the Protestant churches make it clear that the Hebrew Bible is useful for reading but is not canonical, that it is not to be put on the same level as the New Testament, and that it has no compelling authority for Christians.

Harnack's view of first-century Judaism may be characterized as radically negative. Judaism plays only a minor role in the history of early Christianity and contributes nothing of significance to the theology. Although there are similarities between Jewish teachings and the teaching of Jesus, there are no grounds for any meaningful comparisons. One would need to dig through mountains of valueless Jewish teachings in order to find what presents itself in purity and simplicity in the teaching of Jesus. Judaism emphasizes the external duties of correct worship and ritual. It teaches the doctrine of works righteousness, the very opposite of the Pauline doctrine of righteousness by faith. Thus, Christianity is new, and its relation to Judaism and to the Hebrew Bible is not essential. Even if New Testament documents speak of Jesus as the fulfillment of law and prophets, this fulfillment is to be understood as a severance from Judaism, a separation that should result in the Christian rejection of law and prophets as canonical.

In the first volume of his study of the history of Christianity, Harnack has a revealing statement about the relationship of Christianity to Judaism. He raises the question of justice in consideration of the appropriation of the Hebrew Bible by the Gentile Christian church on the one hand, and the rejection of Judaism on the other:

> The Gentile church stripped it [Judaism] of everything; she took away its sacred book; herself but a transformation of Judaism, she

---

83. Ibid., 133.
84. Ibid., 134.

cut off all connection with the parent religion. The daughter first
robbed her mother, and then repudiated her! But, one may ask, is
this view really correct? Undoubtedly it is, to some extent, and it is
perhaps impossible to force anyone to give it up. But *viewed from
a higher standpoint*, the facts acquire a different complexion. By
their rejection of Jesus, the Jewish people disowned their calling
and dealt the death-blow to their own existence.[85]

One may reasonably ask what the "higher standpoint" is from which
Harnack is making this judgment, and if this standpoint is appropriate
for the kind of historical investigation he intends. The answer is obvious.
The "higher standpoint" is nothing other than the Christian conviction
about Jesus, not that of an unbiased historian.

Harnack on Luke-Acts

In order to make a fair assessment of Harnack's judgments about the
treatment of Judaism in Luke-Acts, we must be aware of his considerations about the authorship and sources of these documents. Without
attending to the details of his arguments, we should note that, for Harnack, Luke and Acts were written by the physician and fellow-worker
with Paul, Luke by name. Further, he has confidence in Luke's abilities
to write history. Harnack adopted the two-document hypothesis, which,
by his time, had become the dominant solution to the synoptic problem among Protestant critics. In addition, Luke found it necessary to
use sources for the first part of Acts, which describes pre-Pauline Christian history. Indeed, according to Harnack, in this part of Acts, Luke
used two sources: one (in Acts 3:1–5:16; 8:5–40; 9:31–11:18; 12:1–
23) derived from Philip or his daughters, in which we can have great
confidence as to its historicity; the other (represented in Acts 2:1–47;
5:17–42) is historically worthless. After Acts 15:35, however, the author is, according to Harnack, no longer dependent on sources; he is
writing from personal memory.

Harnack's high regard for the historical competence of the author of
Luke-Acts and for the general accuracy of his work affects his consideration of this author's treatment of Judaism and the Jewish people. He
characterizes Luke as unbiased. On the one hand Luke accepts the divine
rejection of the Jewish people, but on the other he includes favorable
notes about Jews whenever he can. Harnack remarks that "this impartiality of the narrative, in a point where there was such an extraordinary

---

85. Harnack, *Expansion of Christianity*, 1:81–82 (italics added).

temptation to partiality, is a valuable proof of the careful sense of justice of the historian St. Luke."[86] If one should object that Luke is not consistently unbiased and should, for example, call attention to his picture of Jews as constantly stirring up Roman authorities against Paul, Harnack has a ready response: *"This bias is in accordance with actual fact."*[87] Harnack's confidence in Luke's historical competence and the eyewitness character of his report serve to underline the anti-Jewish emphases in his narrative.

What Harnack calls Luke's impartiality may also be termed his ambivalence; that is, there are both pro-Jewish and anti-Jewish tendencies discernible in the narrative. Ferdinand Christian Baur was able to address this issue by positing multiple stages in the composition of the Gospel and by assuming Luke's need in writing Acts to please both Pauline and Jewish Christians.[88] Harnack, however, cannot follow this route. He notes that Luke is sometimes more pro-Jewish than Paul, but in other places the reverse is the case. In his answer to those who think that the author of Acts misrepresented Paul, Harnack admits that Paul was a complex figure. He also notes Luke's pro-Jewish stance, vis-à-vis Paul: "And we must also remember that St. Luke as a 'theologian,' like all Gentile Christians, was more a man of the Old Testament than St. Paul, because he had never come to a real grip with the problem it presented."[89]

For Luke, the Jewish rejection of the Christian message was not, according to Harnack, the problem that it might become for later generations. Jewish rejection was not a sign of the weakness of the gospel, since it was the result of divine predestination that had been foretold in the prophets. Jewish rejection of the gospel has not only led to divine rejection of the Jewish people but also assured the legitimacy of Gen-

---

86. Adolf von Harnack, *The Acts of the Apostles,* NTS 3, trans. J. R. Wilkinson (London: Williams and Norgate, 1909), xxiv–xxv.

87. Adolf von Harnack, *Luke the Physician: The Author of the Third Gospel and the Acts of the Apostles,* NTS 1, trans. J. R. Wilkinson (London: Williams and Norgate, 1908), 135 (italics original).

88. See Ferdinand Christian Baur, *Kritische Untersuchungen über die kanonischen Evangelien, ihr Verhältnis zu einander, ihren Charakter und Ursprung* (Tübingen: Ludw. Fr. Fues, 1847), 391–531; see also idem, *Paul, the Apostle of Jesus Christ, His Life and Work, His Epistles and His Doctrine: A Contribution to a Critical History of Primitive Christianity,* 2 vols., trans. by Allan Menzies (London: Williams and Norgate, 1876).

89. Harnack, *Luke the Physician,* 127. But in a note in the preface to *The Acts of the Apostles* (p. xxv), Harnack seems to suggest that Luke is slightly more anti-Jewish than Paul. Here he addresses the question of anti-Judaism in early Christianity generally and ranks various writers in an order ranging from no anti-Judaism to extreme anti-Judaism. The order is Paul, Luke, John, the apologists, the *Epistle of Barnabas,* and Marcion.

tile Christianity. "This negative theme, which runs like a scarlet thread through the whole book, is summarised once again with impressive emphasis in the antepenultimate verse of the Acts: 'Be it known therefore unto you that this salvation of God is sent unto the Gentiles; they will also hear.' "[90] This means that, for the most part, Jews are treated unfavorably in the text of Luke-Acts; but Harnack is careful to note a major difference between Luke and John at this point.

> The Jew is in a sense the villain in this dramatic history, yet not — as in the Gospel of St. John and the Apocalypse — the Jew in the abstract who has almost become an incarnation of the evil principle, but the real Jew without generalisation and exaggeration in his manifold gradations of Pharisee, Sadducee, aristocrat, Jew of Palestine or of the Dispersion.[91]

For the most part, Harnack stresses a balance in Luke-Acts between anti-Judaism and admiration for the Hebrew Bible: "In hostility to the Jews — so far as that people had rejected the gospel — he [Luke] certainly cannot be surpassed; but just as certainly (see also the gospel, especially chaps. i and ii) he had a theoretical reverence for Old Testament ordinances and Old Testament piety."[92] In addition, Harnack denies that Luke thought of Christians as the new people of God, replacing the Jews. "According to St. Luke there is no new 'People' which takes the place of the old; the Jewish nation still remains the People, to the believing section of which the Gentiles are added."[93]

As a radical theologian who sympathized with Marcion, and a conservative biblical critic who was convinced that a companion of Paul wrote Luke-Acts, Harnack is a fascinating study. Despite his own bias against the Hebrew Bible, he is not blind to Luke's reverence for it. What he calls Luke's lack of bias counts for him as a confirmation of the historical character of Luke-Acts.

Harnack recognizes the deep ambivalence in the attitude toward Jews and Judaism to be found in the text of Luke-Acts, and he sometimes counts it as evidence for the author's impartiality. But his explanation for the presence of both pro- and anti-Jewish tendencies seems remarkably thin. In fact, I could find only one sentence that attempts to provide

---

90. Harnack, *Acts of the Apostles*, xxiv.
91. Ibid.
92. Harnack, *Luke the Physician*, 128.
93. Adolf von Harnack, *The Date of the Acts and of the Synoptic Gospels*, NTS 4, trans. J. R. Wilkinson (London: Williams and Norgate, 1911), 112.

an explanation. The sentence (quoted above and again here) suggests a comparison between Luke and Paul on the issue of the Hebrew Bible: "And we must also remember that St. Luke as a 'theologian,' like all Gentile Christians, was more a man of the Old Testament than St. Paul, because he had never come to a real grip with the problem it presented."[94] The evidence cited for this contention presumably is to be found in Luke 16:17, to which Harnack calls attention in a footnote.[95] Apparently we are to conclude that Luke is representative of typical post-Pauline Gentile Christians who, because they were not Jewish and had not had the experience of Paul, held a higher view than he of Jewish religion. This suggestion seems remarkably inadequate as an explanation for the deep ambivalence to be found in Luke-Acts on the issue of Israel. And when we recall Harnack's almost total neglect of any description of first-century Judaism, we gain the impression that the whole issue had little importance for this great scholar.

HANS CONZELMANN

To move from the time of Adolf von Harnack to that of Hans Conzelmann is to experience severe culture shock. Between them lie two world wars and the Holocaust, events that affected the entire planet, but Germany in particular. Hans Conzelmann (1915–1989) was beginning his university-level education at the start of the Third Reich. Little is known about any public stands that he might have taken on National Socialism or on the program of genocide that led to millions of deaths in Auschwitz, Treblinka, and other camps. It is known that he had difficulties in obtaining his first faculty position, probably because of differences with the director of the Tübingen Foundation, who seems to have been sympathetic with National Socialism. Conzelmann was a member of the Church Theological Society in Württemberg, which Dietz Lange describes as "a group corresponding to the confessing church elsewhere in Germany"; and thus Conzelmann "stood clearly in opposition to the current regime."[96] Conzelmann was a draftee in the German

---

94. Harnack, *Luke the Physician*, 127.

95. Elsewhere Harnack observed that the author placed Luke 16:17 where he did in order to correct the apparent antinomianism of Luke 16:16. See Adolf von Harnack, *The Sayings of Jesus: The Second Source of St. Matthew and St. Luke*, NTS 2, trans. J. R. Wilkinson (London: Williams and Norgate, 1908), 198.

96. Dietz Lange, "In Memoriam Hans Conzelmann," in *Gentiles/Jews/Christians: Polemics and Apologetics in the Greco-Roman Era*, by Hans Conzelmann, trans. M. Eugene Boring (Minneapolis: Fortress Press, 1992), xiv.

military and was seriously wounded on the western front in 1945. One leg had to be amputated. But after the war he taught at Zurich and then at Göttingen. He died in 1989 after a number of serious health problems.

There is not much from Conzelmann's writing that exhibits his understanding of early Judaism. His practice of speaking and writing in brief sentences is well known and has probably led to some misunderstanding that might have been prevented by a more ample and extended discussion. Conzelmann did not publish a comprehensive study of early Judaism, but the topic was addressed in a number of publications on a variety of subjects related to the New Testament and early Christianity.

The article on grace (χάρις) in Kittel's *Theological Dictionary of the New Testament* was written jointly by Walther Zimmerli and Conzelmann, with the latter contributing the section on the meaning of the concept in Judaism. The article suggests that Conzelmann at that time (1964) followed the lead of the dominant school of German New Testament scholarship in picturing Judaism as legalistic and casuistic. For example, he acknowledges the use of the word "grace" in the rabbinic writings but points out the connection with law. On the uses of the term in rabbinic writings, Conzelmann writes, "The central problem is the relation between grace and works. The principle applies: 'One receives a reward only for an act.' ... 'Grace is what thou hast done to us because there were no good works in our hands.' ... That is, grace arises only where there are no good works; it is supplementary."[97] And he concludes, "Basically, however, the concept of grace remains caught in the schema of the Law. In the understanding of grace no line can be drawn from the Synagogue to the NT. Judaism cannot accept the alternative of works or grace."[98]

Perhaps the fullest analysis of early Judaism by Conzelmann is to be found in his *Outline of the Theology of the New Testament.*[99] As a part of the introduction to this volume, Conzelmann devotes some three pages to the Hellenistic environment of early Christianity and thirteen to the Jewish. In his analysis he supports many of his contentions by reference to the New Testament and often moves from Jewish to Chris-

---

97. Hans Conzelmann, χάρις, *TDNT* 9:388.
98. Ibid.
99. Hans Conzelmann, *An Outline of the Theology of the New Testament,* trans. John Bowden (London: SCM Press, 1969). The English edition is translated from the author's *Grundriß der Theologie des Neuen Testaments,* 2d ed. (Munich: Christian Kaiser, 1968). Quotations here are from the English edition.

tian ideas without warning. He introduces the section on the Jewish environment by noting that "Judaism not only provides the setting for Jesus and the primitive community, but is also their religion."[100] He recognizes that Jewish thought and practice in the period before 70 C.E. was not a unity, but he nevertheless intends to concentrate on those points of general consensus. On the idea of God he repeats a frequently noted theme in critical New Testament scholarship, namely, that Jewish thinking about God had emphasized transcendence and distance, as shown in the avoidance of the divine name and the reliance on intermediate beings. And in speaking of God as judge, he says that the idea of a double judgment has found its way into both Jewish and Christian eschatology from Persian religion. Then he writes, "The idea of an individual judgment means that the individual bears the whole weight of responsibility.... The idea of a general resurrection, however, makes it clear that the final victory falls to the good. This guarantees the certainty of salvation."[101] Then in the next paragraph Conzelmann claims, "The view that man is justified only by his works is carried through consistently. There is no room for grace. The judge is bound by his own law."[102] In the section on "Man and Salvation," Conzelmann cautions against making "the Reformation's dogmatic judgment on the law as a means to salvation into a historical verdict on the Jewish understanding of the law."[103] He adds, "For Judaism, the law is not primarily a sum of precepts, but the sign of the election of Israel, the ratification of the covenant. It is not a burden but a delight."[104] But then he asks, "Can obedience be achieved by legalistic casuistry at all?"[105] Attempts to obey law always involve casuistry, and not all things are covered by law. "There is also the limitation of all law; what is not prohibited is permissible."[106] But obedience to law can never suffice, says Conzelmann, because God demands the whole person; and by obedience to law, salvation can never be certain. And thus Judaism must resort to dependence on cult and apocalyptic expectation.

In another book, what appears to be a revision of this section of *An Outline of the Theology of the New Testament* has some different emphases and nuances to be noted. It is, however, difficult to know

---

100. Ibid., 13.
101. Ibid., 14.
102. Ibid.
103. Ibid., 21.
104. Ibid.
105. Ibid.
106. Ibid.

here what specific contributions come from Conzelmann and what come from his co-author, Andreas Lindemann.[107] Near the beginning of this section there is a note on terminology, a vigorously discussed topic in Göttingen at the time. Conzelmann and Lindemann disavow both terms, "late Judaism" and "early Judaism."

> Judaism of the NT era is often called "late Judaism." This is not a legitimate concept; it creates the impression that Judaism, existing alongside the church, is an anachronism up to the present time. Equally erroneous is the apologetic designation "early Judaism," which creates the impression that the OT is not part of Judaism. It is best to speak of Judaism in late antiquity or of Judaism in the hellenistic-Roman era.[108]

In the section on law in Judaism, the authors emphasize the inaccuracy of the concept that obedience to Torah was considered to be a difficult burden, and they maintain that "the law is not to be construed as motivation for external legalism and, especially for the Jew, is not a nuisance."[109] In a paragraph that is remarkable when viewed against earlier statements by Conzelmann, the authors write,

> Jewish obedience to the law must not be misinterpreted: The issue is not formal obedience but the attitude behind that obedience. What matters is not the human efforts alone, but the disposition to obedience. Even if one hopes for a reward for keeping the commandments, it is not permissible at all to use the law selfishly.[110]

The contrast between the teaching of Jesus and that of contemporary Judaism is emphasized in Conzelmann's article on Jesus in the third edition of *Die Religion in Geschichte und Gegenwart,* published in 1959.[111] Although even here Conzelmann did not provide an in-depth analysis of early Judaism, he characterized it as "dominated by the problems of

---

107. See Hans Conzelmann and Andreas Lindemann, *Interpreting the New Testament: An Introduction to the Principles and Methods of N.T. Exegesis,* trans. Siegfried S. Schatzmann (Peabody, Mass.: Hendrickson, 1988). The translation is from the 8th rev. ed. of *Arbeitsbuch zum Neuen Testament* (Tübingen: J. C. B. Mohr [Paul Siebeck], 1985).

108. Ibid., 130.

109. Ibid., 131.

110. Ibid.

111. For an English translation, see Hans Conzelmann, *Jesus: The Classic Article from RGG Expanded and Updated,* trans. Raymond Lord, ed. John Reumann (Philadelphia: Fortress Press, 1973). Quotations here are from this translation.

law and eschatology."[112] And, as in traditional Christian writing about Judaism, law and casuistry go together:

> For Judaism, the interpretation by which one can recognize and fulfill the will of God belongs to the law. This leads either to casuistry or to a heightening of the torah in the sense of the "Rule of the Community" (1QS) at Qumran.... Over against this interpretation and practice, Jesus places a new and peculiarly dialectical method of exposition. He assumes the law is intelligible by itself and needs no interpretation at all. Such interpretation is the work of men and obscures the matter; it is a question of getting back behind the human precepts to the commandments themselves.[113]

For Conzelmann, this is an explanation of the conflict between Jesus and the scribal community: "This understanding of God and law must lead to a conflict with the entire scribal casuistry in which, according to Jesus, God's will is not explained but distorted (Mark 7:6–7) and to a protest against the division of outer and inner which is unavoidable in legalism."[114] Thus the conflict between the teaching of Jesus and the teaching of the scribes inevitably led to conflict. Indeed, Conzelmann maintains, "It is immediately obvious that this preaching had to lead to a fundamental conflict with *all* the trends within Judaism."[115]

But in this same article, Conzelmann is emphatic and clear in denying that Jesus was put to death by Jews: "It is established that Jesus was executed by the Romans (and not by the Jews) since crucifixion is a Roman form of capital punishment and not a Jewish one."[116] Anything beyond this is speculation, and, although he does not deny that there was a session of the Sanhedrin involved in the proceedings, he concludes that the reports in the Gospels cannot be used to reconstruct the actual history. About the New Testament report of the Sanhedrin trial he says, "Methodologically it is misleading to interpret the present report as such a record [of the trial of Jesus]. It is a witness of faith."[117] Conzelmann is consistent in making this point about the death of Jesus. In an article on the Passion narratives of the synoptic Gospels, published in German in 1967, he makes the point quite directly. On the historical substratum of the narratives he says, "The assured core is that Jesus

---

112. Ibid., 18.
113. Ibid., 52–53.
114. Ibid., 53.
115. Ibid., 54.
116. Ibid., 84–85.
117. Ibid., 86.

was crucified. From that we can conclude that he was arrested and that
a court proceeding followed (and, to be sure, a Roman one). Crucifixion
is a Roman, not a Jewish, means of capital punishment."[118] Conzelmann
adds in the next paragraph, "All the rest in the course of events is debatable."[119] It is clear, however, that Conzelmann's chief interest in this
article is theology rather than history: "A contemporary approach to
the passion narrative is not to be gained from single facts but only from
the interpretation."[120] Granted that his main interest is in the interpretation, it is understandable that he does not want to engage in a sustained
discussion of the historical substratum of the Gospels. This means that,
even though any historical conclusion beyond the contention that Jesus
was crucified after a Roman trial is a matter of speculation, the inclusion
of a Jewish trial of Jesus in the synoptic Gospels is part of the interpretation of his death. And so Conzelmann includes the narratives about
Jewish involvement in the death of Jesus as part of the interpretation.
What is notable, however, is that he makes no effort in this article to call
attention to the anti-Jewish character of this interpretation. It is simply
Christian interpretation, which he says is "not a secondary addition to
primary facts of salvation."[121]

Conzelmann did, however, come closer to addressing this question
in a paper delivered in New York at the 1964 meeting of the Society
of Biblical Literature. In this paper Conzelmann demonstrated an acute
awareness of what he called the "historical consequences of this charge
[about the death of Jesus] against the Jews and the sufferings of the
Jewish people caused by a perverted understanding of the creedal formulations. There is no excuse for crimes Christians committed against
Jews."[122] Conzelmann points out that the original debates — reflections
of which made their way into the New Testament — were between two
groups of Jews, "the Jews of the old and the Jews of the new faith,"
both of which maintain "that they are the true people of God, the true

---

118. Hans Conzelmann, "History and Theology in the Passion Narratives of the Synoptic Gospels," *Int* 24 (1970): 179. The English version was translated by Charles B. Cousar
from "Historie und Theologie in den synoptischen Passionsberichten," in *Zur Bedeutung
des Todes Jesu,* ed. Fritz Viering (Gütersloh: Gerd Mohn, 1967), 37–53.

119. Ibid.

120. Ibid., 197.

121. Ibid.

122. Hans Conzelmann, "The First Christian Century as Christian History," in *The
Bible in Modern Scholarship: Papers Read at the 100th Meeting of the Society of Biblical
Literature, December 28–30, 1964,* ed. J. Philip Hyatt (Nashville: Abingdon Press, 1965),
222.

Israel."[123] He also felt it important to point out that, at this time and in this context, the Christian Jews constituted the weaker group that felt itself to be persecuted by the majority.

In one of his last books, written in 1981 but not translated into English until 1992, Conzelmann produced an exhaustive study of anti-Judaism in the ancient period, as seen in the literature of Greco-Roman writers, Christian writers, and Jewish apologists.[124] The discussion of the ancient sources, admirable and helpful as it is, appears to have a subtext in which Conzelmann urges caution about contemporary Christian-Jewish dialogue. As early as the introduction he attacks the tendency in such discussions to picture Jesus as a Jew and to use this picture as a mediating device between Christians and Jews.[125] At a later point he makes it clear that the continuing history of the Jewish people has no theological significance for Christians.[126] After a discussion of anti-Judaism in the earliest Christian writings, Conzelmann judges that the conflict between synagogue and church was inevitable: "The conflict is inherent in the existence of the church itself. It will last as long as church and synagogue exist side by side."[127] At the end he repeats that the "only issue between Jews and Christians is the issue of faith."[128] And he concludes, "All are justified before God in exactly the same way, by faith alone, which Paul in Rom. 3:30 bases on the confession that God is *one*."[129]

Scholars who knew Conzelmann well insist that it is a misunderstanding to take these remarks as anti-Jewish. Conzelmann's main intent was to raise questions about a kind of Christian-Jewish dialogue that blurs the real distinctions between the two groups. Christians should be Christians, and Jews should be Jews. Indeed, Conzelmann, while discouraging the attempt to find religious agreements between Christians and Jews, encouraged attempts to come together on human grounds. He wrote, "But instead of attempting to find a basis for religious agreement, it is thoroughly possible to attempt a rapprochement on human grounds, since Christians stand under the commandment of love, which is the end

---

123. Ibid., 220.
124. See Conzelmann, *Gentiles/Jews/Christians*. The original publication was *Heiden-Juden-Christen: Auseinandersetzungen in der Literatur der hellenistisch-römischen Zeit* (Tübingen: J. C. B. Mohr [Paul Siebeck], 1981). References here are to the English edition.
125. See ibid., 1–5.
126. See ibid., 253–54.
127. Ibid., 257.
128. Ibid., 342.
129. Ibid.

of the law."[130] I take this to mean that Christians should respect those things that make Jews different from Christians and should love Jews, because to do so is to observe the command of Jesus. Nevertheless, there is a certain unresolved tension between the "human" and the "theological" concerns that Conzelmann offers. The concluding statement of the book about the justification of all humans must be considered carefully:

> The Jews cannot be seen as some special *eschatological* category. Within this definition, all human beings, Christian and non-Christian, are directly confronted by God. . . . They are confronted by this Word not as Jews or Gentiles, Greeks or barbarians, but simply as human beings, i.e., as sinners who must renounce all boasting before God, including boasting that they are Christians, since the renunciation of all such boasting is inherent in faith. All are justified before God in exactly the same way, by faith alone, which Paul in Rom. 3:30 bases on the confession that God is *one*."[131]

I take this to mean that the faith by which all human beings may be justified is faith in the God and Father of Jesus Christ. If the issue between Jews and Christians is the issue of faith, and if, as Conzelmann says, Christians should not be expected to surrender their faith, then the implication about Jews is clear. The God of the Law is the God and Father of Jesus Christ. Although he never says so explicitly, I regard Conzelmann as implying that, if they are to become right with God, Jews must accept the faith by which Christians have come to God.

Against this background it should be fruitful to examine Conzelmann's understanding of the ways in which Judaism and the Jewish people are treated in the New Testament, specifically in Luke-Acts. For this examination I will focus attention on his pathbreaking book, *Die Mitte der Zeit.*

Conzelmann on Luke-Acts

Hans Conzelmann wrote *Die Mitte der Zeit* in 1954 as his *Habilitationsschrift.*[132] The significance of his work, as a demonstration of the possibilities of redaction criticism, was quickly perceived by European

---

130. Ibid., 133.
131. Ibid., 342.
132. See Hans Conzelmann, *Die Mitte der Zeit: Studien zur Theologie des Lukas,* BHT 17 (Tübingen: J. C. B. Mohr [Paul Siebeck], 1954); English translation, *The Theology of St. Luke,* trans. Geoffrey Buswell (New York: Harper and Brothers, 1960). References here are to the English edition.

and North American scholars. The German title focuses attention on one of Conzelmann's main contentions about Luke's theology, namely, the conviction that, for Luke, the time of Jesus was not to be understood as an eschatological sign. According to Conzelmann, Luke presented the history of salvation as a process that took place in three ages. The age of Jesus was the second of the three ages, and so the ministry of Jesus was not the precursor of an imminent kingdom of God. The three ages in the history of salvation were that of Israel, that of Jesus, and that of the church. The effect of seeing Jesus in the middle of this history is to claim that the period of the church, in which the reader of Luke-Acts is situated, should be presumed to be an indefinite and not necessarily brief period of time prior to the consummation of all things.

Not only did Conzelmann forge new ground in the conception of salvation history, but he introduced a new way of studying the Gospels. Acknowledging the contributions of form and source criticism, he distinguished his own contribution as an attempt "to elucidate Luke's work in its present form, not to enquire into possible sources or into the historical facts which provide the material."[133] He understood the process by which the Gospels were formed as one of the filling in of a basic kerygma with materials drawn from the traditional lore of Jesus' teachings and from the narrative material about him. Form criticism had clarified the first phase of this process by focusing attention on the primitive oral materials that made up this collection of teaching and narrative material. "Now a second phase has to be distinguished, in which the kerygma is not simply transmitted and received, but itself becomes the subject of reflection."[134] And so Conzelmann presents his study of Luke's theology as dependent on the results of form and source criticism, but going beyond them to ask questions about the Gospel in its present form.

A clarification in terms of method must be made at this point. Conzelmann maintains from the beginning that his work is not dependent on a particular source theory: "This study of St. Luke's theology is, by its approach to the problems, for the most part not dependent on any particular literary theories about St. Luke's Gospel and the Acts of the Apostles, for it is concerned with the whole of Luke's writings as they stand."[135] But in this same opening paragraph, Conzelmann acknowledges a significant dependence on source theory.

---

133. Conzelmann, *Theology of St. Luke,* 9.
134. Ibid., 12.
135. Ibid., 9.

A variety of sources does not necessarily imply a similar variety
in the thought and composition of the author. How did it come
about, that he brought together these particular materials? Was
he able to imprint on them his own views? It is here that the
analysis of the sources renders the necessary service of helping to
distinguish what comes from the source from what belongs to the
author.[136]

Clearly, Conzelmann accepts the view that Luke, in his Gospel, made use
of Mark and Q, and this theory undergirds his redaction criticism at a
number of points. In regard to Acts, however, he is much more circum-
spect about source theories. In both cases, however, it is important to
distinguish between Conzelmann's redaction criticism and narratological
or literary approaches that have been utilized more recently.

For Conzelmann, the key to the division in salvation history between
the age of Israel and that of Jesus is to be found in Luke 16:16: "The
law and the prophets were in effect until John came; since then the good
news of the kingdom of God is proclaimed, and everyone tries to enter
it by force" (NRSV). This verse "provides the key to the topography of
redemptive history. According to this passage, there is no preparation
before Jesus for the proclamation of the Kingdom of God, that is, of the
'Gospel' in Luke's sense."[137]

With this general scheme in mind, I want to focus now on some
specific aspects of Conzelmann's study that provide us with an understanding of Luke's treatment of Jews and Judaism. Initially, one might
suspect that an analysis of the first period of salvation history, the
epoch of Israel, would be useful for Conzelmann's project. In fact, however, Conzelmann says next to nothing about this period. He assumes
that it is characterized by "law and prophets" (cf. Luke 16:16), and
it obviously is intended to be coterminous with the history covered by
the Hebrew Bible. But beyond this, Conzelmann has no interest in describing the period of Israel. On his assumption, this is a period that
continues up through the time of John the Baptist, and so the reader
of Luke should be able to assume that the evangelist covers at least
some part of the period of Israel in the opening chapters, or up to the
point where Jesus makes his first public appearance in Luke 4:1. The
opening chapters of Luke, including the birth and infancy narratives of
Jesus and John in Luke 1–2, constitute a veritable mine of impressions

---

136. Ibid.
137. Ibid., 23.

of Jewish religious life. Here, if anywhere, Luke has a significant opportunity to describe Jewish religious life apart from and prior to Jesus, and the remarkable thing about the description is its positive character. Although the author shows no intention to provide a full description of Jewish religious life, Luke 1–2 focuses the reader's attention on a number of devout Jewish people, whose piety is described in positive fashion. Zechariah and Elizabeth are described as "righteous before God, living blamelessly according to all the commandments and regulations of the Lord" (Luke 1:6). Simeon is said to be "righteous and devout, looking forward to the consolation of Israel, and the Holy Spirit rested on him" (Luke 2:25). Anna "never left the Temple but worshiped there with fasting and prayer night and day" (Luke 2:37). These characters are noted not only for their powerful convictions and expectations, but for their quiet devotion, their obedience to the Law, and their engagement in prayer and fasting. Nothing emerges from these chapters about a religion that is drying up in enthusiasm or suffering the agonies of legalism and casuistry.

But Conzelmann almost entirely omits any discussion of these opening chapters of Luke. The one paragraph in *The Theology of St. Luke* in which he discusses Luke 1–2 is brief enough to be quoted in full:

> The introductory chapters of the Gospel present a special problem. It is strange that the characteristic features they contain do not occur again either in the Gospel or in Acts. In certain passages there is a direct contradiction, as for example in the analogy between the Baptist and Jesus, which is emphasized in the early chapters, but deliberately avoided in the rest of the Gospel. Special motifs in these chapters, apart from the typology of John, are the part played by Mary and the virgin conception, the Davidic descent and Bethlehem. On the other hand there is agreement in the fact that the idea of pre-existence is missing.[138]

Conzelmann's refusal to take account of the birth narratives has been frequently noted and criticized.[139] Paul Minear claims that "if Conzelmann had taken full account of the nativity stories, I believe his position would have been changed at several major points."[140] Indeed, says, Min-

---

138. Ibid., 172.
139. See H. H. Oliver, "The Lucan Birth Stories and the Purpose of Luke-Acts," *NTS* 10 (1964): 202–26; Paul S. Minear, "Luke's Use of the Birth Stories," in *Studies in Luke-Acts,* ed. Leander E. Keck and J. Louis Martyn (Nashville: Abingdon Press, 1966), 111–30.
140. Minear, "Luke's Use of the Birth Stories," 121.

ear, "I believe that it is only by thus ignoring the birth narratives that Conzelmann can appear to establish his thesis that Luke visualized the story of salvation as emerging in three quite distinct stages: the period of Israel, the period of Jesus' ministry, the period since the ascension."[141]

It is difficult to avoid Minear's contention, and what is surprising is the absence from *The Theology of St. Luke* of any genuine argument against the authenticity of Luke 1–2, especially since Conzelmann announced at the beginning of the book that his concern was "with the whole of Luke's writings as they stand."[142] In the absence of such an argument it is inappropriate to presume the reasons that may have led Conzelmann to neglect these narratives. But the neglect produces a result that has a definite bearing on the issue of Judaism in Luke-Acts. The omission of any attention to Luke 1–2 means that Conzelmann forfeited an opportunity to discuss a section of canonical Luke that would support a positive image of Judaism at the time of Jesus. More problematic from his own point of view, neglect of these chapters means that there is no significant discussion of what Conzelmann thought Luke meant by the period of Israel. Although the period of Israel is characterized as that of law and prophets, there is little description of it from Luke's perspective, except in those sections where Conzelmann draws on other parts of Luke-Acts to show that the evangelist's portrait of Jews and Judaism is totally negative.

And it is a negative picture indeed. We should keep in mind Conzelmann's own historical analysis of the crucifixion of Jesus, namely, that it came as a result of a Roman judicial process. His analysis of the Lukan narrative, however, shows that Luke took special pains to remove responsibility for Jesus' execution from Rome and point it toward the Jews. He notes that Pilate pronounced Jesus innocent more than once in Luke's version of the Roman trial and that the governor did not condemn him. "Jesus does not die by the decision of the Roman judge — he is killed by the Jews, to whom he is 'delivered' by the Roman (xxiii, 25)."[143] Conzelmann reads the Lukan narrative of Jesus' crucifixion as saying that Jesus is not executed by the Romans, since Pilate plays only a passive role in the story. "In so far as there is any suggestion that the Romans take part, it is a survival from the sources and is not part of the plan of Luke's account, but, rather, contradicts it."[144] Luke draws

---

141. Ibid.
142. Conzelmann, *Theology of St. Luke*, 9.
143. Ibid., 87.
144. Ibid., 90.

on the earlier tradition but develops it in a one-sided way to "put all the blame on to the Jews."[145]

The guilt of the Jews in putting Jesus to death results in a forfeiting of their election. Still, in Conzelmann's view of the perspective of Luke-Acts, they are offered an opportunity "to make good their claim to be 'Israel.' If they fail to do this, then they become 'the Jews.' "[146] So, although Luke establishes the guilt of the Jews in the death of Jesus, the Christian sermons in Acts concede that they acted in ignorance, and they are given another opportunity. They nevertheless refuse to repent and accept the Christian message, and so through most of Acts they are called "Jews." The terminology is important for Conzelmann, who emphasizes the claim that in Luke-Acts, because of their guilt in the execution of Jesus and their unrelieved obduracy and opposition to the Christian preachers, the Jews have forfeited the right to be Israel.

Although Conzelmann notes that the idea of the "true Israel" has not yet developed in Christian thought, he nevertheless insists that according to Luke-Acts, the church takes over "its inheritance of redemptive history."[147] He emphasizes the links that the earliest community had with Israel, in that it observed the Law and occupied the Temple. That the first generation of Christians observed the Law does not mean that subsequent generations must follow this model. It is only necessary for the first generation to observe Torah in order to provide a link between the church and Israel: "The fact that the primitive community keeps the Law . . . is proof that it is bound up with Israel."[148] Moreover, it is significant that loyalty to the Temple continues on into the Christian period. Conzelmann maintains that the Temple has ceased to be an institution for Jews, "because since Jesus' occupation of the Temple they [the Jews] have no right to possess it."[149] Conzelmann is quite clear about Luke's judgment on the Jews: "The idea of tradition is applied to Israel only in the general sense, that the Church is now the people of God."[150]

In many respects Conzelmann's views on Judaism in the time of Jesus are those of traditional prewar biblical scholarship. His emphasis on Judaism as legalism, casuistry, and works-righteousness is as dreary as those of his predecessors. His views are relieved, however, by his con-

---

145. Ibid.
146. Ibid., 145.
147. Ibid., 147.
148. Ibid., 160.
149. Ibid., 165.
150. Ibid., 167.

viction that it is the Romans who must bear the guilt for the execution of Jesus. And at least on one occasion he exhibited a consciousness of the possible relationship of Christian theology and the *Shoah*. In his important book on Luke, however, the most significant questions remain: How might his views of Luke's treatment of contemporary Judaism have been affected if he had devoted the attention to Luke 1–2 that he did to other parts of this text? Would his description of Luke's portrait of Jews and Judaism have been quite so unrelieved as it is, or might he have been able to see this portrait as ambivalent?

CONCLUSION

Contemporary interest in anti-Judaism in critical New Testament scholarship is partly due to the continuing effort to understand the first-century historical and religious contexts, an effort that has been enhanced by the discovery of new texts and the introduction of new approaches to old texts. But the interest is also due, to a significant extent, to reflection on the Holocaust of 1933–45. That Jews were the chief targets of oppression during these years inevitably forces us to question the religious and intellectual dimensions of the culture in which such events could occur. The judgment that critical New Testament scholarship is responsible for the Holocaust is, of course, indefensible. But the tendencies in this tradition to portray Judaism with unrelieved negativity almost certainly contributed toward the shaping of a culture that harbored sentiments against Jews and provided a justification for widespread anti-Judaic concepts. Thus the Holocaust provides a moral dimension to the study of anti-Judaism and the New Testament.

We must conclude that the major interpreters of the Christian Gospels, from Weber to Bultmann, created a tradition of interpretation that saw in early Judaism the antithesis of Christianity: It was a legalism, without heart and spirit; it emphasized external things; it imposed heavy burdens on adherents; it produced an endless casuistry; and if some gems were to be found in it, they were so covered up with worthless material that they were lost.

As we saw earlier, Hoheisel believed that there was a genuine change in critical approaches after 1947. Since it was not my purpose to provide an exhaustive analysis of critical scholarship either before or after 1947, the examination here should not be regarded as an attempt either to confirm or reject Hoheisel's hypothesis. Nevertheless, this limited examination of the work of Harnack and Conzelmann does little to confirm the thesis. To be sure, nothing like Harnack's antipathy toward the Hebrew Bible or his devastating and degrading descriptions of first-century Judaism appear in Conzelmann's work. But Conzelmann's scholarship shows that some traditional concepts about early Judaism have a tendency to hang on for a very long time and to die slowly if at all. It is painful to hear his judgment, written in 1981, that the continuing history of the Jewish people has no theological significance for Christians.[151]

Critical New Testament scholarship continues, and similar studies of more recent scholarship should be encouraged. This book and the conference that preceded it may at least serve to demonstrate a deep concern that now exists not only for discerning the truth about the foundational Christian documents but also for the moral dimensions of our scholarship.

---

151. See Conzelmann, *Gentiles/Jews/Christians*, 253–54.

RESPONSE TO
JOSEPH B. TYSON

James O. Duke

THE FIRST WORD should be one of appreciation to Professor Tyson for his essay "Anti-Judaism in the Critical Study of the Gospels." His voice is a welcome addition to the chorus warning that anti-Judaism remains a clear and present danger for Christian scholars today. To this end, he offers a brief review of what by now should be widely known about anti-Judaism in New Testament criticism as well as two detailed case studies of makers of Luke-Acts scholarship, Adolf von Harnack at the turn of the twentieth century and Hans Conzelmann following the Second World War and the Holocaust.

My response to his work is that of a historian of theology and church rather than that of a biblical scholar. Hence I will direct my comments less to his reading of their readings of Luke-Acts than on his warning of the continuing legacy of anti-Judaism that he detects in Christian critical biblical scholarship.

It is of course sad to say that Tyson's finding are by no means startling, certainly not to Jews or even to Christians who bother to look into the ever expanding body of literature exposing the church's *adversus Judaeos* tradition. The basic ingredients of that tradition are reasonably clear. Examples of it are so abundant that only exceptions to the rule count as real news, precisely because they are exceptional. Studies that Tyson cites, as well as many others, give no one reason to expect any other result. Time alone will prove whether such exposés will induce Christian scholars generally to learn how to study and love Christian origins without defaming Judaism. There is clear and present danger that in the absence of a secure disciplinary home, this literature will become yet another sideline specialty or interest group area in the now vast but fragmented field of religious studies.

In this regard, the tack taken by Tyson seems well advised indeed. Alerts about Harnack have been given before, but not to my knowledge

252

so amply or with such care. And Tyson is the first I have come across (though I may have missed it) to subject Conzelmann to close scrutiny along these lines. What pleases me about his approach is that by focusing on a theme — portrayals of first-century Judaism — with specific reference to issues of Luke-Acts interpretation, his study is one that (like the works of E. P. Sanders he cites) may well find its way into listings of standard resources for Gospel and Pauline studies.

Tyson's quick historical sketch is a reminder that the tradition of Christian anti-Judaism is neither a passing nor even a recurrent theme in Christian scholarship but an element so pervasive, so entrenched, so resilient, and so protean that it endures even when virtually all else passes away. His two case studies illustrate, in addition, that this tradition insinuates itself into what may be termed Christianity's DNA code, becoming so natural and taken for granted that it influences critical as well as uncritical readings of the biblical texts. It makes itself known where Christian critical scholars seek to be most Christian, that is, at pains to identify and commend the distinctiveness of an "authentically biblical" Christian faith. It also makes itself known, however, when they seek to be most critical and most scholarly — when, for example, they appeal behind or beyond the canonical texts to their reconstructions of Christian origins; when they attend to sources, forms, parallels, redactions, and trajectories of the texts; and when they investigate the literary and/or theological structure, forms, and effects of the final compositions.

All this — and more — is shown here. And it needs to be shown, in the hope that if only Christians were better informed about their Scriptures and their Christian faith, the legacy of anti-Judaism might finally, at this late date, come to its end. Perhaps the analytical approach and restrained tone that Tyson has taken to the issue can gain him a hearing in quarters that more strident voices cannot reach.

Given this measure of agreement, I am not inclined to contest what Tyson has done. I wish instead to invite him to think out loud with me about a few open-ended comments and questions relating to the history of critical New Testament studies, both past and present.

The first has to do with his selection of case studies. Of course, case studies need not be anything other than arbitrary. And here it may be that once on the lookout for superstar interpreters of Luke-Acts, the choice seemed a virtually foregone conclusion. One value happens to be that his study directs attention to critical scholarship at its presumably most critical pitch. Though honored by church and state, Harnack represented a liberalism that no one in his day mistook for more of that "old time religion." Conzelmann — although hardly Bultmann's most radical heir — represented cutting-edge criticism of the day. Hence, if devotion to the Christian faith alone were incapable of challenging anti-Judaism, then perhaps dedication to critical thinking would do so, and if not before form criticism, dialectical theology, the confessing church, the war, and the Holocaust, then surely thereafter. The case studies are therefore also test cases, and Tyson's chief finding is all the more telling because the cases fail the test: "Some traditional concepts about early Judaism have a tendency to hang on for a very long time and to die slowly if at all."[1]

Even so, the data base that is chosen is limited, and the limitation is such that it runs the risk of limiting the moral of the story as well. Pacesetting critics as they were, Harnack and Conzelmann tell us of the tendency of some traditional concepts to hang on for a very long time within continental European criticism, and German Lutheran scholarship in particular. From Sanders and others comes the suggestion, giving G. F. Moore a respectful nod, that treatments of Judaism in British and American circles are if not invariably better then at least somewhat less predictable than those by the grand Teutons. The hypothesis is worth testing.

The result, I suspect, may be a somewhat larger number of exceptions but little if any serious challenge to the rule itself. The several church traditions most supportive of critical scholarship in those lands were — and are — not free of anti-Judaism, and of course until recently English-language biblical scholars have been massively beholden to German models. Indeed, Conzelmann's thesis of three distinct but interrelated epochs of salvation history in Luke-Acts sounds not at all distinctively German or Lutheran but very much like covenantal or dispensational schemata common in Reformed thought — British and American as well as continental — that have brought with them irrepressible supersessionism.

Hence, without complaining because Tyson chose these case studies rather than some others, I can't help but invite him to say more about his selection process and his estimate of how generalizable his findings are. He will agree, I know, that the problems he points out in these Christian biblical critics are by no means specific to Germans, Lutherans, historical critics, or what Anglo-Americans often term lib-

---

1. Joseph B. Tyson, "Anti-Judaism in the Critical Study of the Gospels," in this volume, 251.

eral or modernist in contrast to evangelical views. Why, then, these two case studies? If focus falls on Luke-Acts, why not pre-1947 H. J. Cadbury rather than Harnack or, focusing more on postwar dating than Luke-Acts, why not W. D. Davies rather than Conzelmann?

The other point to be mentioned likewise presses to gauge the full force of Tyson's presentation. But it is of a very different order. It has to do with the model of hermeneutics that readers are to draw from his account. His is a historical-critical study of a number of biblical historical critics. It shows that certain traditional ideas die slowly if ever. It shows too that there is a moral dimension to biblical scholarship, evident to anyone with eyes to see (certainly after the Holocaust if not before) in studies of anti-Judaism and the New Testament. It does not, however, attempt to show why it is that traditional anti-Judaism ideas are especially long lived or why scholars like Harnack and Conzelmann, who are well aware of the moral dimension of scholarship in so many other respects, are blind to it at precisely this point.

Historicist responses come readily to mind, and they are surely correct so far as they go. Unlike fads, traditions persist over time. When they lodge in church confessions, in the sources that nurture national and cultural identity, and even in the infrastructure of critical scholarship (such as reference works of Weber and Strack-Billerbeck), they secure themselves against likely and easy challenge. Plus, biblical-theological scholars are rarely as creative and daring as they are taken to be. In the main, critical advances come on one or perhaps several fronts, leaving most everything else untouched. And the historic flap over critical methods and their results — the infamous separation between churchly and scholarly Christian thought — has been polemically overplayed for so long that it is regularly accepted without much question. But it is not only with respect to anti-Judaism that the attitudes of village pastors in Germany and those of Schürer or Harnack differed little except in the idiom in which they were (and are) stated. Yes, a higher, critical theological learning counts for something, or should. It is unwise, however, to underestimate how much religious studies in toto and Christian biblical-theological study in particular are driven by home-grown pieties. These and surely many other reasons like them (social location, and so forth) are the makings of a zeitgeist explanation for the fact that neither commitment to Christianity nor to criticism immunized Harnack and Conzelmann from traditional anti-Judaism ideas.

But such explanations, apt so far as they go, go only so far. Christian scholars dare not leave the account at that. The anti-Judaism tradition in Christianity is too deep, broad, and pernicious to be chalked up to an excess of misplaced pious zeal and inadvertent lapses of critical acumen. It may well elude "rational" explanation altogether.

Yet Tyson's essay invites at least some further probing of the issue. His title and his account, for example, seem (to me) to leave the impression that anti-Judaism rests in the critical study of the Gospels rather than the Gospels themselves, as though Harnack and Conzelmann have imposed a set of "traditional" anti-Jewish biases on Luke-Acts, while the texts are, if not innocent, then by no means as bad as its commentators have made them out to be. This may well be — both in the sense that the texts include some materials that are arguably more accurate and/or more appreciative of first-century Judaisms than their later commentators indicate, and in the sense that other, more accurate and/or appreciative readings of the texts are possible.

If so, it remains to be shown — a task for future essays. Are readers to infer from this essay, however, that historico-genetic criticism can remove the *adversus Judaeos* "biases" of the Harnacks and Conzelmanns so that the "unbiased" Luke-Acts may appear? It would be a blessing to demonstrate that Luke-Acts (and the rest of Christianity's biblical canon) did little or nothing to contribute to Christianity's historic anti-Judaism and contains much to counteract it. But a healthy hermeneutic of suspicion is in order. The *Wirkungsgeschichte* of the texts runs, to date, strongly in the other direction.

Here, it seems to me, at least two distinct but invariably interrelated concerns surface, and Tyson shifts (perhaps too adroitly) back and forth between them. One has to do with the effort to reconstruct Christianity's origins, including its backgrounds, environs, and variations in adequate historical terms. The other has to do with the effort to construe the set of one or more features constitutive of what Christians call their Christian faith.

The distinction between these two tasks dawned on Christian scholars gradually — in modern (or let us say, prepostmodern) times — fitfully, and never universally. Its initial effect was to legitimate the emergence of critical biblical-theological studies, which at their bottom line resolve to define the adequacy of accounts of Christian origins by the same methods and evidentiary standards as those pertaining to any other objects of historical inquiry. (This alone, by the way, is cause to cast aside the term "late Judaism.")

The construal of the set of features constitutive of Christian faith is another matter, another order of thinking. The label for this order is by no means obvious, although the term "theological" is ready at hand. Clearly it has to do with theological reflection on Christian faith. Complicating matters is that these two concerns, historical inquiry and theological inquiry, are inextricably interrelated, if for no other reason than because the faith of Christians is bound and beholden, both historically and theologically, to founding events in a time of origins datable in world history. Disentangling the historical and the theological claims of Christianity before rerelating them is an onerous, ongoing, uncertain task, and its results are risky. This is surely why Christians have rarely viewed truly critical biblical scholarship merely as a neutral or harmless diversion but as a threat, a benefit, or a real nuisance. It is surely also why along with the Christian conviction in the "truth" of its faith comes the temptation to accept or revise accounts of this faith's historical origins in keeping with prevailing standards of religious "faithfulness."

Although the results of succumbing to the temptation are by no means always or necessarily baleful, to say that the effects of Christian readings of Jewish history have been just that is to understate the case. The tradition, for example, of arguing the theological point that the Christian faith is not, constitutively, a "law" but a "gospel" has all too often been joined to a (false) historical claim about the "legalism of the Jews." (The countertradition of belatedly exonerating "the Jews" of any legalism by ignoring or obliterating the law/gospel distinction within Christianity itself hardly solves the problem, for it apparently overlooks Jewish diversity and assumes that Christianity's anti-Judaism is due to devotion to salvation by grace through faith rather than overweening works-righteousness.) In such instances we are dealing less with the complex, often subtle, interrelationship between the categories of faith claims and historical claims than with a total collapse of the categorical distinction.

Some of the anti-Judaism in critical Gospel studies is of such a character that more and better scholarly criticism counts against it. This putatively self-corrective testing, however, is not automatic. It must be willed. And in the case of Christian critical scholarship, the will has been weak — bound by the tendency to construe the set of features constitutive of the Christian faith by way of contrast and opposition to the faith of Jews. This tendency is of course occasioned and shaped by historical circumstances. But what is not occasioned and shaped by historical circumstances? Historically speaking, neither Judaism nor Christianity has ever been "one thing." Whatever its historical origins, the tendency persists among Christians to construe the set of features constitutive of the Christian faith by way of contrast and opposition to the faith of the Jews.

This tendency is not strictly or properly speaking historical inquiry at all; it functions as a metahistorical category. It configures the field of history before, during, and after Christian historians set out to survey it. As such, it has gained a place within what some theologians call the grammar of faith, that is, a rule governing Christian discourse about Christianity. Tyson will agree, I'm sure, that it is a mistaken rule of faith's grammar: Anti-Judaism is not one of the features constitutive of Christian faith itself. Hence Christianity is by no means fated to identify its distinctiveness by defaming Judaism, even if certain canonical precedents for doing so can be cited.

Combating Christianity's *adversus Judaeos* tradition requires, then, willful resistance on multiple fronts. Among them are critical biblical studies and critical theology and, above all, a reconsideration of the proper relationship(s) of the two for the sake of critical self-testing.

RESPONSE TO
JOSEPH B. TYSON
Ellen T. Charry

PROFESSOR TYSON has offered us a helpful review of New Testament scholarship from the perspective of a small but persistent group of Christians wanting to move Christian scholarship away from presenting Judaism as a system of legalistic works-righteousness and toward presenting it more in keeping with Christian sensibilities. This new sensibility looks for continuities rather than discontinuities between Christianity and its mother. For it is the Christian — especially Lutheran — antipathy for the Law and preference for faith alone that in part renders Judaism inferior in Christian eyes. Although he does not focus on this issue directly, Tyson has most helpfully pointed out the importance of language. How one puts things is as important as what is said. The age of inflammatory language, all too prevalent in theology, must now come to an end.

While New Testament scholarship has focused on the question of legalism, we should keep in mind that the Jewish-Christian argument is far wider than disagreement about the Law of God. But as a point of information, we should also remember that Judaism never questioned the Law and Jewish faithfulness to it, never saw a tension between faith and the Law. The notion of works-righteousness is foreign to Judaism.

The first part of Tyson's essay reports on current treatments of nineteenth-century scholarship. Thus the picture we get is several degrees removed from the texts in question. Two of the scholars discussed, Susannah Heschel and Geza Vermes, are themselves Jews, skewing a bit what I take to be a basically Christian theological discussion. The Christian scholars E. P. Sanders, Martin Hengel, and Karl Hoheisel, building on the earlier work of G. F. Moore, and, I would add, the surprisingly absent R. Travers Herford are now challenging the older presentations of Judaism of Emil Schürer, Ferdinand Weber, Paul Billerbeck, and others. For example, Tyson tells us that Hoheisel, backed up by Moore, credits Weber with inventing the term "legalism" to describe Judaism. And Sanders attributes to Billerbeck the negative contrast between the so-called Pharisaic teaching on justification and Lutheran doctrine. Whether this was an appropriate contrast in the first place is never asked. The issue at hand is the negative judgment that is rendered.

Another example is Wilhelm Bousset's implicit Marcionism that Moore attributed to his preoccupation with apocalyptic literature and that Sanders traces to Weber. And of course, like the others, Bousset signs on to the legalism argument, with the common note that the ritual and moral law are on a par.

Rudolf Bultmann, although not deviating significantly from the work of Weber, adds the notion that Second Temple Judaism "no longer regarded God as an important factor."[1] And naturally, the autonomy of the Law later reaffirmed this trend.

In the second half of the essay Tyson focuses on the work of two Germans, Harnack and Conzelmann, who wrote on Luke-Acts. Both scholars perpetuate the older problems. Harnack's fascination with Marcion not only renders him an anti-Judaist but also, one might add, a heretic as well. But his real error, Tyson opines, is his insistence on the newness of Jesus' teaching in contrast to Judaism. Again, the theme of discontinuity seems to undergird the anti-Jewish outcome. Jesus is simply too powerful a figure for Judaism to be able to stand. The import seems to be simply that Harnack was too energetically Christian. Even still, Harnack's integrity as a scholar is strong enough for him to respect Luke-Acts' reverence for Scripture, in spite of his own doubts.

The other German scholar is Hans Conzelmann. His work illustrates the standard anti-Jewish themes of New Testament scholarship. Judaism is legalistic, with no room for grace. (Much to my chagrin, I myself once heard a young talmudist in Germany repeat this very point to a group of Christian scholars.) And God is so far away as to be inaccessible, a concomitant of legalism. With his report on Conzelmann, Tyson points out another stock criticism: the Jews killed Jesus.

Yet in his own way Conzelmann is part of the new sensibility. His study of anti-Judaism in the early period tries to undermine the continuity-discontinuity hermeneutic and replace it with what might be called a hermeneutic of self-definition. Let each tradition be itself and let conversation between them be on sociological rather than on theological

---

1. Joseph B. Tyson, "Anti-Judaism in the Critical Study of the Gospels," in this volume, 227.

terms. Indeed, this is the position widely adopted by Jews who partic
ipate in the dialogue, for they do not do theology as Christians do, or
once did. One would expect that a disengaged historical stance would
welcome such fresh air to this age-old conflict.

Tyson, perhaps himself sympathetic to this peace offering, nevertheless points out that Conzelmann was still too much of a Christian to
abide by his own suggestion, "implying that, if they are to become right
with God, Jews must accept the faith by which Christians have come to
God."[2]

Conzelmann, living long after Harnack, his consciousness raised by
Nazism, omits the standard anti-Jewish themes that discolor the work
of older scholars. Still, Tyson is impatient with him for giving scant attention to the Lukan birth narratives, so heavily laden with Jewish piety
and deeply dependent on Scripture. Rather than give a positive assessment of Judaism, Conzelmann concludes that Luke offers as negative a
picture of Jews and Judaism as do other first-century writers.

In short, Tyson's argument is that even when New Testament scholars
are sensitive to Jewish concerns, they are unable to make a break with
anti-Judaism and turn the corner on a new day. Perhaps Tyson himself
has a project regarding Luke-Acts in mind.

Tyson's essay gives us an opportunity to overhear current Christian
and Jewish scholars criticizing nineteenth-century Christian scholars for
their heavy-handed Lutheran dogmatics and dynamic of discontinuity
and contrast with Judaism. Although he doesn't explore the concep-
tual background for this dynamic, it is appropriate to point to the
easy fit between Paul's view of Judaism as *aufgehoben* in Jesus Christ
and the evolutionary and developmental sensibility that dominates the
nineteenth century. One way of putting the problem that Tyson has un-
packed is to note that these earlier scholars were not detached historians
but Christian believers. And their beliefs shaped their historiography.
Now that theology — at least as the writers whom Tyson critiques
understood it — is in decline, and the theological training of New Testament scholars is also in decline, the tenor of the times themselves may
contribute to the resolution of the problem.

In the space remaining I would like to suggest two broader concerns and offer one observation arising as much out of my long-term
engagement with the Jewish-Christian conversation as out of my reading of Tyson's essay. The first concerns the task of historical research. To

---

2. Ibid., 244.

put it in syllogistic terms, Tyson's essay argues that (1) Christians have judged Judaism to be legalist; (2) this judgment has led to anti-Judaism; (3) therefore, in order to address the problem of anti-Judaism we must stop saying that Judaism is legalistic. My qualm with this approach is that I fear it does not raise the question of whether these contrasts between Christianity and Judaism are correct, or even understandable. The political agenda for historical research may inadvertently lead us away from facing up to certain things about ourselves. What if it is the case that Judaism and Christianity are really different from one another, even irreconcilably so? Tyson has not argued that negative assessments of Judaism in modern New Testament scholarship are incorrect because they misunderstand Judaism, but that they are incorrect now because in light of the Holocaust they embarrass Christians and anger Jews who may not be at all interested in what Christians think of them, except for the small fact that Christians have put considerable political muscle behind their criticisms.

My second concern has to do with the theological nature of Christian scholarship. Implicit in Tyson's sympathy with Conzelmann's suggestion of limiting Jewish-Christian conversation to "human grounds" is, as I mentioned, the suggestion that to deal with the problem of Christian anti-Judaism we would do best to set aside theological considerations. Many Jews will, I think, welcome this suggestion. The Christian theological judgment is that the failure of Jews to accept what God has done in Jesus leads them to misread Scripture and misunderstand God. To ask Christians to give up that judgment is, for them to jeopardize their own identity because it suggests that they should be worshiping in the synagogue rather than in the church. Conversely, even though Jews tend to think sociologically rather than theologically, to set aside theological considerations would require Jews to give up their belief that Christians are misguided in their understanding of God, among other things.

These are difficult matters. I would like to offer a process comment that comes not from Tyson's essay but from my reflection on one reason why these matters are so difficult for me as a theologian. This may fall under the category of an uninvited personal tangent, but perhaps it will shed some light on the issue at least for some Christians.

For Christians, theology is very important. How we understand and speak about God is central to how we speak about and understand ourselves as God's children. Judaism does not have an analogous conversation. Perhaps it was less interested in Platonism in the early centuries. Perhaps Jewish leadership decided that the daily living out of God's commands was more important than conceptualizing how to talk about God. Whatever the reasons, Jews have generally been more comfortable talking about Jewish life and Jewish culture than about the vision of God and human life to which *halakah* points. To put it provocatively, Jews today think culturally and sociologically while Christians think theologically (although I think some Christians are now beginning to follow the Jewish lead on this).

Because of Christian atrocities against Jews, issues of Jewish survival and the preservation of Jewish culture are more important to Jews than theological issues. Thus when Christians make theological judgments that disagree with what Christians would understand as Jewish theological judgments, they sound to Jewish ears like indictments of Jewish culture and therefore of the Jewish people itself, rather than straightforward theological disagreements. Since the seventeenth century, Christians have been learning to handle their theological disagreements with one another without bloodshed, and some would be interested in transferring that experience to tackling theological disagreements with Jews. But frequently, the Jewish interlocutor is not equipped for or interested in such an undertaking. For Jews, theological discussion is freighted with the assumption that the Christian interlocutor is convinced that the Jew has no right to exist at all as a Jew. Theological conversation may sound like an invitation to give up being a Jew and become a Christian. And since being a Jew involves more than simply a confession of faith, what is being asked is to cease being oneself and to become someone else, indeed to become one's own worst enemy.

What, then, are Christians to do? One thing is to continue to sensitize Christians to these matters, especially regarding preaching and Scripture interpretation. Another is to approach Jews in a spirit of contrition, taking responsibility for Christian sins against the Jewish people. Robert Wilken and others have suggested that Christians need the physical presence of the Jewish people in the world in order to remind them of whose they really are. This would be a great step forward.

But Christians must also insist on their right to self-definition. They must insist on their right to the Jewish Scriptures and to their claim that they worship the God of Israel, admitting that this is no longer recognizable to Jews. Jews, for their part, must strive to be understanding as well. If they claim that they are not responsible for Christians' spiritual welfare and ask that Christians please return the favor by allowing Jews to determine their own spiritual well-being, then they must acknowledge that if Christians claim that their spiritual welfare requires them to pray

Israel's psalms, read Israel's prophets, and worship Israel's God, they have a right to do so, even if this is nonsensical or offensive to Jews.

All of this is a tall order. Jews and Christians have been at each other for some time now. It doesn't look as if Christians will go away, and Jews must come to terms with this. Perhaps the fact that, despite everything, the Jews are still here is an important sign from God that Christians need to attend to. I do not think that Jews and Christians can pray together. Perhaps, however, they can light a candle and sit together in silence.

❧ S • I • X ❧

REFLECTIONS ON ANTI-JUDAISM IN THE NEW TESTAMENT AND IN CHRISTIANITY

E. P. Sanders

I N THE SPRING OF 1995 I attended the planning conference on anti-Judaism and the Gospels, which was organized by Professor William R. Farmer and Dr. Sarah Baumgartner Thurow and held at the University of Dallas. Unfortunately, I was unable to attend the full conference that resulted in the publication of this volume, but I am pleased to have been associated, if only in a preliminary way, with the project. This book succeeds in giving a comprehensive view of the problem that it addresses, and the essays are clear, forthright presentations that will help the reader see what the issues were when the Gospels were written and what they still are. Professor Farmer asked me to contribute "reflections" on the problem of anti-Judaism, which I hope will not detract from the usefulness of the volume.

I have chosen to offer some background comments on four topics and to treat two others more fully. The background comments are on early Christianity as a Jewish movement; intra-Jewish polemic;[1] the status of Jews and Christians in the Roman empire; and examples of New Testament invective against various groups. The fuller discussions concern whether or not Jesus or Paul can be accused of being anti-Jewish, and anti-Judaism in the Middle Ages and the modern world. My two main topics leap from the period before the Gospels were written to much later periods. This is obviously not a full report on the "Jesus movement" prior to the composition of the Gospels, and even more obviously not a substantial account of anti-Judaism in the medieval and

---

1. Polemic is a warlike argument; the Greek word *polemos* means "war."

modern periods. I hope, however, that these observations and examples will help put the other essays in a larger historical perspective.

EARLY CHRISTIANITY AS A JEWISH MOVEMENT

The first Christians constituted a small group within Judaism.[2] Jesus had devoted his own ministry to Jews (Matt. 15:24), and his followers were Jews. At an early date the apostles began to admit Gentiles to the movement, but the Christians remained a basically Jewish group for a few decades. The new movement separated itself from its parent in the course of the first one hundred or so years of its existence. There is no one point that marks the "divorce," and so we must be vague about dates, but by the end of the first century many (probably most) Christian groups considered themselves not to be Jewish. By the end of the second century relatively few Christians would have identified themselves as Jews. Christianity became a predominantly Gentile religion.

The principal impulses behind the growth and development of Christianity were positive and did not depend on the prior view that Judaism was a bad religion and a regrettable way of life; the apostles and the other early Jewish believers in Jesus were not fleeing *from* a religion that they disliked, but rather turning *to* a new revelation. In retrospect, Paul could say that Moses had carried out a "ministry of condemnation," but he also regarded the Mosaic revelation as "glorious" (2 Cor. 3:9). In Philippians he listed his own merits as a Jew and counted them as "gain," though he added that he regarded everything in his past as "loss" in light of what he by then believed was a superior revelation; that is, retrospectively he viewed Judaism as inferior (Phil. 3:4–9). What it lacked was faith in Christ, which was part of a new revelation. This is what A.-J. Levine, following Hare and Smiga, calls "subordinating polemic":[3] It is an argument that aims only at making one view or system inferior to another. There are many more severe forms of religious polemic, as we shall see. Whatever our name for this sort of argument, we have no reason to believe that Peter, James, John, and Paul had been

---

2. It may be objected that the word "Christian" had not yet been coined, and also that it misdescribes the way Paul (the apostle about whom we know the most) saw the matter. In the view of many, it would be more accurate to say that Paul and the other apostles believed in only one religion, messianic Judaism. They did not conceive of "Christianity" as a religion distinct from Judaism. Even if I completely agreed with this view (which I do not; see the discussion of Paul below), I would still use the word "Christian" for the sake of convenience when speaking of Paul, Peter, James, and the other Jewish members of the new movement.

3. Amy-Jill Levine, "Anti-Judaism and the Gospel of Matthew," in this volume, 14.

deeply dissatisfied with Judaism prior to becoming followers of Jesus, though of course they thought that following Jesus was a superior form of Judaism.[4]

The positive Christian belief — the new revelation — was that the God of Israel had sent his Son, Jesus, to save the entire world and that the principal requirement for salvation was faith in him as Son of God and savior. Most of the earliest Christians held that Gentiles were welcome or even more than welcome to join the Christian movement. Gentile converts had to observe some aspects of the Jewish law — principally forsaking the worship of idols and accepting Jewish ethics, especially sexual ethics — but they did not have to be Jewish in order to worship the God of Israel and to believe that he would save them through faith in his Son.[5] Some of the earliest Jewish Christians, however, thought that Gentiles who believed in Jesus should also become Jewish; we shall return to this debate below.

Although the principal motivation of Christian leaders was positive, there was some pressure to criticize the parent religion. If God had to send his Son to save the world, was there not something wrong with Judaism? Did not this new action by the God of Israel show that Judaism had been lacking a necessary ingredient? The logic of such questions has meant that there have been Christian criticisms of Judaism from a very early date, which continue to the present day. Since Christianity is a historical religion that originated as a Jewish sect, and since Christians regard Christianity as both true and necessary, it has seemed obvious to many that Judaism must have been faulty in some way or other. It is striking that this view has led to criticism of Judaism and of Jews, but only seldom to criticism of God. It would be just as logical to fault God for inadequate revelations of his will as to fault Jews because they remained true to the revelations they had received prior to Jesus. After all, they were "guilty" only of believing the stories of Abraham and Moses and holding fast to those beliefs. Or one might criticize God for taking so long to reveal his full will. The problem of God's tardiness is partially acknowledged and partially masked in the New Testament by the use of such phrases as "in the fullness of time" (Gal. 4:4; Eph. 1:10). I

---

4. On 2 Corinthians 3 and Philippians 3, see my *Paul, the Law, and the Jewish People* (Philadelphia: Fortress, 1983; London: SCM, 1985), chap. 4; on Romans 7, which, some scholars think, shows that prior to his conversion Paul felt that the Law only condemned, see ibid., 70–81.

5. On idolatry, see 1 Thess. 1:9–10; 1 Corinthians 8; 10; on sexual ethics, see 1 Thess. 4:1–8 (which includes the admonition not to be like Gentiles); 1 Cor. 6:9; on both, see Acts 15:29.

suppose, however, that the preference to blame Jews is not too hard to understand. Few people who believe in God are willing to criticize him very substantially.[6] It was much easier for the Christians to say that the Jews were hard-hearted or obtuse.

Criticism of Judaism or aspects of Judaism is not, however, necessarily "anti-Judaism." A Jew, for example, could criticize all other Jews for not living up to Judaism's highest expectations; this would not be anti-Jewish. Judaism has always included a lot of internal polemic and debate, to which we now turn.

Intra-Jewish Polemic

I shall give two examples of Jewish denunciation of other Jews, apart from those in the New Testament.[7] The first is from the *Psalms of Solomon*, a work that has nothing to do with the king of Israel who reigned in the tenth century B.C.E.; it is a group of poems composed at about the time of the Roman invasion and conquest of Judea in 63 B.C.E. According to *Ps. Sol.* 8:9–13, some Jews, and more specifically some priests, committed incest and adultery; they stole from the Temple; they brought impurity into the Temple; they sacrificed to God when they were contaminated with menstrual blood; and, in short, "there was no sin they left undone in which they did not surpass the Gentiles." These iniquities were punished by God, who sent the Roman general Pompey to conquer Jerusalem (*Ps. Sol.* 8.14–22).[8] This passage has a lot of the standard elements of religious polemic. The "bad guys," in this case the leading Jewish priests, are criticized in broad strokes, and with no reservations, for willfully and heinously disregarding the commandments of God; in particular they are accused of sexual misconduct and of defiling the Temple. The author of *Psalms of Solomon* 8 was not anti-Jewish; he belonged rather to a Jewish group that opposed the aristocratic priesthood. It is probably not the case that all the leading priests stole from the Temple and disregarded the purity laws, including the prohibition of intercourse with a menstruant (Lev. 15:24; 18:19; 20:18). Religious polemic is not impartial and judicious. There may be

---

6. In Romans 9 Paul entertains the question of whether or not God has been fair: Having chosen Israel, has he now reversed himself? In the second century, Marcion proposed that the God of the Jewish Scripture was a bad god, and that the good God had sent Jesus. This is an extreme case of criticism of the God of Israel.

7. There is a fuller account of intra-Jewish conflict over the Law in my *Jewish Law from Jesus to the Mishnah* (London: SCM; Philadelphia: Trinity, 1990), 84–89.

8. Pompey is not named, but the author has his invasion in mind.

some basis for these accusations, probably legal disputes about marriage and menstrual laws,[9] but the principal category in which this material fits is "intra-Jewish sectarian polemic."

This is also the case in the Dead Sea Scrolls. The Dead Sea sect, which withdrew from the rest of Judaism, called other Jews "lying interpreters and...the congregation of those who seek smooth things" (1QH 2:31); "teachers of lies and seers of falsehood" (1QH 4:9); those "who have turned aside from Thy covenant" (1QH 4:19). The first two passages in particular may be directed against the Pharisees.[10]

JESUS AND PAUL

It is difficult to accuse the two figures who dominate the New Testament of anti-Judaism, because they were so thoroughly Jewish. Jesus, the initiator of the new movement, was an observant Jew.[11] The man who became the greatest and best-known apostle of Jesus, Paul, was also Jewish. Jesus and Paul believed in the God of Israel, and they thought that God had inspired the Hebrew Bible (the Christian "Old Testament"). There is, therefore, an opening assumption that any criticism of Judaism by Jesus or Paul would be *intra-Jewish* debate and polemic, not *anti-Jewish*. The word "anti-Jewish" usually implies criticism of Judaism from non-Jews.[12] In theory, to be sure, a born Jew could defect and criticize his or her antecedents, and thus be anti-Jewish. We shall consider whether or not this could be true of Paul, which will require a few pages, but we can discuss Jesus very quickly.

If it is true that Jesus accused some Pharisees and scribes of hypocrisy (Matthew 23), his attack should be read in the same light as the passages

---

9. The charges of menstrual blood clinging to priests when they sacrificed (for which, see also CD 5:6) are not eyewitness testimony to blood on the priests' clothing, but rather the result of legal debates about when intercourse is permitted. This is a difficult topic in Jewish law, and there was a lot of room for disagreement. See my *Jewish Law from Jesus to the Mishnah,* 209–13. On disputes over what constituted incest, see, for example, CD 5:7–11; my *Judaism: Practice and Belief* (London: SCM; Philadelphia: Trinity, 1992), 185.

10. In Hebrew, "seekers of smooth things" could be a play on the words "investigators of legal rulings," and thus may be against the Pharisees. For bibliography, see Menahem Mansoor, *The Thanksgiving Hymns* (Grand Rapids: Eerdmans, 1961), 110 n. 6.

11. Some New Testament scholars have claimed that Jesus rejected major aspects of Jewish law or even opposed the Law in principle. The evidence, however, is against this view. See my *Jesus and Judaism* (London: SCM; Philadelphia: Fortress, 1985), chap. 9; *Jewish Law from Jesus to the Mishnah,* chap. 1.

12. Terminology and definitions are discussed in other essays in this volume; the fullest discussion is by Levine, "Anti-Judaism and the Gospel of Matthew," 12–16.

from the *Psalms of Solomon* and the Dead Sea Scrolls that we considered previously. As we noted, Jesus obeyed the Jewish law; he had not left Judaism. And his followers were Jews who thought of themselves as Jews. Thus his whole ministry was intra-Jewish. Many New Testament scholars attribute Matthew 23 to post-Jesus Christian tradition, but that is not presently the point. If Jesus spoke the entire chapter, the criticism would actually be less severe than that cited in the *Psalms of Solomon* and the Dead Sea Scrolls. Matthew 23, after all, includes the statement that followers of Jesus should do what the scribes and Pharisees say, even though the performance of those authorities is flawed (Matt. 23:2). This verse gives the scribes and Pharisees more credit than the authors of the Psalms of Solomon and the Dead Sea Scrolls gave their opponents.[13] Put another way, if Jesus spoke a "woe" over Jerusalem (Matt. 23:37–39; Luke 13:34–35), so did other prophets (e.g., Jeremiah 7).

The criticism of other Jews in Paul's letters is more complicated to sort out, for two quite different reasons. The first is that generations of Christian readers have misunderstood the target of Paul's attacks in Galatians. To this day, scholars write, and students believe, that Paul's condemnation of "works of law" in Galatians 2–3 was an attack on his native religion, or more specifically on "Pharisaic soteriology." This ignores the actual subject of the letter. Other Jewish *Christians* wanted to circumcise Paul's Gentile converts. This challenged Paul's authority and his message, and he hit back very hard. He warned his Gentiles that if they accepted circumcision they would cut themselves off from God and fall away from grace (Gal. 5:4). He then lashed out at his opponents: "I wish that those who trouble you would cut the whole thing off" — that is, mutilate their own genitals (Gal. 5:12). The conclusion of the letter shows quite clearly that he is countering a *Christian* position:

> It is those who want to make a good showing in the flesh that try to compel you to be circumcised — only that they may not be persecuted for the cross of Christ. (Gal. 6:12)

In Phil. 3:2, Paul calls those who "mutilate the flesh" "dogs." These are, again, his Christian opponents. He is not discussing Jews and Judaism as such.

---

13. As Levine ("Anti-Judaism and the Gospel of Matthew," 23, 31–33) points out, when Matthew 23 is read in the context of Matthew (rather than the historical Jesus), it may be construed as anti-Jewish, though possibly it is only against Jewish leaders. She approves of regarding sayings by Jesus as "in-house" or "prophetic polemic."

While on the subject of intra-Christian polemic in Paul's letters, we should note that one of the other extreme pieces of invective in Paul's letters also is directed against other Christian leaders: Paul calls his enemies in Corinth "false apostles" and ministers of Satan (2 Cor. 11:13–15).

These cases of severe criticism (*Psalms of Solomon* against the leading priests; the Dead Sea Scrolls against other Jews, especially Pharisees; Jesus against scribes and Pharisees; Paul against his Christian competitors) are what we should expect. People become angriest when they disagree with those who are closest to them. Christian abuse has periodically been as severe or even more severe against other Christians than against Jews, while pagans and others have been treated more leniently. Christians seldom bother to attack Buddhists, and various groups of Jews criticize one another while paying little attention to Hindus.

Although Paul's attacks on the "circumcision party" are not directed against Jews or Judaism as such (but rather against other Jewish Christians), there are passages in Paul's letters where he distances himself from his compatriots and treats them as not being in his own group. This is the second difficulty in assessing whether or not Paul could be "anti-Jewish": We must ask if, when he distinguished himself from the Jews, he explicitly or implicitly attacked Judaism.

Paul wrote to the Galatians that they had heard of his "earlier life in Judaism," including that he had "advanced in Judaism" beyond his contemporaries (Gal. 1:13–14). This implies that he was no longer "in Judaism," and if this were our only information, we would be forced to assume that Paul actually had left Judaism — that he no longer considered himself Jewish. In 1 Cor. 10:32, where he urges his converts to "give no offense to Jews or to Greeks or to the church of God," we see another indication of distance from Judaism. This verse reveals that Paul's Gentile converts were not Jews and were no longer idolaters. They belonged to a third entity, "the church of God," and thus they had to consider how to relate themselves to both Jews and pagans (here specified as "Greeks"). That is, on the ground, in Asia Minor and Greece, Paul was helping to create a third group, the church, which was neither Jewish nor idolatrous, and he naturally identified himself with his converts, at least to some extent. That is doubtless why he wrote of his "earlier life in Judaism": He wanted his Gentile converts not to accept circumcision and become Jewish, and he distanced himself from his Jewish past in an effort to persuade them. They should not accept what he had given up. In light of information yet to be cited, we can say that here Paul was employing persuasive rhetoric, and that he still considered himself Jewish. The rhetoric is nevertheless striking: On at least one occasion he could depict his Judaism as being in the past.

Paul's churches, however, were definitely not Jewish. 1 Cor. 10:32, just cited, correctly indicates that his churches constituted a third entity, neither Jewish nor pagan. This becomes even clearer when we consider Paul's discussions of the election. In Galatians 3 he argues that the heirs of Abraham are not those who accept circumcision and the Law, but rather those who belong to Christ (see especially Gal. 3:29). This implies that there are Jews who are not elect — that is, who are not descendants of Abraham. In this case, Christians, who *are* descendants of Abraham, are distinct from both non-Christian Jews and pagans. This view is tempered in Romans 4, where Paul proposes that Abraham has two groups of heirs, one circumcised and one not — provided that both "have faith" (Rom. 4:11–12). Nevertheless, being Jewish — that is, accepting circumcision and the rest of the Law — does not make one a descendant of Abraham. Thus in these chapters Paul challenges the core of Judaism: the doctrine of election.

In Romans 9 he *worries* about the election of Israel, not wishing to deny it, but nevertheless not finding it to be a satisfactory account of the way God chooses.

> They are Israelites, and to them belong the sonship, the glory, the covenants, the giving of the Law, the worship, and the promises. (Rom. 9:4)

These are the blessings of Israel, but Paul then turns to his doubts:

> It is not as though the word of God had failed. For not all Israelites truly belong to Israel, and not all of Abraham's children are his true descendants. (Rom. 9:6–7)

Again, there are nonelect Jews. Paul would not classify them as pagans, and so there are three groups: the elect (those who are in Christ), nonelect Jews, and idolaters.

We have now seen three points: Paul sometimes distanced himself from "Judaism" and spoke of his Jewish past; he was creating churches that were neither Jewish nor pagan, and to some degree he identified himself with his non-Jewish converts; he wished to redefine the doctrine of the election. I do not think that any of this is necessarily anti-Jewish. The first two points, while true, are incomplete. Despite the passages in which Paul seems to separate himself from Judaism, he was well aware of being deeply Jewish. Five times he was punished in synagogues (2 Cor. 11:24), which indicates that during his career as apostle to the Gentiles he continued to attend the synagogue. In Romans 9, he agonizes over the Jewish rejection of Jesus, and wishes that he himself could be cut off "for the sake of [his] own people, [his] kindred according to the flesh" (Rom. 9:3). Further, his description of his own task in Romans 15 reveals that he saw himself as fulfilling some of the prophecies in the Bible (see further below).

The third point (redefinition of the election) is also subject to at least some modification. Paul does exclude many born Jews from the covenant with Abraham (which might be regarded as being anti-Jewish), but he simultaneously says that to the Israelites belong the covenants (Rom. 9:4). Moreover, at the end of Romans 11 he states that "all Israel will be saved" and that "the gifts and the calling of God are irrevocable" (Rom. 11:26–29), statements that are not at all anti-Jewish. The exclusion of many Jews from the elect in Galatians 3, Romans 4, and Romans 9 is, I think, a by-product of his desire to include Gentile Christians; it seems not to be derived from hostility toward his own people. In these passages Paul does not denigrate his compatriots, he does not call them nasty names, he does not exaggerate, he does not invent bad motives and characteristics. Could we say, then, that this is the beginning of a theological breach between Judaism and the Christian movement, but that, from Paul's point of view, it is still an "in-house" debate and is thus not an instance of "anti-Judaism"?

The second part of this possibility is not entirely persuasive. In and of itself, a debate about who is elect could be entirely intra-Jewish, and we find such a debate in the Dead Sea Scrolls. But when Paul describes his own group, including especially his Gentile converts, as heirs of the covenant with Abraham, while excluding many Jews from that status, he goes beyond the Dead Sea Scrolls. In the latter, not all Jews are elect, but all the elect are Jews. The Dead Sea sectarians were circumcised, they observed the Sabbath, they rigorously obeyed the Law of Moses. This was not true of Paul's converts. They were not Jewish at all, except in Paul's terminology ("descendants of Abraham") — and sometimes not even then (1 Cor. 10:32). There is more than a slight trace of "supersessionism" in Paul: Those in Christ are really in the covenant, though they do not keep the covenantal laws, while the people who were born into it and have done everything that the Law of Moses requires are not thereby included among the elect. People in Christ supersede loyal Jews. The latter must do something else, beyond what the Hebrew Bible requires: They must have faith in Christ, and then they are truly elect, along with the Gentiles who have faith in Christ — the true elect are a third group, neither Jewish nor pagan.[14] This is certainly an *argument against the adequacy of the covenants between God and Israel,* especially the Abrahamic and Mosaic covenants, and so it is *against two of the pillars of Judaism* (the call of Abraham and his descendants; the giving of the Law). Paul's argument about election, in short, is in favor of a new definition of "the people of God" and *against* the biblical and standard Jewish understanding.

Let me repeat that in these passages Paul is not hostile to Jews or to his native religion. Paul's argument is *against traditional Judaism,* but not against *Jews,* election, or the Law as such. Paul wanted to redefine the election, and he also argued that Gentiles did not have to obey the entire Law; but the term "anti-Jewish" seems to me to be essentially misleading. He sometimes deliberately *distanced* himself from what traditionally counted as Judaism, and he created communities that were neither Jewish nor Greek. But even so, he was not an apostate in the usual meaning of the word, since he believed in the God of Israel and he accepted Jewish Scripture as the word of God.

This distance from Judaism, nevertheless, made it possible for him to attack "the Jews," and on at least one occasion he did so:

> For you, brothers, became imitators of the churches of God in Christ Jesus that are in Judea, for you suffered the same things from your own compatriots [i.e., from other Gentiles] as they did from the Jews, who killed both the Lord Jesus and the prophets, and drove us out; they displease God and oppose everyone by hindering us from speaking to the Gentiles so that they may be saved. Thus they have constantly been filling up the measure of their sins; but God's wrath has overtaken them at last. (1 Thess. 2:14–16)

Here we see accusations in which Paul speaks about "the Jews" in distinction from "us." He has a bill of particulars: He proposes that *the Jews killed Jesus;* this was not actually the case, though the high priest did recommend Jesus' execution to Pilate. He also states that they *killed the prophets.* This charge originated, as far as I know, in Neh. 9:26, where it is a piece of intra-Jewish polemic. It also lies behind the apocryphal *Martyrdom of Isaiah.* It is repeated in the New Testament: Acts 7:52 (attributed to Stephen); Matt. 23:30–37 par. (attributed to Jesus).

---

14. See further my *Paul, the Law, and the Jewish People,* chap. 6.

Something like it is implied in the parable of the wicked tenants (Matt. 21:33–41 pars.). As far as we know, it is not true that "the prophets" were killed by Jews or Jerusalemites.[15] Next, Paul charges that "the Jews" *"drove us out"*; this may refer to a flight of some followers of Jesus from Jerusalem, such as that mentioned in Acts 8:1, according to which "all except the apostles were scattered throughout the countryside of Judea and Samaria" (it was apparently a very partial eviction). Finally, the Jews *displease God and oppose everyone* by *hindering "us"* from converting Gentiles. One suspects that this is the point that had recently offended Paul and that brought forth these accusations. Some Jews opposed Paul's conversion of Gentiles, presumably because they did not think that he was actually converting them to worship the God of Israel. The result of these "crimes" — which are not stated with historical accuracy — is that *"God's wrath has come upon them at last"* (or "to the utmost"). We do not know to what punishment these words refer.[16]

What is anti-Jewish about this is the contrast between "the Jews" and "us" in connection with a list of exaggerated or erroneous accusations. In my view, we need both elements: To write an anti-Jewish statement Paul must distinguish himself and the Christian movement from Judaism, and he must level criticisms against the Jews that are either unfair or untrue. 1 Thess. 2:14–16 meets both requirements. One might argue against this conclusion by noting the similar language in Neh. 9:26:

15. Many commentators on the New Testament, of course, accept the charge that "the Jews" killed "the prophets." The only New Testament passage that undertakes to give details is Luke 11:50–51: "This generation [will] be charged with the blood of all the prophets shed since the foundation of the world, from the blood of Abel to the blood of Zechariah. Yes, I tell you, it will be charged against this generation." Matthew's version of the saying lacks "the prophets," having only "all the righteous blood" (Matt. 23:35–36). The Zechariah in question is depicted in 2 Chron. 24:17–22 as delivering an oracle of God before being executed by King Joash; thus he does count as a prophet. It is not, however, fair to say that the case of Cain and Abel proves that "the Jews" killed "the prophets" (since Cain was not a Jew, and Abel was not a prophet), which leaves us with only one example of a prophet being executed, and even in this case it is precarious simply to identify the king with "the Jews." Moreover, the statement that "this generation" will be charged with all the blood of the prophets (or, as in Matthew, all the blood of the righteous) does not reflect well on the justice of God, who, one would like to think, will be less capricious in meting out punishments.

16. Some scholars have suggested that this entire passage was added to the letter by a later hand. One of the considerations in favor of this view is that, when Paul wrote the letter, nothing had recently happened to the Jews that could have been described as the final demonstration of God's wrath. On the other hand, Paul's eschatological mind could have found large significance in a relatively minor event. In any case, I am not inclined to delete individual passages from Paul's letters. On the inaccuracies (which may be described as hyperbole), see C. J. Schlueter, *Filling up the Measure: Polemical Hyperbole in 1 Thessalonians 2:14–16*, JSNTSup 98 (Sheffield: JSOT Press, 1994).

. "*They* were disobedient and rebelled against you [God] and cast your law behind their backs and killed your prophets." Here the speaker sets himself against "them," who are Jews. In Nehemiah 9, however, the speaker does not belong to a group that can be defined as distinct from Judaism and that in part is not Jewish. Nehemiah 9 is more like the Dead Sea Scrolls; it is clearly intra-Jewish polemic. Moreover, Neh. 9:26 is part of a standard catalogue of Israelite failure, repentance, and restoration, and so it does not have the final note of punishment without restoration that seems to be implied in 1 Thess. 2:16 (wrath has come upon them at last). This note of final rejection, though it is only a rhetorical flourish, confirms the character of this passage as anti-Jewish. When one combines final rejection with (1) the inaccurate list of charges, (2) Paul here and elsewhere distancing himself and the Christian movement from the Jews, and (3) the social separation of Paul's churches from Judaism, one might even argue that we should think of Paul as someone who *left Judaism and who then attacked and vilified his former co-religionists.* This view understands the fact that Paul "distanced" himself from Judaism as meaning that he "left."

In light of Romans 9–11 in particular, I think that this is inaccurate as an overall view of Paul. I can imagine the following statement, though I would not wish to offer it as my final view of the subject: Paul was an apostate — not from God, but from Jewish custom and practice — who, having left, turned and attacked Judaism. Such a statement would be neither fair to Paul nor entirely true, since it would obscure how Jewish he was, how committed to the God of Israel, how faithful he wanted to be to the Jewish Scripture, how deeply he sympathized with the Jewish people, and how highly he valued "the sonship, the glory, the covenants, the giving of the Law, the [Temple] worship, and the promises" (Rom. 9:4). But I also think that those who wish to be sensitive to the question of whether or not Paul broke with Judaism, as well as to the painful subject of subsequent Christian anti-Judaism, should see the anti-Jewish possibilities in Paul's letters. They are, to repeat, that in 2 Corinthians 3 and Philippians 3 he engaged in "subordinating polemic" that resulted in his calling the Mosaic covenant a "dispensation of condemnation"; that he distanced himself and the Christian movement from the Jews (though not from the God of Israel or Jewish Scripture); that his own converts were neither Jewish nor pagan (which makes Jews "the other" and potentially the enemy of "us"); that he wanted to redefine the election so that not all Jews were elect, while all those in Christ superseded the nonelect Jews; and that he wrote a rather nasty couple of verses in which he set "us" in contrast to "the Jews," whom he inaccurately depicted as committing numerous evil deeds.

Did Paul break with Judaism? That was not his intent. Paul's mission to the Gentiles, which helped lead to the eventual separation of the Christian movement to Gentiles, and which was the principal factor that led Paul to distance himself from Judaism, was in accord with a common Jewish view: in "the last days," according to the expectations in Isaiah and other biblical prophets, the Gentiles would turn to worship the God of Israel (e.g., Isa. 2:2–3). In Romans 15, Paul refers to several passages in the Hebrew Bible that look forward to the inclusion of Gentiles among the worshipers of the God of Israel. Thus Paul was not motivated by any sort of animus against his own people. Put positively, what he wanted was a "new creation" in which all Jews and all Gentiles would be joined together through faith in Christ. Since that did not come about, however, the *result* was a break between Pauline Christianity and Judaism. In the course of history, Paul's redefinition of the election became fully supersessionist, and his creation of churches that were neither Jewish nor pagan became the norm.

Our conclusion of asking about Jesus and Paul in connection with anti-Judaism is this: It would be entirely erroneous to say that Jesus was anti-Jewish, and it would also be untrue to say that Paul was *basically* and *intentionally* anti-Jewish (though I regard 1 Thess. 2:14–16 as an anti-Jewish passage, and the redefinition of election as constituting a break with Judaism). Subsequently in Christianity any sort of negative statement that might possibly include some Jews would be used in an anti-Jewish way. Thus not only 1 Thess. 2:14–16, but also Paul's attack on the circumcisers and his redefinition of the election, as well as Matthew 23 may serve anti-Jewish purposes. Of the New Testament passages discussed thus far, however, I regard only 1 Thess. 2:14–16 as being truly anti-Jewish. The historian must make distinctions between full anti-Judaism, intra-Jewish criticism, the rhetoric employed in the formation of a new group (Gentile heirs of Abraham), and the anti-Jewish use of those debates and arguments.

The Status of
Jews and Christians in the Roman Empire:
The Context of Christian Polemic

A further historical point to bear in mind when assessing anti-Judaism in Christianity is a focal point of some of the other essays in this volume,

and I shall mention it only briefly in order to provide background information. In the first century, Jews in the Roman empire, though they were
sometimes criticized and ridiculed for their "odd" customs and beliefs
(especially monotheism, circumcision, the Sabbath, and avoidance of
pork), nevertheless had a fairly favorable position. Under the leadership
of the Jewish ethnarch and high priest, Hyrcanus II, and his right-hand
man, Antipater (the father of Herod the Great), Palestinian Jews supported Julius Caesar in his conflict with Pompey. Subsequently Herod
ingratiated himself with Octavian, who soon became Augustus. The
consequence of these two adroit political moves was that both Julius
Caesar and Augustus issued several decrees friendly to Jews, not just
in Palestine, but throughout the empire. These privileges were then repeated in separate decrees issued by Roman governors and city councils
in various parts of the empire.[17] The decrees gave Jews a number of special rights, which included freedom from military service (because of the
Sabbath law); the right to send money to the Temple; the right to gather,
even in Rome (freedom of assembly, especially in Rome, was a privilege); the right to try their own cases; and the right to follow their own
customs. These rights implied another one that is not mentioned explicitly: Jews who lived in the western Diaspora could refrain from civic
ceremonies that included worship of pagan gods — as all or most city
ceremonies did. The early Christian communities in Asia Minor, Greece,
and Italy had no such rights, and consequently they were in a vulnerable
position. From the point of view of the citizens of Greco-Roman cities,
Christians were not good citizens, because they did not participate in
the principal civic activities. Jews could appeal to ancient customs in a
world that respected antiquity, as well as to the special decrees in their
favor. The Christians had no basis for exemption from civic worship and
ceremonies. They could, of course, claim loyalty to the God of Israel, but
it was perfectly obvious that they were not Jews, and so that claim did
not work. Religiously, the Gentile Christians had no status; they were
not Jews and they were no longer pagans. This sometimes led to "persecution," which in the first century was usually harassment, ostracism,
arrest, and interrogation, not execution.[18] Nevertheless, it was unpleasant. Both the Acts of the Apostles and the *Martyrdom of Polycarp* depict

---

17. For the decrees, see Josephus, *Antiquities* 14.190–264; 16.162–73. See the summary of main points in my *Practice and Belief*, 212.

18. According to *Mart. Pol.* 12.2, both the pagans and Jews of Smyrna accused the
Christians of not sacrificing or worshiping. In this case, the accusations led to execution.
(Polycarp lived ca. 69–155 C.E. The story of his martyrdom was written shortly after his
death.)

the Jews as being at least partly responsible for pagan persecution of Christians (e.g., Acts 13:50; 14:2; *Mart. Pol.* 13.1). This is such a regular theme in Acts that one suspects it to be editorial, but it is intrinsically probable that some Jews were eager to protect their own privileges and did not wish Gentiles to pass themselves off as worshipers of the God of Israel. The Christians often resented the Jews, either because they had special standing or because they used it against the Christians. In any case, this produced a certain amount of anti-Jewish propaganda. In the first century, Christian anti-Judaism probably helped solidify the Christian communities; they were neither pagans nor Jews, and criticizing both helped them define who they were.[19] The Christians, however, were completely powerless. This situation could lead to "free" polemic against the Jews; it had no effect, except the psychological support of the Christian communities, and so it could be quite vicious.[20] The Christian critics of Judaism, in other words, could speak irresponsibly. Coupled to the motive of resentment was the continuing attraction that Judaism had, which Christian leaders such as John Chrysostom felt compelled to combat.[21]

The previous paragraph skips from the first into the second, third, and fourth centuries, where I do not intend to stay. Nor do I intend to excuse Christian attacks on Jews. Viciousness is viciousness, no matter what the circumstances, and viciousness is unchristian. The historian, however, must note the conditions in which Christian vituperation against Jews grew.

NEW TESTAMENT INVECTIVE AGAINST VARIOUS GROUPS

Let us now return to the New Testament and polemic. Three groups are the targets of invective in the New Testament. The first group, other Christians, we have already noted in the discussion of Paul (his wish that his opponents in Galatia would mutilate themselves; his description of opponents in Corinth as servants of Satan, and so forth). The second target was pagan society and government. The book of Revelation, which

---

19. For the distinction of Christians from both Jews and pagans, see, for example, *Diogn.* 1.1; both are wrong because they sacrifice (chap. 3); Jewish practices are superstitious, fraudulent, and ridiculous (chap. 4). (The date of the *Epistle to Diognetus* is uncertain, but it is probably second or third century.)

20. This is my own reading of the most anti-Jewish statements in the Gospel of John, two of which are cited below.

21. See Marcel Simon, *Verus Israel: A Study of the Relations between Christians and Jews in the Roman Empire (AD 135–425)* (Oxford: Oxford University Press, 1986), 321–28.

is the most bloodthirsty book in the Christian canon (exceeding Joshua by a good margin), heaps invective on Rome, using "Babylon" as a code word for the imperial city. Babylon "made all nations drink of the wine of the wrath of her fornication" (Rev. 14:8); she is "mother of whores and of earth's abominations" (Rev. 17:5); Babylon is "a dwelling place of demons, a haunt of every foul and hateful bird, a haunt of every foul and hateful beast" (Rev. 18:2); "the kings of the earth, who committed fornication and lived in luxury with her, will weep and wail over her when they see the smoke of her burning" (Rev. 18:9); "Babylon the great city will be thrown down, and will be found no more" (Rev. 18:21).

Of the third group, the Jews, we read, "you are from your father the devil" (John 8:44); "you are not from God" (John 8:47); and the people who call themselves Jews are not actually Jews, but rather "a synagogue of Satan" (Rev. 2:9).

Thus there are passages in the New Testament that reveal more-or-less equal hostility toward three different groups. The results, however, have not been the same. Today, no one cares what Paul thought of the Christian circumcision party; his wish that his enemies would mutilate their own genitals is amusing — a piece of nastiness that had no effect and that applies to no one today. Similarly, no one cares what the author of Revelation thought of Rome. The author did not offer unbiased and judicious criticism, but he was powerless to persecute Romans, and his hatred of the city did not lead Christians subsequently to persecute Romans.

From this we may conclude that the occasional pieces of Christian invective against Jews in the New Testament would not matter very much if these statements had never had any effect. If subsequent Christians had exercised tolerance and love when dealing with or thinking about Jews and Judaism, we could now say that it was not nice of the author of John to state that Jews were sired by the devil, and that such an attitude does not correspond very well to the gospel of love and mercy, but we would not now have conferences on the problem of anti-Jewish statements in the New Testament. Unfortunately, however, Christians, partly inspired by attacks on Jews in the New Testament, have repeatedly come up with *new* anti-Jewish views, and they have developed a remarkable number of ways to persecute Jews. Although some statements in the New Testament played a role (including several in the Gospels, which are discussed in other essays in this volume), we have to put a lot of the blame on the people who went looking for passages that would justify their own anti-Judaism. Fourth-century Christians living in Rome did not turn to Revelation and decide to burn down the city and kill the pagan inhabitants. When Christians accepted the Gospels of John and Matthew as Scripture, they did not thereby foreordain that Christianity would be anti-Jewish. That depended on the free will of subsequent Christians.

In 2 Corinthians 3 and Philippians 3 (discussed above), Christians could have found an alternative view of Judaism: glorious and good, though not as good as Christianity. If they did not find it, it was because they were not looking.

ANTI-JUDAISM IN THE MIDDLE AGES AND MODERN WORLD

I shall give only two examples of Christian anti-Jewish creativity after the period of the New Testament. The first is the policy of medieval European Christians not to allow Jews to own land. This had a lot of pernicious effects. When this policy was combined with the dogma that it was unchristian to lend money at interest, the result was that Jews became the financiers of Europe. Even prior to the rise of capitalism, Europeans sometimes needed to borrow money, and they could turn only to the Jews. Jews did not really fit into the feudal system, which was based on ownership of land, and so were outside of normal society. Financiers who are outsiders are bound to be unpopular. Worse, in the absence of a real place in feudal society, Jews were answerable directly to the king, who could use them quite cynically, and who often did so. At the king's direction, for example, they could be forced to extend too much credit to a nobleman; the king could then require them to foreclose on the mortgage. The result would be that the king would have the property, since the Jewish lender or lenders could not hold the land. This, in turn, created even more hostility — not against the king, but against the Jews. There is nothing in the New Testament that dictates this situation. In the modern world, the entire arrangement is almost incomprehensible, since modern people cannot understand the dogma that Christian money must not earn interest. Yet modern Christians not infrequently criticize Jews for being overly concerned with commerce and finance. The effect of this medieval creation lingers to this day.[22]

---

22. I have heard this criticism of Jews, but I have not read it in a recent scholarly book. I shall, however, cite an example from a nineteenth-century British scholar whom I admire, but who was influenced by the biases of his day. J. B. Lightfoot, discussing Jewish settle-

The second example of creative anti-Judaism is the invention of the
idea that first-century Judaism was "legalistic" and therefore that Jews
were "legalists." Since modern Judaism derives from first-century Judaism, it was (and often still is) assumed that modern Judaism is legalistic
as well. The history of the charge of legalism is a very large topic, many
aspects of which are explained in the essay by Professor Tyson in this
volume. I hope in the not-too-distant future to do a full study; right
now I wish only to add a few words to Tyson's excellent discussion.

Those who charge Judaism with being legalistic intend to say something extremely negative about Judaism and Jews. Many people do not
understand how serious the charge is, since they do not know precisely what Protestant scholars mean when they say that Jews were
(and, by implication, still are) legalistic. Jews sometimes agree with their
Protestant critics that they are legalistic, by which the Jews mean that
they follow the divine law. Therefore I shall offer a list of legalism's
component parts to indicate the weight and tone of the accusation.

1. In legalism, a person stands alone before God, with the obligation
   of doing enough good deeds to earn God's favor. There is no prior
   grace; there are no group benefits. Each individual starts out with a
   clean slate, but with 100 percent of the responsibility of salvation.

2. Salvation is attained by doing more good deeds than bad deeds.
   People must be obedient at least 51 percent of the time.

3. Legalists believe that God is basically an accountant, a judge who
   is inflexibly controlled by human performance and who spends his
   time keeping score. He has, however, a power possessed by no ac-
   countants (though possibly desired by some): He reigns supreme at
   a final judgment of humanity, and he sends people with 51 percent
   good deeds to eternal bliss, people with 49 percent good deeds to
   eternal damnation.

4. To meet the 51 percent requirement, legalists tend to pile up a lot
   of easy good deeds, which are necessarily minor. This leads to the
   pursuit of trivial acts of piety.

5. Trivial acts of piety lead to hypocrisy: showing off minor external
   actions while ignoring the most important religious principles.

---

ment in Galatia, wrote that the Jews, like the Phoenicians, had "commercial instincts"
and that Galatia was attractive to Jews because it "afforded great facilities for commercial enterprise" (*Saint Paul's Epistle to the Galatians*, 10th ed. [London: MacMillan and
Company, 1890, repr. 1892], 10.

6. Psychologically, the legalist is either *anxious* because he or she does not know whether or not enough good deeds have been compiled, or *arrogant* because he or she has done so many trivial good deeds that God will be forced to save her or him. There is no happy confidence in God because of his love and mercy, since the legalist's God lacks these qualities. The only psychological possibilities are anxiety and arrogance.

7. The legalist believes in repentance in a very deficient way. Each act of repentance offsets one bad deed; that is, repentance is only one more meritorious work. There is no such thing as thoroughgoing repentance.

8. Within legalism, only one factor offers relief from strict judgment in accord with the number of good and bad deeds: a treasury of merits based on works of supererogation. Saintly legalists have more good deeds than they need, and God will apply some of these to offset the deficiencies of others. In particular, these supererogatory deeds may tip the scale in favor of people whose deeds are precisely 50 percent good and 50 percent evil.

This would certainly be a dreadful religion if anyone belonged to it. When Christians say that Judaism is a legalistic religion, they are saying that, from the point of view of the subject — the religious person — being a legalist is absolutely terrible (it leads to anxiety or arrogance), and moreover that legalism induces bad behavior (triviality and hypocrisy).

There is so much to say about this portrayal of Judaism that I hardly know where to start. I shall make only four points, and I shall be as brief as possible.

First, the accusation that Jews were legalistic comes from nineteenth-century German Protestant scholarship, though it has been widely adopted by other Christian scholars, especially New Testament scholars. It was partly derived from Protestant attacks on Roman Catholicism, as is evident from the use of the terms "treasury of merits" and "works of supererogation." That is, the accusation is originally only religious polemic, hurled first at this enemy and then at that, and it is about as fair and unbiased as was first-century religious polemic. Protestant scholars, of course, produced handbooks in which they purported to "prove" from Jewish sources that first-century Judaism really was legalistic. In fact, the supposed proof vanishes on examination (Professor Tyson's essay in this volume refers to some of the literature on this topic). Ancient

Jewish literature emphasizes the love and mercy of God, grace, repentance, and all the features that Protestant polemicists fondly believe not to be there. Moreover, it lacks the supposed theology of legalism. The charge of legalism is no more than creatively malignant religious polemic, and it is sad to see that it especially disfigures pietist Christian biblical studies. As sometimes happens, those who intend to be the most pious are the most vicious.

Second, I offer a hypothesis as to why this charge arose. At one time, Christians were distinguished from Jews by *creedal* statements. Christians believed the various statements contained in the great creeds of the fourth and fifth centuries, such as that Jesus was "of one substance with the Father as regards his Godhead, and at the same time of one substance with us as regards his manhood...one and the same Christ...recognized in two natures, without confusion, without change, without division, without separation...."[23] Jews, obviously, did not hold these opinions. In the eighteenth and nineteenth centuries, however, religion began to adopt the great principles of humanism, and these started to replace the philosophical formulations of late antiquity. Christian clergy became less willing to expound how there are two substances in one person, or three persons in one Godhead, and more willing to discuss love, mercy and grace. This, no doubt, was a great improvement; I am glad not to have to sit through explanations of how two natures could be combined in one person without being either mingled or separate. The new liberal, humanistic Christians, as they lost confidence in the creeds, did not, however, give up the idea that their religion was best. When nineteenth-century scholars combined the view that Christianity *consists of* divine love and mercy, human love, and humble repentance, with the view that Christianity was completely superior to all other religions, especially its parent, Judaism, it seemed self-evident that Judaism lacked the human virtues that characterized Christianity. Thus arose the accusation that Jews were legalistic: They did not believe in grace, love, mercy, or true repentance; all they had was anxious or arrogant striving to save themselves by performing a lot of trivial works.

The conclusion of this point is the same as the first: The accusation of legalism is nothing but religious polemical propaganda. It has nothing to do with the study of Jewish sources, but arises from a change in Christianity and the assumption that Judaism was (and is) the opposite of Christianity.

---

23. From the Definition of Chalcedon (451 C.E.).

Third, it is noteworthy that these are theological charges and that the Protestant literature in which they are found is quite abstract. The reader has the impression that none of the people who wrote this rubbish knew any Jews. I was taught such things in divinity school, but I had the good fortune to be introduced to some leading Jews in Dallas by the editor of this volume. This very quickly led me to doubt the theological abstractions. Only later did I study the material and see the lack of connection between early Jewish literature and the charge of legalism.[24]

Fourth, we should note that *no one has ever been a legalist* (except, perhaps, a few modern existentialists). The ancient world, like the modern, knew hypocrites, and I assume that they could be found in all groups, as they are now; the ancient world knew about self-righteousness, triviality, and the like. But the crucial first item on our list of legalism's components was entirely absent. No first-century Jew thought that he or she stood alone before God, with the obligation to do enough good deeds to earn God's favor. No first-century Jew believed that there was no prior grace and that there were no group benefits. This sort of individualism is a modern idea. Even today, individualism this rugged would be rare among religious people. But the ideas that are most basic to Judaism include the election and the covenant between God and Israel. All the ancient sources show the importance of the Jewish people as a group. Jews were famous for their adherence to one another and to their ancestral practices, observance of which maintained their place within the covenant; the question of the situation and fate of Israel is prominent in ancient Judaism, much more prominent than the question of individual salvation. The charge of legalism, to be true, requires that Jewish individuals be engaged in the anxious or arrogant effort to save themselves by their own personal achievements. In fact, Judaism is the antithesis of this extremely individualistic way of thinking.

It almost goes without saying that the accusation of legalism is not derived from the New Testament. It is for the most part the creative work of nineteenth-century Protestant scholars, who tried to give some kind of theological coherence to their assertion that Judaism was an inferior religion when judged by the canons of modern liberal humanism. The charge is, I think, Hegelian: If Christianity consists of love and so forth, there must be a polar opposite. Since Christianity broke away from Judaism, Judaism must be that polar opposite; thus Judaism must

---

24. *Paul and Palestinian Judaism* (London: SCM; Philadelphia: Fortress, 1977), part 1.

be the negation of everything that is Christian. That is all there is to the charge of legalism: a fantastic web-spinning of opposites that exist only in theory, not in real life.

CONCLUSION

What is most to be deplored is that so many Christians have been unable to rise above one of the more unfortunate human characteristics: the desire to prove that one belongs to a good group by claiming that another group is awful. Surely, our brains are wired to compare and contrast. But we are also intelligent, and we should be able to avoid the wicked desire to invent contrasts that make us look good. And that is what the history of Christian anti-Judaism is: a history of invented contrasts. The truth is that Christians have more in common with Jews than with any other group. Both religions believe in one good God; both believe in love, mercy, and grace. One, at least in my experience, has done a more consistent job of producing kind and charitable people than the other. I hope that all readers of this work, and especially the Christians, who have so often been deficient in this regard, resolve to do better at fostering the human virtues in which we all believe.

CONTRIBUTORS

WILLIAM R. FARMER, *University of Dallas*

AMY-JILL LEVINE, *Vanderbilt University*

PHILIP L. SHULER, *McMurry University*

WARREN CARTER, *St. Paul School of Theology*

DARYL D. SCHMIDT, *Texas Christian University*

DAVID L. BALCH, *Texas Christian University*

ALLAN J. MCNICOL, *University of Texas (Austin)*

DAVID RENSBERGER, *Interdenominational Theological Center*

MARK GOODWIN, *University of Dallas*

THOMAS D. LEA, *Southwestern Baptist Theological Seminary*

ROBERT LOUIS WILKEN, *University of Virginia*

EVERETT FERGUSON, *Abilene Christian University*

D. JEFFREY BINGHAM, *Dallas Theological Seminary*

JOSEPH B. TYSON, *Southern Methodist University*

JAMES O. DUKE, *Texas Christian University*

ELLEN T. CHARRY, *Southern Methodist University*

E. P. SANDERS, *Duke University*

287

INDEX OF ANCIENT SOURCES

MEDIEVAL AUTHORS

GRECO-ROMAN LITERATURE

Index of Names

INDEX OF SUBJECTS